Ice Age Trail Guidebook 2014

More than 100

Detailed

Segment-by-Segment

Descriptions and

Maps to Help You

Connect with the

Thousand-Mile

Ice Age National Scenic Trail

A Publication of the
Ice Age Trail Alliance

Cover photo: Skunk and Foster Lakes Segment, Waupaca County. Photo by Eric Sherman.

Cover design by Celtic, Inc. (**celticinc.com**), Brookfield, WI.

Interior design by Sue Knopf.

Cartography by Mapping Specialists Limited (**mappingspecialists.com**), Fitchburg, WI.

Printed by Versa Press, Inc. (**versapress.com**), East Peoria, IL.

*Dedicated to the thousands of volunteers
who have contributed their time and effort
to the Ice Age Trail for more than 50 years.*

Hike Locator

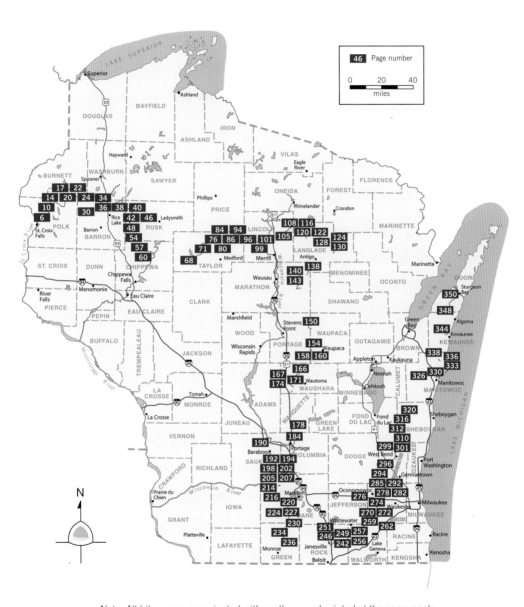

Note: All hike maps are oriented with north up and printed at the same scale.

Contents

Regional Map: Washington County 289

Regional Map: Fond du Lac & Sheboygan Counties 307

Regional Map: Manitowoc County 323

Regional Map: Kewaunee & Door Counties 341

Acknowledgments

Without the contributions of the following individuals publication of this book would not have been possible.

Volunteer Field Editors

As with most Ice Age Trail Alliance projects, publication of this book relied on the contributions of volunteers. The following individuals served as Field Editors, hiking segments of the Trail and checking drafts of this book for accuracy:

Ed Abell, Dave Ammend, Patty Amsrud, Dan & Diane Anderson, Nancy Bahling, Diane Balmer, McLynda Batterman, Sande Becker, Sharon Bloodgood, James Bolitho, Jennifer Boudreau, Wanda Brown, Bob & Cindy Burtley, David Busse, Kitrina Carlson, Jeana Church, Jean Clark, Tobi Clark, Marcy Conklin, Jim Cousin, Dan Crouse, Fred & Edith Dalleksa, Tim Dickinson, Jeff & Shelly Dohlby, Sharon Dziengel, Chris Einwalter, Roger Elver, Gary Ertl, Lynn Eschenburg, Tim Eschers, Jacqueline Frank, Barb Frey, Jenna Gilles, Tom Gross, Clayton Grow, Eileen Hannigan, Gary & Sandy Hegeman, Dave Henning, Bill Herbold, Gordon Herz, Mary Jacobson, Ruby Jaecks, Kris Jensen, Bob Jozwowski, Evelyn Kain, Elaine Klein, Jean Klein, Sue Knopf, Dan & Pat Kohler, Matt Kolinski, Paul Kuhlmann, Lisa Laudolff, Becky Leclair, Will Luedtke, Pete May, Tom May, Josh Mayer, Derrick Mayoleth, Jim Meinhardt, Glen Mercier, Steve Meurett, Buzz Meyer, Cary Mui, Tess Mulrooney, Gary Nelson, Carol Neuhoff, Anna Nirva, Dave & Mariette Nowak, Alexa O'Brien, Dave O'Brien, Jefren Olsen, Ginny Pease, Gail Piotrowski, Jim Popp, Joe Rickert, Bob & Sue Root, Judy Rose, Julie Rudolph, Jim Runge, Terry Schnapp, Betty Schraith, Jen Scott, John Singer, Ryan Singh, Phil Sower, Bryan Stewart, Larry Swanson, Susan Sweeney, Terri Tacheny, Tammy Vanden Heuvel, Lila Waldman, Mike Walters, Jonah Westrich, Nick Wilkes, Erika Wittekind, Glenn Wobick, Kattie Zappia and Jeff Ziegler

Ice Age Trail Alliance Chapter Leaders

Volunteers who lead the Ice Age Trail Alliance's 21 chapters offered valuable input to field editors and the IATA's Guidebooks Team both through personal insights and by soliciting book review assistance from fellow chapter members:

Andrew Bent, Dale Crisler, Dean Dversdall, Gary Ertl, Joanna Kramer Fanney, Sally Freckmann, Gary Fredrick, Tom Gross, Mike Guisleman, Bob Held, Bruce & Ruby Jaecks, Kris Jensen, Joe Jopek, Debbie Krogwold, Jim Kurz, Lynn Larson, Randy Lennartz, Tim McRaith, Donna & Neal Meier, Buzz Meyer, Dan Mitchell, David Mix, Fred Nash, Carol Prchal, Craig Sanford and Richard Smith

Guidebooks Team

Publication of the *Ice Age Trail Guidebook 2014* was coordinated by the Ice Age Trail Alliance's Guidebooks Team:

Sharon Dziengel, volunteer
Gary Hegeman, volunteer
Sue Knopf, volunteer
Eric Sherman, IATA staff
Tiffany Stram, IATA staff

The Guidebooks Team extends a special thank you to:

- Volunteer Andrew Hanson III and IATA staff member Matt Kaufmann for their valuable contributions to the guidebooks-revision project for both this current edition and past editions.
- Volunteer Sandy Hegeman for substantial proofreading help on field editor comments.
- All IATA staff members for support and a wide variety of contributions throughout the guidebooks-revision process.

Introduction

The Ice Age National Scenic Trail, one of only eleven such trails in the country, is a thousand-mile footpath that immerses users in fascinating, world-renowned Ice Age features and the outdoor playground that is Wisconsin. The Trail offers a little something for everyone. Long stretches of uninterrupted tread through quiet North-woods forests meet the demands of backpackers looking for a multi-day adventure away from it all. Closer to home, the Trail weaves in and around more populous areas, such as West Bend, Janesville and St. Croix Falls, satisfying those seeking a brief, after-dinner jaunt to recharge life's batteries with plenty of fresh air. For the scientific-minded, the story behind the kames, drumlins, eskers and erratics seen along the Trail invites a lifetime of investigation, while for the artistic crowd, there are innumerable spots, both quiet and grand, that will inspire the author to pick up her pen and the artist to grab his sketchpad or camera. And, perhaps most impor-tantly, the Ice Age Trail provides an outlet for those who like to give as well as receive, with volunteer opportunities to match most any talent.

Given the Ice Age Trail's broad appeal, a critical task for the Ice Age Trail Alliance (IATA), the nonprofit volunteer and member-based organization that works to cre-ate, support and protect the Trail, is to make sure people can find it! The two most common questions received by staff at the IATA main office are "Where can I find the Trail?" and "What will I see when I get there?" We here at the IATA are proud to say that this book will provide the answers to those two questions and just about any other head-scratcher related to hiking the Ice Age Trail.

The *Ice Age Trail Guidebook 2014* breaks down the thousand-mile Trail into shorter segments and describes each hike in great detail. This book is built on previous editions of the *Ice Age Trail Companion Guide*, but improves on that book in several ways:

- The Guidebook includes a map for each segment taken from our popular *Ice Age Trail Atlas* (available at **iceagetrail.org**).

- The Guidebook has been rewritten to flow from west to east, matching the direction of the maps in the Atlas.

- The Guidebook describes each segment based on consistent criteria, includ-ing elevation, ruggedness and availability of drinking water, camping and rest-rooms, to name a few.

No matter how you approach the Ice Age Trail, please keep in mind that it is a work in progress and there is much to be done. If these books are helpful and you find yourself having one enjoyable Ice Age Trail adventure after another, consider joining the effort to maintain what we've built so far, complete what we haven't and protect the Trail for future generations. Please visit **iceagetrail.org** or give us a call to discover how you can provide financial support (through an IATA membership) or "sweat equity" (through volunteer effort) to enable others, both present and future, to enjoy the remarkable Ice Age National Scenic Trail.

Background Information

Ice Age Trail Landscapes

Through the eons, the landscapes along the Ice Age Trail have been shifted, shaped and eroded by wind, sedimentation, hardening of molten rock and the movement of water and glacial ice. The Trail showcases the dramatic effects of continental glaciers.

Colossal ice sheets repeatedly gripped the Earth during the Ice Age of the past two million years. Ice sheets are the largest glaciers, and unless you travel to Greenland or Antarctica, it may be hard to imagine their immensity. They can be two miles thick and stretch for more than 1,000 miles. The modern glaciers found at some of America's national parks are mountain glaciers—mere rivers of ice. Ice Age ice sheets were like oceans of ice with lobes along their margins similar to gulfs or bays.

Glaciers scrape, sculpt, carry and drop materials of all sizes, from tiny particles of clay to huge boulders. During the last period of the Ice Age, more than a third of the Earth's land was impacted. Some materials were deposited directly by the ice while others were transported by the meltwater that flowed over and away from the ice sheets. Glaciers and their meltwater piled material into particular landforms that we call moraines, drumlins, kames and eskers.

The Ice Age Trail is one of the best places to witness many of the landforms created by continental glaciation. The most recent period of the Ice Age, which slowly ended about 10,000 years ago, is known as the Wisconsin Glaciation.

Most of the landforms of the Ice Age Trail were created near the end of the Wisconsin Glaciation. Some features are much older. Along eastern segments of the Trail are occasional outcrops of 400-million-year-old dolomite. The bedrock at Dells of the Eau Claire and Grandfather Falls is approximately 1.8 billion years old.

Rounded boulders scattered along the Trail (sometimes piled in fencerows by farmers) were likely carried by glaciers from sources far to the north. These are known as erratics. Some erratics were carried from as far away as Canada. Rocks that look like and come from local bedrock are not erratics.

As you hike the Ice Age Trail, look for evidence of past glaciation. Take the time to speculate how far an erratic traveled to reach its resting place. Guess how large the block of ice was that created a kettle. Envision a torrent of sand-laden meltwater gushing through a valley. Imagine a thousand feet of glacial ice above a kame.

There are stories in the land...

Glacial Lobes

This is an illustration of the glacial lobes during the Late Wisconsin Glaciation. All but the southwestern corner of Wisconsin was glaciated. The last glaciation was not as extensive as some that had preceded it. Arrows indicate the direction of ice flow.

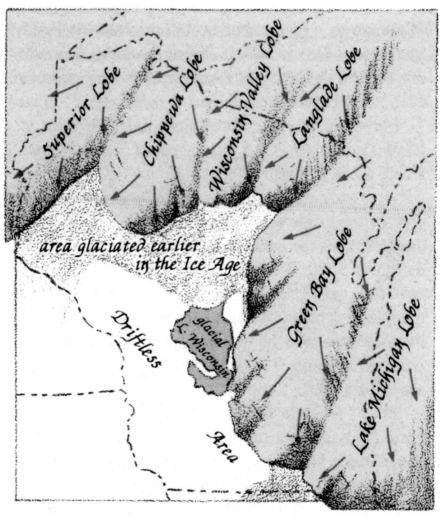

Image from The Ice Age Geology of Devil's Lake State Park, *John W. Attig et al., Wisconsin Geological and Natural History Survey, 1990.*

Ice Age Trail
Elevation Chart

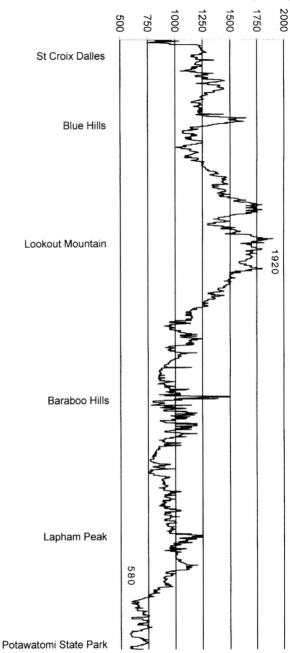

The topography along most of the Ice Age Trail is gently rolling, although some sections, like the Baraboo Hills (Sauk County) and Harrison Hills (Langlade and Lincoln counties), have steep climbs and descents. The highest point along the Trail is Lookout Mountain (1,920 feet), with a fire tower in Lincoln County. The lowest point, 580 feet, is along the shore of Lake Michigan in Manitowoc, Kewaunee and Door counties.

The Ice Age Trail Alliance

The Ice Age Trail Alliance is a nonprofit volunteer- and member-based organization whose mission is to create, support and protect a thousand-mile foot trail tracing Ice Age formations across Wisconsin. Established in 1958 (and then known as the Ice Age Park & Trail Foundation), the IATA has more than 3000 members across the nation. Working cooperatively with the Wisconsin Department of Natural Resources (DNR), National Park Service, local governments, businesses and private landowners, the IATA works to protect, promote, build and maintain the many segments of the Ice Age National Scenic Trail.

Check out **iceagetrail.org** for an in-depth look at the organization. You can also get more information by calling or writing:

Ice Age Trail Alliance
2110 Main Street
Cross Plains, WI 53528
800-227-0046 • info@iceagetrail.org

Supporting the Ice Age Trail

Become a Member of the Ice Age Trail Alliance

As a member of the IATA, your dues will provide critical support for Ice Age Trail volunteer activities, trailway protection and land stewardship. As a member, you'll receive:

- A subscription to our magazine, *Mammoth Tales*, with features on new Ice Age Trail segments, chapter events, land acquisitions, trail-building activities and more.

- Discounts on Ice Age Trail merchandise.

- Membership (and voting privileges) in your local volunteer chapter and invitations to participate in chapter hikes, Trail improvement events and social activities.

- An invitation to the IATA Annual Conference & Membership Meeting and other special events.

To support the Ice Age Trail through an IATA membership, please visit **iceagetrail.org** or call us at **800-227-0046**.

Become a Volunteer

In addition to supporting the Ice Age Trail through an IATA membership, you can also support the Trail by becoming a volunteer. Because the Trail is built and maintained almost exclusively by volunteers, they are the heart, soul, hands and backbone of the Ice Age Trail. New faces are always welcome and no experience is necessary!

CHAPTER EVENTS

With more than 20 IATA volunteer chapters organized throughout Wisconsin, if you live near the Trail there is an opportunity to get involved right in your own backyard. Chapters are active throughout the year, organizing activities such as Trail construction, maintenance, hikes, campouts, land stewardship, promotion and education. Check the IATA website (**iceagetrail.org**) for chapter contact information and a calendar of events.

MOBILE SKILLS CREW PROGRAM

In addition to the local events at the chapter level, the IATA also organizes statewide trail-building projects each year through its Mobile Skills Crew (MSC) program. Whether you are a seasoned trail builder or just starting to learn about the Trail, MSC events offer a great opportunity for all types of volunteers to give back to the outdoors, visit new landscapes and make new friends. Volunteers at MSC events work hard, earn a sound education in trail building and, perhaps most importantly, have fun!

Though the goal of the MSC program is to educate and empower volunteers on methods of building high quality, sustainable trail, no previous background in trail construction is needed to participate. Those who just want to check out what Ice Age Trail volunteering is all about are welcome to lend a hand at any time during the event. Further, other help is welcome in many areas, including food preparation, community outreach, publicity, administration and entertainment.

Check out **iceagetrail.org** for more information about the Mobile Skills Crew program and a calendar of events.

Volunteers crafted a new section of the Cross Plains Segment during a recent trail-building event. As shown in these before, during and after photos, Ice Age Trail volunteers skillfully opened up the landscape for hikers to enjoy. More help is always needed...join us for some of the most rewarding volunteer work around!

Property Types

The Ice Age National Scenic Trail is uniformly marked with yellow blazes, but as a "partnership" project the land ownership and management for the Trail are anything but consistent. The Trail crosses a wide variety of property types, including private land and lands owned and managed by municipal, county, state and federal agencies. Generally speaking, lands open to public access are shown on the maps in this book with green shading, while those not open to general public access are shown in beige.

From a hiker's perspective, the experience of navigating the Trail doesn't change substantially when passing over varying land types, with a few key exceptions related to private lands. Hikers should be mindful of these points to help ensure the continued good relations with private landowners that are so critical to the Ice Age Trail.

- While hiking a portion of the Trail crossing private lands, hikers must stay on the Trail. Sticking to the Trail tread is a general recommendation for the entire Trail but a **requirement** on private lands.

- Portions crossing private lands may be closed during some hunting seasons. See p. xxv for more information on hunting.

The patchwork of land management also yields different regulations for camping, hiking with pets, parking and so on. Because blanket statements for a particular aspect of hiking on a particular property type can be difficult to formulate, this book attempts to identify both "rules of thumb" and instances where there are exceptions to the rule.

Using the Ice Age Trail Guidebook 2014

This book is broken down by region, county and then Ice Age Trail segment.

Each region is introduced with an Ice Age Trail Alliance Series D map that shows the approximate location of each segment relative to major roads and municipalities.

Each county section is introduced with a page including a general description of the landscape in that area and information on the Ice Age Trail Alliance volunteer chapter that is active in the county.

The description for each Ice Age Trail segment in this book includes the following elements.

SEGMENT SNAPSHOT

The snapshot for each segment starts with distance. Distance in some cases includes not only established Ice Age Trail, marked with yellow blazes, but also portions of "connecting route" (CR), unmarked sections not officially part of the Ice Age Trail that typically follow quiet country roads. *Disclaimer: Roads on connecting routes, while legally open to pedestrians, may not have been designed for safe use by pedestrians (in contrast to Ice Age Trail segments). By identifying these routes, neither the Ice Age Trail Alliance, National Park Service, Wisconsin Department of Natural Resources nor the local governmental body are implying any guarantee about their safety or suitability for Ice Age Trail hikers.*

After distance, the snapshot includes a one- or two-sentence general description of the segment that describes the hiking experience.

From there, the snapshot uses a variety of icons and accompanying notes to describe "need to know" information about the segment. **A key to these symbols is found on p. 371.**

Online Extra! An Excel file with "snapshot" ratings for all segments is available for download from the Ice Age Trail Alliance's website, **iceagetrail.org**. Hikers can sort the file by various criteria to help identify segments that may be suitable for the type of hike they are seeking.

This symbol provides a general idea of how much elevation change (and physical challenge) there is on the segment. The range is 1 (mostly flat) through 5 (very hilly). A higher number may be the result of one very steep climb or the accumulation of many shorter climbs over the full length of a segment.

This symbol provides a general idea of how challenging the segment may be to a hiker. The range is 1 (not rugged) through 5 (very rugged). The number takes into account (i) Ice Age Trail signage, maintenance and/or layout challenges; (ii) water hazards or crossings; (iii) remoteness and (iv) presence of logging activities. Users of this book should recognize that these numbers may mean different things to hikers of different abilities and expectations. Generally speaking, though, anyone hiking a segment with a higher ruggedness rating should be prepared for a challenging and, perhaps, difficult, adventure.

This symbol indicates that a pump or spigot with potable water is available on or near the segment. The water source may be available only seasonally.

Of special interest to long-distance hikers, this symbol indicates the presence of a natural source from which hikers may draw water for filtration/chemical treatment.

This symbol provides an important "heads up" that all hikers should plan on packing plenty of drinking water before arriving at the segment, as no source of water is available in the area.

Of interest to backpackers, this symbol indicates that the segment has hike-to camping options that are further defined by map symbols. A map symbol key is on page 370. In terms of hike-to camping, four map symbols are used:

This symbol indicates a hike-to campsite developed for backpackers. These sites have varying levels of development but typically include a flat spot to pitch a tent and a fire ring.

This pattern of shading on the maps indicates areas where hikers may practice Leave No Trace primitive camping (see p. xxvi for more details on Leave No Trace). These areas are found scattered along only the northern tier of the Ice Age Trail, from the Trail's Western Terminus east through Langlade County.

This symbol denotes a Dispersed Camping Area (DCA). To help increase camping opportunities for Ice Age Trail long-distance hikers, the Ice Age Trail Alliance and its partners are working to establish Dispersed Camping Areas (DCAs), especially in areas (i.e., the southern two-thirds of the Trail) where convenient camping options are otherwise limited for long-distance hikers. DCAs are not "campgrounds" or even "campsites" in the traditional sense...instead, they are typically nothing more than a cleared area where hikers may legally camp for a night. Use of DCAs is restricted to those on multi-night long-distance hikes.

This symbol shows the location of trailside shelters in the Northern and Southern Units of the Kettle Moraine State Forest on the southeastern leg of the Trail. As an exception to the general rule for other hike-to camping resources, reservations are required and only one group per site per night is permitted. Reservations can be made only by calling **888-947-2757** and often need to be made weeks in advance.

This symbol indicates that a traditional "car-camping" campground is located on or within a few miles of the segment. Reservations and/or a fee are often required at these campgrounds.

For those interested in having some relaxing meal or social time before or after a hike, this symbol indicates that a picnic area is available on or near the segment.

Bring the kids! For those looking for something fun to do with children before or after hitting the Trail, this symbol indicates that child-friendly amenities like playgrounds and/or swim areas are available on or near the segment.

This symbol indicates that a toilet is available on or near the segment. Amenities vary (from a pit toilet to a heated restroom with running water) and may be available only seasonally.

For those who are uncomfortable hiking in the presence of hunting, this symbol indicates that hikers will not have any interaction with hunting on the full length of a particular segment. Most of these segments are in urban areas and may include long stretches of multi-use paths, sidewalks and/or roads.

This symbol indicates that the segment crosses private land and portions or the full segment may be closed to hikers during hunting season(s). The Ice Age Trail relies on the generosity of private landowners. Respect these Trail closures at all times. **One irresponsible hiker can jeopardize the future of an entire Ice Age Trail segment by hiking a closed portion of the Trail.**
See p. xxv for more information on hunting and the Ice Age Trail.

The general guideline for hiking with dogs on the Ice Age Trail is that the dog should be leashed (8-ft maximum length) and under control at all times. This symbol indicates that the segment has **additional** special regulations for hiking with dogs. In some areas, dogs are prohibited entirely; in others, they must be leashed by law.

This symbol indicates that portions of the segment overlap with biking, snow-mobiling or groomed cross-country skiing trails or roads and/or sidewalks. The message behind this symbol is twofold: (i) hikers can expect to see non-hikers during the hike and (ii) the segment may include wide paths or roads that may not conform to the traditional idea of a hiking path.

This symbol indicates that other hiking trails (spurs, loops or lollipops) are present off the main segment route. The message behind this symbol is twofold: (i) hikers should pay close attention to Trail signage to stay on the main segment route and (ii) those looking for additional miles to explore on foot may have opportunities **from** this segment.

For those using a wheelchair or similar device, this symbol identifies segments that may have portions suitable for wheelchair use. The list of segments flagged with this symbol is not exhaustive and does not attempt to identify segments meeting legally defined criteria of "accessible." Those seeking more specific accessibility information for a particular segment should contact the Ice Age Trail Alliance (**800-227-0046, info@iceagetrail.org**).

TRAIL ACCESS AND PARKING

This section includes driving directions to the Trail access points at the start and end of each hike. Also included is a description of the parking on or near the segment(s).

Parking Area (indicated by a 🅿 icon on the maps) denotes a space where cars can be parked legally and fully off the road. There is quite a wide range within this category, from "a grassy, open space" to a full-fledged paved parking lot.

Roadside Parking (no accompanying map icon) denotes an area where cars may be parked along a road but still within relatively close contact with road traffic. Those uncomfortable with parking in these areas should seek out the nearest Parking Area instead.

Additional considerations for parking:

- A Wisconsin State Parks day pass or annual sticker is required when parking at any State Park or State Forest parking area.

- If parking overnight, park in a Parking Area only and avoid roadside parking. Some parking areas are more suitable than others; in all cases, hikers should notify the county sheriff's department with overnight parking dates and location. Parking areas not open to overnight parking are noted for each segment.

- Those feeling uncomfortable with the parking situation on a particular segment may want to try contacting the Ice Age Trail Alliance volunteer chapter leader for that area. Chapter leader contact information is available at **iceagetrail.org** or from the IATA main office, **800-227-0046**. In some cases, chapter leaders may be able to find a volunteer in the area who will generously donate time, vehicle usage and fuel costs to help you with a shuttle to and/or from the Trail access. Those benefiting from this type of help are strongly encouraged to provide a generous gratuity to the volunteer.

THE HIKE

This section describes significant geological, historical and natural information of the area and provides hikers with turn-by-turn directions for areas where the Ice Age Trail route is not immediately evident based on Trail signage. GPS waypoints are included in this section for all waypoints except those at the start and end of each segment. The waypoints are listed in parentheses and in bold type, e.g., (**MN2**). See the section below and **iceagetrail.org** for more information on waypoints.

POINTS OF INTEREST

Some segments include an additional listing for an attraction on or near the Trail route that would be an interesting side trip for hikers.

AREA SERVICES

This section includes nearby amenities (e.g., restaurants, grocery stores, lodging) that hikers may find helpful. Businesses listed by name support the Ice Age Trail Alliance. Inns and B&Bs listed as part of the IATA's INN Style program have teamed up with the Ice Age Trail Alliance to offer hikers access to first-rate hospitality and accommodations. See **iceagetrail.org** for more information on the INN Style program.

SEGMENT MAP

For each segment a map from the Ice Age Trail Alliance's popular *Ice Age Trail Atlas* is included. The map includes a green dot corresponding to the start of the segment as described in "THE HIKE" section and and a red dot corresponding to the end. Info boxes on the map point the way to the next segment in either direction; brief driving directions are included for those segments separated by a connecting route of less than 5 miles.

GPS waypoints are included on the map for all waypoints except those at the start and end of each segment. See the section below for more information on waypoints. **A map symbol key is located on p. 370.**

Other Recommended Resources

The Ice Age Trail Alliance's website, **iceagetrail.org**, includes Trail navigation information as well as updates on current Trail conditions and route changes. As the Ice Age Trail route evolves continually from year to year as volunteers build new segments and upgrade existing ones, this is a great resource to consult to learn how the Trail has changed relative to the information presented in this book.

The volunteers who head up the 21 Ice Age Trail Alliance chapters are passionate about helping people get out and enjoy the Trail. Contact info for chapter leaders is available on the IATA's website. Hikers are urged to get in touch with these folks (especially ahead of longer hikes and/or those in remote areas) to get a clear picture of the state of the Trail in a particular area. Chapter leaders are volunteers with busy lives outside of the Trail; therefore, hikers should be ready to wait a few days for a response to inquiries. Hikers who strike out with email are urged to try calling instead. Those who hit a dead end should call the IATA main office to see if another chapter leader in the area is available to answer questions.

The *Ice Age Trail Atlas* has more than 100 color hiking maps of the Trail route, including not only established Ice Age Trail segments but also unofficial connecting routes. Each Atlas page is 8.5" x 11"; those who like a little more contextual information for the area around the Ice Age Trail route may enjoy the larger maps more than the excerpts included in this book. The Atlas also includes a gazetteer that describes many place names along the Trail. To order the Atlas, visit **iceagetrail.org** or call the IATA at **800-227-0046**.

Long-distance hikers will want to check out the *Ice Age Trail Databook*, due out late in 2014. The book has highly detailed mileage breakdowns for hundreds of access points along the entire thousand-mile Ice Age Trail route. It also includes in-depth resupply and town service info. For more info visit **iceagetrail.org** or call the IATA at **800-227-0046**.

DeLorme's *Wisconsin Atlas and Gazetteer* also offers a larger view of the surrounding area along the Ice Age Trail and access to it.

Those looking for highly detailed descriptions of the glacial processes that shaped the Wisconsin landscape and the Ice Age Trail landforms left behind will want to get a copy of *Geology of the Ice Age National Scenic Trail*, by David M. Mickelson et al. The book is published by UW Press and widely available through both bookstores and online book sellers.

Hikers are urged to contact tourism boards listed in this book for county road maps and local points of interest beyond the Ice Age Trail.

GPS Waypoints and the ColdCache Program

Global Positioning System (GPS) waypoints listed in the text and on the maps highlight glacial, natural or historical landmarks along the Ice Age Trail. In addition, some waypoints identify critical navigational points such as Trail junctions, stream crossings and Trail access points difficult to see or find from the road.

GPS waypoints appear in the text as a "footnote," listing the county's two-letter abbreviation followed by a number. For example: (**DK1**) indicates Door and Kewaunee counties Waypoint 1.

Online Extra! All waypoints are available for download to GPS devices from the Ice Age Trail Alliance's website, **iceagetrail.org**. Also available for download from the IATA website is an Excel file with waypoint coordinates and descriptions.

New and experienced users of GPS technology may be interested in the IATA ColdCache award program. ColdCaching is a family-friendly activity that provides the opportunity to experience the thrill of a treasure hunt, learn important navigational skills and develop an appreciation for Wisconsin's fascinating Ice Age history. The concept of Ice Age Trail ColdCaching is based on the popular activities of geocaching and earthcaching. Participants seek out natural features along the Ice Age Trail, identify the landmark, record the GPS coordinates and leave only footprints on the landscape. The ColdCache program awards patches based on the number of identified ColdCaches logged in. For more information and to download the award program log, go to **iceagetrail.org** or email **coldcache@iceagetrail.org**.

Trail Signage

Yellow blazes are the official indicator used to mark the Trail route. These are seen as painted or plastic 2- by 6-inch vertical rectangles placed on trees and posts along the Trail. Other shapes of yellow blazes may be found along the Trail, but these are being phased out and replaced by the standard 2- by 6-inch blaze.

- **Blue blazes** indicate a spur or access trail.

- **White blazes** indicate a loop trail.

- **Directional arrows** indicate sharper Trail turns. They are yellow set against a brown background on a 4- by 4-inch plastic sign and can be found on posts or trees. Older-style wood-routed arrows occasionally can be found along the route.

The Trail route in some state and county parks shares existing park trails and may have no blazes. For an additional navigational aid in these cases, consult local park maps.

Trail Conditions

Trail conditions change constantly. Nature and animals impact the Trail as much as humans do. Some parts of the Trail are better maintained than others. Volunteers do their best to maintain the Trail, but storm damage or vandalism can occur any time of the year. Some segments are well maintained and easy to follow, while others may become overgrown or more difficult to follow due to recent logging, storms or beaver activity.

Not all streams or creeks have bridges, especially in remote areas. Some waterways require fords or crossing on beaver dams. Use caution at all water crossings without a structure. The easiest and safest place to cross may not necessarily be where the Trail meets the waterway.

As trailway protection and volunteer trail-building progress, the Ice Age Trail evolves toward completion. The Trail route changes regularly. Some of these changes are small, such as a slight relocation to take a more sustainable route. Other changes are more dramatic, such as when a new segment is opened following the acquisition of a large property. For Trail updates and conditions, visit **iceagetrail.org**.

On the website, you will also find a list of Ice Age Trail Alliance chapter coordinators. Mike Rotter, an Ice Age Trail "Thousand-Miler," provided this helpful advice on communicating with chapter coordinators about Trail conditions:

- Call the coordinator before hiking in a chapter's territory for information and advice. The coordinators can often provide the most up-to-date Trail conditions (including news about logging in the area and suggested alternate routes). They can also tell you if others are hiking at this time.

- Call the chapter coordinator after hiking with information about Trail conditions you encountered. Tell them the good things you saw and experienced along with your thoughts on where improvements could be made.

Seasonal Variation

Each moment of the year has its own beauty.
RALPH WALDO EMERSON

The Ice Age Trail can be enjoyed in all four seasons and provides a fresh perspective for the hiker with each passing month.

During spring, the land comes alive with a wide variety of wildflowers and migrating birds. Seasonal rains and winter snowmelt can result in wet areas along some sections of the Trail and raise river water levels. Hikers should be extremely cautious when fording rivers and streams.

The warm temperatures of summer encourage hikers to reward themselves with a refreshing dip in one of the many lakes or rivers along the Ice Age Trail's route. Wildflowers continue to bloom, especially in the many finely restored prairies through which the Trail passes. May and June represent the onset of tick, mosquito and black fly seasons, though in many years these pests become less of a bother by August. Ripened blackberries, raspberries, blueberries and thimbleberries encourage the hiker to slow his or her pace and enjoy a trailside treat.

There is no better way to enjoy Wisconsin's fall colors than by trekking the Ice Age Trail. The state's many hardwood forests provide a visually stunning array of hues for the hiker to enjoy. During late fall, hunters take to the woods, and hikers should check for Trail closures or special considerations before heading out. Refer to p. xxv for more information on hunting and the Ice Age Trail.

The Ice Age Trail provides a cure for cabin fever during winter, with ample opportunities for snowshoeing and cross-country skiing along the Trail. The leafless landscape offers views of the Trail's famous glacial topography, enabling the user to better witness the legacy of the Ice Age.

Safety

Personal safety is a concern when one ventures to unfamiliar places. Always use common sense and take precautions. It is best to not hike alone. Do not be lulled into a false sense of security, even with a partner or a group. Two or more can be just as vulnerable as one. The following are some suggestions:

- Leave an itinerary of your trip with family and friends.
- Stay in contact with home or friends on longer hikes. Call from towns to update them on your location.
- When parking at Trail access areas, secure your vehicle. Do not leave anything of value in plain sight.
- Carry a cell phone, but realize it may not work in remote sections of the Trail.
- Avoid camping within a half-mile of road crossings.
- Do not tell strangers where you are headed or plan to camp.
- If you run into a suspicious person, consider moving on to another location.
- Always trust your instincts.

If you are a victim of crime or witness a crime, report the incident to the police or local sheriff's department and notify the IATA. Call **911** for emergencies.

Be prepared for natural dangers. Hiking anywhere for any length of time, including day hikes, can expose you to dehydration, hypothermia, heat exhaustion, contaminated water, lightning, dangerous water crossings, rabies, insect-borne diseases and poison ivy. To steer clear of these hazards, read and learn about backcountry travel and safety before you go. Knowledge, experience and common sense are your best tools. Be prepared with a map, compass, appropriate weather gear, water, light, matches, first aid kit, signal whistle and food, even for day hikes.

Special Concern: Mosquito and Tick-Borne Illnesses

Mosquito and tick-borne diseases typically first cause flu-like symptoms and usually can be treated with antibiotics if caught early. Untreated, they may cause serious health problems, including death in rare cases. Three notable illnesses transmitted by ticks or mosquitoes found in Wisconsin are Lyme disease, Ehrlichiosis and the West Nile virus.

Lyme disease is caused by bacteria that are transmitted to humans by the bite of infected deer ticks. The deer tick, at its largest, is only about half the size of the common wood tick, and is about the size of a pinhead or speck of black pepper. There are more than 16,000 Lyme disease infections in the United States each year. Symptoms include a characteristic "bull's-eye" rash and flu-like symptoms such as fever, malaise, fatigue, headache, muscle aches and joint aches. Infrequently, Lyme disease may have long-term severe, chronic and disabling effects, but it is rarely, if ever, fatal.

Ehrlichiosis is also caused by bacteria transmitted by certain species of ticks. Symptoms generally include fever, headache, malaise and muscle aches. Other signs and symptoms may include nausea, vomiting, diarrhea, cough, joint pains, confusion and occasionally a rash, particularly in children. Ehrlichiosis can be a severe illness, especially if untreated, and as many as half of all patients require hospitalization. It can be fatal.

West Nile Virus is an infection caused by the bite of a mosquito infected with the virus. Mosquitoes are infected with the West Nile virus by feeding on infected birds. Approximately 80% of people infected with West Nile virus do not become ill. Most of the remaining 20% of infected people may experience a mild illness that can present with fever, headache, eye pain, muscle aches, joint pain, a rash on the trunk, swollen lymph nodes, nausea and vomiting. Less than 1% of people infected with West Nile virus will become severely ill and require hospitalization. In rare cases, the infection may be fatal, particularly in the elderly and people with other medical conditions. There is no specific treatment for West Nile virus infection. A physician may provide treatment to relieve the symptoms of the illness.

The following precautions can reduce the risk of acquiring these and other possible tick and mosquitoes infections.

- Wear shoes, high socks, long pants with cuffs tucked into socks and a long-sleeved shirt with shirttails tucked in to keep ticks off your skin and on the outside of clothing.
- Light-colored clothing will make ticks easier to find.
- Insect repellents containing 0.5% permethrin or 20–30% DEET have been

shown to be effective in repelling deer ticks. If such products are used, follow the manufacturer's directions on the label.

- Walk in the center of mowed trails to avoid brushing up against vegetation. Avoid hiking at dusk and dawn when mosquitoes are most active.

- Conduct thorough "tick checks" on yourself and your children after spending time outdoors. Inspect all parts of your body carefully, including your armpits, scalp, back of neck, groin and places where clothes are close to skin, like the belt-line or cuffs.

Prompt removal of ticks can drastically reduce the chance of disease transmission. If a tick is found, remove it by grasping it as close to the skin as possible with a narrow-bladed tweezers. Pull straight out slowly and firmly until the tick lets go. If the tick's mouthparts stay embedded in the skin, remove them with a sterile needle as you would a sliver. After removing it, thoroughly wash the site with soap and water and apply an over-the-counter antibiotic cream like Neosporin or Bacitracin. Save the tick in a jar or plastic bag and make a note of the day you removed it. Let your doctor know you were bitten by a tick for any necessary follow-up care and treatment especially if you develop any flu-like symptoms over the next several weeks.

For more information on mosquito and tick-borne diseases, visit:

cdc.gov/ticks/diseases
cdc.gov/westnile
dhs.wisconsin.gov/communicable

Hunting

Many public and private lands along the Ice Age Trail are open to hunting during a variety of hunting seasons. Hikers should keep the following in mind while the state's major hunting seasons are happening:

Hunting Season Dates and What to Wear

The Wisconsin Department of Natural Resources annually sets a range of season dates for a wide range of game species. The most popular hunting seasons include deer (bow and gun), turkey, small game and waterfowl. Season dates vary from year to year and in different locations around the state. Get the most updated information on the Wisconsin Department of Natural Resources' Season Dates page (**dnr.wi.gov/topic/hunt/dates.html**).

The nine-day gun deer-hunting season is in late November. This is the most popular hunting season and the one during which Ice Age Trail hikers are most likely to see their hiking options limited.

For your safety, consider this time of year "Blaze Orange Season"—wear blaze orange (or other bright colors) from October through March when you and your pet are on the Trail.

Hiking on Private Lands

The private landowners who generously serve as Ice Age Trail hosts may close the portion of the Ice Age Trail that runs through their property during hunting season. This is most common during the nine-day gun deer season, but closures can be in place during other seasons as well.

"Private Land" signs are placed at any point where the Ice Age Trail enters private land, most often at a road crossing. Landowners and/or Ice Age Trail Alliance volunteers also often place "Segment Closed" signs (with dates of the closure) at Trail access points.

Respect signs that announce a closed portion of Trail and be cognizant when you pass "Private Land" signs. This will help ensure the continued good relations with private landowners that are so critical to the Ice Age Trail.

In advance of your hike, consider calling the chapter coordinator or the IATA office (**800-227-0046**) for more details on sections of the Trail that are closed. Visit iceagetrail.org to find chapter coordinator contact information.

Hiking on Public Lands

Just about all segments of the Ice Age Trail that cross public lands remain open for hiking during hunting season, including the Chequamegon-Nicolet National Forest, state and county forests and state parks.

Wisconsin Act 168 allows hunting in most state parks and State Ice Age Trail Areas (SIATAs) from Nov. 15 to Dec. 15 and from April 1 to the Tuesday nearest May 3.

In these locations, no hunting or trapping is allowed within 100 yards of the Ice Age Trail. Note that this rule does not apply to other trails in state parks.

Visit the Wisconsin DNR's Hunting and Trapping in State Parks page (**dnr.wi.gov/topic/parks/hunt**) for more information and for hunting and trapping maps for each state park and SIATA.

Leave No Trace Ethics

You are encouraged to get out and enjoy the gifts the Ice Age has left us. To preserve and protect the natural beauty of Wisconsin, low impact camping and "leave no trace" ethics should be followed. The purpose of these guidelines is to help decrease the impact of humans on the Trail.

- Plan ahead and be prepared. Call for Trail conditions, carry maps, know the regulations of the area and plan or reserve your overnight camping.

- Remember to carry out what you carried in, including all garbage and leftover food. Repackage food to minimize waste. Leave the natural environment better than you found it. Inspect your campsite and rest areas for trash or spilled food before leaving.

- Leave only footsteps. Take only photos. Do not pick flowers, plants or bark off trees.

- Preserve the past. Observe and do not disturb or take historical artifacts such as arrowheads, historical or cultural structures, rock walls or sensitive natural resources. Do not build structures or furniture or dig trenches.

- Travel and camp on durable surfaces. Durable surfaces include established trails and campsites, rock, gravel, dry grasses or snow.

- Stay on the Trail at all times. Do not cut switchbacks. Walk single file in the middle of the Trail, even when it is wet or muddy.

- Be considerate of other hikers. Let nature prevail. Avoid loud voices and noises. Be courteous and yield to other users on the Trail.

- Limit groups to 20 on day hikes and 10 for overnight trips.

- Where primitive camping is permitted, camp off trail, at least 200 feet from lakes and waterways and out of sight of developed areas. Good campsites are found, not made. Altering a site is not necessary.

- Make low impact fires at existing fire rings only and use only downed wood. Drown out fires thoroughly before breaking camp. Never leave a fire unattended. Campfires can cause lasting impact to the backcountry. Use a portable stove for cooking instead of a campfire.

- Dispose of human waste properly. Dig a 6-inch-deep cat hole at least 200 feet from trails or water. Cover and disguise the cat hole when finished. Pack out toilet paper and feminine hygiene products.

- Avoid using soap within 200 feet of any waterway. Sand makes an excellent scrubber. Use biodegradable soap and scatter strained dirty dishwater at least 200 feet from any waterway.

- Respect wildlife. Observe wildlife from a distance. Do not follow or approach them. Do not damage their habitat. Never bait or feed wild animals. Feeding wildlife damages their health, alters natural behaviors and exposes them to predators and other dangers.

- Store food and trash securely to avoid rodents or bears. Do not eat in or around your sleeping area. Hang your food properly in bear country.

- Some Ice Age Trail segments intersect or use cross-country ski trails that are groomed in winter. Proper hiking etiquette asks for winter hikers and snowshoe users to walk well to the side of the groomed ski tracks.

- Respect private property. The Trail relies heavily on support of private landowners. Respect their rights. Stay on the Trail at all times. The Trail often crosses private property to get to public or IATA land. Do not camp on or vandalize private land. It is a privilege to access the Trail through private landowners' property.

For more on Leave No Trace ethics, visit **LNT.org** or call the Leave No Trace Center for Outdoor Ethics at **800-332-4100**.

Invasive Species Impact

Each year IATA volunteers and partners exert great effort combating invasive or non-native plant species along the Ice Age Trail corridor and throughout the state. Without these efforts, the non-native plants, animals and pathogens can displace native species, disrupt ecosystems and harm recreational activities. Invasive species can spread rapidly and aggressively because they lack the predators and competitors. Controlling invasive species is difficult and getting rid of them is often impossible.

Anyone who spends time in the outdoors is a potential vector of undesirable plant material. To minimize the introduction and spread of invasive species, hikers should:

- Minimize disturbance by staying on the Trail and if possible stay out of heavily infested areas entirely.

- Before and after a hike on the Trail, inspect and clean clothing, footwear and gear. Make sure that your gear, especially your footwear, is clear of plant materials. Remove and discard any plant material or soil in the garbage. Use boot brushes where available, or bring your own brush to scrape off dirt.

- Firewood can harbor many different kinds of invasive pests and diseases that are harmful to Wisconsin's trees in both forest and urban settings. Follow the DNR regulations on firewood which prohibits bringing firewood onto any DNR properties from more than 50 miles away or from outside of Wisconsin.

- Be a proactive land steward. If a new patch of invasives is discovered, please let the IATA staff know. Do not attempt to remove it on your own as much of the Trail is on private lands.

For more information visit **dnr.wi.gov/topic/Invasives.**

Chapter and Thousand-Miler Certificates

Many Ice Age Trail Alliance volunteer chapters have programs that acknowledge hikers who have completed all Ice Age Trail miles and connecting routes in their territory. More information about these programs can be found at **iceagetrail.org** or by contacting the local chapter.

The IATA recognizes anyone who reports having hiked the entire Trail and completes a recognition application as a "Thousand-Miler." The IATA policy operates on the honor system, assuming anyone who applies for recognition has hiked all 1000+ miles between Interstate State Park and Potawatomi State Park. To qualify, it is necessary to have hiked all current Ice Age Trail segments and connect all Trail segments by walking the connecting route of your choice. Not considered are issues of speed, length of time from start to finish, sequence, direction or whether or not one carries a pack. Visit **iceagetrail.org** to obtain a Thousand-Miler application.

Ice Age Trail Guidebook 2014

Point Beach Segment, Manitowoc County.

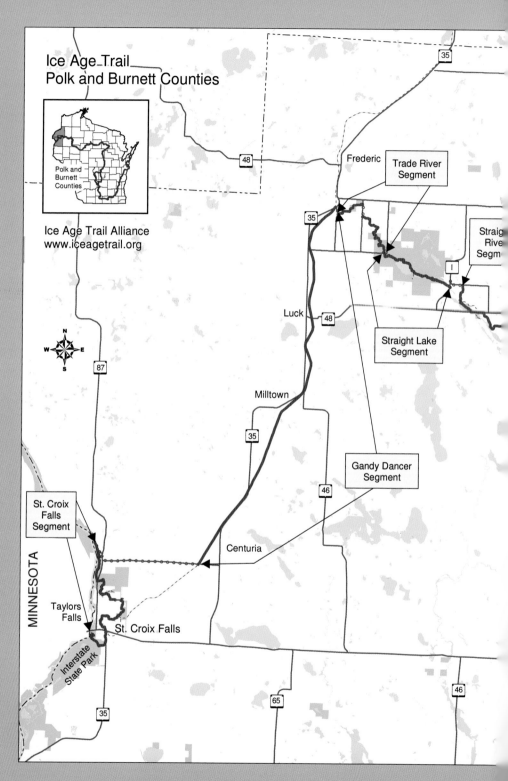

Ice Age Trail
Polk and Burnett Counties

Polk and
Burnett
Counties

Ice Age Trail Alliance
www.iceagetrail.org

MINNESOTA

Frederic

Trade River
Segment

Straig
Rive
Segm

Straight Lake
Segment

Luck

Milltown

Gandy Dancer
Segment

St. Croix
Falls
Segment

Centuria

Taylors
Falls

St. Croix Falls

Interstate
State Park

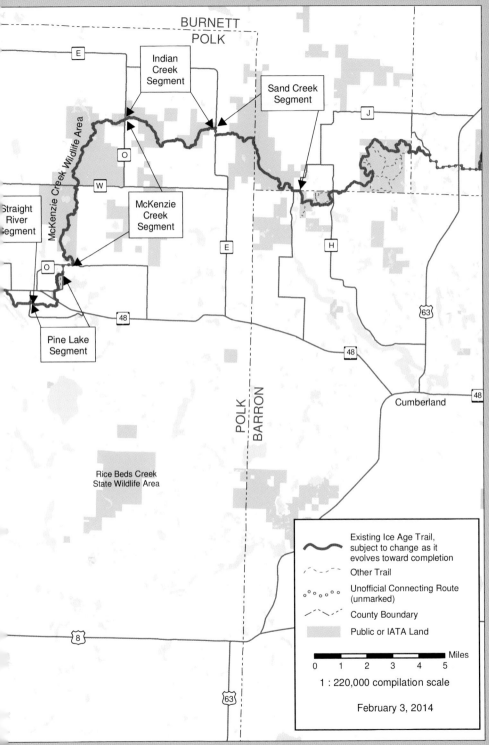

Polk & Burnett Counties

Trail miles: 57.1
Connecting route miles: 7.3

The Superior and Des Moines lobes largely shaped Polk and Burnett counties. First, the Superior Lobe came from the northeast. Later, the Des Moines Lobe moved south through Minnesota and branched northeast into the St. Croix Falls area, through the present-day towns of Atlas, Cushing and Grantsburg. The Superior Lobe had numerous ice margins where eskers and ridges of glacial till and boulders were deposited.

Most of the Ice Age Trail through Polk County is confined to the hilly and forested moraines. The exception is on the Gandy Dancer State Trail from Centuria to Milltown. Here the Trail is on a glacial outwash plain along some of Polk County's best cropland.

The Ice Age Trail's western terminus overlooks the St. Croix River in Interstate State Park. Glacial potholes are featured trailside with the Trail's terminus perched above the riverway and the Dalles of the St. Croix gorge. The state park is an Ice Age National Scientific Reserve unit with an interpretive center containing educational displays about the Ice Age. The park is also Wisconsin's oldest state park, established in 1900. Polk County is also home to one of Wisconsin's newest state parks, Straight Lake State Park, designated in 2004.

Much of the Trail covers remote areas of the county. Finding water can be a problem during the summer. Logging in the county forest and private lands occurs regularly and can make it a challenge to locate Trail blazes. Take your time, pay close attention to blazes and carry a map and compass.

Primitive camping is allowed on Polk and Burnett County Forest land. Please camp at least 200 feet from trails and waterways. Burnett County officials request that campers call in advance for permission.

CHAPTER INFORMATION

The Indianhead Chapter hosts numerous hikes, work outings and presentations by glacial geologists throughout the year. The chapter's "Traprock Trekkers" program rewards hikers who hike all the Ice Age Trail miles in the chapter's territory. Upon completion, Trekkers receive a certificate, attractive patch and, of course, memories to last a lifetime. Contact the chapter for more details.

COUNTY INFORMATION

Burnett County Department of Tourism and Information: 715-349-5999 or
800-788-3164, burnettcounty.com

Burnett County Forest Department: 715-349-2157; call for primitive camping permission

Polk County Visitor Information Center: In St. Croix Falls, on the Ice Age Trail, at the intersection of STH-35 and USH-8; 715-483-1410 or 800-222-7655, polkcountytourism.com

Straight Lake Segment.

St. Croix Falls Segment (Atlas Map 1f)

SNAPSHOT

7.8 miles (7.6 IAT, 0.2 CR): Ice Age Trail Western Terminus in Interstate State Park to River Rd.

> **Note:** It is anticipated that volunteers will build a new section of Trail in 2014 between Louisiana Street and Ray Zillmer Park. The new route is shown as "Future Trail" on the accompanying map. Check with the Ice Age Trail Alliance (800-227-0046, iceagetrail.org) for more details.

🔷🔶🔷 *This segment features both a state park and a "Trail Town" and highlights several outstanding features including the Dalles of St. Croix River, Hospital Esker and Riegel Park.*

 At the Ice Age Trail Interpretive Center and other locations in Interstate State Park, the Polk County Tourist Information Center and Lion's Park (seasonal).

 From the St. Croix River, Big Rock Creek and other small streams/creeks. Do not take water from Mindy Creek as the headwaters are at the site of an old landfill.

 Walk-to campsite (**BP20**) in the St. Croix National Scenic Riverway.

 Two campgrounds in Interstate SP.

 At Interstate SP and Lion's Park.

 At Interstate SP (incl. Interpretive Center), Polk County Tourist Info Center, Lions Park and St. Croix National Scenic Riverway campsite.

 By law, dogs must be leashed in Interstate SP.

 Portions overlap with bike trails, ski trails, roads and sidewalks.

 Interstate SP and the Wert Family Nature Center have a network of trails; Riegel Park and Ray Zillmer Park each have white-blazed loop trails.

 Portions of this segment may be suitable for those using wheelchairs or similar devices.

TRAIL ACCESS AND PARKING

Western Terminus in Interstate State Park: From St. Croix Falls at the intersection of USH-8 and STH-35, take STH-35 south for 0.6 mi. Turn right, enter Interstate State Park and follow park roads 1.5 mi to the Pothole Trail parking area. A brief walk clockwise on the Pothole Trail leads to the western terminus marker.

River Rd.: From St. Croix Falls at USH-8 and STH-87, take STH-87 north for 3.0 mi. At River Rd. turn left and go northwest 0.5 mi to the Trail access. Roadside parking.

Additional Parking: (i) Interpretive Center and other parking areas in Interstate State Park. (ii) Polk County Visitor Information Center at STH-35 and USH-8. (iii) East Georgia St. parking area near its intersection with Vincent St. (iv) Riegel Park on Louisiana St. (v) Ray Zillmer Park on Day Rd. (vi) Wert Family Nature Preserve on east side STH-87. (vii) Lions Park on STH-87.

THE HIKE

The St. Croix River valley that hikers pass through on this segment was formed when the glacial lobe in the area retreated. Meltwater created Glacial Lake Duluth. Then giant floods drained the lake and cut the valley through billion-year-old volcanic basalt bedrock.

Access to the Ice Age Trail's western terminus is via Interstate State Park's Pothole Trail, a loop trail that was built shortly after the park was created in 1900 and is one of Wisconsin's oldest recreational footpaths. From the Pothole Trail

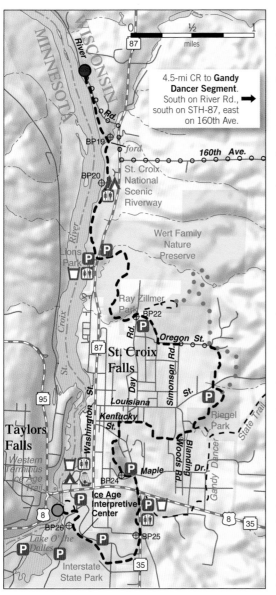

parking area, hikers can reach the Ice Age Trail's western terminus either by trekking on the northern non-Ice Age Trail portion of the loop or along the Ice Age Trail southern portion of the loop. The glacial potholes and Dalles of St. Croix River highlighted on the Pothole Trail were formed when torrential glacial meltwater scoured the riverside bedrock cliffs with rock and silt in a drilling-type motion. The potholes vary in size and depth, with one 16 feet deep and 3 feet wide. Additional larger potholes are located in Minnesota's Interstate State Park on the other side of the St. Croix River.

Upon reaching the Ice Age Trail's western terminus, hikers will find the official terminus marker (similar to the marker found at the Trail's eastern terminus in Potawatomi State Park, Door County), affixed to a large glacial erratic on a basalt cliff overlooking the 100-foot-deep gorge of the Dalles of the St. Croix River. From just below the terminus marker, looking upriver, one can see the famous rock face of the "Ol' Man of the Dalles." Looking downriver, one can see a rare 90 degree turn in the river. This basalt rock protrusion, hard enough to stop the roaring outflow of the prehistoric lake and river, was the site of the world's largest log jam in 1886. It took three months to dynamite the river clear for log traffic coming from the logging forests to the saw mills.

From the segment starting point at the western terminus, hikers will head back to the Pothole Trail parking area on the southern portion of the loop, cross Park Road and head southwest and then southeast on the state park's Horizon Rock Trail. The segment ascends steeply, passing by a stone shelter near a rock-ledge overlook (**BP26**) with views of the river as it makes its way to the Ice Age Interpretive Center. At the center, hikers can pick up a park map for detailed information on the park's trails and facilities.

From the interpretive center, the segment briefly shares the northern portion of the Skyline Nature Trail loop then departs the nature trail by heading eastward toward the state park entrance road. The segment then links up with a paved bike path and turns north along STH-35, quickly leaving (**BP25**) Interstate State Park and soon bringing hikers to the Polk County Tourist Information Center, located across STH-35 just south of the STH-35/USH-8 intersection.

After crossing USH-8 the segment ascends the Hospital Esker (**BP24**). From here hikers can enjoy excellent views of the city of St. Croix Falls and the glacial lake plain left behind by the drained Glacial Lake Duluth.

The segment descends the esker to the hospital parking area on State Street and continues north on Roosevelt Street, then turns east on Kentucky Street. The segment leaves Kentucky Street and continues east then southeast up a bluff into a wooded area, then connects with a paved city bike path heading east through a school grounds.

After passing through the school grounds, the segment enters another wooded area, intersects with Blanding Woods Road and then enters the city-managed Florence Baker Riegel Memorial Park. The segment makes its way northeast through the park on its way to a parking area on the south side of Louisiana Street. Hikers can explore the park further by departing the Ice Age Trail and following a white-blazed loop trail that departs the yellow-blazed route just east of a parking area at Louisiana Street.

In late summer 2014, volunteers are planning to build a new section of the Ice Age Trail from the current intersection with the white-blazed loop. The new route will arch east, pass over basalt knobs and interpret a wonderful basalt-walled drainageway, cross Louisiana Street east of the current parking area, continue north through upland woods to Oregon Street, then head north to eventually hook up with the current Trail route at Ray Zillmer Park/Day Road.

The segment's route (at the time of publication of this book) continues north from Louisiana Street up a hill; from the top, hikers will spot the local fairgrounds, community gardens and an old red barn. The segment drops down the hill and, at the intersection of Oregon Street and Sunrise Road, continues west on an unmarked connecting route along Oregon Street before veering northwest on Mindy Creek Court.

Departing from Mindy Creek Court, the segment makes its way northwest toward Day Road. Near the intersection with Day Road hikers will find Ray Zillmer Park, which is dedicated to the founding father of the Ice Age Trail and includes a half-mile white-blazed loop trail that at its highest point offers fine views of the St. Croix River valley.

At Day Road, the segment crosses a 26-foot-long footbridge. Look carefully at the bridge's limestone landing (**BP22**) closest to Day Road; when the limestone is wet, two 6-inch nautilus fossils appear. The segment continues west through woods and follows downhill alongside boulder-strewn Mindy Creek, named after a Native American woman from the Bad River Band of the Ojibwe who was the last of the Native Americans to live and work by the St. Croix River in the area.

After leaving Mindy Creek, the segment heads north as it continues to descend toward the STH-87 Trail access through the Wert Family Nature Preserve. The segment crosses STH-87 and passes through part of Lions Park, then turns north and takes hikers to the scenic shoreline of the St. Croix River. There are several social trails ("unofficial" trails created by meandering hikers) in the area; hikers should pay close attention to signage and stay close to the riverbank.

Heading north, hikers will soon come across a shoreline primitive campsite (**BP20**). The campsite is part of the St. Croix National Scenic Riverway and is available on a first-come, first-served basis. After passing by the primitive campsite, the segment reaches bridgeless Big Rock Creek (**BP19**), which hikers can usually cross on steppingstones, but may have to ford in high waters. Once across the creek, hikers will continue north along the St. Croix River to the segment terminus at River Road.

Mobile Skills Crew project site, 2005, 2014

AREA SERVICES

Interstate State Park: Camping. On Trail (715-483-3747, dnr.wi.gov/topic/parks/name/interstate; reservations: 888-947-2757, reserveamerica.com).

St. Croix Falls: Restaurant, grocery store, convenience store, general shopping, lodging, camping, library, medical care. On Trail. Most services in downtown on Washington St., USH-8 and STH-35. Medical services at St. Croix Regional Medical Center (235 State St., 715-483-3261 or 800-642-1336, scrmc.org). Outfitter/boot repair at St. Croix Falls Cobbler Shop (102 S. Washington St., 715-483-5798). For area info, contact the Falls Chamber of Commerce (715-483-3580, fallschamber.org) or the Polk County Tourist Information Center (715-483-1410, polkcountytourism.com).

St. Croix National Scenic Riverway: Primitive camping. On Trail (715-483-2274, nps.gov/sacn).

Overlooking the St. Croix River near the Ice Age Trail's western terminus.

Gandy Dancer Segment (Atlas Maps 1f, 2f, 3f)

SNAPSHOT

15.6 miles (15.2 IAT, 0.4 CR): 160th Ave. to 150th St.

 This segment follows the multi-use Gandy Dancer State Trail (GDST) on a level, crushed-rock surface.

 At village parks in Centuria, Milltown and Luck.

From the Trade River and a few intermittent streams/creeks.

 At nearby Big Butternut Lake Park in Luck, 1.0 mi east of the Trail (see Area Services).

 At village parks in Milltown and Luck.

 By law, dogs must be leashed on the GDST.

 Segment overlaps with the GDST and also includes a short roadwalk. The GDST is open to biking and snowmobiling.

 The GDST continues both north and south.

 Portions of this segment may be suitable for those using wheelchairs or similar devices.

TRAIL ACCESS AND PARKING

160th Ave.: From Centuria at the intersection of 8th St. and STH-35, take STH-35 south 0.5 mi. At 160th Ave. turn right and go west 0.9 mi to the Ice Age Trail/Gandy Dancer Trail access. No parking. Nearest parking is at the Gandy Dancer State Trail parking area in Centuria.

150th St.: From Frederic on STH-35/48, take STH-35/48 south 2.0 mi. At 150th St. turn left and continue south 0.3 mi to the parking area.

Additional Parking: Gandy Dancer State Trail trailheads in the towns of Luck and Milltown.

THE HIKE

From 160th Avenue, this segment heads northeast along the Gandy Dancer State Trail (GDST). The 98-mile, multi-use GDST crosses the Wisconsin–Minnesota border twice on its way from St. Croix Falls to Superior. The crushed limestone–surfaced trail was converted from the abandoned Soo Line railway. The name "Gandy Dancer" was chosen to honor the men who built and maintained railroad tracks. "Gandy Dancers" used tools manufactured by the Gandy Manufacturing Company and, while working, followed songlike calls and melodies that helped synchronize the

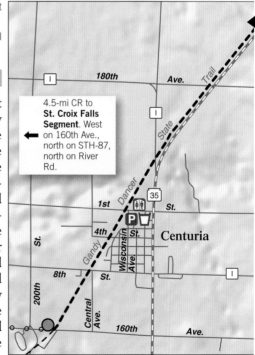

4.5-mi CR to **St. Croix Falls Segment**. West on 160th Ave., north on STH-87, north on River Rd.

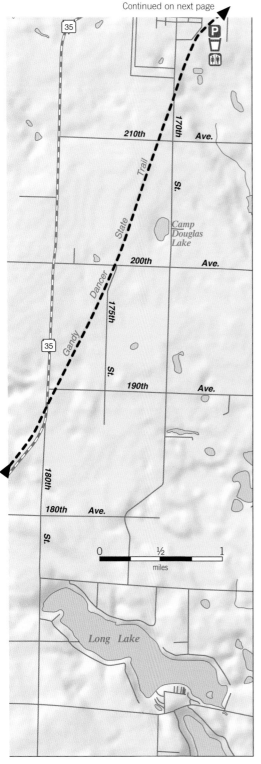

Continued on next page

swinging of tools and the movement of feet as they "danced" to the next rails. The GDST connects with the North Country National Scenic Trail south of the city of Superior.

The segment takes hikers through three small towns: Centuria, Milltown and Luck. Founded at the turn of the 20th century, Centuria has a rest stop along the segment with restrooms and vending machines. This log-sided structure is fully enclosed, affording all-weather protection for the hiker. Between Centuria and Milltown, the segment crosses from the west side of STH-35 to the east side. In Milltown, named for the sole building for a number of years, there is a picnic area with restrooms at the intersection of Milltown Avenue and STH-35. Milltown services are located on Main Street two blocks west of the segment. In Luck hikers will find picnic tables at the segment's intersection with STH-48. This village near Butternut Lake was a stopover for travelers between Cumberland, WI, and Taylor Falls, MN. Travelers felt that if they made it here by nightfall they were "luck"-y.

Between towns, the segment is largely sheltered on both sides by trees. While the Gandy Dancer State Trail does get used by bikers and snowmobilers, a hiker may walk for long stretches without encountering others.

The segment departs from the GDST where the GDST crosses STH-35/48 about 5 miles north of Luck. The segment follows an access path along the highway to 150th Street, where it heads south on an unblazed connecting route for 0.3 miles to the segment's terminus.

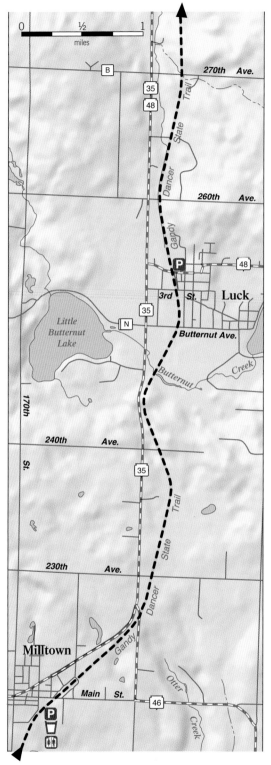

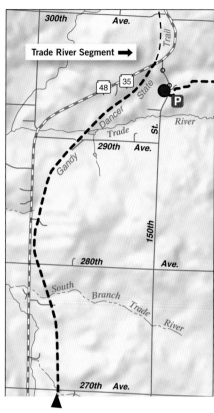

Trade River Segment ➡

AREA SERVICES

Gandy Dancer State Trail: On Trail (715-485-9294, dnr.wi.gov/topic/parks/name/gandydancer).

Centuria: Restaurant, convenience store, lodging, library. On Trail. Meals at Al's Diner (101 STH-35, 715-646-2931).

Milltown: Restaurant. On Trail.

Luck: Restaurant, grocery store, convenience store, lodging, camping, library, medical care. On Trail. Meals and internet at Café Wren (2596 STH-35, 715-472-4700, cafewren.com. From the Trail turn west on 260th Ave. At STH-35 turn left and go south. The cafe is on the east side of STH-35. Camping on business grounds by permission; call 715-472-2922). Additional camping at Big Butternut Lake Park 1.0 mi east of the Trail crossing with Butternut Ave.

Lodging and meals at Luck Country Inn and Oakwood Café (STH-35 and STH-48, 715-472-2000 or 800-544-7396, luckcountryinn.com).

Frederic: Restaurant, convenience store, camping, library, medical care. From the Gandy Dancer State Trail near 150th St. go 1.5 mi north on GDST or STH-35. Meals at Bean's Country Griddle (715-327-5513) and Jimmy's Drive In (715-566-0963).

Siren: Restaurant, lodging. From the Gandy Dancer State Trail near 150th St. go ~12 mi north on STH-35. Meals at Adventures Restaurant and Pub (7710 Park Rd. W., 715-349-8500) and Chattering Squirrel Coffee Café (715-349-8282). Lodging at Best Western Motel (715-349-7800) and The Lodge at Crooked Lake (715-349-2500).

St. Croix Falls: See St. Croix Falls Segment, p. 6. From 160th Ave. go west and south ~5 mi.

GREG SEITZ

Straight Lake Segment.

Trade River Segment
and Straight Lake Segment (Atlas Map 3f)

Trade River Segment—4.3 miles (3.9 IAT, 0.4 CR):150th St. to 280th Ave.

Straight Lake Segment—3.6 miles: 280th Ave. to 100th St. (CTH-I)

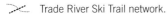 The **Trade River Segment** highlights the Trade River and its headwaters area, which hikers will explore on serpentine boardwalks.

 From the Trade River and headwaters wetlands.

 At Coon Lake Park in Frederic, ~2 mi north of the Trail.

 Portion of the segment crossing private land between 150th St. and the SIATA property east of 140th St. is closed during gun deer season.

 Segment includes connecting route roadwalk. Portions overlap with cross-country ski trails and logging/forest roads.

Trade River Ski Trail network.

The dramatic **Straight Lake Segment** highlights wild Straight Lake State Park and beautiful, pristine Straight Lake.

 From the Straight River, Straight Lake and other small lakes and wetland areas.

 Portion of segment crossing private land between the eastern boundary of Straight Lake State Park and CTH-I is closed during gun deer season.

Park access road leading to 120th Street parking area.

TRAIL ACCESS AND PARKING

150th St.: From Frederic on STH-35/48, take STH-35/48 south 2.0 mi. At 150th St. turn left and continue south 0.3 mi to the parking area.

100th St. (CTH-I): From Luck at the intersection of STH-35 and STH-48, take STH-48 east 5.2 mi. At 100th St. (CTH-I) turn left and go north 0.9 mi to the parking area on the west (left) side of the road.

Additional Parking: (i) 140th St. roadside parking. (ii) 280th Ave. parking area on the south side of the road. (ii) 120th St. Straight Lake State Park parking area 0.1 mi north of the intersection of 120th St. and 270th Ave.

THE HIKE

Prominent features in this area are knobs of basalt bedrock. During the pre-Cambrian era, 1.1 billion years ago, the Earth's crust split across part of the

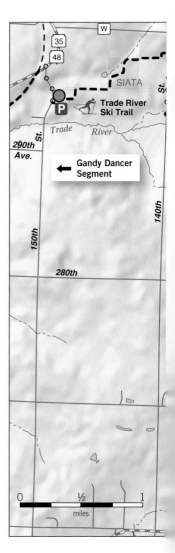

North American continent. Known as the mid-continent rift, the split extended from Kansas to Lake Superior. Huge volumes of molten lava flowed to the surface and cooled, forming the basalt bedrock seen here. For most of that distance the basalt is beneath sedimentary rock, but from St. Croix Falls to Lake Superior outcroppings of exposed bedrock can be found.

The **Trade River Segment** begins at 150th Street at the parking area for the Trade River Ski Area, which offers 4 km of groomed ski trails in winter. The segment briefly overlaps with the ski trail route; those hiking here in winter should hike well off to the side of the groomed track.

When the segment reaches 140th Street, hikers should turn right and head south for 0.4 miles along the unmarked connecting route before departing 140th Street and continuing eastward on the off-road portion of the segment. Here, the segment passes through a prairie, along the Trade River and through a wooded area. A notable waypoint is the big basalt rock (**BP17**) dropped here by the Superior Lobe.

Because of impermeable bedrock, for the last half-mile before the segment's endpoint on 280th Avenue the route has to navigate wetlands (and accompanying beaver dams) that make up the headwaters of the Trade River. The segment design incorporates the uniqueness of the terrain, saturating the hiker's senses by meandering next to, around and over some of the bedrock and serendipitously coursing above the perpetually wet ground on a serpentine, elevated boardwalk.

*Mobile Skills
Crew project site,
2010, 2011*

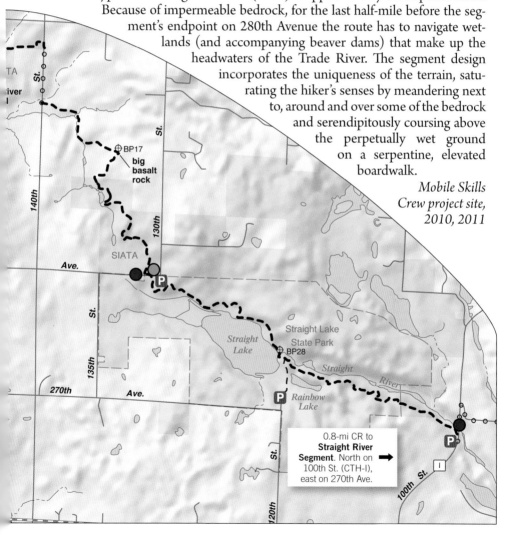

The **Straight Lake Segment** travels through the heart of 3000-acre Straight Lake State Park, which contains the headwaters of two river systems: the Straight River draining southeast and the Trade River draining to the northwest. The landscape is hummocky with outcroppings of basalt bedrock. Because the bedrock is close to the surface, the terrain contains numerous ephemeral ponds, perched wetlands and marshes.

The park exists in a transition zone between two vegetative communities: the northern hardwood forest and the prairie forest. One finds an intermingling of species from both communities and here many plants and animals reach their northern and southern limits. The extensive block of oak forest approaches old-growth status. Black bear, red fox, river otter, gray tree frog, leopard frog and four-toed salamander are common.

(Note: The DNR bans all glass containers in Straight Lake State Park.)

From its starting point on 280th Avenue the segment makes its way past the north shore of 107-acre Straight Lake, a shallow drainage lake with a small dam (**BP28**) at its outlet to the Straight River. Shortly after crossing the dam the Trail intersects with a gravel road that leads south to the state park's 120th Street parking area. The segment continues east through the Straight River tunnel channel, the finest example of a glacial tunnel channel in the Midwest. During the Ice Age, a subglacial river flowed rapidly as it exited beneath the receding glacier. The sediment it collected was carried away from the glacial margin, leaving the channel intact.

The segment passes near the eastern end of Rainbow Lake and glimpses of the lake can be seen through the trees. Soon after hikers will cross a unique, curving boardwalk. As the segment makes its way to its endpoint on 100th Street (CTH-I), hikers are treated to a number of spectacular views of the valley of the Straight River tunnel channel.

Mobile Skills Crew project site, 2007, 2009, 2010, 2011

AREA SERVICES

Oak Forest Retreat Center: Lodging (2824 130th St., Frederic, 715-327-4500, oakforestcenter.org). From the intersection of 280th Ave. and 130th St., go north 0.7 mi on 130th St. Call before visiting. Limited availability.

Frederic: See Gandy Dancer Segment, p. 10. From 150th St. go north 1.5 mi. Also see Trail Access and Parking directions, above.

Siren: See Gandy Dancer Segment, p. 10. From 150th St. go north ~12 mi.

Luck: See Gandy Dancer Segment, p. 10. From 120th St. Trail access go west ~5 mi. Also see Trail Access and Parking directions, above.

Straight River Segment and Pine Lake Segment (Atlas Maps 3f, 4f)

SNAPSHOT

Straight River Segment—3.4 miles: 270th Ave. to Round Lake Rd.

Pine Lake Segment—2.9 miles: Round Lake Rd. to 70th St.

 The **Straight River Segment** highlights the Straight River tunnel channel and includes an enjoyable loop trail.

 From the Straight River and Long Lake.

 Primitive camping near the 95th St. parking area (**BP14**).

The segment is closed during gun deer season.

 Portions overlap with a snowmobile trail, STH-48, a private gravel driveway and some logging/forest roads.

 Two white-blazed loop trails: one along the east side of the Straight River and the other off the 95th St. parking area.

 The **Pine Lake Segment** is rich in variety, highlighting glacial remnants, restored prairies and hummocky woodlands.

 No reliable sources of water.

Portion of the segment crossing private land between Round Lake Rd. and STH-48 is closed during gun deer season.

 Portions overlap with snowmobile trails, logging/forest roads and 260th Ave.

 A white-blazed loop trail crossing a debris field.

TRAIL ACCESS AND PARKING

270th Ave.: *From Luck* at the intersection of STH-35 and STH-48, take STH-48 east for 5.2 mi. At 100th St. (CTH-I) turn left and go north 1.3 mi. At 270th Ave. turn right and go east 0.6 mi to the Trail access. Roadside parking.

70th St.: *From Cumberland* at the intersection of STH-48 and STH-63, take STH-48 west 15.7 mi. At 260th Ave. turn right and go east 0.7 mi. At 70th St. turn left and go north 0.7 mi to the parking area on the west side of the road. *From Frederic* at the intersection of STH-35 and CTH-W, take CTH-W east 9.0 mi. At 60th St. (CTH-O) turn right and go south 3.0 mi and follow CTH-O to the west on 270th St. for 0.9 mi. At 70th St. turn left and go south 0.3 mi.

Additional Parking: "Moh's Mountain" (**BP14**) on 95th St.

THE HIKE

The **Straight River Segment** starts out by heading south from 270th Avenue, passing through a dry kettle as it makes its way toward the Straight River tunnel channel. Dropping down from the rim of the tunnel channel the segment intersects (**BP12**) with a white-blazed loop trail. A side trip on the white-blazed trail leads to an enormous white pine on private land and then continues along the east side of the Straight River to STH-48. The white-blazed trail is at river level and therefore offers excellent bird viewing opportunities of eagles and nesting Canadian geese, sandhill cranes and trumpeter swans.

From the intersection with the white-blazed trail the segment continues south, going up and down a small kame, crossing the Straight River and switchbacking

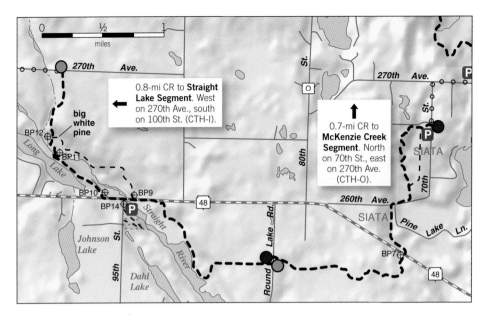

up an esker (**BP11**) that separates the Straight River and Long Lake.

The segment continues a short distance southeast on the esker above the shore of Long Lake before reaching a private gravel drive and several private cabins. From here, hikers can see both the Straight River to the east and Long Lake to the west. The segment follows the gravel drive southeast to its intersection (**BP10**) with STH-48.

At the intersection of the private drive and STH-48, hikers should head east for 0.3 miles along the southern shoulder of STH-48. In the process, the route intersects with 95th Street. Hikers looking for primitive camping can head a short distance south on 95th Street to a parking area (**BP14**) for an IATA-owned property. The property is open to primitive camping and has a white-blazed loop trail leading to the wooded hilltop known as "Moh's Mountain."

Back on STH-48, the segment crosses the wide Straight River, where a hiker may see otters and water birds, and intersects (**BP9**) on the north side of STH-48 with the southern access to the white-blazed loop trail encountered earlier in the segment. Shortly, the segment departs from STH-48 and heads southeast through a pine plantation back toward the shore of the Straight River. The route hugs the shore of the river for nearly half a mile before turning east, climbing a hill and traversing along field edges to the segment's endpoint on Round Lake Road.

The **Pine Lake Segment** continues east from Round Lake Road, passing mostly through wooded areas on its way to STH-48. After 0.5 miles, the segment reaches a gated cattle field. Hikers may enter the field through the gate if it is unlocked (please make sure gate is closed) or by using fence stiles on the adjoining fences. Once in the field, the Trail hugs the forest edge before heading east into the forest over another fence stile. From here, the segment occasionally shares a snowmobile trail; hikers should pay close attention to blazes and directional arrows on posts.

Upon reaching STH-48 (**BP7**), hikers should cross with caution and continue on the segment as it bends to the northwest and then north along a field edge to 260th Avenue. The segment turns right and heads east for 0.2 miles on 260th Avenue before going off-road and heading north again.

The portion of the segment between 260th Avenue and its endpoint on 70th Street crosses land that is a veritable glacial dumping ground, with hilly, open fields, restored prairie areas and hummocky woods that highlight many glacial features. Shortly after the segment leaves 260th Avenue, it intersects with a white-blazed loop trail that offers a side trip to explore these many glacial features in greater depth.

AREA SERVICES

Frederic: See Gandy Dancer Segment, p. 10. From 270th Ave. Trail access go north ~10 mi. Also see Trail Access and Parking directions, above.

Luck: See Gandy Dancer Segment, p. 10. From STH-48 Trail access go west ~7 mi. Also see Trail Access and Parking directions, above.

Cumberland: See Grassy Lake Segment, p. 34. From 70th St. Trail access go east ~17 mi. Also see Trail Access and Parking directions, above.

Straight Lake Segment.

Polk & Burnett Counties

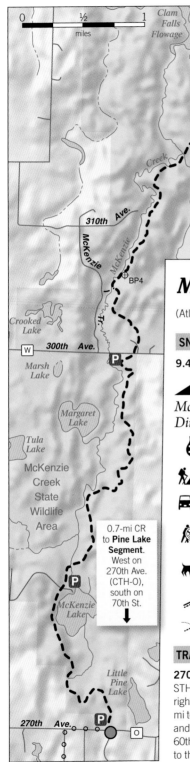

McKenzie Creek Segment

(Atlas Maps 4f, 5f)

SNAPSHOT

9.4 miles: 270th Ave. (CTH-O) to 50th St. (CTH-O)

4 3 *This wild and scenic segment highlights the McKenzie Creek tunnel channel and McKenzie and Dinger kettle lakes.*

 From McKenzie Creek, the Clam River, Dinger Lake, McKenzie Lake and other smaller streams/creeks.

 County forest land west of CTH-O only. Primitive camping is not permitted in the State Wildlife Area.

 In Clam Falls, ~2 mi north of the 60th St. parking area.

 Portion of segment crossing private land between 60th St. parking area and 50th St. (CTH-O) is closed during gun deer season.

 By law, dogs must be leashed April 15 to July 31 in the State Wildlife Area.

 Portions overlap snowmobile trails and logging/forest roads.

Intersects with a few side trails.

TRAIL ACCESS AND PARKING

270th Ave. (CTH-O): *From Cumberland* at the intersection of STH-48 and STH-63, take STH-48 west 10.0 mi. At 40th St. turn right and go north 2.0 mi. At 270th Ave. turn left and go west 2.5 mi to the parking area. *From Frederic* at the intersection of STH-35 and 300th Ave. (CTH-W), take 300th Ave. (CTH-W) east 9.0 mi. At 60th St. (CTH-O) turn right and go south 3.0 mi and follow CTH-O to the west on 270th Street for 0.6 mi.

50th St. (CTH-O): *From Cumberland* at the intersection of STH-48 and USH-63, take STH-48 west for 8.0 mi. At 10th St. (CTH-E) turn right and go north, west then north 4.7 mi. (Please note when CTH-E turns west then north, it becomes 15th St.) At 300th Ave. (CTH-W) turn left and go west 4.0 mi. At 50th St. (CTH-O) turn right and go north 2.5 mi to the parking area on the west side of the road. *From Frederic* at the intersection of STH-35 and 300th Ave. (CTH-W), take 300th Ave. (CTH-W) east 10.0 mi. At 50th St. (CTH-O) turn left and go north 2.5 mi.

Additional Parking: (i) 280th Ave. at McKenzie Lake boat launch parking area. (ii) 300th Ave. (CTH-W) parking area. (iii) 60th St. Clam River parking area.

THE HIKE

The McKenzie Creek Segment highlights the steep and hilly topography of the 5,497 acre McKenzie Creek State Wildlife Area. Established in 1945, the wildlife area provides watershed protection and access to four trout streams and six lakes. Often growing near the lakes and in bog areas are tamarack, alder and black spruce, with occasional white spruce and balsam fir. The remainder of the forest is mostly red oak, aspen and pine, with some maple, ironwood, basswood, hickory and elm. The forest is reestablishing from years of logging and fire. Growing beneath the forest canopy is a wide variety of ferns, wildflowers like yellow lady's slipper, wild geranium, Solomon's seal and trillium and an assortment of fungi. Wild strawberries and raspberries can also be found along the Trail.

From 270th Avenue, the segment heads north, enters a northern hardwood forest and follows a logging road down a slope. Soon the Trail leaves the logging road for a well-defined single track trail that follows the gentle ups and downs of the kettle topography in this area. Hikers may experience the feeling of being in a very diverse and remote wilderness. After passing a Leopold bench overlooking an ephemeral wetland hikers will climb a slope to catch a first glimpse at McKenzie Lake through the woods.

Continuing through forest and meadow, the Trail skirts the shore of spring-fed McKenzie Lake and crosses a gravel road leading to a boat ramp. This is the only lake in the wildlife area to have a developed access for boaters. The serene, undeveloped kettle lake is a prime example of an end product of the glacial activity in the area.

North of McKenzie Lake, the segment cuts through an area of towering white pines, crosses McKenzie Creek and then climbs a ridge overlooking the creek. Hikers may notice a change in species as the segment covers rolling topography, sticking mostly to a ridge. This area is also home to undevleoped Margaret Lake and Tula Lake, which are accessible from a trail west of where the segment crosses 300th Avenue (CTH-W).

North of 300th Avenue (CTH-W), the segment joins a sandy logging road through an older logging harvest area. Hikers should pay close attention to signage as the Trail intersects with other logging roads and a few side trails. The segment soon meets McKenzie Creek again and follows the creek north as it winds along the tunnel channel of McKenzie Creek (**BP4**), a pristine Class I trout stream with a naturally sustaining wild trout population. Pass another Leopold bench on top of a hummock with great views of the creek below and the valley of the tunnel channel.

Eventually, the Trail crosses a small tributary of McKenzie Creek on a wooden bridge and climbs out of the tunnel channel. The segment then drops down to lower elevations as it passes along the west shoreline of Dinger Lake, one of many remote kettle lakes in the area. As the segment curves around to the north of the lake, hikers will pass another Leopold bench offering views across the lake. The segment continues through forest and shortly crosses the scenic Clam River, a Class III trout stream, just before reaching the 60th Street Trail access and parking area.

From the Clam River parking area, hikers will climb up a hill and follow a wide snowmobile trail. Near a tributary of the Clam River, the segment route leaves the snowmobile trail and continues on well marked and maintained single track trail through northern hardwood forest. Here the Trail crosses a section of private lands and then enters a State Ice Age Trail Area (SIATA). The segment crosses another small ephemeral stream shortly before reaching its terminus on 50th Street (CTH-O).

AREA SERVICES

Clam Falls: Restaurant, camping. From the Clam River Trail access on 60th St. go north ~2 mi. Meals at Clam Falls Tavern (647 335th Ave., 715-653-2518).

Frederic: See Gandy Dancer Segment, p. 10. From CTH-W Trail access go west ~13 miles. Also see Trail Access and Parking directions, above.

Cumberland: See Grassy Lake Segment, p. 34. From CTH-W Trail access go east and south ~20 mi. Also see Trail Access and Parking directions, above.

Indian Creek Segment (Atlas Map 5f)

SNAPSHOT

5.4 miles: 50th Street (CTH-O) to 15th St. (CTH-E)

  This segment explores rolling, remote Polk County Forest lands.

 From the headwaters of the Indian Creek (**BP31**).

Primitive camping on county forest lands.

 Portion of the segment crossing private land west of 30th St. is closed during gun deer season.

 Portions overlap snowmobile trails and logging/forest roads.

TRAIL ACCESS AND PARKING

50th St. (CTH-O): *From Cumberland* at the intersection of STH-48 and USH-63, take STH-48 west for 8.0 mi. At 10th St. (CTH-E) turn right and go north, west then north 4.7 mi. (Please note when CTH-E turns west then north, it becomes 15th St.) At 300th Ave. (CTH-W) turn left and go west 4.0 mi. At 50th St. (CTH-O) turn right and go north 2.5 mi to the parking area on the west side of the road. *From Frederic* at the intersection of STH-35 and 300th Ave. (CTH-W), take 300th Ave. (CTH-W) east 10.0 mi. At 50th St. (CTH-O) turn left and go north 2.5 mi.

15th St. (CTH-E): *From Cumberland* at the intersection of STH-48 and USH-63, take STH-48 west for 8.0 mi. At 10th St. (CTH-E) turn right and go north, west then north 7.4 mi to parking area on west side of the road. (Please note when CTH-E turns west then north, it becomes 15th St.) *From Frederic* at the intersection of STH-35 and 300th Ave. (CTH-W), take 300th Ave. (CTH-W) east 14.0 mi. At 10th St. (CTH-E) turn left. Follow directions from above to the Trail access parking area.

Additional Parking: 30th St. Trail access. Parking area on the east side of the road.

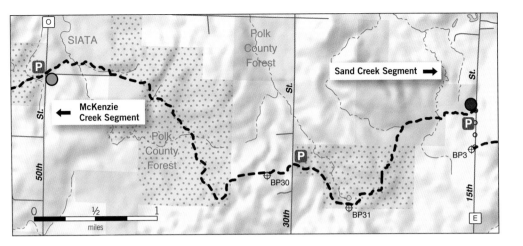

THE HIKE

The Indian Creek Segment passes through thickly forested and hummocky areas of a State Ice Age Trail Area, Polk County Forest and private land. The majority of the segment is on public land and the forest is mostly managed for larger stands of hardwoods by select cutting.

The segment heads east from 50th Street (CTH-O) through mostly softwood lowlands, crossing numerous creek beds on generally level terrain. Hikers should be aware that this portion of the Trail can be wet in spring and at times of rainy weather. Thick berry bushes are common in late summer.

The segment then travels through a high-relief hummocky area. This terrain was created when sand and gravel, carried by under-the-ice rivers and streams, were left behind after the ice sheets melted. These hummocks will challenge hikers with steep climbs and descents and provide nice views of the surrounding forest. Shortly before reaching 30th Avenue, a Leopold bench (**BP30**) sits on top of a hummock.

Crossing 30th Avenue marks the approximate midpoint and the start of a trek through more open woods and a few rocky creek beds. A short climb up a ridge puts the segment above a small picturesque lily-filled lake (**BP31**), the headwaters of Indian Creek. Waterfowl and herons can be spotted from the forested ridge as the Trail winds north and east. The habitat is ideal for wildlife and hikers may spot deer, grouse, various birds and signs of black bear.

The final mile of the segment consists of narrow hand-carved trail, a short bridge crossing and an open meadow, dotted with young white pines, as the segment makes its way to its terminus on 15th Street (CTH-E).

AREA SERVICES

Clam Falls: See McKenzie Creek Segment, p. 20. From 50th St. (CTH-O) Trail access go north and west ~3 mi.

Frederic: See Gandy Dancer Segment, p. 10. From 50th St. (CTH-O) Trail access go north and west 12.5 mi. Also see Trail Access and Parking directions, above.

Cumberland: See Grassy Lake Segment, p. 34. From 15th St. (CTH-E) Trail access go south and east ~15.5 mi. Also see Trail Access and Parking directions, above.

Sand Creek Segment (Atlas Maps 5f, 6f)

6.0 miles (5.7 IAT, 0.3 CR): 15th St. (CTH-E) Northern Trail Access to Lake 32 Rd.

 This segment highlights the Sand Creek tunnel channel while exploring county forest lands and frequently sharing logging roads.

 From Sand Creek and some smaller streams/creeks and wetland areas.

 Primitive camping on county forest lands.

The portion of the segment crossing private land between 15th St. (CTH-E) and Polk County Forest boundary is closed during gun deer season.

 Segment includes a short connecting route roadwalk. Small portions overlap snowmobile trails and gravel/dirt roads; a significant portion overlaps logging roads.

TRAIL ACCESS AND PARKING

15th St. (CTH-E) Northern Trail Access: From Cumberland at the intersection of STH-48 and USH-63, take STH-48 west for 8.0 mi. At 10th St. (CTH-F) turn right and go north, west then north for 7.4 mi to a parking area on the west side of the road. (Note: When CTH-E turns west then north, it becomes 15th St.).

Lake 32 Rd.: From Cumberland at the intersection of STH-48 and USH-63, take STH-48 west for 5.0 mi. At 2nd St. turn right and go north 1.6 mi. At 26th Ave. turn left and go west 1.0 mi. At 1st St. turn right and go north 1.5 mi. At 27th Ave. turn right and go east 0.5 mi. At 1st St. turn left and go north 2.5 mi. At 30th Ave. turn right and go east 0.2 mi to the junction with Lake 32 Rd. and the parking area on the corner.

THE HIKE

Starting from the 15th St. (CTH-E) northern Trail access and parking area, hikers should walk 0.3 miles south to the point where the segment heads off road (**BP3**). Here, the segment makes its way east over private land for the first half-mile before entering Polk County Forest lands. The segment bends to the southeast and follows the Sand Creek tunnel channel over hummocky sand and gravel. Sand Creek flows southeast through the bottom of the tunnel channel in a valley that extends to the town of Cumberland and includes several large lakes.

At a point just southeast of the Polk/Burnett county line, the segment reaches a bridge over Sand Creek (**BP2**). The creek has a wide variety of fish including largemouth bass, smallmouth bass and walleye. Shortly after the creek crossing the segment hooks up with a dirt forest road as it makes its way south and then southeast. The segment turns left off the road and meanders along on old logging roads through the woods. Hikers should pay close attention to signage as these logging roads can become overgrown.

The segment reaches a crossing of an old but well-preserved beaver dam. The Trail in this area may be wet or flooded in spring or during rainy periods. The segment passes along the south side of a wetland before reaching the intersection (**BP1**) of 1st Street and 30th Avenue. Hikers should continue east on 30th Avenue to the segment's endpoint at the 30th Avenue/Lake 32 Road intersection.

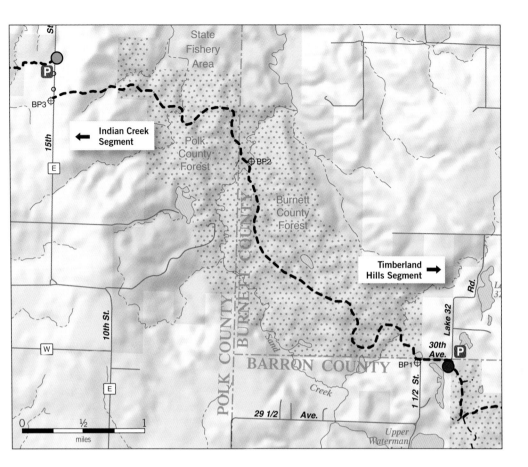

AREA SERVICES

Frederic: See Gandy Dancer Segment, p. 10. From 15th St. (CTH-E) Trail access go north and west ~18 mi.

Cumberland: See Grassy Lake Segment, p. 34. From Lake 32 Rd. Trail access go east 12.3 mi. Also see Trail Access and Parking directions, above.

I hiked with eager anticipation. I rounded a corner and saw the western terminus! I made it and not a soul was there to witness it. People told me to hike my own hike so it was fitting I ended alone. My feelings were all mixed up, should I feel happy, sad, relief or pride. I think they all came out. Pete showed up a few minutes later and he took some pics of me at the end trying to look stoic. Stoic comes easy after two months in the woods.

DAVE CALIEBE, ICE AGE TRAIL THOUSAND-MILER

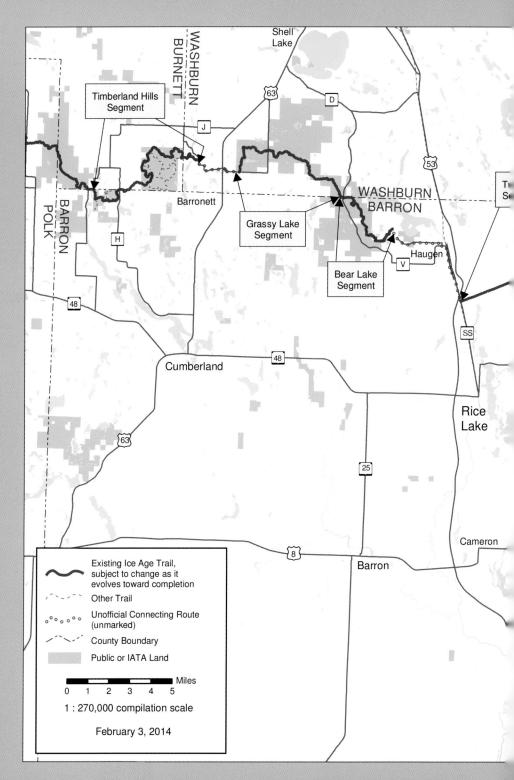

Timberland Hills
Segment

WASHBURN
BURNETT

Shell
Lake

63

D

53

J

POLK
BARRON

Barronett

Grassy Lake
Segment

WASHBURN
BARRON

H

Bear Lake
Segment

Haugen

V

T
S

48

SS

Cumberland

48

Rice
Lake

63

25

Cameron

8

Barron

Existing Ice Age Trail,
subject to change as it
evolves toward completion

Other Trail

Unofficial Connecting Route
(unmarked)

County Boundary

Public or IATA Land

Miles

0   1   2   3   4   5

1 : 270,000 compilation scale

February 3, 2014

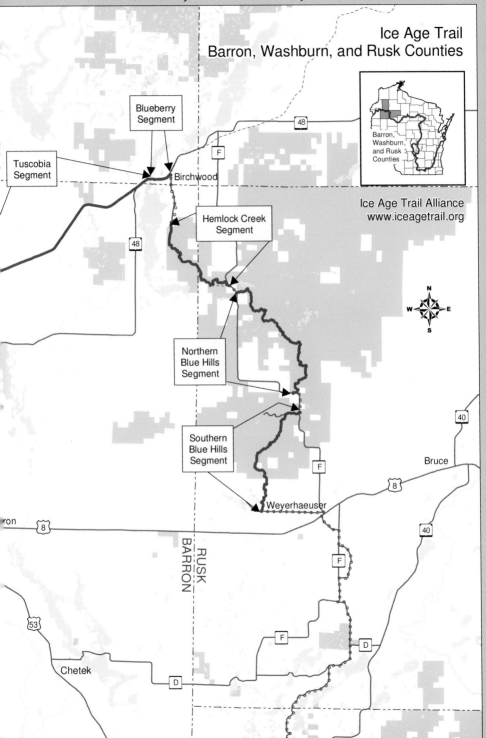

Ice Age Trail
Barron, Washburn, and Rusk Counties

Blueberry Segment

Tuscobia Segment

Birchwood

Hemlock Creek Segment

Barron, Washburn, and Rusk Counties

Ice Age Trail Alliance
www.iceagetrail.org

Northern Blue Hills Segment

Southern Blue Hills Segment

Bruce

Weyerhaeuser

RUSK
BARRON

Chetek

Barron & Washburn Counties

Trail miles: 41.8
Connecting route miles: 10.5

The Ice Age Trail route in Barron and Washburn counties winds through three different landscapes. To the west and north is the Superior Lobe end moraine, a lakes studded zone dominated by steep kettle topography. To the east are the Blue Hills, a 1.6-billion-year-old quartzite range. Between the two is an outwash plain created by meltwater from the Chippewa and Superior glacial lobes. The Ice Age Trail shares the Tuscobia State Trail, a multi-use rail-trail, across the outwash plain.

Primitive camping is allowed on Washburn and Barron County Forest land. Please camp at least 200 feet from trails and waterways.

CHAPTER INFORMATION

The Superior Lobe Chapter was formed in 2001 and meets regularly at the University of Wisconsin-Barron County in Rice Lake. The chapter maintains area Ice Age Trail segments and sponsors seasonal hikes, including snowshoe hikes, bird walks and the Woolly Mammoth Classic Run/Walk. The chapter also offers the "Superior Lobetrotter" award to hikers who pre-register and complete all Ice Age Trail segments from Lake 32 Rd. in Burnett County to CTH-F in Rusk County. Contact the chapter for details.

COUNTY INFORMATION

Barron County Visitor Information: 715-637-6871, barroncountywi.gov

Barron County Forest and Recreation Department: 715-537-6295

Washburn County Forest Department: 715-635-4490, www.co.washburn. wi.us

Ferns and equisetum (horsetail) lining the banks of Tuscobia Creek on the Tuscobia Segment.

Barron & Washburn Counties

Timberland Hills Segment (Atlas Map 6f)

SNAPSHOT

10.9 miles: Lake 32 Rd. to Leach Lake Rd.

  This segment mostly follows ski and snowshoe trails on hilly terrain through the Timberland Hills Ski Area, passing some scenic small lakes and wetland areas along the way.

From some small lakes and small intermittent streams/creeks.

Primitive camping on county forest lands.

Two portables available near the crossings of CTH-H and Boyd Ln.

Portion of segment crossing private land (i) east of the end of the gravel road to the Timberland Hills Ski Area western boundary and (ii) east of the Timberland Hills Ski Area eastern boundary to Leach Lake Rd. are closed during gun deer season.

 Dogs should stay off portions that overlap with groomed ski trails in winter.

Small portions overlap logging/forest roads and a gravel road. Large portions overlap with ski and snowshoe trails. Hike to the side of groomed ski trails in winter. Ski-area trails are open to horseback riding during the non-ski season.

 Ski/snowshoe network trails are open to hiking.

TRAIL ACCESS AND PARKING

Lake 32 Rd.: From Cumberland at the intersection of STH-48 and USH-63, take USH-48 west for 5.0 mi. At 2nd St. turn right and go north 1.6 mi. At 26th Ave. turn left and go west 1.0 mi. At 1st St. turn right and go north 1.5 mi. At 27½ Ave. turn right and go east 0.5 mi. At 1½ St. turn left and go north 2.5 mi. At 30th Ave. turn right and go east 0.2 mi to the junction with Lake 32 Rd. and the parking area on the corner.

Leach Lake Rd.: From Cumberland at the intersection of STH-48 and USH-63, take USH-63 north for 8.3 mi, ~1 mi past Barronett. At Brickyard Rd. turn left and go west 0.9 mi. At Leach Lake Rd. turn right and go north then west then north 0.7 mi to the Trail access (look for yellow arrow). Roadside parking.

Additional Parking: (i) 3rd St. (CTH-H): Timberland Hills West Lighted Cross Country Ski Trails parking area on the west side of the road. (ii) Boyd Ln.: Timberland Hills Cross-Country Ski Area main parking area.

THE HIKE

This segment traverses hummocky topography of the Superior Lobe's St. Croix Moraine. From its starting point on Lake 32 Road, the segment heads south on the Waterman Lakes Snowshoe Trail through a recent selectively logged area on a logging road and then east on narrower snowshoe trail. The segment weaves through mixed hardwood forests and crosses an old beaver dam (BW15) between two wet-

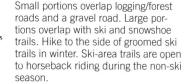

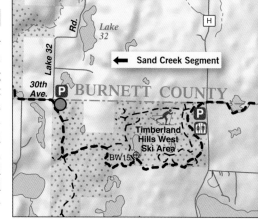

lands. The Trail then transitions to the wide grassy path of the Timberland Hills West Lighted Cross Country Ski Trails.

The segment crosses CTH-H (about 500 feet north of the Timberland Hills West parking area) and continues east on a gravel road for about a quarter mile where the road ends at two driveways. The Trail leaves the road and follows the southern edge of an open field before heading northeast across the field and re-entering the woods. The segment enters Burnett County Forest lands and at a signed junction (**BW14**) connects with the wide, mowed trails of the Timberland Hills Cross-Country Ski Area. This portion of Trail through the ski area is quite hilly, often steep and may have wet areas at the bottom of the hills. The segment continues about a mile north to the ski area's main parking lot and winter warming hut off Boyd Lane.

The segment generally continues north then east from Boyd Lane through a fine stand of white pine and over a bridge. From this point to a spot just north-west of Offers Lake, the segment ascends and descends frequently as it goes in and out of two tunnel channels, one of which flowed from the area of the present-day South Fork of the Clam River and the other from Leach Lake.

Reaching the east side of the ski area the segment leaves the ski trail (**BW13**) to follow a narrow track alongside some wetlands and beaver ponds. The segment passes by a Leopold bench (**BW17**) overlooking a scenic pond and then goes through a blueberry patch and down a steep hill to intersect with a grassy

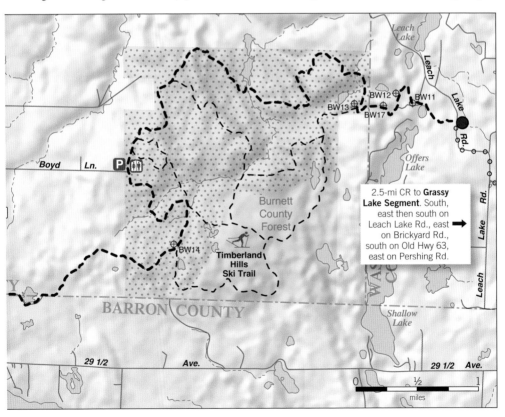

2.5-mi CR to **Grassy Lake Segment**. South, east then south on Leach Lake Rd., east on Brickyard Rd., south on Old Hwy 63, east on Pershing Rd.

Boyd Ln.

Burnett County Forest

BW14

Timberland Hills Ski Trail

BARRON COUNTY

BW12 BW11
BW13 BW17

Leach Lake

Offers Lake

Shallow Lake

29 1/2 Ave.

29 1/2 Ave.

0   ½   1
miles

road (**BW12**) near a red gate.

From here the segment follows grassy roads for about a quarter of a mile. Hikers should pay close attention to signage as there are intersecting roads and a right turn. The Trail abruptly leaves the grassy road to the left (**BW11**) and enters a brushy area (site of clear-cut), skirts the shoreline of a pond and climbs the side of a steep ravine. The segment then meanders a short distance through the woods to its terminus on Leach Lake Road.

AREA SERVICES

Barronett: See Grassy Lake Segment, p. 34. From Leach Lake Rd. Trail access go south ~2.5 mi.

Cumberland: See Grassy Lake Segment, p. 34. From Leach Lake Rd. Trail access go south ~10 mi. Also see Trail Access and Parking directions, above.

Shell Lake: See Grassy Lake Segment, p. 34. From Leach Lake Rd. Trail access go north ~8.5 mi.

Hiking trails provide the entire American family with perhaps the most economical, most varied form of outdoor recreation.

GAYLORD NELSON, WISCONSIN SENATOR AND GOVERNOR
AND FOUNDER OF EARTH DAY

Enjoying the cooling waters of Hemlock Creek on the Hemlock Creek Segment.

Barron & Washburn Counties

Grassy Lake Segment (Atlas Map 7f)

SNAPSHOT

8.2 miles: Pershing Rd. to 30th Ave.

  This remote segment crossing through Washburn County Forest is almost entirely on logging roads and features several small and scenic beaver-inhabited lakes.

From several small lakes, streams/creeks and other wetland areas.

 Primitive camping on county forest lands.

At nearby private campground 2.2 mi north of 30th Ave. Trail access (see Area Services for Sarona).

 Nearly the full segment is on logging/forest roads, portions of which are open to snowmobiling. A portion overlaps with primitive Shingle Camp Road, which is open to cars and ATVs.

TRAIL ACCESS AND PARKING

Pershing Rd.: From Cumberland at the intersection of STH-48 and USH-63 take USH-63 north for 8.3 mi. At Brickyard Rd. turn right and go east 0.1 mi. At Old Highway 63 turn right and go south 0.1 mi. At Pershing Rd. turn left and go east 0.7 mi just past W8661 Pershing Rd. to the Trail access parking area.

30th Ave.: From Haugen at the intersection of CTH-SS and CTH-V, take CTH-V (3rd St.) west 0.5 mi. Curve south on CTH-V (now 18th St.) and go 0.7 mi. Join 27th Ave. where CTH-V curves west and follow it west 1.7 mi. When CTH-V curves south, continue west on 27th Ave. for another 0.3 mi. At 16th St. turn right and go north 4.0 mi joining 13¾ St. (Shallow Lake Rd.). At 30th Ave. turn left and go west 0.1 mi to the parking area on the north side of the road.

Additional Parking: (i) Lehman Lake Rd. parking area. (ii) Shingle Camp Rd. parking area (**BW8**).

THE HIKE

Like the Timberland Hills Segment, the Grassy Lake Segment continues through hummocky topography of the Superior Lobe's St. Croix Moraine and skirts beaver-inhabited lakes and wetlands. Wildflowers include hepatica, violets, columbine, geraniums and carpets of trillium. Hikers should pay close attention to signage and the map while navigating through this segment as Ice Age Trail signage can be knocked down by animals or concealed by foliage. Low lying signs could also be covered by high water. A significant portion of the segment may be wet or flooded during rainy periods so appropriate gear for wet travel is recommended.

From its starting point on Pershing Road the segment heads north around a gate and soon passes near the west side of Grassy Lake (**BW9**). From here the segment heads

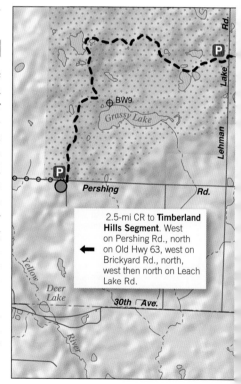

2.5-mi CR to **Timberland Hills Segment**. West on Pershing Rd., north on Old Hwy 63, west on Brickyard Rd., north, west then north on Leach Lake Rd.

north and then east on to Lehman Lake Road through generally forested terrain and past some small lakes and wetlands.

East of Lehman Lake Road the segment enters the Washburn County Forest Welsh Lake Unit. For the first 1.3 miles the segment shares the route with primitive Shingle Camp Road; this portion of the segment is open to car and ATV traffic. The segment leaves Shingle Camp Road at a point (**BW8**) where the road turns north; the segment continues southeast from this junction around a gate.

The segment makes its way to its terminus on 30th Avenue through more wetland areas and some hummocky terrain. Hikers will encounter several low-lying washouts of varying sizes that may have standing water. No footbridges exist on the segment. Some washouts can be easily stepped over while others may produce wet feet.

AREA SERVICES

Barronett: Restaurant, grocery store, convenience store. From Pershing Rd. Trail access go west 0.7 mi. At Old Hwy 63 turn right and go north 0.1 mi. At Brickyard Rd. turn left and go west 0.1 mi. At USH-63 turn left and go south 1.5 mi.

Cumberland: Restaurant, grocery store, convenience store, lodging, camping, library, medical care. From Pershing Rd. Trail access go west 0.7 mi. At Old Hwy 63 turn right and go north 0.1 mi. At Brickyard Rd. turn left and go west 0.1 mi. At USH-63 turn left and go south 8.3 mi. Area information from Cumberland Chamber of Commerce (715-822-3378, cumberland-wisconsin.com).

Shell Lake: Restaurant, grocery store, convenience store, lodging, library, medical care. From Pershing Rd. Trail access go west 0.7 mi. At Old Hwy 63 turn right and go north 0.1 mi. At Brickyard Rd. turn left and go west 0.1 mi. At USH-63 turn right and go north 7.0 mi.

Sarona: See Bear Lake Segment, p. 36. From 30th Ave. Trail access go north ~8 mi.

Haugen: See Tuscobia Segment, p. 38. From 30th Ave. Trail access go south and east 7.3 mi. Also see Trail Access and Parking directions, above.

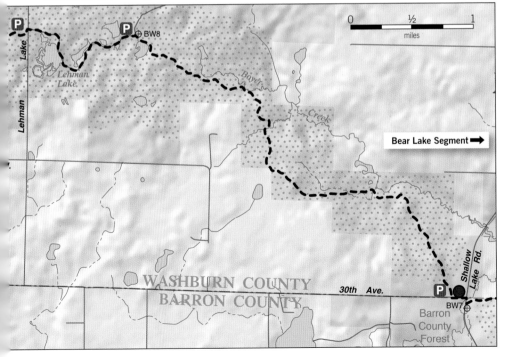

Bear Lake Segment (Atlas Map 8f)

SNAPSHOT

5.3 miles: 30th Ave. to 28th Ave. (CTH-VV)

 This segment crosses hummocky terrain and highlights several lakes and scenic wetlands.

 At Camp Phillips near Round Lake.

From Bass Lake, Round Lake, Crooked Lake and other small lakes, intermittent streams/creeks and wetland areas.

Primitive camping on county forest lands.

 At nearby private campgrounds 2.2 mi north of the 30th Ave. Trail access and 2.2 mi east of the 28th Ave. (CTH-VV) Trail access (see Area Services).

 Small portions overlap with a bike trail, gravel roads and logging/forest roads.

 Scout camp trail network.

TRAIL ACCESS AND PARKING

30th Ave.: From Haugen at the intersection of CTH-SS and CTH-V, take CTH-V (3rd St.) west 0.5 mi. Curve south on CTH-V (now 18th St.) and go 0.7 mi. Join 27th Ave. where CTH-V curves west and follow it west 1.7 mi. When CTH-V curves south, continue west on 27th Ave. for another 0.3 mi. At 16th St. turn right and go north 4.0 mi joining 13¾ St. and becoming Shallow Lake Rd. At 30th Ave. turn left and go west 0.1 mi to the parking area on the north side of the road.

28th Ave. (CTH-VV): From Haugen at the intersection of CTH-SS and CTH-V (3rd St.), take CTH-V west 0.2 mi. At Norvin Ave. turn right and go north 0.2 mi. At 5th St. (CTH-VV), which becomes 28th Ave., turn left and go west then north 2.2 mi. Look for the Ice Age Trail sign on the east side of the road. No parking at the Trail access on 28th Ave. (CTH-VV). Instead, park at Camp Phillips' "Cub World" parking area 0.2 mi south of the 28th Ave. (CTH-VV) Trail access.

THE HIKE

This segment continues through hummocky topography of the Superior Lobe's St. Croix Moraine, the outer edge of which is about 1.5 miles southeast of the segment's endpoint on 28th Avenue (CTH-VV).

From its starting point on 30th Avenue the segment heads east on the road for 0.1 miles to an intersection with Barron County's 13¾ - 16th Street (a road that changes names to Shallow Lake Road a short distance north, at the Barron/Washburn county line). The segment route turns south at the intersection and follows 13¾ - 16th Street (a Rustic Road) for 0.1 miles to a point (**BW7**) where the segment leaves the road and continues east through a mix of forests and marsh on Barron County Forest land. Hikers may catch a glimpse of Bear Lake through the woods in the distance to the east as they cross the hummocky terrain, especially when leaves are off the trees.

As it nears the southern shore of Crooked Lake the segment leaves Barron County Forest land and enters the Boy Scouts' L.E. Phillips Scout Reservation. The segment soon crosses a cattail-lined wetland on a 16-foot puncheon and 190-foot boardwalk (**BW6**) constructed by volunteers in 2003. This portion of the segment is a haven for northern waterfowl and dragonflies and often features a nightly chorus of frogs.

Heading south from Crooked Lake and Round Lake hikers may see in the trees

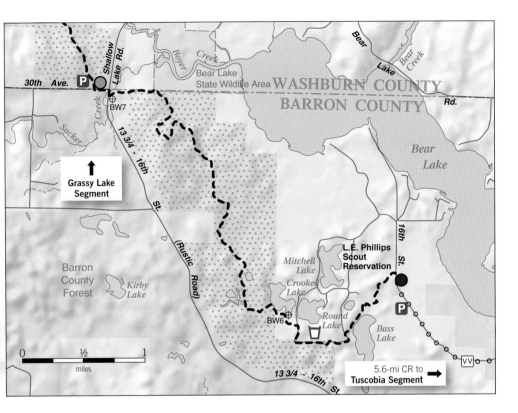

one of the camp's framed platform tent areas and can obtain drinking water from a faucet located between the tent area and Round Lake. From this area the segment continues east and then northeast, passing by the camp's Bass Lake beach before reaching the segment endpoint on 28th Avenue (CTH-VV)

Mobile Skills Crew project site, 2003

AREA SERVICES

Barronett: See Grassy Lake Segment, p. 34. From the 30th Ave. Trail access go west ~6 mi.

Haugen: See Tuscobia Segment, p. 38. From 28th Ave. (CTH-VV) Trail access go east 2.6 mi. Also see Trail Access and Parking directions, above.

Rice Lake: See Tuscobia Segment, p. 38. From the 28th Ave. (CTH-VV) Trail access go east and south ~11 mi.

Sarona: Camping. From the 30th Ave. Trail access, take Shallow Lake Rd. north 2.2 mi to White Tail Ridge Campground and RV Park, which has 6 tent sites (715-469-3309, whitetailridgecampground. com).

I'm convinced that a person could walk the same 10 miles every day of the year and see something beautiful.

MARK COOK, ICE AGE TRAIL THOUSAND-MILER

Tuscobia Segment (Atlas Maps 8f, 9f, 10f)

10.3 miles: CTH-SS to Tuscobia State Trail at Balsam Lake Rd.

🔺1🦫 *This segment follows the multi-use Tuscobia State Trail (TST) and features glacial erratics, several small kettle lakes, and views across an outwash plain.*

🚰 At the Brill baseball field and park (seasonal).

💧 From several small lakes, the Brill River and other small intermittent streams/creeks.

🚗Ⓐ At nearby private campground ~4 mi north and west of the CTH-SS Trail access and Waldo Carlson County Park 1.5 mi south of the Balsam Lake Rd. Trail access (see Area Services).

🧺 At Waldo Carlson County Park.

🚻 At the CTH-SS parking area, the Brill baseball field and park (seasonal) and Waldo Carlson County Park.

🐕! By law, dogs must be leashed while hiking on the TST.

🚴 Portions of the TST are open to biking, horseback riding, ATVs and snowmobiling.

-·-· The western end of the segment intersects with the Wild Rivers State Trail. The TST continues east from Balsam Lake Rd.

♿ Portions of this segment may be suitable for those using wheelchairs or similar devices.

TRAIL ACCESS AND PARKING

CTH-SS: From Rice Lake at the intersection of STH-48 and CTH-SS, take CTH-SS north 4.5 mi. A large gravel parking area for the Tuscobia State Trail, with a kiosk and restrooms, is on the right side of the road.

Tuscobia State Trail at Balsam Lake Rd.: From Birchwood at the intersection of Main St. and STH-48 take STH-48 west 2.0 mi. At Balsam Lake Rd. turn right. No parking available. Alternatively, park roadside on Featherstone Rd. on the south side of STH-48.

Additional Parking: (i) 21st St., parking area. (ii) Town of Brill, parking area. (iii) 26th St., roadside.

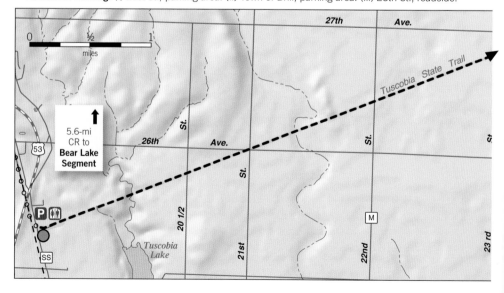

Ice Age Trail Guidebook 2014

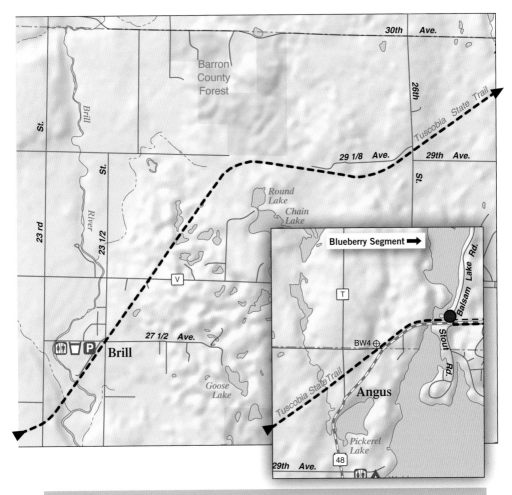

THE HIKE

This segment follows a portion of the 74-mile Tuscobia State Trail, which in 1966 became the second abandoned rail line in the state to be converted for recreational use. During its rail days the route was called the Omaha Line and at its peak operation, one passenger, one freight and 11 logging trains traveled each way—a total of 26 trains passing a given point every day. When the line was abandoned in 1965 after years of decline in the railroad and logging industries, the corridor land was to be parceled out to farmers. Hulda Hilfiker, a local resident, was instrumental in persuading neighbors and the State of Wisconsin to convert the railroad grade to a recreational trail. The portion of the Ice Age Trail that shares the Tuscobia State Trail is open to walking, bicycling, horseback riding and snowmobiling in winter. A short section on the bridge crossing the Red Cedar Narrows and the eastern approach to the bridge is open to ATVs.

Between the segment's western terminus on CTH-SS and the town of Brill, the segment links the terminal moraines of the Superior and Chippewa lobes as it crosses their outwash plain. The segment maintains a level even grade, with one exception: an area about a mile east of CTH-SS where the segment dips into a valley and crosses scenic Tuscobia Creek flowing south into Tuscobia Lake.

Upon reaching Brill, the segment crosses onto the Chippewa Moraine. Between Brill and Angus the segment passes numerous erratics and several small kettle lakes.

Soon after crossing CTH-T the segment enters into Washburn County (**BW4**) and crosses "The Narrows" connecting Balsam Lake and Red Cedar Lake, which are part of a tunnel channel of the Chippewa Moraine. Hikers should note that the portion of the Tuscobia State Trail in this area is open to ATV use; caution is advised. The segment ends a short distance east of The Narrows where the Tuscobia State Trail intersects with Balsam Lake Road.

Mobile Skills Crew project site, 2011

AREA SERVICES

Tuscobia State Trail: On Trail (715-266-7032, dnr.wi.gov/topic/parks/name/tuscobia).

Haugen: Restaurant, grocery store, camping. From the CTH-SS Trail access go ~2.5 mi north on CTH-SS. Meals at Lona's Corner Café (715-234-6110), Hanson's Hideaway (715-234-6555) and the Country Inn (715-234-4803). Camping at Shady Rest Campground (715-234-7339); from Haugen go west on 28th Ave. (CTH-VV). At 17¾ St. turn right and go north 0.2 mi.

Rice Lake: Restaurant, grocery store, convenience store, general shopping, lodging, library, medical care. From the CTH-SS Trail access go 4.5 mi south on CTH-SS. Meals at Adventures Sporting Café & Pub (715-234-4040). Outfitter/camping supplies at the Bear Paw Company (715-236-7300) and Surplus Outfit Stores (715-234-3491). Area info from the Rice Lake Area Chamber of Commerce (715-234-2126 or 877-234-2126, rice-lake.com).

Brill: Meals at Wagon Wheel (715-234-1823). On Trail.

Mikana: Restaurant, grocery store, lodging, camping. From the crossing at CTH-T go 3.0 mi south on CTH-T/STH-48. Lodging at Mikana Marine & Resort (715-234-3008). Camping at Waldo Carlson County Park (29th Ave. on Red Cedar Lake, 715-354-3353 or 715-537-6295).

Birchwood: See Blueberry Segment, below.

Blueberry Segment (Atlas Map 10f)

SNAPSHOT

0.9 miles: Tuscobia State Trail at Balsam Lake Rd. to Featherstone Rd. at Loch Lomond Blvd. (28¾ St.)

 This short segment follows part of the historic Blueberry Line railway.

 At nearby Doolittle County Park north of Birchwood (see Area Services).

 A 1.0-mi blue-blazed spur from the eastern end of the segment goes into Birchwood.

TRAIL ACCESS AND PARKING

Tuscobia State Trail at Balsam Lake Rd.: From Birchwood at the intersection of Main St. and STH-48 take STH-48 west 2.0 mi. At Balsam Lake Rd. turn right. No parking available. Alternatively, park roadside on Featherstone Rd. on the south side of STH-48.

Featherstone Rd. at Loch Lomond Blvd. (28¾ St.): From Birchwood at the intersection of Main St. and STH-48, take STH-48 west 1.0 mi. At Loch Lomond Blvd. (28¾ St.) turn left and go south 0.1 mi to the intersection with gravel Featherstone Rd. Roadside parking.

Additional Parking: "Big Fish Wayside" parking area in Birchwood. Located on STH-48 1.0 mi east of Loch Lomond Blvd. (28¾ St.) at Vance St.

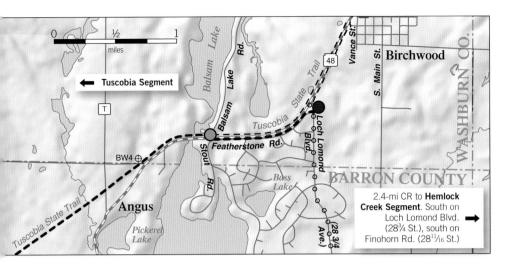

THE HIKE

Although wishful hikers may be drawn to this segment in hopes of finding wild blueberries, the name actually comes from the original Blueberry Line railway that was refurbished and converted to a foot-travel-only path in 2011.

The Blueberry Line and similar smaller rail lines were important links between communities and the rest of the world at the turn of the century. Everything was brought in and shipped out by rail and if people wanted to travel—for shopping, visiting relatives or vacation—it was by rail. Eventually rail travel gave way to the automobile and the Blueberry Line ceased passenger service to Birchwood in 1936.

From the segment starting point at the intersection of the Tuscobia State Trail and Balsam Lake Road next to STH-48, hikers should head south and carefully cross STH-48. Shortly after crossing STH-48 the segment turns east and parallels Featherstone Drive and STH-48 as it makes its way to its endpoint at Loch Lomond Boulevard (28¾ Street).

East of the segment's endpoint, a blue-blazed spur trail continues northeast parallel to STH-48 into the village of Birchwood. This spur ends at the "Big Fish Wayside" parking area, where IATA volunteers and workers from local Dobiehill Timberworks engineered a 14th-century-style, timber-framed structure that acts as a depot for hikers arriving or departing from Birchwood.

Mobile Skills Crew project site, 2011

AREA SERVICES

Birchwood: Restaurant, grocery store, convenience store, lodging, camping. From Loch Lomond Rd. (28¾ St.) and STH-48 go 1.0 mi northeast on STH-48. INN Style program lodging at Cobblestone B&B (715-354-3494, cobblestonebb.com), The Farm B&B (715-354-3367) and Tagalong Golf & Resort (715-354-3458, tagalonggolf.com). Other lodging at the Birchwood Motel (715-354-7706). Camping at Doolittle County Park (715-354-3300). Meals at Birchwood Café (715-354-3000), Shannon's Trailside Restaurant (715-354-3969), Paul's Pizza Den (715-354-7058) and Tagalong Golf Resort Restaurant. Area info available from the Birchwood Area Chamber of Commerce (800-236-2252, birchwoodwi.com).

Mikana: See Tuscobia Segment, above. From Balsam Lake Rd. at STH-48 go west and south 4.0 mi.

Hemlock Creek Segment (Atlas Map 10f)

SNAPSHOT

6.2 miles: Finohorn Rd. (28¹¹⁄₁₆ St.) to CTH-F

> **Note:** It is anticipated that volunteers will build a new section of Trail in 2014 south of Murphy Flowage Picnic Area that will connect with the current white blazed trail. The Trail access on CTH-F will be relocated farther south to the intersection of CTH-F and Bucks Lake Road. The new route is shown as "Future Trail" on the accompanying map. Check with the Ice Age Trail Alliance (800-227-0046, iceagetrail.org) for more details.

 *This scenic segment through rolling county forest highlights a heron rookery, the western edge of the Blue Hills and a loop around Hemlock Creek.*

At the Murphy Flowage Picnic Area and Murphy Flowage Campground.

From Pigeon and Hemlock creeks and a few small intermittent streams and lakes/wetland areas.

Primitive camping on county forest lands.

At the campground across CTH-F from the Murphy Flowage Picnic Area and at Rusk County Remote Campsite 6 on Bucks Lake Rd. (see Area Services).

Small portions overlap with a snow-shoe trail and logging/forest roads.

White-blazed loop south of Hemlock Creek.

TRAIL ACCESS AND PARKING

Finohorn Rd. (28¹¹⁄₁₆ St.): From Birchwood at the intersection of Main St. and STH-48, take STH-48 west 1.0 mi. At Loch Lomond Blvd. (28¾ St.) turn left and go south then west 2.5 mi. At Finohorn Rd. (28¹¹⁄₁₆ St.) turn left and go south 0.1 mi to the Trail access. Roadside parking.

CTH-F: From Birchwood, at the intersection of Main St. and STH-48, take STH-48 east 2.3 mi. At CTH-F turn right and go south 8.0 mi. No parking. Park at the Murphy Flowage Picnic Area, 200 yd. north of the CTH-F Trail access on the west side of the road. Follow the access road to the picnic area.

Additional Parking: Bolger Rd. (25½ Ave.) parking area, 1.2 mi west of CTH-F.

THE HIKE

From its starting point on Finohorn Road (28¹¹⁄₁₆ St.) the segment heads south and crosses Pigeon Creek, then passes over flat terrain to an abandoned blue heron rookery (**BW3**), now home to nesting osprey.

South of the rookery the segment reaches a boardwalk; hikers should use caution when passing through this area and will likely come out with wet feet, especially in times of rainy weather and high water. One alternative for navigating through the area is to use a beaver dam that parallels the segment route; prior to boardwalk construction the dam was the main route of passage.

As the segment makes its way to Bolger Road, it ascends into Barron quartzite hills, the first taste of the Blue Hills highlighted on segments farther east in Rusk County. Hikers should watch carefully for signage in this area as the route intersects many grassy logging roads.

Now in Rusk County, south of Bolger Road the segment drops steeply toward Hemlock Creek. Along the way the Trail passes some small, quickly flowing creeks. After paralleling Hemlock Creek for a half-mile the segment reaches a

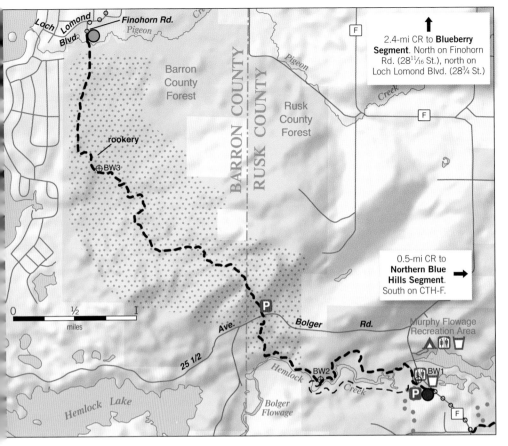

junction (**BW2**) with a white-blazed trail that turns south from this junction and highlights the southern side of the creek. Pairing this white-blazed trail with the main segment creates an enjoyable 2.75-mile loop.

From the junction with the white-blazed loop, the main segment continues east along the north side of Hemlock Creek with several trailside benches presenting scenic views of the wetland below. The segment crosses the creek on an abandoned road bridge and enters the Murphy Flowage Picnic Area.

The segment continues southeast along the access road for the picnic area. Shortly before reaching its endpoint at CTH-F, the segment intersects (**BW1**) again with the white-blazed trail that follows the south side of Hemlock Creek.

Mobile Skills Crew project site, 2007, 2008, 2014

AREA SERVICES

Murphy Flowage Recreation Area: Picnic area (west side of CTH-F) and camping area (east side of CTH-F) (715-532-2113). On Trail.

Birchwood: See Blueberry Segment, p. 40. From the CTH-F Trail access go north ~10 mi. Also see Trail Access and Parking directions, above.

Rusk County Remote Campsite 6: Camping. From Murphy Flowage Picnic Area take CTH-F south 0.5 mi. At Bucks Lake Rd. (recommend 4WD) go west to the end of the primitive road. For more information contact Rusk County Forestry Department (715-532-2113, RuskCounty.org/department/forestry/camping-information).

Rusk County

Trail miles: 16.5
Connecting route miles: 17.5

Two distinct landscapes dominate the Ice Age Trail route through Rusk County. In the northern half of the county are the Blue Hills, once a mountain range of quartzite bedrock older than the Appalachian Mountains and most of the Rocky Mountains. The 1.6-billion-year-old quartzite peaks wore down over time. The Chippewa Lobe, flowing south and southwest, came to a halt as it reached the Blue Hills. It left a legacy of scattered lakes that offer an enticing habitat for an abundance of wildlife. Seen in the county forest have been white-tail deer, wolf, black bear and on rare occasion moose, who travel from as far away as Michigan's Upper Peninsula. The southern half of Rusk County is a land of lakes, which extends into Chippewa County.

On Rusk County Forest land, primitive camping is permitted at least 200 feet from trails and waterways.

CHAPTER INFORMATION

The Blue Hills Chapter formed in 1992 after the Rusk County Chapter, formed in 1975, reorganized. Most of the Ice Age Trail through this area was designed and built in the late 1970s and early 1980s by Adam Cahow, a professor at the University of Wisconsin-Eau Claire. The chapter members continue his pioneer trailblazing with ongoing Trail maintenance projects and construction of new Trail routes.

COUNTY INFORMATION

Rusk County Visitor Center: 715-532-2642 or 800-535-7875, ruskcounty.org

Rusk County Forestry and Parks Information: 715-532-2113 or 800-535-7875

ERIC SHERMAN

Devils Creek on the Northern Blue Hills Segment.

Rusk County   45

Northern Blue Hills Segment (Atlas Map 11f)

SNAPSHOT

9.3 miles: Bucks Lake Road at CTH-F to CTH-F Southern Trail Access

Note: It is anticipated that volunteers will build a new section of Trail in 2014 north of Bucks Lake Road. The new route is shown as "Future Trail" on the accompanying map. Check with the Ice Age Trail Alliance (800-227-0046, iceagetrail.org) for more details.

 This remote and rugged segment crossing through the Blue Hills features a number of scenic stream crossings and several beautiful wetland areas.

At the nearby Murphy Flowage Picnic Area and Murphy Flowage Campground.

From Devil's Creek and other small streams/creeks and lakes/wetland areas.

 Primitive camping on county forest lands.

 Nearby campgrounds at Rusk County Remote Campsite 6 and Murphy Flowage Recreation Area and at Audie Flowage-Perch Lake Recreation Area, ~5 mi east (see Area Services).

 Portions overlap with logging/forest roads and gravel Bucks Lake Rd.

TRAIL ACCESS AND PARKING

Bucks Lake Rd. at CTH-F: From Birchwood at the intersection of Main St. and STH-48, take STH-48 east 2.3 mi. At CTH-F turn right and go south 8.5 mi. Roadside parking on Bucks Lake Rd. Alternatively, park at the Murphy Flowage Picnic Area located on CTH-F 0.5 mi north of the Bucks Lake Rd./CTH-F intersection on the west side of the road. Follow access road around to the picnic area.

CTH-F Southern Trail Access: From Weyerhaeuser on USH-8 take CTH-F north then west 6.6 mi. Roadside parking.

Additional Parking: (i) Bucks Lake Rd. where the Trail goes off-road (**RU8**). Roadside parking. (ii) Stout Rd. Trail access parking area (**RU6**).

THE HIKE

The segment starts at the intersection of Bucks Lake Road and CTH-F. Hikers should head east on Bucks Lake Road for 0.6 mi. *This distance will be shorter once volunteers construct a new section of Trail north of Bucks Lake Road. Watch for signage at approximately 0.2 mi east of CTH-F that will direct hikers to the new route.* The current segment route leaves (**RU8**) Bucks Lake Road and heads south on a logging/forest road. The segment traverses rolling hills through a mixed hardwood forest in an area showing evidence of extensive beaver activity.

Reaching the wide, grassy road/spur trail to the Stout Road parking area, the segment continues southward through rolling, hummocky glacial topography in a mix of hardwood forest. This portion of the segment is mostly on a two-track footpath, occasionally mixing in short sections of current and old logging roads. Hikers should pay close attention to Trail signage at intersecting logging/forest roads. After reaching the outlet of a large wetland (**RU5**), the Trail follows a branch of Devil's Creek through a scenic and peaceful shallow valley, crossing a series of bridges.

The segment continues its southward course through hummocky terrain. Eventually the segment makes its way to a ridge overlooking Devil's Creek. The

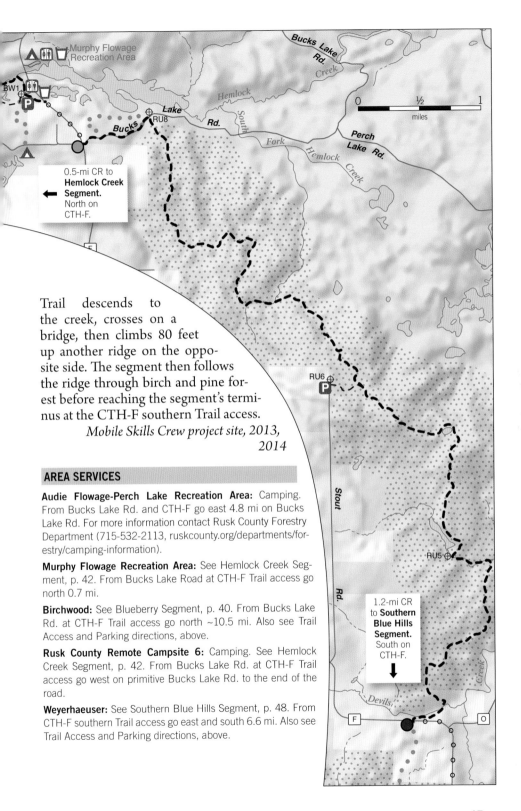

Murphy Flowage
Recreation Area

0.5-mi CR to
**Hemlock Creek
Segment.**
North on
CTH-F.

Trail descends to the creek, crosses on a bridge, then climbs 80 feet up another ridge on the opposite side. The segment then follows the ridge through birch and pine forest before reaching the segment's terminus at the CTH-F southern Trail access.

Mobile Skills Crew project site, 2013, 2014

AREA SERVICES

Audie Flowage-Perch Lake Recreation Area: Camping. From Bucks Lake Rd. and CTH-F go east 4.8 mi on Bucks Lake Rd. For more information contact Rusk County Forestry Department (715-532-2113, ruskcounty.org/departments/forestry/camping-information).

Murphy Flowage Recreation Area: See Hemlock Creek Segment, p. 42. From Bucks Lake Road at CTH-F Trail access go north 0.7 mi.

Birchwood: See Blueberry Segment, p. 40. From Bucks Lake Rd. at CTH-F Trail access go north ~10.5 mi. Also see Trail Access and Parking directions, above.

Rusk County Remote Campsite 6: Camping. See Hemlock Creek Segment, p. 42. From Bucks Lake Rd. at CTH-F Trail access go west on primitive Bucks Lake Rd. to the end of the road.

Weyerhaeuser: See Southern Blue Hills Segment, p. 48. From CTH-F southern Trail access go east and south 6.6 mi. Also see Trail Access and Parking directions, above.

1.2-mi CR
to **Southern
Blue Hills
Segment.**
South on
CTH-F.

Southern Blue Hills Segment (Atlas Map 12f)

7.2 miles: Yuker Rd. at CTH-F to Old 14 Rd. (Bass Lake Rd)

  This remote and rugged segment continues through the Blue Hills, traversing ridges, kettles and ravines.

From North Lake, Moose Ear Creek and other small intermittent streams/creeks and wetlands.

Primitive camping on county forest land and at a primitive campsite (**RU2**) on the south shore of North Lake.

 The portion of the segment south of the Rusk County Forest boundary to Old 14 Rd. (Bass Lake Rd.) is closed during gun deer season.

 Portions overlap with logging/forest roads and dirt access road.

TRAIL ACCESS AND PARKING

Yuker Rd. at CTH-F: From Weyerhaeuser on USH-8 take CTH-F north 5.4 mi. to Yuker Rd., an unmarked dirt road heading west. Roadside parking on Yuker Rd.

Old 14 Rd. (Bass Lake Rd.): From Weyerhaeuser on USH-8, take CTH-F (2nd St.) north 0.1 mi. At the first street north of the railroad tracks, unmarked Railway Ave., turn left. Railway Ave. transitions into Old 14 Rd. (Bass Lake Rd). Go west 1.0 mi, angle left across the railroad tracks and continue west 1.9 mi to the Trail access. Roadside parking along the north side of the road.

THE HIKE

This segment starts at the intersection of CTH-F and Yuker Road, an unmarked dirt road used by fishermen and hunters for access to Rusk County Forest land. Hikers should head west on Yuker Road for 0.7 miles to a point (**RU9**) where the Trail leaves Yuker Road and heads south on a logging/forest road. Shortly, the segment splits off to the right on a narrow tread. Within the first few miles, the Trail twice crosses scenic Moose Ear Creek on primitive wooden and log bridges (second crossing: **RU4**). As the route makes its way to North Lake it follows or parallels forested ridges with views of trailside kettles and down glacial-formed ravines on a mix of two-track footpath and logging roads. Low-lying areas may be soggy. Hilly, forested terrain characterizes this portion of the segment, most of which is on Rusk County Forest land. During growing season dense vegetation hugs the Trail; pay close attention to Trail signage.

The segment eventually emerges into a clearing and soon after intersects and briefly follows to the east a dirt access road. The segment curves around to the west and south of North Lake, a local fishing hole, then reaches the south shore of the lake and a primitive campsite (**RU2**). The south shore offers scenic views of the lake and is a perfect place to view the many birds, including loons, who use the lake.

South of North Lake, the Trail soon comes to a gate and fence stile and enters private land. The segment crosses the outlet/small stream (**RU1**) from a small, unnamed lake then weaves in and out of woods, skirts daisy pastures and crosses the small stream two more times on a combination of forest roads, farm roads and narrower tread. Eventually the Trail climbs a ridge overlooking a lake through the forest, crosses another fence stile and comes to a gravel farm road (**RU13**) with excellent views of agricultural fields through an opening in the trees.

From here on its way to its terminus on Old 14 Road (Bass Lake Road), the segment includes a trek through a forested, more hummocky area, the crossing of a set of railroad tracks, the skirting of another wetland/lake and a pine, oak and birch forest with an undergrowth of ferns.

Mobile Skills Crew project site, 2013, 2014

AREA SERVICES

Audie Flowage-Perch Lake Recreation Area: See Northern Blue Hills Segment, p. 46. From Yuker Rd. at CTH-F go north and east ~9 mi.

Murphy Flowage Recreation Area: See Hemlock Creek Segment, p. 42. From Yuker Rd. at CTH-F go north ~10.5 mi.

Birchwood: See Blueberry Segment, p. 40. From Yuker Rd. at CTH-F Trail access go north ~20 mi.

Weyerhaeuser: Restaurant, grocery store, convenience store, lodging. From Old 14 Rd. (Bass Lake Rd) Trail access go east 3.0 mi. Lodging at Country View Motel (715-353-2780).

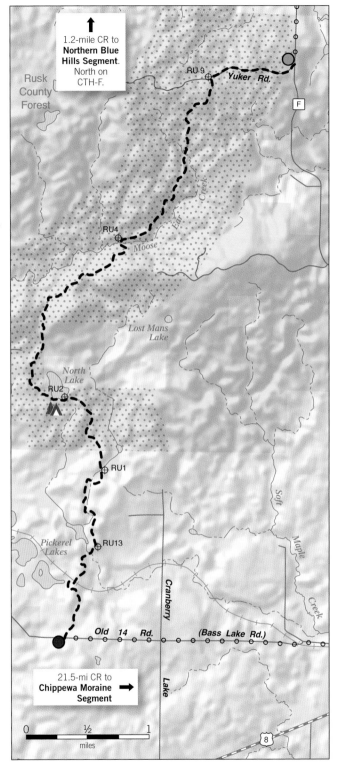

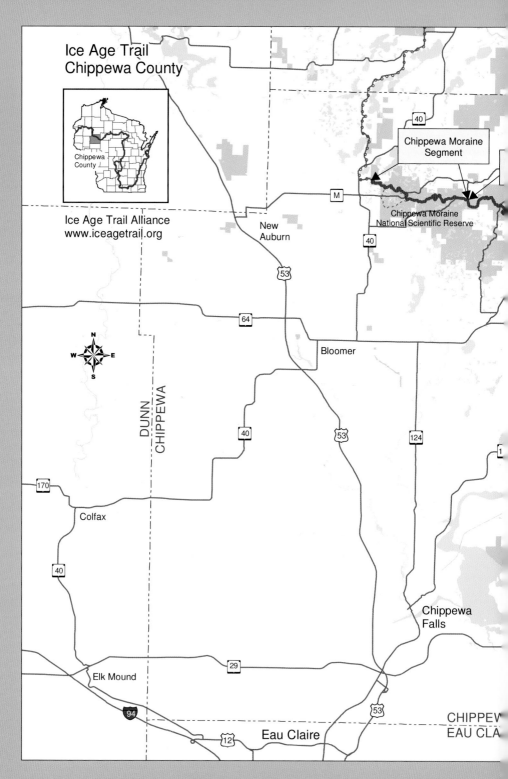

Ice Age Trail
Chippewa County

Chippewa
County

Ice Age Trail Alliance
www.iceagetrail.org

Chippewa Moraine
Segment

Chippewa Moraine
National Scientific Reserve

New
Auburn

Bloomer

DUNN
CHIPPEWA

Colfax

Chippewa
Falls

Elk Mound

Eau Claire

CHIPPEW
EAU CLA

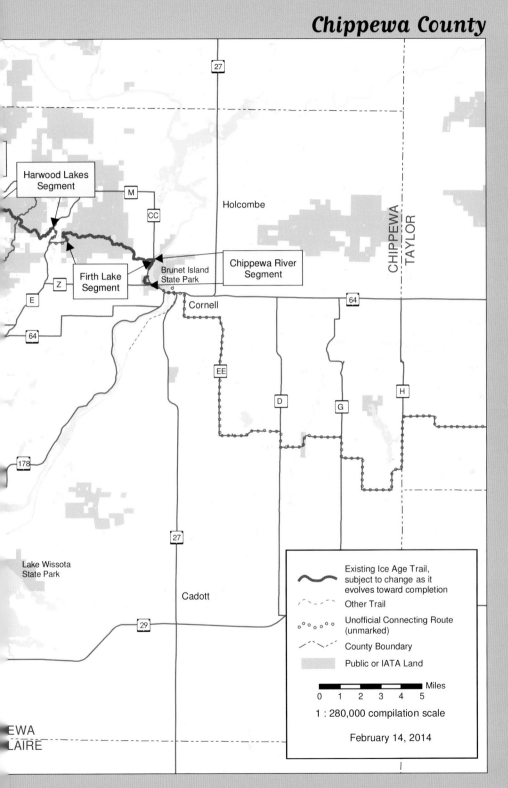

Chippewa County

Harwood Lakes Segment

M

CC

Holcombe

CHIPPEWA

TAYLOR

Firth Lake Segment

Z

Brunet Island State Park

Chippewa River Segment

E

Cornell

64

64

EE

D

G

H

178

27

Lake Wissota State Park

Cadott

29

Existing Ice Age Trail, subject to change as it evolves toward completion

Other Trail

Unofficial Connecting Route (unmarked)

County Boundary

Public or IATA Land

Miles

0 1 2 3 4 5

1 : 280,000 compilation scale

February 14, 2014

EWA
LAIRE

Chippewa County

Trail miles: 21.3
Connecting route miles: 33.6

The Chippewa Lobe formed Chippewa County's prominent glacial features, including the Chippewa Moraine. The terminal moraine stands above the surrounding cultivated plains, with lakes and ponds set in a forested jumble of hills. Unlike the higher hills of the interlobate Kettle Moraine in southeastern Wisconsin, the features of the Chippewa Moraine are characterized by gentler hills of "dead ice" moraine. As the ice ceased to move, fissures crisscrossed the glacier. Surface debris, transported by sliding ice and flowing meltwater, filled many cracks and formed a variety of sharp ridges after the ice melted. When debris-covered blocks of ice melted, kettles formed, producing the area's knob-and-swale landscape. Ice-walled lake plains, flatter-topped areas formed by glacial lakebeds, are peculiar to this area.

The Chippewa Moraine National Scientific Reserve's David R. Obey Ice Age Interpretive Center is perched high atop an ice-walled lake plain and offers views of the lake-dotted countryside. It has a 4.5-mile Circle Trail with interpretive signs and shorter nature trails that explore the area. Inside, modern in-depth displays and hands-on exhibits describe the Wisconsin Glaciation and its legacy in the area. Both the reserve and nearby Brunet Island State Park are waypoints on the Great Wisconsin Birding & Nature Trail.

Primitive camping is permitted on Chippewa County Forest land. Please camp at least 200 feet from waterways and trails. There are also two developed walk-to campsites on the Chippewa Moraine National Scientific Reserve property; some portions of the reserve are open to primitive camping but others are not. Refer to the maps for more details on camping locations and county forest boundaries.

CHAPTER INFORMATION

The Chippewa Moraine Chapter officially formed in 1988 and sponsors hikes, work outings and presentations on glacial geology. The chapter maintains a close relationship with the Chippewa Moraine National Scientific Reserve's David R. Obey Ice Age Interpretive Center, where many events take place, such as the chapter's annual Parade of Colors hike in autumn. In addition to its chapter pages at **iceagetrail.org**, the chapter maintains its own external website, **iatchippewa. org**. The site features a wealth of information, including news items, detailed parking information, an archive of the chapter's *Trail Dispatch* newsletters and information for member volunteers and hikers. There is also information about the trail-related merchandise that the chapter offers for sale at the interpretive center. The chapter periodically broadcasts announcements on trail conditions and events via email and Twitter (**twitter.com/iatachippewa**).

COUNTY INFORMATION

Chippewa County Tourism: 866-723-0331, chippewacounty.com

Chippewa County Facilities and Parks Division: 715-726-7882

Chippewa County Land Conservation and Forest Management Division: 715-726-7920

North of North Shattuck Lake on the Chippewa Moraine Segment.

Chippewa Moraine Segment (Atlas Map 15f)

7.6 miles: 267th Ave. (Oak Ln.) to 167th St. (Plummer Lake Rd.)

 This very scenic segment passes nearby more than 20 kettle lakes and highlights several significant ice-walled lake plains, including the one the Obey Ice Age Interpretive Center is built on.

 At the Obey Interpretive Center.

 From numerous lakes.

 Primitive camping on portions of the Chippewa Moraine Reserve. Two walk-to campsites (**CH13, CH14**) near the Interpretive Center.

A small private campground on Salis-bury Lake on STH 40, 0.7 mi from the western end of the segment.

 Restrooms available at the Obey Interpretive Center and at the two primitive campsites (privy) just off the Trail. Please respect those who have reserved the sites.

 Small portion overlaps with 260th Ave. (Rattlesnake Hill Rd.).

 Chippewa Moraine National Scientific Reserve trail network.

TRAIL ACCESS AND PARKING

267th Ave. (Oak Ln.): From USH-53 take the CTH-M/New Auburn exit. Follow CTH-M east for 7.0 mi. At STH-40 turn left and go north 0.7 mi. At 267th Ave. (Oak Ln.) turn right and go east 0.7 mi to the Trail access on the south side of the road. Roadside parking just west of the Trail access. No overnight parking.

167th St. (Plummer Lake Rd.): From USH-53 take the CTH-M/New Auburn exit. Travel east 12.6 mi on CTH-M. At 167th St. (Plummer Lake Rd.) turn right and go south 1.0 mi to the parking area on the west side of the road near the boat landing area. No overnight parking. The segment begins 0.2 mi north on Plummer Lake Rd. just south of the intersection with 260th Ave. (Rattlesnake Hill Rd.).

Additional Parking: (i) Circle Hiking Trail parking area on CTH-M near western boundary of Chippewa Moraine National Scientific Reserve. (No parking at CTH-M Trail access farther east.) (ii) Chippewa

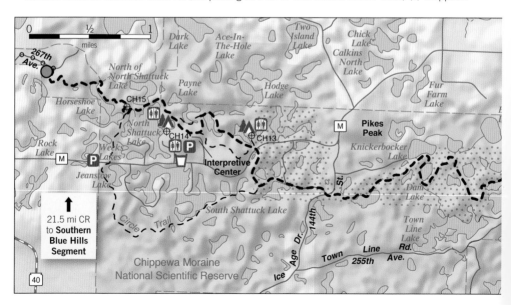

Moraine National Scientific Reserve's David R. Obey Ice Age Interpretive Center off CTH-M. (iii) 260th Ave. (Rattlesnake Hill Rd.) parking area 0.2 mi west of where the Trail heads off on the north side of the road. Parking area in the corner of a field. Overnight parking permitted.

THE HIKE

This segment traverses dramatic high-relief hummocky terrain with numerous scenic kettle lakes. The first portion of the segment travels through the North of North Shattuck Lake State Natural Area, a southern dry mesic forest. This area is heavily used by birds during spring migration, including red-headed woodpeckers, hairy woodpeckers, scarlet tanagers, American redstarts, yellow-throated vireos and eastern wood-pewees.

From its starting point on 267th Avenue (Oak Lane) the segment heads east and soon reaches the northern tip of the first of two lakes named "Horseshoe" that hikers will pass while hiking the segment. On the way toward the southeastern corner of the lake the segment climbs a hill; during leaf-off seasons hikers can see five bays from this point (**CH15**). Coming down from the hill the segment soon intersects with the Chippewa Moraine Reserve's Circle Trail. To stay on the Ice Age Trail, hikers should turn left at this junction and continue east. This is the first junction with the reserve's "other" trails; signage is excellent throughout the trail network making it easy for hikers to navigate.

After the segment passes between North Shattuck Lake and the aptly named North of North Shattuck Lake, the route bends south and soon intersects with a spur trail that leads 750 feet to a walk-to primitive campsite (**CH14**). This is one of two primitive campsites on the reserve, each with a privy and fire ring. Hikers wanting to spend a night at either site should first check in at the interpretive center; there is a small fee.

A short distance south of the campsite spur the segment intersects with the reserve's Dry Lake Trail and Mammoth Nature Trail, which branch off the Ice Age Trail route to the east. From this junction the Ice Age Trail continues southeast toward the interpretive center.

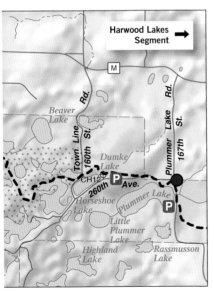

From the interpretive center, the segment heads north and wraps around the northern tip of a small lake, then continues southeast toward CTH-M. A short distance before the CTH-M crossing a 300-foot spur trail leads north to the reserve's second walk-to primitive campsite (**CH13**).

East of CTH-M the segment reaches the eastern junction with the Circle Trail and passes by another scenic cluster of lakes before crossing 144th Street (Ice Age Drive). As the segment makes its way east, it skirts the north shore of the segment's second Horseshoe Lake and crosses 160th Street (Town Line Road).

The Trail shortly arrives at a bench overlooking Dumke Lake (**CH12**). The view here can give a hiker a visual appreciation of how ice-walled lake plains formed.

During the Wisconsin Glaciation period, small lakes filled depressions in the ice surface and became walled off by enormous ice blocks. Lakes often formed on debris-covered parts of the glacier, and over time, fine sediment accumulated on the lake's floor. When the ice surrounding the lake melted, the sediment that accumulated in the lake remained. This formed a high, flat-topped area on the landscape. Often dish-shaped, these plateau-like areas have rich soil for farming. The coarse material deposited near the ice block wall and glacial lake's shoreline forms a higher "rim-like" ridge around the lake plain. After the glacial lake drained, parts of the ice wall continued to melt and water flowed across the now dry lakebed, carving a channel that the segment crosses just east of the bench. The channel actually flowed away from Dumke Lake, demonstrating that the ice wall continued to melt long after the original glacial lake was dry. The ice block disappeared last, leaving Dumke Lake well below.

From Dumke Lake the segment continues east, intersects and briefly follows 260th Avenue (Rattlesnake Hill Road) and passes by one final lake (Plummer) before reaching the segment's terminus at 167th Street (Plummer Lake Road).

Mobile Skills Crew project site, 2004

POINTS OF INTEREST

Chippewa Moraine National Scientific Reserve and the David R. Obey Ice Age Interpretive Center: On Trail (13394 CTH-M, New Auburn; 715-967-2800, dnr.wi.gov/topic/parks/name/chipmoraine/naturecenter.html).

The Ice Age Interpretive Center has many hands-on and interactive activities, including activity books, short films and various displays about geologic, cultural and natural history. The Center is generally open year-round Tuesday to Sunday from 8:30 a.m. to 4:00 p.m. (closed Monday) and has maps, drinking water and helpful staff. Hikers should stop here for information and check-in for the property's two walk-to primitive campsites. Three loop trails start here and share parts of the Ice Age Trail: the Circle Trail (4.5 mi), Dry Lake Trail (1.8 mi) and Mammoth Nature Trail (0.7 mi). These trails feature numerous interpretive signs described in Hiking Field Trip Guide for Glacial Landforms, available at the center.

AREA SERVICES

New Auburn: Convenience store, restaurant, camping. Restaurant and convenience store at the intersection of STH-40 and CTH-M, 2.0 mi west of the Obey Interpretive Center. Camping at Salisbury Campground (715-967-2782) on Salisbury Lake, 1.0 mi north of the intersection of STH-40 and CTH-M. Convenience store in town, ~8 mi west of the Interpretive Center.

Cornell: See Firth Lake Segment and Chippewa River Segment, p. 60. From the Obey Interpretive Center on CTH-M go east ~19 mi.

> *Favorite noises were my nightly forest bedrooms that would "come alive" after sunset, with all kinds of noises and every crunch of forest floor or snap of a branch seeming to be caused by a huge critter, probably a 400-pound bear. One of the most memorable night awakenings was from an hourly tail slap by the resident beaver of a pond 25 feet from my tent.*
>
> TIM OBUKOWICZ (AKA "REX"), ICE AGE TRAIL THOUSAND-MILER

Harwood Lakes Segment (Atlas Maps 15f, 16f)

5.8 miles: 167th St. (Plummer Lake Rd.) to CTH-E

> **Note:** It is anticipated that volunteers will build a new section of Trail in 2014 between the southern boundary of the Chippewa County Forest and the Picnic Lake bridge. The new route is shown as "Future Trail" on the accompanying map. Check with the Ice Age Trail Alliance (800-227-0046, iceagetrail.org) for more details.

  This beautiful segment features large beaver dams, a massive glacial erratic and several scenic pristine lakes and wetland areas.

From numerous lakes, streams/creeks and wetland areas.

A walk-to primitive campsite (**CH11**) between the two Harwood Lakes, a Dispersed Camping Area (DCA) (**CH7**) on the west shore of Picnic Lake and primitive camping on county forest lands.

 Portion of segment crossing private land between the southern boundary of the Chippewa County Forest and the Picnic Lake bridge is closed during gun deer season.

 Small portion overlaps with Plummer Lake Road.

 Spur trail to primitive campsite at Harwood Lakes, blue-blazed spur trail to DCA and Girl Scout Camp Nawakwa trail network.

167th St. (Plummer Lake Rd.): From USH-53 take the CTH-M/New Auburn exit. Travel east 12.6 mi on CTH-M. At 167th St. (Plummer Lake Rd.) turn right and go south 1.0 mi to the parking area on the west side of the road near the boat landing area. No overnight parking. The segment begins 0.2 mi north on Plummer Lake Rd. just south of the intersection with 260th Ave. (Rattlesnake Hill Rd.).

CTH-E: From Cornell take STH-64 west across the Chippewa River. At CTH-CC turn right and go north 1.0 mi. At CTH-Z turn left and go west 5.0 mi. At CTH-E turn right and go north 3.0 mi. Roadside parking.

Additional Parking: Deer Fly Trail. From CTH-M and Deer Fly Trail (gravel road), go south 2.6 mi on Deer Fly Trail to the parking area on west side of road.

From the segment's starting point on 167th Street (Plummer Lake Road) just south of the road's intersection with 260th Avenue (Rattlesnake Hill Road) hikers should head south along the road for 0.2 miles across a narrow causeway between Plummer Lake and a wetland. Across from the Trail access parking area the segment then departs from the road and heads east through the easternmost portion of the Chippewa Moraine Reserve property, which is relatively flat compared with the dramatic high-relief hummocky topography of the remainder of the segment. The wide path enters a second-growth forest with a high canopy and diverse understory of ferns and woodland plants. Hikers should note that primitive camping is not permitted on this part of the Reserve, but is permitted on county forest lands farther east.

The segment leaves the Reserve and enters Chippewa County Forest lands just before arriving at a bench (**CH17**) that provides lovely views of the Harwood Lakes. About 200 feet east of the bench, a spur trail leads north steeply downhill

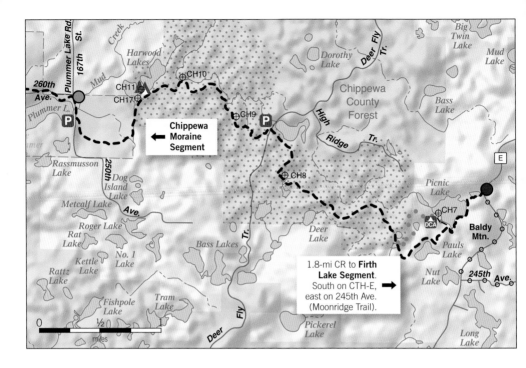

to a small but picturesque primitive campsite (**CH11**) (no privy) on the narrows between the two Harwood Lakes.

East of the Harwood Lakes in rolling topography, the segment crosses Mud Brook on a series of bridges offering a view of the Mud Brook Valley (**CH10**). The Trail climbs steeply to the top of a well-defined hummocky ridge then drops down to follow alongside a swamp. Along the north side of the Trail, hikers may detect ruts from when loggers cut trenches in the ground and filled them with water to create iced tracks to run their logging sleds on.

The segment crosses a boardwalk/bridge (**CH9**) over a low wet area and passes a bench offering a quiet respite as it sits near the boardwalk surrounded by several old white pine trees.

The Trail climbs up out of the swamp and crosses a distinctive county ATV trail. It then outlines the edge of another swamp/wetland area with toppled trees exposing their roots and soon arrives at Deer Fly Trail (a gravel road).

East of Deer Fly Trail, the segment passes a massive glacial erratic just 40 feet off trail and shortly crosses a footbridge at the base of an enormous beaver dam. The dam creates a flowage to the south with several heron nests. The segment then continues along to another bridge (**CH8**), known as "Kim's Crossing," spanning a small gulch. The spot is named "Kim's Crossing" in memory of Kim Heidtke. Kim's family funded the bridge project to commemorate her love of the Ice Age Trail. This spot was home to an earthen beaver dam until backed up water overtook the dam and carved the gulch in its place. A wetland pond remains as habitat for waterfowl and other wetland creatures.

The segment continues along through mixed forest of aspen, pine, maple, hemlock, oak and fir. Before the segment exits Chippewa County Forest lands, the Trail offers multiple views of a tamarack bog.

Volunteers will be building a new section of the Trail here in 2014 that will stay in Chippewa County Forest and swing north then east toward Picnic Lake.

The current segment route crosses onto private property, climbs a ridge and continues northeast to the south shore of Picnic Lake. The segment intersects a blue-blazed spur trail that leads to a Dispersed Camping Area (DCA) (**CH7**) on the west shore of Picnic Lake. The campsite comes complete with a rustic crafted "loveseat" and "couch."

Back on the Trail, the segment reaches a bridge on private property spanning an intermittent stream draining into Picnic Lake. *It is immediately west of the bridge that the new section of Trail will intersect the existing Ice Age Trail.* Continuing on the current route, the segment crosses the bridge and wraps around the eastern edge of Picnic Lake on Girl Scout Camp Nawakwa property, offering many views of the pristine lake. The segment intersects with and shares portions of the Camp Nawakwa trail network. Just before reaching its terminus on CTH-E, the Trail skirts above a scenic hemlock-rimmed pond.

Mobile Skills Crew project site, 2013, 2014

AREA SERVICES

New Auburn: See Chippewa Moraine Segment, p. 54. From the 167th St. (Plummer Lake Rd.) Trail access go north and west ~13 mi. Also see Trail Access and Parking directions, above.

Cornell: See Firth Lake Segment and Chippewa River Segment, p. 60. From the CTH-E Trail access go south and east 9.0 mi. Also see Trail Access and Parking directions, above.

AARON CARLSON

Enjoying a backpacking adventure in the Chippewa Moraine.

Firth Lake Segment and
Chippewa River Segment (Atlas Map 16f)

SNAPSHOT

Firth Lake Segment—6.5 miles: 245th Ave. (Moonridge Trail) to CTH-CC

Chippewa River Segment—1.8 miles (1.4 IAT, 0.4 CR): CTH-CC to CTH-Z

> **Note:** It is anticipated that volunteers will sign a new section of the Chippewa River Seg-ment in 2014 on the west side of CTH-CC. The new route is shown as "Future Trail" on the accompanying map. Check with the Ice Age Trail Alliance (800-227-0046, iceagetrail.org) for more details.

 The **Firth Lake Segment**, *an interesting and scenic hike, crosses an ice-walled lake plain and beaver dams in a generally forested setting and highlights beautiful Firth Lake.*

 From Firth Lake and a few intermittent streams/creeks.

Primitive camping on county forest lands.

Eastern portion of the segment cross-ing private land is closed during gun deer season.

 Portions overlap with logging/forest roads.

A short spur trail leads to a parking area next to Firth Lake.

 The short **Chippewa River Segment** highlights Perch Lake and features dramatic views of the Chippewa River.

 From the Chippewa River and Perch Lake.

 At nearby Brunet Island State Park (see Area Services).

 At nearby Millyard Park, Brunet Island State Park and the Cornell Visitor Center.

Small portion overlaps with CTH-CC.

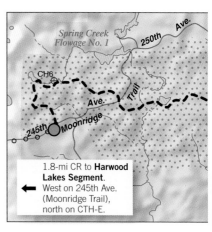

1.8-mi CR to **Harwood Lakes Segment**.
← West on 245th Ave. (Moonridge Trail), north on CTH-E.

TRAIL ACCESS AND PARKING

245th Ave. (Moonridge Trail): From Cornell take STH-64 west across the Chippewa River. At CTH-CC turn right and go north 1.0 mi. At CTH-Z turn left and go west 5.0 mi. At CTH-E turn right and go north 2.0 mi. At 245th Ave. turn right and go 0.9 mi. Roadside parking; use caution as this is a narrow, curvy road.

CTH-Z: From Cornell take STH-64 west across the Chippewa River. At CTH-CC turn right and go north 1.0 mi. At CTH-Z turn left and go west 0.2 mi to the Trail access on the north side of the road. Roadside parking.

Additional Parking: (i) 250th Ave. parking area and boat launch, located south down a gravel drive. From the parking area, walk around a gate and follow the access trail ¼ mile to the Ice Age Trail. (ii) CTH-CC parking area on east side of road, 1.2 mi north of CTH-Z intersection. *Note: The CTH-CC parking area is the main parking area serving these two segments.* (iii) Perch Lake parking area on the west side of CTH-CC, 0.3 mi north of CTH-Z intersection.

The **Firth Lake Segment** traverses a second-growth northern mesic forest of birch, red maple, ash and balsam, with an understory of fern, clintonia, blue bead lily, bloodroot, Indian pipe and red baneberry. This segment can be very wet in spring due to beaver activity in the many lakes and ponds. There are fence stiles and board bridges throughout.

From its starting point on 245th Avenue (Moonridge Trail) to Firth Lake, the segment traverses rolling high-relief hummocky topography. Heading north and then east, the segment reaches a bridge (**CH6**) near a small stream; just beyond the bridge hikers can look north to a view of trailing arbutus on the north slope of the moraine.

After crossing 245th Avenue (Moonridge Trail) and continuing south the segment intersects with logging roads while meandering through old-growth forest of white and red pine, spruce, aspen and oak. As the segment nears Firth Lake, it enters a nice ravine just before coming to the lake, then intersects with a spur trail (**CH5**) heading north to the 250th Avenue parking area and boat launch. From the spur trail junction the segment turns sharply to the south.

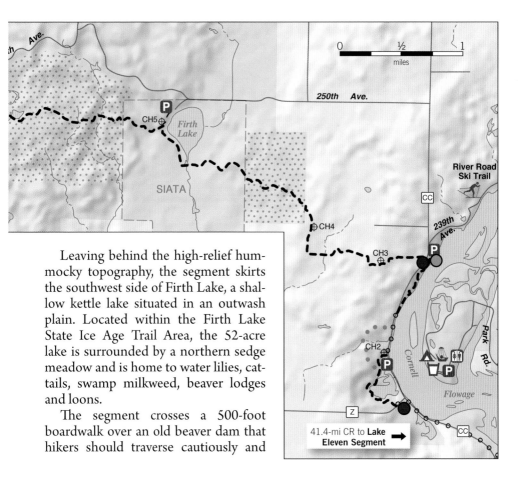

Leaving behind the high-relief hummocky topography, the segment skirts the southwest side of Firth Lake, a shallow kettle lake situated in an outwash plain. Located within the Firth Lake State Ice Age Trail Area, the 52-acre lake is surrounded by a northern sedge meadow and is home to water lilies, cattails, swamp milkweed, beaver lodges and loons.

The segment crosses a 500-foot boardwalk over an old beaver dam that hikers should traverse cautiously and continues east into low-relief hummocky topography, re-entering Chippewa County Forest and passing through an alder swamp. The segment's final 1.3 miles are on private property and feature a 0.3-mile walk through an extensive ice-walled lake plain (**CH4**) and a crossing of part of the Maple Hill End Moraine (**CH3**).

The **Chippewa River Segment** starts out from the large CTH-CC parking area and heads south through a forest featuring stunning Chippewa River views from the edge of rolling bluffs, with braided, steep topography and vertical gains up to 70 feet. Several deep ravines transect the segment west to east and water drains seasonally to the river. The forest cover includes various species of ash, oak and maple, with an undergrowth of several varieties of seasonal woodland flowers.

After passing through the thin strip of land between the road and river, the segment reemerges onto CTH-CC, where hikers will follow the road south for 0.4 miles.

Volunteers will be building a new section of the Trail in 2014 on the west side of CTH-CC that will eliminate most or all of the road walk to the Perch Lake parking area.

About 400 feet north of the DNR's Perch Lake parking area, the current segment route resumes an off-road course (**CH2**), heading west from CTH-CC. The segment bends around the western shore of Perch Lake, then steers southeast away from the lake, crossing an open power line area before reaching the segment's endpoint on CTH-Z.

Mobile Skills Crew project site, 2006, 2014

AREA SERVICES

Cornell: Restaurant, grocery store, convenience store, lodging, library. From the CTH-Z Trail access, go east 0.2 mi. At CTH-CC turn right and go south 1.0 mi. At STH-64 turn left and go east 0.6 mi. Most services are on Bridge St. (STH-64/27) or 1 block north on Main St.

Brunet Island State Park: Camping. In Cornell, from Park St. and STH-64 (just east of Millyard Park), go north on Park St. 1.8 mi (715-239-6888, dnr.wi.gov/topic/parks/name/brunetisland; reservations: 888-947-2757, reserveamerica.com).

Hiking on my own, I enjoyed the solitude and independence it offered. My constant companions were "Woodrow," a hiking stick made of locust, and "Sweetheart," my backpack, with whom I had an on-again, off-again love affair. (Our relationship was dependent on her weight.)

TOM TEEPLES (AKA "LRRP"), ICE AGE TRAIL THOUSAND-MILER

Firth Lake Segment.

Chippewa County

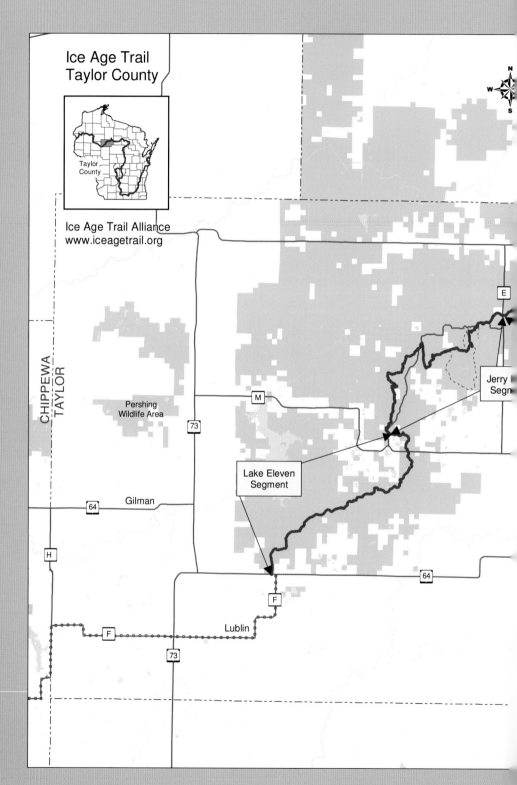

Ice Age Trail
Taylor County

Taylor
County

Ice Age Trail Alliance
www.iceagetrail.org

E

CHIPPEWA
TAYLOR

Jerry
Segn

Pershing
Wildlife Area

M

73

Lake Eleven
Segment

64   Gilman

H

64

F

F

Lublin

73

Taylor County

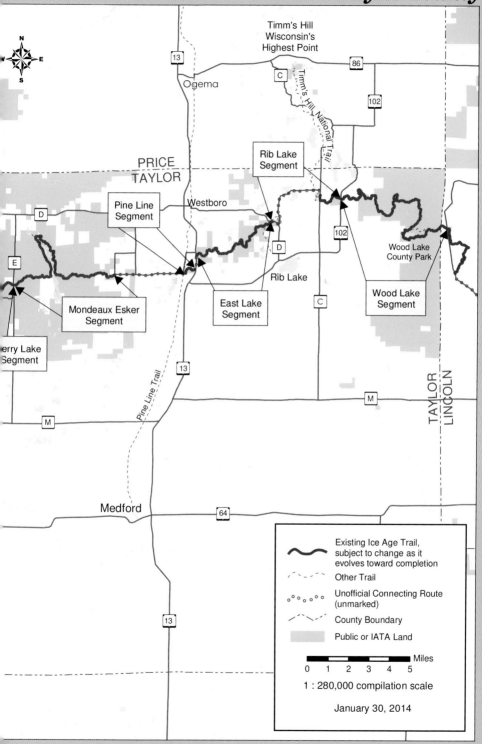

Timm's Hill
Wisconsin's
Highest Point

13

Ogema

86

C

102

PRICE
TAYLOR

Rib Lake
Segment

Timm's Hill National Trail

Pine Line
Segment

Westboro

D

D

102

Wood Lake
County Park

E

Rib Lake

Mondeaux Esker
Segment

East Lake
Segment

Wood Lake
Segment

erry Lake
Segment

C

M

Pine Line Trail

13

TAYLOR
LINCOLN

M

M

Medford

64

13

Existing Ice Age Trail,
subject to change as it
evolves toward completion

Other Trail

Unofficial Connecting Route
(unmarked)

County Boundary

Public or IATA Land

Miles

0 1 2 3 4 5

1 : 280,000 compilation scale

January 30, 2014

Taylor County

Trail miles: 63.0
Connecting route miles: 24.0

The Chippewa Lobe had the greatest influence on the present-day topography of Taylor County, sculpting all but the eastern edge of the county (shaped by the Wisconsin Valley Lobe, as seen in the Wood Lake moraine) and the southern part of the county (shaped by earlier glaciations). Glaciers left behind a hilly terrain with kettle lakes, erratics, ice-walled lake plains and eskers. Most of Taylor County lies within the end moraine zone near the recent glacier's southernmost extent.

The Menominee, Ho-Chunk, Chippewa and Sioux nations, French trappers, early missionaries and loggers once inhabited the area. Area forests thrive with hemlock, sugar maple, yellow birch and red and white pine trees. The Ice Age Trail goes through the Chequamegon National Forest and highlights the Mondeaux Dam Recreation Area, with the historic Mondeaux Lodge and Dam. The national forest is more than 850,000 acres and is rich in geologic and human history. Approximately 2,100 known archeological sites, containing more than half of the archeological sites recorded in northern Wisconsin's 15 counties, are present in the forest. Sites range from 10,000-year old prehistoric native American campsites to 20th century homesteads. The North Country National Scenic Trail also passes through the Chequamegon National Forest about 100 miles north of the Ice Age Trail.

Primitive camping is allowed on Taylor County Forest lands and in the national forest. Please camp at least 200 feet from trails and waterways.

CHAPTER INFORMATION

The High Point Chapter was officially organized in 1986. The chapter is working with Taylor County officials, Wisconsin Department of Natural Resources and the National Park Service to identify the Ice Age Trail corridor for western Taylor County. The proposed corridor will line up with eastern Chippewa County's proposed corridor.

COUNTY INFORMATION

Medford Area Chamber of Commerce: 715-748-4729, medfordwis.com

Price County Tourism Department: 800-269-4505, pricecountywi.net

Chequamegon National Forest Medford—Park Falls District Ranger: 715-748-4875

Taylor County Forestry & Recreation Department: 715-748-1486

East Lake Segment.

Taylor County

Lake Eleven Segment (Atlas Maps 21f, 22f)

14.1 miles: STH-64 to Sailor Creek Rd. (FR-571)

   This varied segment in the Chequamegon National Forest, with a distinct Northwoods feel, highlights the clear, deep kettle Lake Eleven and many other glacial features associated with the Perkinstown End Moraine.

From South Fork of the Yellow River, Lake Eleven, Beaver Creek and other small intermittent streams/creeks, lakes and wetland areas.

Primitive camping on national forest lands. Several walk-to campsites (**TA22, TA28**) are located at Lake Eleven.

At Kathryn Lake Campground ~3 mi west of CTH-M Trail access (see Area Services).

Small portions overlap with horseback and snowmobile trails and logging/forest roads.

Short side trails lead to campsites around Lake Eleven.

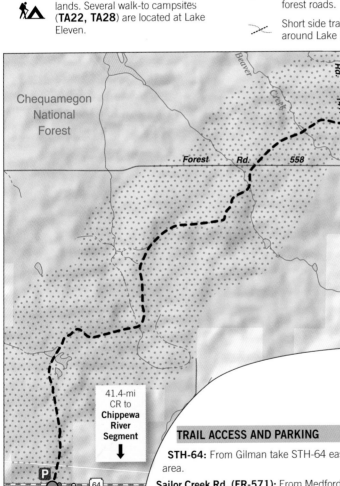

Chequamegon National Forest

41.4-mi CR to **Chippewa River Segment**

TRAIL ACCESS AND PARKING

STH-64: From Gilman take STH-64 east for 8.0 mi to the parking area.

Sailor Creek Rd. (FR-571): From Medford at the intersection of STH-64 and STH-13 take STH-13 north 4.5 mi. At CTH-M turn left and go west 13.0 mi. At Sailor Creek Rd. (FR-571) turn right and go north 0.7 mi to the parking area.

From its starting point on STH-64 the segment heads north and east and after 2.8 miles skirts around a beaver dam; hikers should watch for signage and avoid crossing the actual dam. A significant portion of the forest between STH-64 and FR-558, covering approximately the first 3.5 miles of the segment, was flattened by a tornado in 2002. The area's once towering hardwoods and pines have been replaced with underbrush, rapidly growing raspberry bushes and poplars. Due to lack of trees in some places, yellow-blazed Carsonite posts mark the Trail route. The area is beginning to return to its original state but caution is still recommended. This challenging portion of the segment can potentially be difficult to navigate and footing is rough in areas. Hikers should move slowly and pay close attention to signage. Hikers should also note that throughout the segment, depending on the season, creek crossings can be treacherous with moving water after

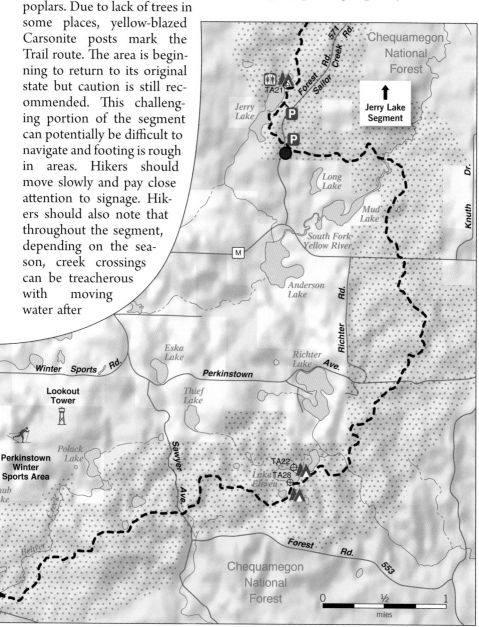

periods of snow melt or heavy rain.

North of Forest Road 558, the segment continues to make its way northeast toward Lake Eleven on dramatic high-relief hummocky topography through a mix of conifers and hardwoods. Hikers can experience a true remote feeling in this area. The segment highlights a classic ice-walled lake plain as it passes by the south shore of a small pond, roughly a half-mile west of the Sawyer Avenue crossing. Beaver dams are in ponds, creeks, bogs and marshes. Boardwalks are well placed, but some traversing of bogs and wet crossings is required. This area is full of logging history; logging railroads penetrated the interior lands between the rivers around 1890.

As the segment passes by Lake Eleven, a snowmobile trail that leads west of the Ice Age Trail provides access to several primitive campsites on the north shore of the lake (**TA22**) that offer benches and fire rings. The area is also used by fishermen, equestrian groups and hunters. Water for filtration is easily accessible. A primitive campsite (**TA28**) located on the south side of Lake Eleven is accessed by a short side trail about 100 feet west of the wooden bridge. It is marked by a very large boulder. The camp is in a hemlock grove up the hill along the lake. It has a stone fire ring with a log bench and many good places for tents.

As the segment makes its way to Perkinstown Avenue (FR-116) it passes through Richter Lake Hemlocks State Natural Area. Highlighted in this area is a collapsed ice-walled lake plain that holds a northern mesic forest consisting mainly of sugar maples, white ash, basswood and hemlock along with some yellow birch and red maple. At the base of the lake plain, a small white cedar swamp progresses into a northern wet forest that surrounds a small kettle bog lake, which formed in an ice-block depression.

North of Perkinstown Avenue (FR-116) the segment continues through rolling, forested terrain to CTH-M and then to a crossing of the South Fork of the Yellow River, which the Ice Age Trail crosses again farther north on the Jerry Lake Segment. About a mile after the river crossing the segment reaches its endpoint at Sailor Creek Road (FR-571).

AREA SERVICES

Gilman: Restaurant, grocery, convenience store, camping, library. From the STH-64 Trail access go west 8.0 mi.

Chequamegon National Forest Medford–Park Falls District Kathryn Lake Campground: Camping. From the CTH-M Trail access go west 2.5 mi on CTH-M. At FR 102 go south 0.5 mi to campground entrance. 8 campsites, vault toilets, water, swimming and fishing (715-748-4875; reservations: ReserveAmerica.com or Recreation.gov, 877-444-6777).

Medford: See Pine Line Segment and East Lake Segment, p. 80. From the STH-64 Trail access go east 18.2 mi. Also See Trail Access and Parking directions, above.

Perkinstown: Restaurant, convenience store. From CTH-M Trail access, go west ~3 mi.

Jerry Lake Segment (Atlas Maps 22f, 23f)

SNAPSHOT

15.1 miles: Sailor Creek Rd. (FR-571) Southern Trail Access to CTH-E

 This segment features Jerry Lake, the mile-long Hemlock Esker and crossings of the two forks of the Yellow River. The segment traverses the Chippewa Moraine over crevasse fills and across several glacial ice-walled lake plains.

 From Jerry Lake, South and North Branches of the Yellow River, Sailor Creek and other small intermittent streams/creeks and lakes.

 Primitive camping on national forest lands and many walk-to campsites.

Pit toilets at the primitive campgrounds located at the northeast end of Jerry Lake (**TA21**) and the southern end of the Chippewa Lobe Interpretive Loop (**TA17**).

 Small portions overlap with numbered forest roads and other primitive logging/forest roads.

 Partially shares the Chippewa Lobe Interpretive Loop, intersects and crosses the White Birch Trail and intersects parking area and road access spur trails.

TRAIL ACCESS AND PARKING

Sailor Creek Rd. Southern Trail Access: From Medford at the intersection of STH-64 and STH-13 take STH-13 north 4.5 mi. At CTH-M turn left and go west 13.0 mi. At Sailor Creek Rd. (FR-571) turn right and go north 0.7 mi to a small parking area. Additional parking area is available 0.3 mi north on Sailor Creek Rd. (FR-571), where a short side trail connects to the Ice Age Trail and Jerry Lake.

CTH-E: From Medford at the intersection of STH-64 and STH-13, take STH-13 north 15.0 mi to Westboro. At CTH-D turn left and go west 8.5 mi. At CTH-E turn left and go south 3.5 mi to the parking area.

Additional Parking: (i) Roadside parking along Lake 19 Rd. (FR-108). (ii) White Birch Trail parking area on Mondeaux Ave. (FR-102). The White Birch Trail (Forest Trail 567) leads 1.1 mi south to the Ice Age Trail. (iii) Small parking area on Mondeaux Ave (FR-102) where the Ice Age Trail leaves the road just west of the crossing of the North Branch of the Yellow River.

THE HIKE

From its starting point at the Sailor Creek Road (FR-571) southern Trail access the segment angles northwest to the shore of Jerry Lake. The segment passes by a side trail that leads back to a parking area on the road and then makes its way a bit farther north to a trailside primitive campsite (**TA21**) located on the northeast end of the lake. The campsite has a pit toilet and a steel fire grate. This is the best place to access the lake to get water as the rest of the shoreline is marshy and has receded over the years.

After crossing Hay Meadow Road (FR-572) the segment brings hikers to a crossing of the South Fork of the Yellow River on an impressive 67-foot-long bridge that volunteers constructed in 2012. The segment then bends northwest, following the river to a primitive campsite (**TA20**) situated on a ridge overlooking the river valley.

As the segment makes its way north from the river crossing it passes through an area that can be confusing for hikers to navigate thanks to two (and almost three)

crossings of the same road. The segment (a) passes just west of the terminus of primitive FR-576, then (b) bends back south to cross the road just east of its terminus, then (c) makes its way east and crosses the road a second time.

After the second crossing of FR-576 the segment continues northeast to Sailor Creek. Hikers will find a primitive campsite (**TA26**) on the west side of the segment and north side of the creek about 150 feet northeast from the river crossing. The campsite is marked by a large blue-gray boulder and is situated in a grove of hemlocks. It features a stone fire ring and nice flat area with space for several tents.

After the northern crossing of Sailor Creek Road (FR-571) the segment bends south and traverses the Hemlock Esker (**TA19**) for almost a mile, rising 80 feet above the forest floor. This area is part of Lost Lake Esker State Natural Area, which protects the complex forest and wetland communities associated with the esker and the glacial till surrounding it.

After descending from Hemlock Esker the segment bends northeast and passes a distinct large rock that guards the entrance to a primitive campsite (**TA25**) tucked under a

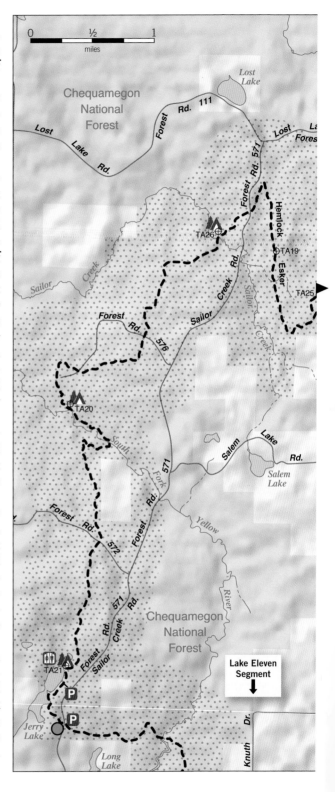

Ice Age Trail Guidebook 2014

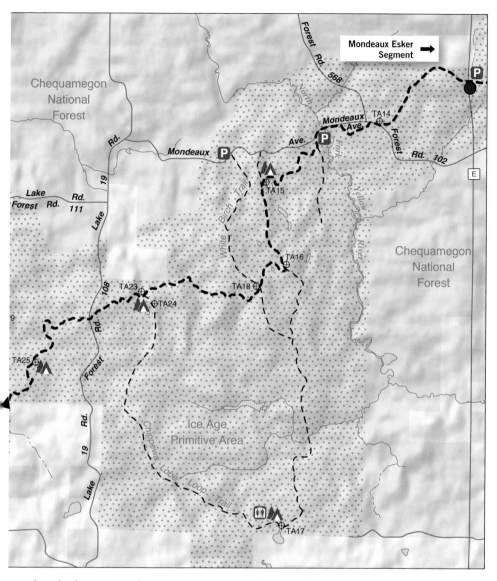

hemlock canopy. The campsite is near a boardwalk crossing, just east but not in sight of where the segment crosses an unnamed creek.

After crossing Lake 19 Road (FR-108) the segment follows the edge of a beautiful, large bog before reaching the western intersection of the Chippewa Lobe Interpretive Loop (see detailed description, below) at an informational kiosk (**TA23**). From this intersection hikers can head south 0.1 miles on the loop trail to a nice primitive campsite (**TA24**). Situated on high, dry ground, the campsite has benches, a stone fire ring and an access trail for water to a small bog lake.

The segment continues east from the junction with the loop trail past marshes, bogs and wetland areas. After about a mile the segment reaches another junction (**TA18**), this one with the White Birch Trail (Forest Trail 567). A walk north on White Birch Trail will take hikers to a parking area on Mondeaux Avenue (FR-

102). A walk southeast on the White Birch Trail offers another access to the Chippewa Lobe Interpretive Loop.

Less than half a mile east of its junction with the White Birch Trail, the segment reaches the eastern junction (**TA16**) with the Chippewa Lobe Interpretive Loop. The segment turns left at the junction and heads due north. After 0.7 miles the segment reaches another junction. From here, hikers can continue due north on Forest Trail 350 to access Mondeaux Avenue. The segment turns right at the intersection and heads east, almost immediately reaching a primitive campsite (**TA56**) located on the west shore of an unnamed, small lake and featuring a stone fire ring and log benches.

Less than a mile east of the primitive campsite the segment intersects with a forest trail and turns north to reach Mondeaux Avenue (FR-102). The segment turns east and follows the road for 100 yards to a crossing of the North Fork of the Yellow River. Benches near the river offer a nice spot to relax and enjoy the tranquil setting. East of the river the segment dips back into the forest, then crosses Mondeaux Avenue (FR-102) (**TA14**) and meanders northeast to the segment's endpoint on CTH-E. This last section, through birch forest with an undergrowth of ferns, is mostly flat and tends to get swampy after heavy rain and during the spring thaw.

Mobile Skills Crew project site, 2003, 2012, 2014

SIDE TRAIL—CHIPPEWA LOBE INTERPRETIVE LOOP

6.1 miles: Includes 4.6 miles of Loop trail + 1.5 miles of Ice Age Trail to close the loop

Access by foot only: (i) From the west, hike the Ice Age Trail 0.5 mi east from Lake 19 Rd. (FR-108) to a kiosk at the start of the Loop (**TA23**). (ii) From the north, hike the White Birch Trail (Forest Trail 567) south 1.1 mi, cross the Ice Age Trail (**TA18**) and continue south another 0.5 mi to its intersection with the Chippewa Lobe Interpretive Loop. This is less scenic than the Ice Age Trail access. (iii) From the east, hike the Ice Age Trail 1.6 mi west of where the Ice Age Trail leaves FR-102 after crossing the North Fork of the Yellow River. A steel sign marks the trail junction (**TA16**).

The Chippewa Lobe Interpretive Loop, also called the "Blue Diamond Trail" due to its blazes, is a rugged route that circles a remote roadless area called the Ice Age Primitive Area. Six posts mark the miles oriented counter-clockwise, starting from the Ice Age Trail's western access to it at the kiosk. During wet weather, the loop may not be passable, as the Yellow River tributaries flow west to east through the entire section, with little structure at critical wet crossings. A primitive campsite (**TA24**) is located on the loop 0.1 miles south of its western intersection with the Ice Age Trail. A second secluded, primitive campsite (**TA17**) is located at the southern end of the loop, 2.7 miles south of the Ice Age Trail's western intersection and 1.9 miles south of the Ice Age Trail's eastern intersection. Situated with pleasant views of the pond and beaver dam, the exceptional site has a log bench, fire pit and small cast iron table made from an old fire grate. A pit toilet is hidden a few yards to the southeast.

AREA SERVICES

Gilman: See Lake Eleven Segment, p. 68. From the Sailor Creek Rd. (FR-571) Trail access go west ~18 mi.

Mondeaux Dam Recreation Area: See Mondeaux Esker Segment, p. 76. From the CTH-E Trail access go north and east ~4 mi.

Medford: See Pine Line Segment and East Lake Segment, p. 80. From the CTH-E Trail access go east and south ~22 mi. Also see Trail Access and Parking directions, above.

Hemlock Esker on the Jerry Lake Segment.

Taylor County

Mondeaux Esker Segment (Atlas Map 23f)

SNAPSHOT

11.4 miles: CTH-E to Shady Dr.

 This segment has two remote, very rugged forested sections split by a trek through the popular Mondeaux Dam Recreation Area.

 At Mondeaux Dam Recreation Area lodge and campgrounds.

 From the Mondeaux Flowage and other small streams/creeks and wetland areas.

 Primitive camping on national forest lands.

 Several campgrounds around Mondeaux Flowage.

Several areas within the Mondeaux Dam Recreation Area including the lodge and Spearhead Point campground.

 At the Mondeaux Dam Recreation Area and campgrounds.

Small portions through the Mondeaux Dam Recreation Area and near Spearhead Point campground overlap with roads or sidewalks. Other portions overlap with logging/forest roads.

 Near Mondeaux Dam the segment passes near the trailhead for the Aldo Leopold Nature Trail.

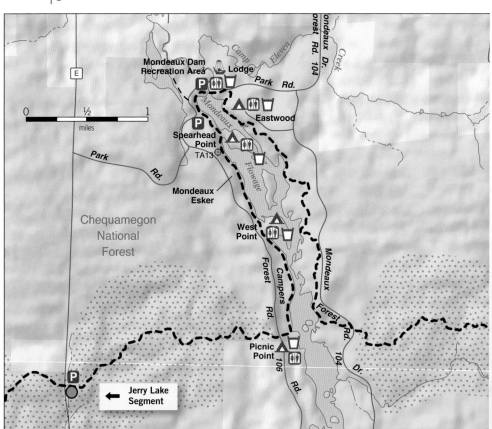

TRAIL ACCESS AND PARKING

CTH-E: From Medford at the intersection of STH-64 and STH-13, take STH-13 north 15.0 mi to Westboro. At CTH-D turn left and go west 8.5 mi. At CTH-E turn left and go south 3.5 mi to the parking area.

Shady Dr.: From Medford at the intersection of STH-64 and STH-13, take STH-13 north 15.0 mi to Westboro. At CTH-D turn left and go west 2.5 mi. At Zimmerman Rd. (FR-101) turn left and go south 2.0 mi. At Rindt Rd. (FR-564) turn right and go west 1.0 mi. At Shady Dr. turn left and go south 1.0 mi. No parking.

Additional Parking: Mondeaux Dam Recreation Area. From STH-13 at Westboro take CTH-D west 6.0 mi. At Mondeaux Dr. (FR-104) turn left and go south 1.0 mi. At Park Rd. (FR-106) turn right and follow the signs west to the recreation area.

THE HIKE

The present-day Mondeaux Flowage occupies a seven-mile tunnel channel, which once gushed with meltwater beneath the Chippewa Lobe. The area's well-known landforms of ice-walled lake plains, small kettle lakes and forest-covered glacial knobs were the result of stagnant glacial ice. Multiple eskers form the hogback ridges characteristic of the flowage area. The area is a waypoint on the Great Wisconsin Birding & Nature Trail and birders should look for the state-threatened red-shouldered hawk and other species such as raven, pileated woodpecker, winter wren, hermit thrush, warblers, northern water-thrush and scarlet tanager.

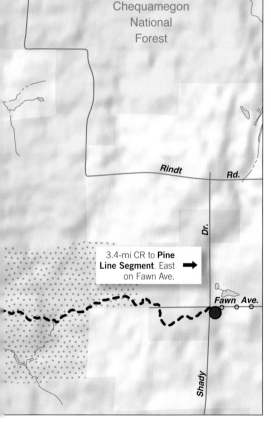

From CTH-E the segment makes its way east through Mondeaux Hardwoods State Natural Area. Beaver activity in the form of fallen trees and dammed creeks is common here and the segment crosses the tops of several well-established beaver dams.

The segment crosses Campers Road (FR-106) to the shore of the Mondeaux Flowage and turns north, paralleling the west side of the flowage. The segment climbs atop and follows the crest of the obvious Mondeaux Esker (**TA13**).

As the segment continues north toward the Spearhead Point campground hikers may want to consider jumping off the Ice Age Trail for two interesting side trips. A year-round glacial spring with cold, clear water can be found by following Park Road west a short distance from its intersection with Campers Road. The Leopold Nature Trail heads northwest from Park Road less than a half-mile north of the Park Road/

Campers Road intersection.

Back on the Trail, hikers should pay close attention to signage at the somewhat confusing crossing of the campground road near Spearhead Point. Toward the northern end of the flowage the segment passes by the facilities of the Mondeaux Dam Recreation Area. In addition to several developed campgrounds around the Mondeaux Flowage, the Mondeaux Dam Recreation Area has picnic shelters, a swimming beach and boat rentals. The segment passes by a historic lodge built by the Civilian Conservation Corps, which today houses a seasonal grill and concession stand. On summer weekends the lodge is often the site of back-patio concerts.

The segment crosses the Mondeaux Dam and parallels Park Road briefly before continuing south past the Eastwood Campground. As the segment continues south along the east side of the flowage it passes through recently logged areas where hikers should follow signage carefully. A mix of exposed roots and overgrown vegetation can make for poor footing.

The segment turns east and crosses Mondeaux Drive (FR-104) and continues east to its endpoint at the Shady Drive/Fawn Avenue intersection. This last portion of the segment can be exceptionally challenging even for experienced hikers and all who pass through here should be prepared for a tough trek. The segment follows "troads" (old two-track logging roads) in some sections and parallels wetland areas and crosses unnamed creeks with no bridges. Some areas may require a wet ford due to occasional flooding caused by beaver activity and seasonally changing water levels. Signage can be sparse at times, especially in open areas, and cell phones do not always work in this remote area.

Mobile Skills Crew project site, 2005

AREA SERVICES

Mondeaux Dam Recreation Area: Camping, restaurant (seasonal), lodging (seasonal). On Trail. Meals and cabin rental (seasonal) at Mondeaux Dam Lodge (W7969 Park Rd., Westboro, 715-427-5746, 715-748-4875, mondeauxdamlodge.com). Camping at Chequamegon National Forest Campgrounds: Eastwood, Spearhead Point, Picnic Point (group), West Point (first come, first serve) and nearby North Twin Lake (877-444-6777, ReserveAmerica.com or Recreation.gov).

Chequamegon National Forest Medford—Park Falls District: Information (715-748-4875, www.fs.usda.gov/cnnf).

Medford: See Pine Line Segment and East Lake Segment, p. 80. From the CTH-E Trail access go south and east ~18 mi. Also see Trail Access and Parking directions, above.

Westboro: See Pine Line Segment and East Lake Segment, p. 80. From the Mondeaux Dam Recreation Area go east ~8.5 mi. Also see Trail Access and Parking directions, above.

Mondeaux Esker Segment.

Taylor County

Pine Line Segment and East Lake Segment (Atlas Maps 24f, 25f)

SNAPSHOT

Pine Line Segment—0.9 mile: Fisher Creek Rd. at Fawn Ave. to STH-13

0.7-mi Connecting Route

East Lake Segment—6.4 miles: STH-13 Wayside to CTH-D

 The very short **Pine Line Segment** *retains a remote, deep-woods feeling.*

At Chelsea Lake County Park.

A walk-to campsite (**TA29**).

 Segment is closed during gun deer season.

 Crosses Pine-Line multi-use rail-trail at western end of segment.

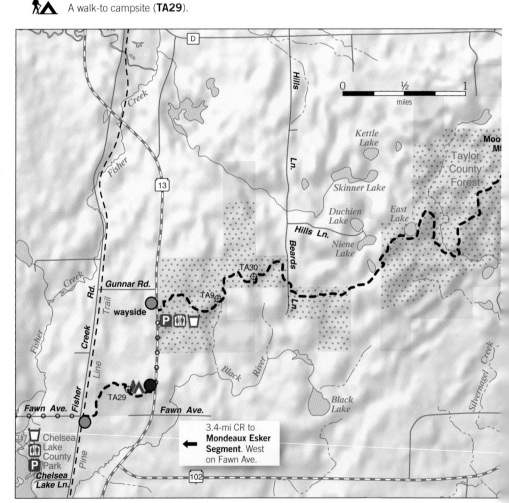

The remote, hilly and scenic **East Lake Segment** *highlights the head-waters of the Black River, historic logging sites and Moose Mountain and features signs along the route demarcating points of interest.*

 At the STH-13 wayside (seasonal).

 From East Lake and a few other small lakes and intermittent streams/creeks.

Primitive camping on county forest lands.

 Portion of the segment crossing private land east of Beards Ln. is closed during gun deer season.

 Portions overlap with cross-country ski/bike trails and with logging/forest roads.

Rib Lake Nordic Ski Trails network.

TRAIL ACCESS AND PARKING

Fisher Creek Rd. at Fawn Ave.: From Medford, at the intersection of STH-64 and STH-13 take STH-13 north 13.0 mi. At Gunnar Rd. turn left and go west 0.5 mi. At Fisher Creek Rd. turn left and go south 1.0 mi. The Ice Age Trail is on the east side of the road at the Fawn Ave. intersection. No parking.

CTH-D: From Rib Lake at the intersection of STH-102 and CTH-D, take CTH-D north for 2.0 mi to the parking area on the right side of the road. A spur trail leads to the Ice Age Trail.

Additional Parking: (i) Chelsea Lake County Park. (ii) STH-13 wayside.

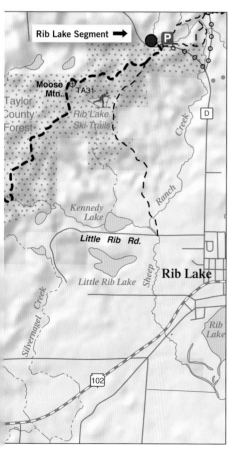

THE HIKE

From its starting point at the Fisher Creek Road/Fawn Avenue intersection, the 0.9-mile **Pine Line Segment** crosses the Pine Line multi-use trail and then makes its way east along the edge of a farm field. The segment turns north and soon enters a wooded property owned by the Ice Age Trail Alliance. A small primitive campsite (**TA29**), built by local Boy Scouts, is located in a wooded clearing west of the segment's endpoint on STH-13.

Upon reaching STH-13, hikers should head north on the shoulder of the highway for 0.7 miles to a wayside on the east side of the road. The wayside has water and restrooms available from late May to mid-September.

From the STH-13 wayside the **East Lake Segment** heads east through hilly terrain and mixed hardwood forest. Look for signs noting points of interest or identifying trees, including a sign at the beginning of the segment detailing the Wisconsin Conservation Corps' help in building the Ice Age Trail in Taylor County. The segment soon reaches the headwaters of the Black River (**TA9**) in a scenic hemlock grove. Farther on, the Trail enters (**TA30**) a Taylor County aspen regeneration project area. The segment follows a swath cut through the trees and crosses Beards Lane.

From here the segment continues northeast through a mix of Taylor County Forest and private lands, soon passing by the shore of East Lake, a classic kettle lake, in a landscape of dramatic high-relief hummocky topography. After passing by East Lake, the segment continues northeast through forested but slightly less hilly terrain and eventually climbs to the top of Moose Mountain (**TA31**). Here, hikers can enjoy a nice panoramic view of the area when leaves are off the trees. Hikers will notice erratics of various sizes, shapes and colors scattered across Moose Mountain and in some of the surrounding areas. The Trail descends and near its endpoint on CTH-D connects and overlaps with the Rib Lake Nordic Ski Trail network.

Mobile Skills Crew project site, 2002

AREA SERVICES

Chelsea Lake County Park: Water, restrooms, picnic area. From the Fawn Ave. and Fisher Creek Rd. intersection go south on Fisher Creek Rd. 0.5 mi. At the park's gravel road, turn right and go west 0.3 mi to the county park.

Westboro: Restaurant, library. At the STH-13 wayside go north 2.5 mi on STH-13. Library has limited hours.

Medford: Restaurant, grocery store, convenience store, general shopping, lodging, camping, library, medical care. At the STH-13 wayside go south 12.5 mi on STH-13. For area info, contact the Medford Area Chamber of Commerce (715-748-4729, medfordwis.com).

Rib Lake: See Rib Lake Segment, p. 84. From the CTH-D Trail access go south 2.0 mi.

We spend millions to go fast; let's spend a little to go slow.
RAYMOND T. ZILLMER, FOUNDER, ICE AGE TRAIL ALLIANCE

A porcupine along the Lake Eleven Segment.

Taylor County

Rib Lake Segment (Atlas Map 25f)

5.8 miles (1.6 IAT, 4.2 CR): CTH-D to STH-102

> **Note:** It is anticipated that volunteers will build a new section of Trail in 2014 and 2015 between Harper Drive and CTH-C in the Ann and Bob Rusch & Martha and Herman Rusch Preserves. The new Trail construction will eliminate the connecting route road walk over time. Check with the Ice Age Trail Alliance (800-227-0046, iceagetrail.org) for more details.

3 3 *This segment, which will evolve considerably starting in 2014, includes a lengthy roadwalk followed by a shorter off-road portion.*

 At Rusch Preserves (**TA5**).

 From Copper Creek, Sheep Ranch Creek and several lakes along the connecting route.

 Three walk-to campsites in the Rusch Preserves.

 At nearby private campground 4.0 mi south of the Trail (see Area Services).

 At South Harper Lake public beach (no facilities) on the west end of the lake.

 Portion of the segment crossing private land between CTH-C and STH-102 is closed during gun deer season.

 A significant portion is connecting route roadwalk. Off-road sections overlap with cross-country ski trails and logging/forest roads.

 The connecting route portion passes the trailhead for the Timm's Hill National Trail.

 Portions of this segment in the Rusch Preserves may be suitable for those using wheelchairs or similar devices.

TRAIL ACCESS AND PARKING

CTH-D: From Rib Lake at the intersection of STH-102 and CTH-D, take CTH-D north for 2.0 mi to the parking area on the right side of the road.

STH-102: From Rib Lake at the intersection of STH-102 and CTH-D, take STH-102 east then north 5.5 mi. No parking.

Additional Parking: CTH-C Rib Lake Nordic Ski Trails handicap-accessible parking area in front of the Nordic Ski Trails kiosk. A second parking area is located at the large Rusch Preserves parking area slightly north of the kiosk area. Pick up the Ice Age Trail on the east side of CTH-C across from the parking areas.

THE HIKE

This segment starts with a connecting-route roadwalk east on CTH-D, north on Harper Drive and east on Rustic Road #1. This road takes hikers past a swimming beach on South Harper Lake and then an access point for the Timm's Hill National Trail (**timmshilltrail.com**), which heads north to Timm's Hill, Wisconsin's highest point at 1951.5 feet.

Upon reaching CTH-C hikers should turn right and head south to where the segment departs the road and continues toward STH-102. Before heading off-road, hikers can cross to the west side of CTH-C and explore the 30-acre IATA-owned Ann and Bob Rusch & Martha and Herman Rusch Preserves, which features three primitive campsites with a well water pump (**TA5**). While visiting hikers should watch carefully for private property markers and must stay within the preserve's boundaries. *Volunteers will undertake a multiyear effort to construct a*

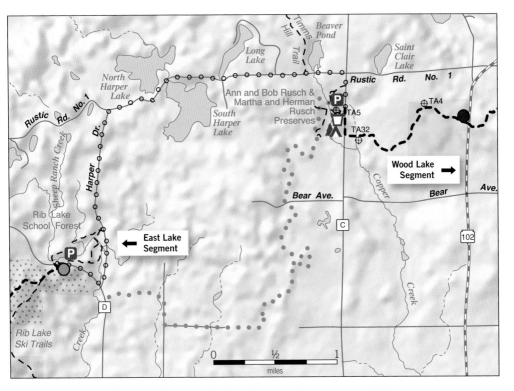

new section of the Trail westward from this area beginning in 2014.

Between CTH-C and its endpoint on STH-102, the segment passes over private lands featuring areas of open fields and mature hardwoods. The segment briefly cuts through an area of pine trees and a field before entering the woods and crossing a creek on a curving boardwalk (**TA32**). The segment climbs a hill and continues through alternating areas of woods and fields, intersecting with several logging roads on its way to the segment's terminus at STH-102. Two of these open areas were once part of quarries, but little evidence of quarry activity remains today. In the second quarry area, however, hikers will pass a small cinder block cairn (**TA4**), which stands in contrast with the more natural surroundings.

Mobile Skills Crew project site, 2008, 2011, 2014, 2015

AREA SERVICES

Rib Lake: Restaurant, grocery store, convenience store, lodging, camping, library, medical services. From the CTH-D Trail access go 2.0 mi south on CTH-D. Camping at Lakeview Tourist Park (300 Park Row, Rib Lake, 800-819-5253). For area info, contact Town of Rib Lake (715-427-5404, riblakewisconsin.com).

Medford: See Pine Line Segment and East Lake Segment, p. 80. From CTH-D Trail access go south ~18 mi.

Wood Lake Segment (Atlas Maps 25f, 26f)

SNAPSHOT

13.5 miles: STH-102 to Tower Rd.

 This wild, remote segment highlights scenic Gus Johnson Creek, Wood Lake, wetlands and historic logging camp sites.

 At Wood Lake County Park.

From Gus Johnson Creek (**TA1**), Wood Lake, and other small streams/creeks, small lakes and wetland areas.

Primitive camping on county forest lands.

 Campgrounds at Wood Lake County Park and Camp 8 Flowage.

 A portion of the segment crossing private land east of STH-102 is closed during gun deer season.

 Portions overlap with logging/forest roads.

A white-blazed loop north of Wood Lake.

TRAIL ACCESS AND PARKING

STH-102: From Rib Lake at the intersection of STH-102 and CTH-D, take STH-102 east then north 5.5 mi. No parking.

Tower Rd.: *From Rib Lake* at the intersection of STH-102 and CTH-D, take STH-102 east for 2.0 mi. At CTH-C turn right and go south 7.0 mi. At CTH-M turn left and go east 8.0 mi. At Tower Rd. turn left and go north 9.0 mi to the parking area on the west side of the road. *From Merrill* at the intersection of I-39/USH-51 and STH-64, take STH-64 west for 3.0 mi to the junction with STH-107. Continue west on STH-64/107 6.6 mi. At CTH-M continue west for 10.9 mi. At Tower Rd. turn right and go north 9.0 mi.

Additional Parking: (i) CTH-C. See Rib Lake Segment for description. (ii) Second Bear Ave. Trail access (**TA33**) parking area. (iii) Wood Lake County Park. (iv) North Loop Rd. Trail access parking area.

THE HIKE

Note: At the time of this book's publication the Trail crossing of Gus Johnson Creek was impassible due to flooding from beaver dams. Until this situation is resolved and this portion of the Trail is reopened, hikers should

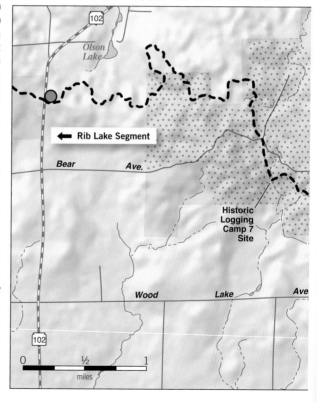

take the following alternate route: From the second ("central") crossing of Bear Avenue (TA33) turn right and follow Bear Avenue east then north 0.7 miles to the Trail's third ("eastern") crossing of Bear Avenue (TA34). At this point hikers can rejoin the Trail heading east into the woods.

This segment is in a very remote area that provides welcoming habitat for deer, black bear, wolf, grouse and coyote. Wetlands and lakes are home to eagles, sandhill cranes, loons and beaver. The area has recovered from extensive logging since the early 1900s, when logging camps (remains of which are found along the segment) dotted the forest landscape and were symbolic of the Northwoods way of life during the early part of the past century. Wayfinding can present a challenge in some areas and hikers can expect to cross unbridged creeks and seasonally flooded wetlands that occasionally swamp portions of the segment.

From its starting point on STH-102 the segment heads through an area that embraces the western end moraines left by the Wisconsin Valley lobe. The segment climbs one end moraine, drops to cross an intermittent stream at Six Stone Crossing, then courses along the outer side of another end moraine.

The segment continues east through a mix of Taylor County Forest and private lands, crosses Bear Avenue for the first time ("western" crossing), skirts by the historic Logging Camp 7 site and reaches the second ("central") crossing of Bear Avenue (TA33). From here the segment traverses the scenic and steep-sided valley of Gus Johnson Creek, set between two ice-walled-lake plains and formed

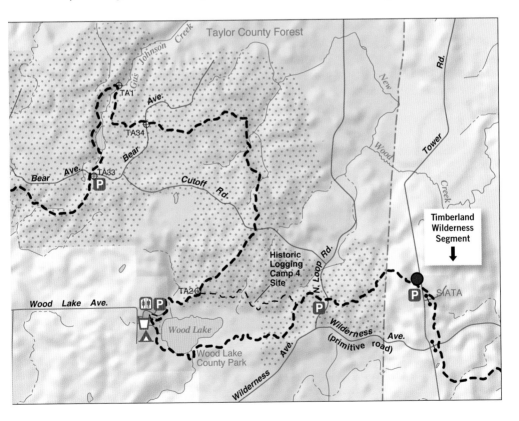

by water gushing from under the ice at the outer edge of the Wood Lake Moraine. The segment has an especially intimate wilderness character along Gus Johnson Creek (**TA1**). East of the creek near the third crossing of Bear Avenue (**TA34**), hikers may notice how the forest dramatically changes from hemlock, birch and maple to maple, oak and poplar.

The segment turns south, crosses Cutoff Road, travels through an area of spectacular high-relief hummocky topography and then reaches the western junction (**TA2**) with a 2.5-mile loop trail circling Wood Lake. The 67-acre lake is spring-fed with clear, blue waters. The Ice Age Trail uses the western and southern portions of the loop trail, passing through Wood Lake County Park's swimming, picnic and camping areas, where water and restrooms are available seasonally. The white-blazed northern portion of the loop highlights the historic Logging Camp 4 site, which was in operation from 1906 to 1910.

From the eastern junction with the Wood Lake loop trail the segment crosses North Loop Road and continues eastward through high-relief hummocky topography toward the segment's endpoint on Tower Road, crossing from Taylor County into Lincoln County along the way.

Mobile Skills Crew project site, 2008, 2009, 2011

AREA SERVICES

Wood Lake County Park: Camping, water, restroom. On Trail. For information contact Taylor County Forestry & Recreation Department (715-748-1486). From Rib Lake at the intersection of STH-102 and CTH-D take STH-102 east and north 4.0 mi. At Wood Lake Rd. turn right and go east 3.3 mi.

Rib Lake: See Rib Lake Segment, p. 84. From the STH-102 Trail access go south 5.5 mi. Also see Trail Access and Parking directions, above.

Medford: See Pine Line Segment and East Lake Segment, p. 80. From the STH-102 Trail access go south ~22 mi.

Merrill: See Turtle Rock Segment and Grandfather Falls Segment, p. 101. From Tower Rd. Trail access go south and east ~30 mi. Also see Trail Access and Parking directions, above.

I am thrilled to be a Thousand-Miler. I am delighted I accomplished this feat with my best friend, my husband Rick. I couldn't and wouldn't have hiked the entire Ice Age Trail without him. Together we experienced the best of Wisconsin, the part you can only see by taking a hike.

ROBERTA BIE (AKA "FREIDA"), ICE AGE TRAIL THOUSAND-MILER

Wood Lake Segment.

Taylor County

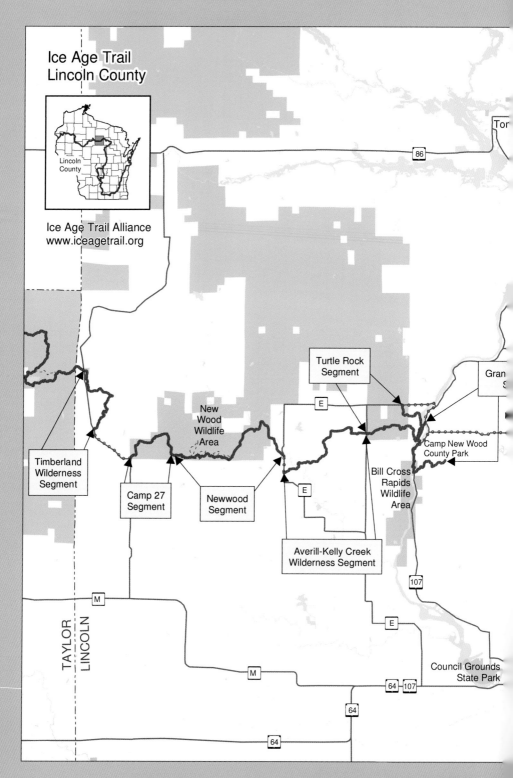

Ice Age Trail
Lincoln County

Lincoln
County

Ice Age Trail Alliance
www.iceagetrail.org

86

Tor

Turtle Rock
Segment

New
Wood
Wildlife
Area

E

Gran
S

Camp New Wood
County Park

Timberland
Wilderness
Segment

Camp 27
Segment

Newwood
Segment

E

Bill Cross
Rapids
Wildlife
Area

Averill-Kelly Creek
Wilderness Segment

107

TAYLOR

LINCOLN

M

E

Council Grounds
State Park

M

64   107

64

64

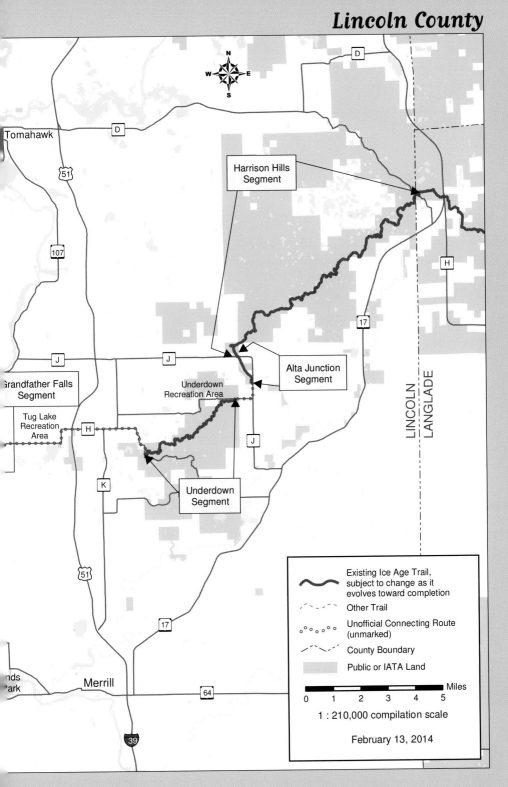

Tomahawk

Harrison Hills
Segment

Grandfather Falls
Segment

Tug Lake
Recreation
Area

Underdown
Recreation Area

Alta Junction
Segment

Underdown
Segment

LINCOLN
LANGLADE

Merrill

Existing Ice Age Trail,
subject to change as it
evolves toward completion

Other Trail

Unofficial Connecting Route
(unmarked)

County Boundary

Public or IATA Land

Miles

0   1   2   3   4   5

1 : 210,000 compilation scale

February 13, 2014

Lincoln County

Trail miles: 49.1
Connecting route miles: 16.2

Lincoln County lies within the Northern Highlands. This was once a mountainous region that eroded away before the Ice Age. The Ice Age glaciers further scoured the higher peaks and filled the valleys with glacial till and debris. The subsequent geographical feature of this area is the Wisconsin Valley Lobe which covers most of central and northern Lincoln County. Aerial views of the land would reveal parallel moraine ridge "waves" formed by the receding glacier 15,000 to 18,000 years ago. A spectacular band of high-relief hummocky topography marks the maximum southern extent of this lobe. The county is bookended by the Wood Lake Moraine on the west and the Harrison Moraine on the east side of the advancing lobe. Within the Harrison Moraine are the Harrison Hills and Underdown segments, where the terrain often varies by more than 200 feet. This top-notch topography is marked by deep kettles, fragmented ridges, irregular hummocks and ice-walled lake plains. The Wisconsin River at Grandfather Falls provides an opportunity to see 1.8-billion-year-old exposed bedrock and large boulders smoothed by thousands of years of water flow.

The segments in Lincoln County provide some of the most isolated experiences on the Ice Age Trail. The forest uplands include hemlock, maple, yellow and white birch, white cedar, balsam fir, poplar, black ash, white pine and tamarack. Black bear are common and timber wolves are present in the large tracts of public land in the area.

Dogs should be kept on a leash as they have been known to chase bear and deer and could be attacked should they wander near a den of cubs or wolf pups. Bringing dogs to these areas during hunting season may endanger the use of these lands.

For overnight parking contact the chapter coordinator for best locations and notify the county sheriff department. Primitive camping is permitted on county forest land. Please camp at least 200 feet away from waterways and trails.

A navigational note: Throughout the county there are yellow paint markings found in areas about to be or recently logged. These markers are not Ice Age Trail navigational aids and differ from the traditional Ice Age Trail yellow blaze by their irregular shape and randomness.

CHAPTER INFORMATION

The Northwoods Chapter is one of the oldest IATA chapters. The chapter has a Trail segment "adoption" program which divides Trail segments into manageable distances for volunteers to maintain. It also has a rich history of working with youth groups, the Wisconsin Conservation Corps, Mobile Skills Crew program and volunteers from throughout the state to build new Trail segments and maintain existing ones in the county.

COUNTY INFORMATION

Lincoln County: co.lincoln.wi.us

Lincoln County Forestry, Lands & Parks Department: 715-539-1034

Lincoln County Sheriff's Office: 715-536-6272; contact for overnight parking permission.

CAROL NEUHOFF

Wisconsin River on the Grandfather Falls Segment.

Timberland Wilderness Segment (Atlas Map 26f)

3.9 miles: Tower Rd. Northern Trail Access to Tower Rd. Southern Trail Access

  This very remote segment through hardwood forests features ice-walled lake plains, ravines and several small streams.

💧 From several small intermittent streams/creeks.

🚃 Portions overlap with logging/forest roads.

TRAIL ACCESS AND PARKING

Tower Rd. Northern Trail Access: *From Merrill* at the intersection of I-39/USH-51 and STH-64, take STH-64 west for 3.0 mi to the junction with STH-107. Continue west on STH-64/107 6.6 mi. At CTH-M continue west for 10.9 mi. At Tower Rd. turn right and go north 9.0 mi to the parking area on the west side of the road. *From Rib Lake* at the intersection of STH-102 and CTH-D, take STH-102 east for 2.0 mi. At CTH-C turn right and go south 7.0 mi. At CTH-M turn left and go east 8.0 mi. At Tower Rd. turn left and go north 9.0 mi.

Tower Rd. Southern Trail Access: *From Merrill* at the intersection of I-39/USH-51 and STH-64, take STH-64 west for 3.0 mi to the junction with STH-107. Continue west on STH-64/107 6.6 mi. At CTH-M continue west for 10.9 mi. At Tower Rd. turn right and go north 7.0 mi to the Trail access on the east side of the road. Roadside parking. No overnight parking. *From Rib Lake* at the intersection of STH-102 and CTH-D, take STH-102 east for 2.0 mi. At CTH-C turn right and go south 7.0 mi. At CTH-M turn left and go east 8.0 mi. At Tower Rd. turn left and go north 7.0 mi.

THE HIKE

This segment passes through a 35,000-acre privately owned property that is a large, undeveloped tract. Timber production and harvest have not hindered the eastern timber wolf, black bear, bobcat, deer, red fox, or fisher populations. The signs of wildlife and the isolation of the region make for a true wilderness feeling. The state purchased a linear easement on this property to permanently protect the Ice Age Trail in 1999 and in 2002 the state purchased a Forest Legacy Easement over the entire 35,000 acres that prevents the land from being developed or subdivided.

The segment starts off from a point on Tower Road directly across from the Wood Lake Segment Trail access and crosses a grassy forest road after a quarter-mile. This is the first of four crossings of logging roads. Logging operations have occurred in the recent past moving generally from the south to the north. Some clear-cutting of aspen and the timber stand improvement cutting of hardwoods are evident along the route. Prior to more recent logging operations, this area was last logged in 1938.

After the second logging road crossing, the segment passes through an area with several trailside erratics then traverses the top of a crescent-shaped ridge before reaching an old railroad grade.

As the segment makes its way southeast, it follows the edge of an ice-walled lake plain (**LI35**). Hikers can peer through the forest to see creek-filled ravines and forested lowlands of mature hemlock, balsam fir, white cedar and yellow birch. Pass a Leopold bench dedicated to Herb Schotz, volunteer and former coordinator of the Ice Age Trail Alliance's Northwoods Chapter, as the segment turns to the southwest.

Continuing on, the segment crosses a two-plank native material bridge (**LI36**) made on-site that spans a ravine. Here steam engines moved timber via the old railroad grade to the main line south and east.

After crossing the third logging road (also an old railroad grade) the segment follows rolling ridges of two more ice-walled lake plains before crossing the final logging road and reaching its terminus at Tower Road.

Mobile Skills Crew project site, 2004, 2007

AREA SERVICES

Merrill: See Turtle Rock Segment and Grandfather Falls Segment, p. 101. From the Tower Rd. southern Trail access go south and east ~27.5 mi. Also see Trail Access and Parking directions, above.

Rib Lake: See Rib Lake Segment, p. 84. From the Tower Rd. southern Trail access go south and west ~9 mi. Also see Trail Access and Parking directions, below.

Medford: See Pine Line Segment and East Lake Segment, p. 80. From the Tower Rd. southern Trail access go south and west ~30 mi.

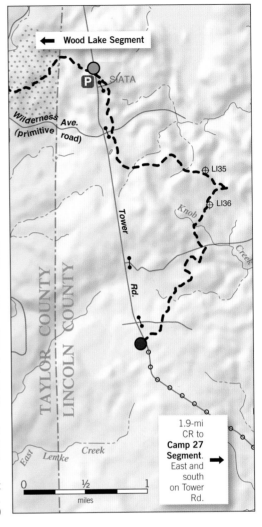

I have a deep sense of gratitude for those who had the vision to establish this Trail and for those who selflessly and quietly maintain the quality of it. I know that our state is enhanced by its presence. It is a corridor of beauty and adventure for many people and a corridor of connection for wildlife of all kinds. Hiking it is a treasured gift which I hope to re-gift to others. As I found on a billboard in Hatley, "Sometimes the best things are right in your backyard."

CHRIS MILLER (AKA "DANCING DOVE"), ICE AGE TRAIL THOUSAND-MILER

Camp 27 Segment
and Newwood Segment (Atlas Maps 26f, 27f)

SNAPSHOT

Camp 27 Segment—2.9 miles: Tower Rd. to Conservation Ave.

Newwood Segment—6.5 miles: Conservation Ave. to CTH-E

 The **Camp 27 Segment** traverses one of the most remote areas in the state—the New Wood State Wildlife Area—and includes the crossing of a large beaver dam and a river ford.

 From the North Fork of the Copper River (**LI31**) and a wetland area (**LI32**).

 By law, dogs must be leashed April 15 to July 31 when crossing State Wildlife Area.

 Portions overlap with logging/forest roads.

Short spur trail (gravel road) to the site of historic Camp 27 lumber camp.

 The remote **Newwood Segment** traverses a wide variety of terrain and highlights the beautiful New Wood River and three towering riverbank pines.

 From the New Wood River, Camp Twentysix Creek and other small streams/creeks and wetland areas.

 Primitive camping on a narrow band of county forest.

Portion of segment crossing private land between the eastern boundary of the Lincoln County Forest and CTH-E is closed during gun deer season.

 By law, dogs must be leashed April 15 to July 31 when crossing State Wildlife Area.

 Portions overlap with logging/forest roads.

A number of hunter access footpaths on old forest roads.

TRAIL ACCESS AND PARKING

Tower Rd.: *From Merrill* at the intersection of I-39/USH-51 and STH-64, take STH-64 west for 3.0 mi to the junction with STH-107. Continue west on STH-64/107 6.6 mi. At CTH-M continue west for

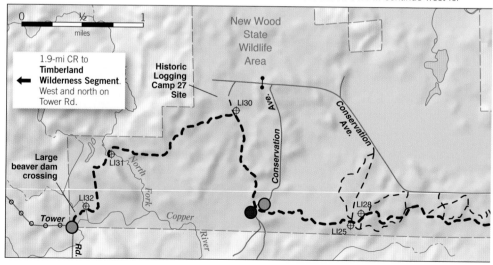

10.9 mi. At Tower Rd. turn right and go north 5.1 mi to the Trail access on the east side of the road. Roadside parking. *From Rib Lake* at the intersection of STH-102 and CTH-D, take STH-102 east for 2.0 mi. At CH-C turn right and go south 7.0 mi. At CTH-M turn left and go east 8.0mi. At Tower Rd. turn right and go north 5.1 mi.

CTH-E: From Merrill at the intersection of I-39/USH-51 and STH-64, take STH-64 west for 3.0 mi. At STH-107 turn right and go north 12.8 mi past Grandfather Falls and Dam. At CTH-E turn left across the Wisconsin River and go west then south for 7.5 mi to the parking area on the west side of the road.

Additional Parking: (i) Conservation Ave.: From the CTH-E access go south 0.2 mi on CTH-E. At Conservation Ave. turn right and go west 2.1 mi to the parking area. (ii) Additional parking areas farther west along Conservation Ave. near hunter access footpaths on old forest roads (see map). These are maintained mostly during hunting season. Note: Toward the south end of Conservation Ave., an old logging road (footpath only) heads west from the road and provides access to the Ice Age Trail.

THE HIKE

Both the Camp 27 and Newwood segments traverse the New Wood State Wildlife Area. The area dates back to 1945 when 960 acres of cutover and burned land were purchased by the state for deer, forest wildlife and waterfowl management and public hunting purposes. Additional state purchases increased the Wildlife Area to today's 4,635 acres. The New Wood State Wildlife Area is one of the most remote areas in the state. Since the early 1980s timber wolf packs have returned and reestablished themselves in the area. The upland forest offers habitat for deer, ruffed grouse, snowshoe hare, timber wolves, hawks, bald eagles and a variety of thrushes and warblers. New Wood State Wildlife Area is featured in the Lake Superior Northwoods Region of the Great Wisconsin Birding and Nature Trail.

From its starting point on Tower Road, the **Camp 27 Segment** quickly reaches a beaver dam more than 100 feet long that is used to cross a large wetland (**LI32**). Hikers will follow atop the narrow earthen embankments of the dam, which are marked on each end. There is a substantial breach in the eastern portion of the dam and wooden planking helps hikers cross the gap. Footing is uneven and parts of the tread across the dam can be unstable and give away underfoot. Hiking poles or sticks are helpful for balance and extreme caution should be used when crossing the dam.

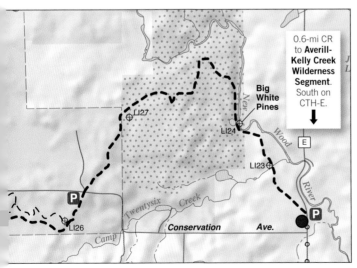

Farther on the segment crosses the North Fork of the Copper River on a rocky creek bed about 30 feet wide (**LI31**). Depending on the season or rainy periods, this may be a relatively dry crossing or require a shallow ford. From here the segment switches back and forth between narrow, tree-lined corridors and wide, grassy logging trails.

About a mile and a quarter past the North Fork of the Copper River crossing, the segment intersects (**LI30**) with a gravel logging road that leads 100 yards north to the site of the historic Camp 27 logging camp. Camp 27 was established in 1940 or 1941 by the Rib Lake Lumber Company of Delaware. Logs were transported by rail to the Company's sawmill in Rib Lake. At the time, hemlocks still grew so large two people could barely reach around the trunks. Logging was done by hand using crosscut saws and axes. Loggers worked in winter, icing the roads to transport the logs by sled. Some winters there were as many as 150 men in Camp 27. The camp was self-sufficient as they even had their own cattle and pigs. By 1945 the area had been cut over and cleared. Little trace of Camp 27 remains at the site, except a small mound on the northern edge of the camp, probably a garbage dump site. This area was more recently used as a staging area for logging.

From the intersection (**LI30**) with the gravel road to Camp 27, the segment continues south, crossing an ice-walled-lake plain just shy of its terminus on Conservation Avenue.

The **Newwood Segment** heads east from Conservation Avenue through a few boggy areas and marshland. Within a mile the segment intersects (**LI25**) with the first of several hunter access footpaths on old forest roads that are primarily used by hunters during hunting season. They offer a way back to Conservation Avenue where there are additional parking areas.

As the segment continues eastward, it traverses a classic esker (**LI28**) and highlights trailside erratics. Portions of the segment follow narrow and lightly treaded footpath sections that enhance the natural, semi-primitive experience. As the segment nears the Conservation Avenue Trail access and parking area, it transitions (**LI26**) from a narrow footpath to wide, grassy "troads" along the edge of an assortment of open meadows.

The eastern half of the Newwood Segment courses rough terrain on state, county and private lands. This area along the entire Wisconsin River valley was logged for large pines from the 1850s through the 1890s. Rivers were used to transport the logs to the mills. In 1906, the logging of hardwoods and hemlock started once the pines were gone and a source of new wood was needed. A network of standard gauge railroad spurs was placed in areas being logged for transportation of the hardwood. The Stange & Kinzel Lumber Company of Merrill put in rail spurs and used them until the area was completely logged off from the 1900s to 1920s. The spurs tied in with a line of the Milwaukee Road which went from the Newwood area into Merrill to the company's lumber mill. Eastern hemlock bark played an important role in the forest and tanning industries of northern Wisconsin from 1885 to 1922. In 1925, the Rib Lake Lumber Company bought the land and held logging operations on it for the next 20 years.

North of Conservation Avenue the segment makes its way across the State Wildlife Area boundary into a mile-wide band of Lincoln County Forest, where primitive camping is permitted. Shortly after crossing into the Lincoln County Forest, hikers will find a Leopold bench (**LI27**) beneath a large pine and a hemlock. After the segment curves around to the south it reaches a point along the New Wood River where hikers will discover three giant white pines (**LI24**). These probably escaped the saw during the logging heyday due to their small size at the time. They have since thrived and offer a scenic, peaceful resting spot under their canopy. There is a bench and access to the New Wood River here.

Farther along, the segment reaches an overlook of the river featuring another Leopold bench in a small grove of hemlocks where hikers can relax and enjoy the memorable view. Hikers must not camp here as this spot and the remainder of the segment are on private land. The segment continues through hummocky glacial terrain to a crossing of Camp Twentysix Creek (**LI23**) before following the flat, grassy rail bed of a historic logging railway that rises above the surrounding wetlands and brings the segment to its terminus on CTH-E. Wolf scat is commonly seen on the old rail bed.

Mobile Skills Crew project site, 2003, 2004, 2005, 2006

AREA SERVICES

Merrill: See Turtle Rock Segment and Grandfather Falls Segment, p. 101. From the CTH-E Trail access go east then south ~23 mi. Also see Trail Access and Parking directions, above.

Rib Lake: See Rib Lake Segment, p. 84. From the Tower Rd. Trail access go west ~8 mi. Also see Trail Access and Parking directions, above.

Medford: See Pine Line Segment and East Lake Segment, p. 80. From the Tower Rd. Trail access go south and west ~30 mi.

Averill-Kelly Creek Wilderness Segment (Atlas Maps 27f, 28f)

SNAPSHOT

4.8 miles: CTH-E to Burma Rd.

2 5 *This segment, entirely on private lands, features three water crossings in a forested, remote setting.*

 From the New Wood River (**LI21**), Averill Creek (**LI19**), Kelly Creek and a few smaller intermittent streams.

 The eastern portion of the segment is closed for all of October, November and December. A reroute is posted during this time. The entire segment is closed for the traditional 9-day gun deer season in November.

 Dogs must be leashed at all times.

 Portions overlap with logging/forest roads.

TRAIL ACCESS AND PARKING

CTH-E: From Merrill at the intersection of I-39/USH-51 and STH-64, take STH-64 west for 3.0 mi. At STH-107 turn right and go north 12.8 mi past Grandfather Falls and Dam. At CTH-E turn left, go across the Wisconsin River and go west then south for 8.1 mi. Roadside parking on the east side of the road.

Burma Rd.: From Merrill at the intersection of I-39/USH-51 and STH-64, take STH-64 west for 3.0 mi. At STH-107 turn right and go north 12.8 mi past Grandfather Falls and Dam. At CTH-E turn left across the Wisconsin River and go west 2.6 mi. At Burma Rd. turn left and go south 1.1 mi. NO PARKING. Instead, find roadside parking next to the Turtle Rock Segment Burma Rd. southern Trail access sign

0.1 mi farther south on the east side of the road. DO NOT park in front of the private road/access gate on the west side of the road.

THE HIKE

From its starting point on CTH-E the segment passes through an open canopy of aspen and birch trees regenerating after a timber harvest from the beginning of this millennium. In 2012 the first half-mile was intermittently logged off and hikers should pay close attention to signage. After a mile the segment reaches and then parallels the peaceful New Wood River before reaching a point where hikers will ford the river (**LI21**). The river is wide but generally only ankle- to knee-deep. After periods of heavy rains, however, it can get as high as hip-deep.

After the ford the segment reaches an open grassy area at an unmarked trail junction (**LI20**) and continues east to a spot where hikers will rock-hop across Averill Creek (**LI19**). Following the creek crossing the segment passes through a large clear-cut timber harvested area regenerating with pioneer plants such as birch, aspen and cherry, along with raspberry bushes, grasses and shrubs. The segment uses portions of an old railroad grade as it makes its way first to Kelly Creek, a trout stream, and then to its endpoint on Burma Road.

AREA SERVICES

Merrill: See Turtle Rock Segment and Grandfather Falls Segment, p. 101. From Burma Rd. go north, east then south ~18 mi. Also see Trail Access and Parking directions, above.

Tomahawk: See Turtle Rock and Grandfather Falls Segment, p. 101. From Burma Rd. go north, east then north ~17 mi.

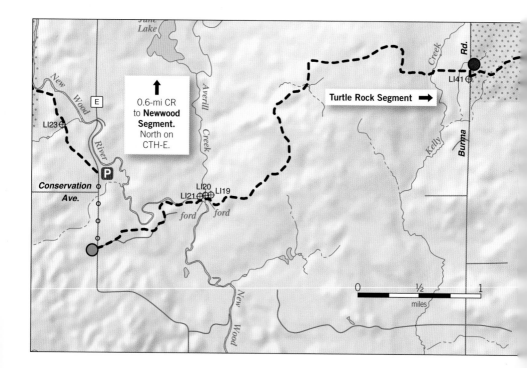

Ice Age Trail Guidebook 2014

Turtle Rock Segment and Grandfather Falls Segment (Atlas Map 28f)

SNAPSHOT

Turtle Rock Segment—5.1 miles: Burma Rd. Northern Trail Access to CTH-E

2.1 mile Connecting Route

Grandfather Falls Segment—4.0 miles: STH-107 Grandfather Falls Hydro Northern Parking Area to Camp New Wood County Park on STH-107

 The **Turtle Rock Segment** *includes a beautiful—and very challenging—trek along and near the banks of the Wisconsin River, where the ceremonial Turtle Rock is found.*

 From the Wisconsin River and other small streams/creeks.

 Primitive camping on county forest lands.

 Eastern portion of the segment crossing private land along and near the Wisconsin River is closed during gun deer season.

 Segment includes brief roadwalk on Burma Rd. Portions overlap with logging/forest roads and multi-use trails open to snowmobiling and cross-country skiing.

 The short but scenic **Grandfather Falls Segment** highlights Ripley Creek, the Wisconsin River, Grandfather Falls and a unique hydroelectric plant.

 At Camp New Wood County Park.

 From the Wisconsin River and Ripley Creek.

 Campground at Camp New Wood County Park.

 At Camp New Wood County Park. Also, portable restroom at STH-107 Grandfather Falls Hydro northern parking area.

 Portions overlap with logging/forest roads and gravel access roads.

 Unmarked spur trails off the northern portion along the Wisconsin River and the Nels P. Evjue Memorial Forest trail network.

TRAIL ACCESS AND PARKING

Burma Rd. Northern Trail Access: From Merrill at the intersection of I-39/USH-51 and STH-64, take STH-64 west for 3.0 mi. At STH-107 turn right and go north 12.8 mi past Grandfather Falls and Dam. At CTH-E turn left across the Wisconsin River and go west 2.6 mi. At Burma Rd. turn left and go south 1.1 mi. NO PARKING. Instead, find roadside parking next to the Turtle Rock Segment Burma Rd. southern Trail access sign 0.1 mi farther south on the east side of the road. DO NOT park in front of the private road/access gate on the west side of the road.

Camp New Wood County Park on STH-107: From Merrill at the intersection of I-39/USH-51 and STH-64, take STH-64 west for 3.0 mi. At STH-107 turn right and go north 10.0 mi to parking area for Camp New Wood County Park day use area.

Additional Parking: (i) CTH-E parking area on the north side of the road across from the Trail access. (ii) Grandfather Falls Hydro northern parking area on west side of STH-107. (iii) Grandfather Falls Hydro southern parking areas on west side of STH-107. (iv) Wisconsin River canoe and tubing/float craft entry point parking area on west side of STH-107, a short distance south of Grandfather Falls Hydro southern parking area.

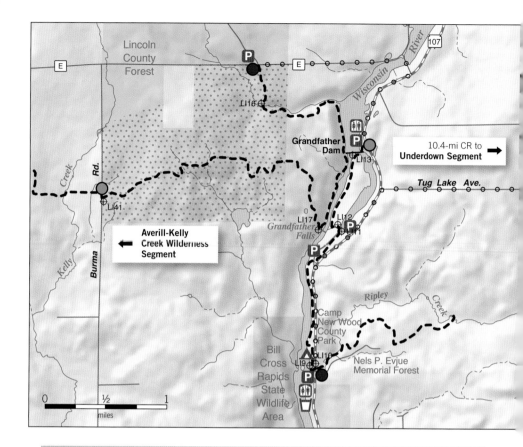

THE HIKE

The **Turtle Rock Segment** was named for a ceremonial rock used by Native Americans. The segment is diverse and rugged, traversing through thickets and isolated forest, along a rocky river shoreline and around a marsh, and may require a few hours to hike going one-way. The segment is lightly used and it is important that hikers watch for blazes and directional arrows to stay on course. Bears in the area are famous for knocking down directional sign posts. This is a prime area for bird watching and wildlife viewing as the DNR maintains several wildlife and game clearings in the area. Expect the sudden rise of grouse, curious forest hawks swooping overhead and the sudden noisy commotion of deer crashing through the undergrowth.

From the endpoint of the Averill-Kelly Creek Wilderness Segment on Burma Road, hikers should head south 0.1 miles to a point where the segment leaves Burma Road (**LI41**) and heads east. Within a half-mile, the segment reaches a 4-acre DNR wildlife clearing which has been used by hikers as a good place for primitive camping.

The first few miles of the segment follow wide, multi-use trails through mixed forest before transitioning to a narrower, winding path.

The segment heads down a steep hill into the valley of the Wisconsin River (**LI17**). The segment tread can become slippery with forest debris as the forest becomes dense near the river and the terrain becomes rocky. A nice but very rocky portion of the segment heads north along the river for about a mile past Grandfather Dam and Falls. This side of the river offers the best view of the Falls and one can climb out on rocks to watch cascading river water. Careful hikers will also spot Turtle Rock, a huge erratic with a "turtle head" protuberance jutting skyward.

The segment intersects with a small, unnamed creek emptying into the Wisconsin River. After heading west and climbing out of the Wisconsin River valley, hikers will find a wooden bench that sits 20 feet above the creek on a scenic bank.

Farther along, the segment crosses the creek (rock hops) (**LI16**) and skirts a wetland area. There may be a few wet spots, but the Trail remains passable even in wet conditions. Shortly after passing through this area, the segment follows a wide multi-use path to its endpoint on CTH-E.

To reach the Grandfather Falls Segment, hikers should head east on a connecting route along lightly travelled CTH-E. After 1.3 miles hikers will reach a bridge and head east across the Wisconsin River to STH-107, then turn right and hike south 0.8 miles along STH-107.

The **Grandfather Falls Segment** starts at the Grandfather Falls Hydro northern parking area on STH-107. From the parking area, the segment heads south past a red gate and crosses a bridge over the inlet of a reservoir that is located east of the Wisconsin River. Once across the bridge, the segment heads west on a gravel drive to the base of Grandfather Falls Dam and the original red brick hydroelectric plant. From here the segment enters woods (**LI13**) and travels south along the river.

Below the dam, hikers can view the unique boulders and sculptured rock formations caused by the thousands of years of cascading water. The sound is thunderous as it is the largest waterfall on the Wisconsin River, with a total drop of 89 feet. The rapids continue for about one mile. Hikers travel through an enormous pre-Cambrian rock outcrop, geologic evidence of a former mountain range exposed by weathering and the more recent scraping of the glaciers.

Native Americans and fur traders portaged here to bypass Grandfather Falls. Later, untold numbers of logs made their way down this stretch of the river. In 1846, history records 24 lumber mills on the Wisconsin River providing 20 million board feet of lumber per year. By 1857, there were 107 mills producing over 100 million board feet per year. The dam itself represents a living history of the taming of the river for hydroelectric power in the early 20th century.

The segment continues south and then turns east to cross a grassy swath and the reservoir's floodgate outlet on a bridge (**LI12**) built by the DNR in 2010. The bridge is engineered to withstand floodwater and is a replacement for several others that were repeatedly washed out over the years. Be mindful of the floodgate warning sirens as the gates are opened once a week.

The segment then proceeds over a short section north of a set of huge wooden tubes called penstocks and south of the reservoir. Once past the penstocks, the segment turns sharply south (**LI11**) paralleling the wooden penstocks. The penstocks carry water hundreds of yards downriver from the reservoir and are made of wood banded with steel. Wood was used because it does not corrode or rot under the constant water pressure. However, the water pressure does create a fascinating tubular fountain effect. Water shoots from hundreds of small leaks occurring at knotholes in the wood. Wooden plugs are used to close the larger leaks.

Toward the downstream end of the penstocks, the segment continues around the east side of the current hydroelectric plant before reaching a Wisconsin River canoe and tubing/float craft entry point and parking area. It continues south through the camping area of Camp New Wood County Park, the historic site of a 1935 Civilian Conservation Corps (CCC) camp named Camp McCord. The segment then reaches a Trail junction (**LI9**) located just north of a bridge over Ripley Creek.

From this junction, hikers can turn left to head east onto a 1.6-mile (one-way) out-and-back portion of the segment. This portion starts out heading east along Ripley Creek to a crossing of STH-107 (**LI10**). East of STH-107, this portion of the segment descends and continues intermittently along a beautiful rocky stretch of Ripley Creek on Merrill School Forest private property. This property came to be the School Forest in 1944 when William T. Evjue, an 1898 graduate of Merrill High School, purchased 598 acres from Lincoln County and donated it to the school. The property became a memorial to William's father, Nels P. Evjue, a pioneer Merrill woodsman. Initially, students planted 2000 conifer trees and after purchase of an additional 80 acres of land, 60,000 more trees were planted on the property.

The out-and-back portion climbs steeply to a meadow above the creek. Trail conditions and markings may vary when the meadow is overgrown with plants. The out-and-back portion intersects with various roads and trails that are part of the Nels P. Evjue Memorial Forest trail network, passes an education center and continues until reaching its terminus at the eastern boundary of the Merrill School Forest property. Here, hikers should turn around and return to the junction point to head south and complete the full segment.

Back at the junction point where the segment splits, hikers will head south over the Wisconsin Conservation Corps bridge crossing Ripley Creek. The segment reaches the entrance drive for the Camp New Wood County Park day use parking area, where an Ice Age Trail kiosk marks the end of the segment.

Mobile Skills Crew project site, 2011

AREA SERVICES

Camp New Wood County Park: Camping. On Trail. Camping for a fee on a first come, first served basis. Contact the Lincoln County Forestry, Lands & Parks Department (715-539-1034) for info.

Council Grounds State Park: Camping. From Camp New Wood County Park on STH-107 go south 7.5 mi on STH-107 (715-536-8773, dnr.wi.gov/topic/parks/name/councilgrounds/; reservations: 888-947-2757, reserveamerica.com).

Merrill: Restaurant, grocery store, convenience store, general shopping, lodging, camping, library, medical care. From Camp New Wood County Park on STH-107 go south 10.0 mi on STH-107. For area info contact the Merrill Area Chamber of Commerce (877-907-2757, merrillchamber.org).

Tomahawk: Restaurant, grocery store, convenience store, lodging, camping, library, medical care. From Camp New Wood County Park go north ~17 mi on STH-107. For area info contact the Tomahawk Area Chamber of Commerce (715-453-5334, gototomahawk.com).

Underdown Segment and
Alta Junction Segment (Atlas Maps 29f, 30f)

Underdown Segment—6.3 miles: Horn Lake Rd. to Copper Lake Ave.

1.2 mile Connecting Route

Alta Junction Segment—1.2 miles: CTH-J Southern Trail Access to CTH-J Northern Trail Access

 The very hilly and forested **Underdown Segment** *passes through the popular Underdown Recreation Area and cuts through the primeval "Enchanted Forest," a beautiful hemlock grove next to a wetland area.*

 At the Underdown Recreation Area main parking area 1.1 mi west of the eastern end of the segment.

 From Dog Lake and Mist Lake.

Primitive camping on county forest lands. Two walk-to campsites in the Mist Lake/Dog Lake area (**LI39, LI5**).

 Campground at the Underdown Recreation Area main parking area. Primitive campground on south end of Horn Lake.

Much of the segment overlaps with bike trails, horse trails, cross-country ski trails, snowshoe trails and logging/forest roads.

 Underdown Recreation Area trail network.

 The short **Alta Junction Segment** *follows a historic railroad grade for much of its route.*

From the North Branch of the Prairie River and a small intermittent creek.

Horn Lake Rd.: From Merrill at the intersection of I-39/USH-51 and CTH-K, take CTH-K north 7.3 mi. At CTH-H turn right and go east 0.5 mi to gravel Horseshoe Lake Drive. As CTH-H turns north, continue east on Horseshoe Lake Dr. for 0.8 mi. At Horn Lake Rd. turn right and go south 1.2 mi. No parking. Parking is available next to the primitive campsites on the south end of Horn Lake (see additional parking below).

CTH-J Northern Trail Access: From Merrill at the intersection of I-39/USH-51 and STH-64, take USH-51 north 13.0 mi to Irma. At CTH-J turn right and go east 5.1 mi. Roadside parking. Roadside parking also available along primitive Alta Springs Rd.

Additional Parking: (i) Horn Lake camping area: From Horn Lake Rd. Trail access take Horn Lake Rd. south and then west at the T intersection 0.4 mi to the primitive campsites on the south end of Horn Lake. (ii) Copper Lake Ave.: From Merrill at the intersection of I-39/USH-51 and CTH-K, take CTH-K north 7.3 mi. At CTH-H turn right and go east then north 1.0 mi to Copper Lake Ave. At Copper Lake Ave. turn right and go east 3.7 mi. Pass the Underdown Recreation Area main parking area and continue an additional 1.1 mi east to reach the Trail access. Roadside parking. (iii) CTH-J southern Trail access: From Merrill at the intersection of I-39/USH-51 and STH-64, take USH-51 north 13.0 mi to Irma. At CTH-J turn right and go east then south 6.6 mi to a DNR parking area on the west side of CTH-J. There is also an additional DNR parking area 0.25-mi north on CTH-J.

The topography traversed by the **Underdown Segment** is part of the Harrison Moraine of the Wisconsin Valley lobe. Glacial debris remnants in the form of hummocks separate deep kettles. Some kettles remain lakes, but most are filled with sphagnum peat. Thick forests including frequent hemlock groves, white pine, mature maples and white birch hide the high-relief hummocky terrain that a hiker may not always see but will certainly feel with the climbs and descents.

From its starting point on Horn Lake Road the segment heads east then north and after about a mile winds through a thick hemlock grove called "The Enchanted Forest." Sphagnum moss bogs lie amid the hemlocks and towering white pines. Steep climbs up and down hummocks greet the hiker as the segment closes in on Mist Lake and reaches a highpoint and Leopold bench (**LI40**) high above the lake. Farther east along the segment another very steep ascent leads to a marked campsite (**LI39**) halfway between Mist Lake and Dog Lake. The site is very primitive and high above the surrounding forest. A sign on the right marks this site. After descending through a mature hardwood forest hikers will encounter another hemlock grove that wraps around the northwest side of Dog Lake. A second campsite (**LI5**) located near the lake can be difficult to find. Hikers can find it by first facing the lake, then turning 180 degrees and going up a small rise. There are two unmarked sites here with two fire rings.

After leaving Dog Lake the segment crosses several small bridges and joins single-track trail. The segment here is well marked. After crossing Loop Road (open to all vehicles including ATVs) the segment enters an open mature white birch forest home to nesting cooper's hawks. The segment continues through open forest and a recently logged area with quickly sprouting poplar trees and

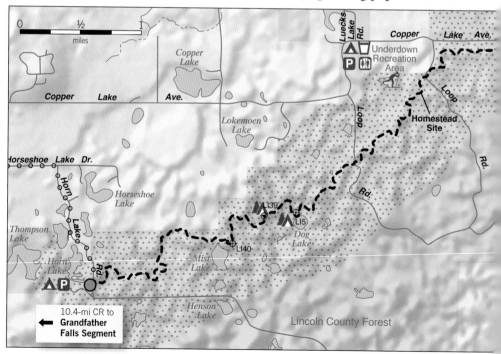

berry bushes, ascending to the high point of the segment. Volunteers have worked hard to make this section easy to traverse with new hand built bench cuts carved into the hillside.

Just prior to crossing Loop Road a second time hikers will reach the location of the original homestead site of Bill Underdown. Remains of the cabin foundation can be found with some extensive exploration of the area. The segment crosses Loop Road and steeply climbs an esker. This very narrow ridge has steep sides falling off on both sides from the narrow ribbon of trail. Another bench here lets the hiker rest and take in the surrounding deep woods. The segment descends down and across a wet intermittent creek and back up and through a recent timber harvest area before reaching its endpoint on Copper Lake Avenue.

To reach the Alta Junction Segment, hikers should head east for 0.7 miles on a connecting route along Copper Lake Avenue, then turn left and head north for 0.5 miles on CTH-J.

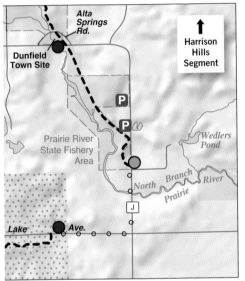

The **Alta Junction Segment** is named after the historic railroad junction of two rail lines at the village of Dunfield (now a ghost town). The segment follows along the east side of the North Branch of the Prairie River. This area is known for the natural springs that bubble up from underground water tables. The Pay Brothers Alta Springs Bottling Company (1930s) and the Alta Springs Bottling Company (late 1800s) bottled and sold the spring water for medicinal purposes.

From the southern Trail access on CTH-J the segment initially crosses a hummocky area, cuts through a parking area and then follows a rail grade built in 1908 that was part of the Milwaukee Road network that mainly serviced the logging industry in the area. Old railroad ties can still be seen in some places. The rail lines served the land Sigmund Heinemann owned and were used to transport timber to the mill town of Heinemann until it burned down in 1910. Traversing the hilly glacial terrain, trains also hauled freight along these lines to the lumber mills in Merrill and Tomahawk until 1931. The segment ends when it again intersects CTH-J near Alta Springs Road.

AREA SERVICES

Underdown Recreation Area: Camping, restrooms, water. From the Cooper Lake Ave. Trail access go west 1.1 mi. Contact the Lincoln County Forestry, Lands & Parks Department (715-539-1034) for info.

Merrill: See Turtle Rock Segment and Grandfather Falls Segment, p. 101. From the Underdown Recreation Area go west then south ~17 mi. Also see Trail Access and Parking directions, above.

Tomahawk: See Turtle Rock Segment and Grandfather Falls Segment, p. 101. From the CTH-J northern Trail access go west then north 15.5 mi.

Gleason: See Harrison Hills Segment, p. 108. From the CTH-J southern Trail access go south then east ~6 mi.

Harrison Hills Segment (Atlas Maps 30f, 31f)

SNAPSHOT

14.4 miles: CTH-J to First Lake Rd.

  This beautiful, remote segment features roller-coaster topography, plentiful primitive camping options and long views from the top of Lookout Mountain.

 From the numerous trailside lakes, a trailside spring near the North Branch of the Prairie River and other small streams/creeks.

Primitive camping on county forest lands. Two walk-to campsites (**LI37, LI38**) on Chain Lake.

At an ATV shelter at the CTH-B Trail access.

Portions overlap with logging/forest roads and two gravel roads.

TRAIL ACCESS AND PARKING

CTH-J: From Merrill at the intersection of I-39/USH-51 and STH-64, take USH-51 north 13.0 mi to Irma. At CTH-J turn right and go east 5.1 mi. Roadside parking. Roadside parking also available along primitive Alta Springs Rd.

First Lake Rd.: From Merrill at the intersection of I-39/USH-51 and STH-64, take STH-64 east 0.3 mi. At STH-17 turn left and go northeast for 21.9 mi. At First Lake Rd. turn left and go north then west 1.5 mi to parking area on the north side of First Lake Rd., just before the intersection of First Lake Rd., Parrish Rd. and Fish Lake Rd.

Additional Parking: (i) Turtle Lake Rd.parking area (**LI42**). (ii) CTH-B large multi-use parking area adjacent to the main Lincoln County ATV trail system parking area and building on the west side of the road. Do not block ATV trail access.

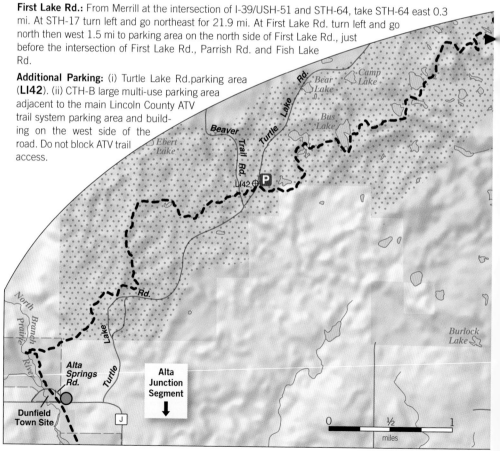

Ice Age Trail Guidebook 2014

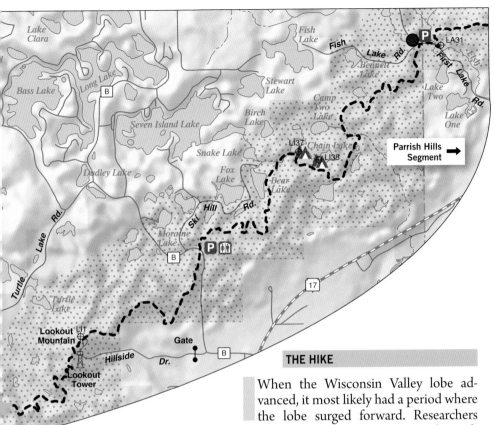

THE HIKE

When the Wisconsin Valley lobe advanced, it most likely had a period where the lobe surged forward. Researchers have found that when today's glaciers rapidly advance they gather sediment on their surface, especially along the marginal edges. When the ice melts it leaves behind deep kettles and high-relief hummocks. The Harrison Moraine that this segment traverses is noted for this spectacular high-relief topography, including many glacially deposited ridges and hills such as Lookout Mountain, the highest point on the Ice Age Trail at 1,920 feet above sea level. Views are especially impressive when leaves are off.

Generally on public forest lands, this segment is remote (the Harrison Hills support a thriving wolf pack) and rugged. Ongoing timber harvest can make navigation challenging at times. The Trail corridor, while generally easy to follow, can be quite narrow in some areas. Watch carefully for Trail signage, especially at intersections and when on logging/forest roads.

This segment starts off at CTH-J, quickly crosses primitive Alta Springs Road and soon brings hikers to a natural spring bubbling trailside and a bench with a view to the North Branch of the Prairie River. The segment follows the river briefly before heading northeast to an area with a network of public ATV trails. ATVs are often seen or heard nearby; however, the segment does not overlap with any of the ATV trails.

The segment crosses Beaver Trail Road and then Turtle Lake Road (**LI42**) before entering a region filled with small, beautiful, undeveloped lakes. It is common to see beavers swimming in some of the lakes at dusk. A few open timber harvest areas on this portion of the segment are reestablishing with what is called a "gap" forest. Pioneer plants, such as grasses, shrubs and raspberry bushes, close in on the Trail and the new growth of aspen and birch trees offers little shade.

The segment reaches the top of Lookout Mountain (LI1), which has numerous buildings, including a fire and radio tower. The old fire tower cabin is usually locked; however, the tower can be climbed almost to the top. From up high, the view to the southeast is of the Antigo Flats, a broad outwash plain formed in front of the melting ice. The view to the northwest is of undeveloped kettle lakes and the hummocky forested landscape.

The segment continues northeast from Lookout Mountain through deciduous forest dominated by oak and maple trees on its way to CTH-B, where the segment passes by an ATV parking area with vault toilets.

A popular fishing destination, the northeastern section of the segment passes many lakes. There are two angler campsites on Chain Lake: the first campsite (LI37) is located between the west and center lobe approximately 100 feet off the Trail; the second campsite (LI38) is located between the east and center lobes approximately 400 feet off the Trail. The second campsite may be flooded when water levels are high.

From Chain Lake, the segment continues for a bit more than a mile to its terminus on First Lake Road, right on the Lincoln/Langlade county line.

AREA SERVICES

Tomahawk: See Turtle Rock Segment and Grandfather Falls Segment, p. 101. From the CTH-J Trail access go west then north 15.5 mi.

Gleason: Restaurant, convenience store. From the CTH-J Trail access, take CTH-J east, south and east 5.6 mi to STH-17. At STH-17, turn left (northeast) and go 1.9 mi. From the CTH-B parking area, take CTH-B east 1.2 mi. to STH-17. At STH-17 turn right (southwest) and go 10.0 mi.

Harrison: Restaurant. From the CTH-B Trail access parking area go west and north ~7 mi.

Merrill: See Turtle Rock Segment and Grandfather Falls Segment, p. 101. From the First Lake Rd. Trail access go east then south ~24 mi. Also see Trail Access and Parking directions, above.

Rhinelander: See Parrish Hills Segment, p. 116. From the First Lake Rd. Trail access go east and north ~18 mi.

I was about to go around a corner in the Trail, when at the same time a bear was coming from the other direction. We were both startled, but the bear turned and was gone in an instant, crashing into the brush that was so thick you wouldn't think it could be penetrated. The bear must have seen something awfully ugly to make it turn tail and run like that, poor thing. (I was glad.)

TOM TEEPLES (AKA "LRRP"), ICE AGE TRAIL THOUSAND-MILER

The Ice Age Trail can be enjoyed at a wide variety of speeds. Jason Dorgan, shown here traversing the Harrison Hills Segment, "thru-ran" the entire Trail in just over 3 weeks.

Lincoln County

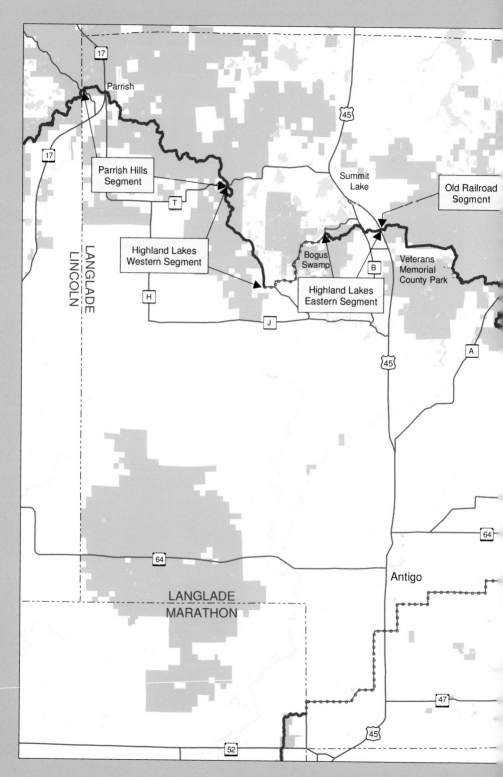

Parrish

17

17

45

Summit
Lake

Parrish Hills
Segment

Old Railroad
Segment

T

LANGLADE
LINCOLN

Highland Lakes
Western Segment

Bogus
Swamp

B

Veterans
Memorial
County Park

H

Highland Lakes
Eastern Segment

J

45

A

64

64

Antigo

LANGLADE
MARATHON

47

45

52

Ice Age Trail Guidebook 2014

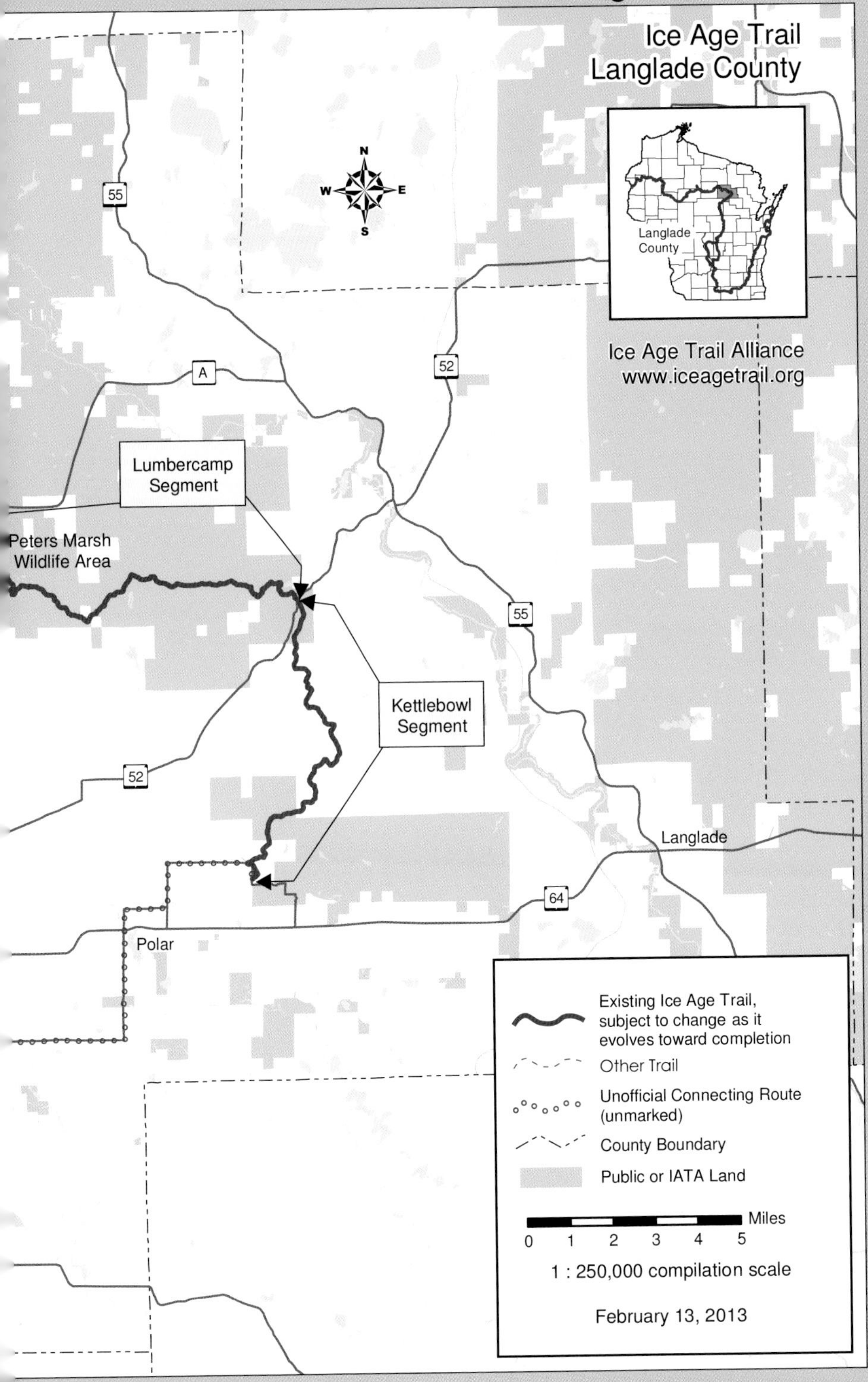

Ice Age Trail
Langlade County

Langlade
County

Ice Age Trail Alliance
www.iceagetrail.org

N
W—E
S

55

A

52

Lumbercamp
Segment

Peters Marsh
Wildlife Area

55

Kettlebowl
Segment

52

Langlade

64

Polar

	Existing Ice Age Trail, subject to change as it evolves toward completion
	Other Trail
	Unofficial Connecting Route (unmarked)
	County Boundary
	Public or IATA Land

Miles
0   1   2   3   4   5

1 : 250,000 compilation scale

February 13, 2013

Langlade County

Trail miles: 52.0
Connecting route miles: 28.7

The Wisconsin Valley, Langlade and Green Bay lobes shaped the landscape of Langlade County. In places, one can imagine the violent movement of the glacial lobes as they carved and crafted the county's landscape. These three glacial lobes deposited a large terminal moraine, 250 feet high in places, when the ice stopped and began to retreat 13,000 to 25,000 years ago. South and west of the end moraine is the broad outwash plain known as the Antigo Flats, named for the city of Antigo, which sits near its center. Langlade County is named for Charles de Langlade, son of a French man and Ottawa woman. He was a leader in the region during the second half of the 1700s. The Ice Age Trail passes through hummocky end moraine terrain on county and private industrial forest lands. The county forest program started in 1928 (the first of its kind in Wisconsin) after local voters approved the establishment of a unit on a large acreage of a tax-delinquent, cutover land. Today, almost 130,000 acres, a fifth of the land area in the county, are managed by the county. The state and federal governments own another 80,000 acres.

Logging is a way of life in this area and has a constant influence on the Ice Age Trail. Therefore, hikers are urged to contact the coordinator of the IATA's Langlade County Chapter before hiking in the area to get updates on logging activities and other issues affecting Trail navigability and wayfinding. Trail users here should carry a compass and topographic map. Yellow metal posts with and without Ice Age Trail signage are used often to signify the route through the county. These are used instead of the traditional wooden posts because wooden posts are often vandalized (by both humans and bears) in the area.

Because of all the county forest land, primitive camping opportunities are widespread. As with all parts of the Ice Age Trail open to primitive camping, hikers should set up their campsites at least 200 feet from trails and waterways. For overnight parking hikers should contact the coordinator of the IATA's Langlade County Chapter for best locations and also notify the county sheriff department. Water sources are scarce on the Kettlebowl and Lumbercamp segments.

CHAPTER INFORMATION

The Langlade County Chapter was formed in 1974 and within its first year mapped and marked five Ice Age Trail segments. Chapter volunteers maintain the Trail with help of area organizations. The chapter promotes the Ice Age Trail with outings, local news articles, a newsletter called the *Langlade Erratic*, service club presentations and exhibits at community events.

COUNTY INFORMATION

Langlade County Visitor Information: 715-623-2085, langladecounty.org/ tourism

Langlade County Forestry Department: 715-627-6300

Langlade County Sheriff Department: 715-627-6411, contact for overnight parking permission

Sharing the Camp Susan nature trails, Highland Lakes Eastern Segment.

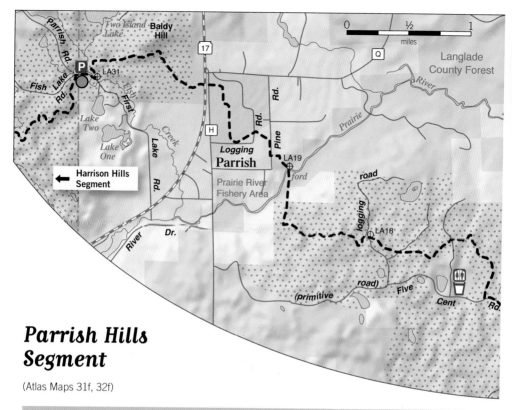

Parrish Hills Segment

(Atlas Maps 31f, 32f)

11.6 miles: First Lake Rd. Western Trail Access to CTH-T

▲3 👢5 *This remote and rugged segment features several wetland areas, scenic Townline Lake, a ford of the Prairie River, the shoulder of Baldy Hill and a scenic ridge with long views.*

 At an enclosed ATV shelter north of Five Cent Rd. (see map icons).

 From Townline Lake, the Prairie River and other small lakes and wetland areas.

 Primitive camping on county forest lands. Camping is not allowed in the immediate vicinity of the enclosed ATV shelter north of Five Cent Rd.

 Townline Lake wayside.

 At an enclosed ATV shelter north of Five Cent Rd. (see map icons) and the Townline Lake wayside.

 Portion of the segment crossing private land west of Pine Rd. is closed during gun deer season.

 Portions overlap with roads, ATV and snowmobile trails, and gravel logging roads.

TRAIL ACCESS AND PARKING

First Lake Rd. Western Trail Access: From Merrill at the intersection of I-39/USH-51 and STH-64, take STH-64 east 0.3 mi. At STH-17 turn left and go northeast for 21.9 mi. At First Lake Rd. turn left and go north then west 1.5 mi to the parking area on the north side of First Lake Rd. just before the intersection of First Lake Rd., Parrish Rd. and Fish Lake Rd.

CTH-T: From Antigo, at the intersection of USH-45/STH-47 and STH-64, take USH-45/47 north 16.6 mi to Summit Lake. At CTH-T turn left and go west 5.2 mi to the Townline Lake wayside parking area.

THE HIKE

This segment is the oldest in the county and was named after the town of Parrish in the northwestern corner of Langlade County and the belt of moraine hills of boulders, sand and gravel deposited by the massive ice sheet over 10,000 years ago. It traverses the Parrish End Moraine, winding its way southeast through the typical hilly, hummocky terrain. The wetlands are so extensive that the Trail layout winds through the landscape to take advantage of beaver dams and narrow, high ridges. The segment is notable for the extent of evergreen forest (spruce, pine, fir, balsam, etc.) traversed by the route.

Several characteristics make this segment potentially challenging for hikers to navigate. Depending on water levels, there may be several wet crossings

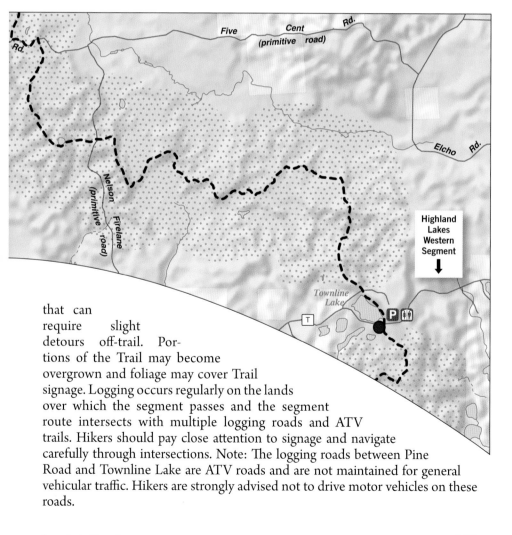

that can require slight detours off-trail. Portions of the Trail may become overgrown and foliage may cover Trail signage. Logging occurs regularly on the lands over which the segment passes and the segment route intersects with multiple logging roads and ATV trails. Hikers should pay close attention to signage and navigate carefully through intersections. Note: The logging roads between Pine Road and Townline Lake are ATV roads and are not maintained for general vehicular traffic. Hikers are strongly advised not to drive motor vehicles on these roads.

From its starting point on First Lake Road, hikers should head east on First Lake Rd. 0.2 miles to a point where the segment leaves the road (**LA31**) and briefly heads north then east through forested terrain, passing by 1831-foot Baldy Hill and then meandering to the STH-17 crossing. Hikers should cross STH-17 cautiously and continue southeast over lands that are part of a glacial outwash fan from the Harrison Moraine. Hikers should note that portions of the segment here cross private lands where primitive camping is not permitted.

After skirting south and eastward along a pine plantation, the segment emerges onto Pine Road, follows the road south for a short distance and then continues southeast to a crossing (river ford) of the Prairie River (**LA19**), which has a fairly firm bottom with water levels typically below the knees. With rocks and vegetation on the river bed, hikers may wish to use footwear appropriate for the crossing.

A little more than a mile east of the river the segment reaches a small wooden Adirondack-style shelter (**LA18**) in a grassy opening along a logging road. Much of the next portion of the segment traverses high-relief hummocky topography. The segment continues east and then bends south to its intersection with primitive Five Cent Road. Hikers can head west approximately 0.25 miles along Five Cent Road, then north on a logging road approximately 0.2 miles to reach an ATV shelter with drinking water and restrooms.

The segment used to continue south across the road, but tornado damage in 2011 necessitated a change in the route. Upon reaching Five Cent Road hikers should turn left and follow the road east for a short distance, less than 0.25 miles, before departing from the road to head south for less than a mile down the primitive Parrish Game Trail. The segment then departs from the Parrish Game Trail and resumes its traditional route eastward.

The segment crosses Nelson Firelane and eventually joins the Parrish Snowmobile and ATV Trail for a short distance. Hikers here should be alert to motorized traffic. The segment continues east, passing by large wetlands and through logged clear-cut areas. At one time, the segment traversed at least two active beaver dams. Reroutes were constructed over the years because the beavers' persistence in dam building caused flooding of the segment. The footbridge that hikers cross a mile north of the segment's terminus on CTH-T replaced one beaver dam.

The segment follows the northeast edge of scenic Townline Lake along the base of a hill through a stand of large hemlock. Townline Lake is one of two trout lakes in the county and loons can be seen here in season. Remains of a bench, fire pit and stairs built by the Civilian Conservation Corps in the 1930s can be seen along the lakeshore. The segment ends at the Townline Lake day-use picnic area on CTH-T, which features a privy, grill, picnic table and fire ring.

AREA SERVICES

Rhinelander: Restaurant, grocery store, convenience store, general shopping, lodging, camping, library, medical care. From the STH-17 Trail access go north 15.5 mi. Area info available from the Rhinelander Chamber of Commerce (715-365-7464, explorerhinelander.com).

Gleason: See Harrison Hills Segment, p. 108. From the STH-17 Trail access go south 10.5 mi.

Merrill: See Turtle Rock Segment and Grandfather Falls Segment, p. 101. From STH-17 Trail access go south ~25 mi. Also see Trail Access and Parking directions, above.

Antigo: See Highland Lakes Eastern Segment, p. 122. From the CTH-T Trail access go east then south 21.7 mi. Also see Trail Access and Parking directions, above.

Alta Lake, Highland Lakes Eastern Segment.

Langlade County

Highland Lakes Western Segment (Atlas Maps 32f, 33f)

SNAPSHOT

5.9 miles: CTH-T to Kleever Rd.

   This segment mostly follows primitive logging roads through hardwood forests along and within the Parrish Terminal Moraine.

From the West Branch of the Eau Claire River (**LA16**).

Primitive camping on county forest lands.

At Townline Lake wayside.

 Portions of the segment crossing private land may be closed during gun deer season.

 Significant portions overlap county forest gravel logging roads open to logging trucks, snowmobiles and ATVs.

TRAIL ACCESS AND PARKING

CTH-T: From Antigo, at the intersection of USH-45/STH-47 and STH-64, take USH-45/47 north 16.6 mi to Summit Lake. At CTH-T turn left and go west 5.2 mi to the Townline Lake wayside and parking area.

Kleever Rd.: From Antigo at the intersection of USH-45/STH-47 with STH-64, take USH-45/47 north 8.5 mi. At CTH-J turn left and go west 4.0 mi. At Forest Rd. turn right and go northwest 2.1 mi. At Kleever Rd. (Sucker Rd.) turn left and go west 0.4 mi to its western end. Roadside parking on Kleever Rd. only. No overnight parking.

THE HIKE

Between CTH-T and the crossing of the West Branch of the Eau Claire River, the segment traverses the Parrish Terminal Moraine's high-relief hummocky topography. East of the river, the segment follows the base of a ridge that is the highest outer moraine ridge anywhere on the entire Ice Age Trail.

As the segment heads south from its starting point on CTH-T hikers will climb a ridge and enjoy a view to the southwest of a large wetland that is a former glacial lake formed behind the Parrish Terminal Moraine. Over thousands of years, the shallow basin filled with soil and organic materials from the surrounding landscape to create the swamp viewed today. Over thousands of years, all lakes eventually become wetlands similar to the swamp seen here. There are a number of intersecting logging roads on this portion of the segment and hikers should watch carefully for blazes and directional arrows.

After 2.6 miles the segment crosses the West Branch of the Eau Claire River (**LA16**). The crossing can be tricky in high water. There is a rudimentary footbridge that will keep feet dry in medium high water and rocks in the river that can be used as stepping stones in low water. A dry crossing of the river can be found by heading upriver approximately 300 yards, crossing over the river on a culvert and returning to the Trail by heading southwest on a logging road.

Just beyond the river crossing, the segment reaches a former rail line junction where five fire lanes or logging roads meet, known as "Five Points" (**LA15**). Eastbound hikers should follow the distinct logging road headed southeast. This is the second lane/road to the left or clockwise. Westbound hikers should follow the logging road headed northwest. Be careful not to follow ATV trail signs. A short side trip on the logging road headed northeast off the main route offers a view of the West Branch of the Eau Claire River dissecting the Parish Terminal Moraine. Massive volumes of glacial meltwater now represented by the tame West Branch made the cut through the moraine.

From Five Points, the segment continues southeast through a mix of county forest and private land along an unimproved forest lane. Just past a second gate, a logging road intersects from the right; bear left to stay on the Trail. The segment ends at the west end of Kleever Road.

AREA SERVICES

Elcho: See Highland Lakes Eastern Segment, p. 122. From the CTH-T Trail access go east then north ~9 mi.

Summit Lake: See Highland Lakes Eastern Segment, p. 122. From the CTH-T Trail access go east then north ~6 mi.

Antigo: See Highland Lakes Eastern Segment, p. 122. From the Kleever Rd. Trail access go east then south ~15 mi. Also see Trail Access and Parking directions, above.

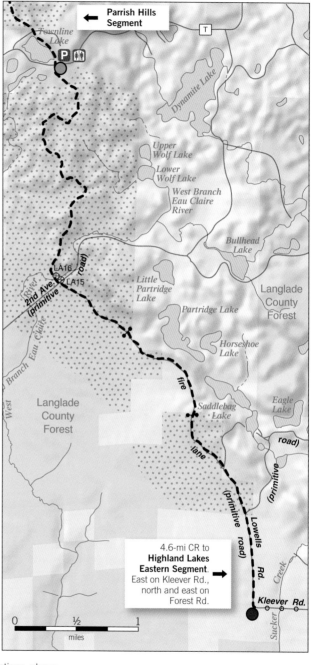

Parrish Hills Segment

Townline Lake

T

Dynamite Lake

Upper Wolf Lake

Lower Wolf Lake

West Branch Eau Claire River

Bullhead Lake

LA16
LA15
2nd Ave. (primitive road)

Little Partridge Lake

Partridge Lake

Langlade County Forest

Horseshoe Lake

Eagle Lake

West Branch Eau Claire River

Langlade County Forest

fire lane

Saddlebag Lake

(primitive road)

4.6-mi CR to **Highland Lakes Eastern Segment.** East on Kleever Rd., north and east on Forest Rd. →

Lowells Rd.

Kleever Rd.

Sucker Creek

0   ½   1
miles

Highland Lakes Eastern Segment (Atlas Map 33f)

3.4 miles: Forest Rd. to USH-45/STH-47

   This segment is named for the abundance of lakes located through the area that serve as the headwaters for the Hunting, Eau Claire and Prairie rivers.

From Deep Wood, Alga, Susan and Alta lakes.

Primitive camping on county forest lands.

Portion of segment crossing private land between CTH-B and USH-45/STH-47 is closed during gun deer season.

 Portions overlap with ATV trails, snowmobile trails and Camp Susan entrance drive.

 Camp Susan's nature trail.

TRAIL ACCESS AND PARKING

Forest Rd.: From the north side of Antigo, at the intersection of USH-45/STH-47 with STH-64, take USH-45/STH-47 north 12.3 mi. At Koepenick Rd. turn left and go 0.8 mi. At CTH-B turn right and go north 1.4 mi. At Bass Lake Rd. turn left and go west 1.5 mi bearing left at intersections. At Forest Rd. turn left and go south 0.2 mi to the Trail access on the east side of the road. The current Trail access is slightly south of the Deep Woods Lake wayside. No parking on the east side of the road. Park at Deep Woods Lake wayside located on the west side of Forest Rd. No overnight parking.

USH-45/STH-47: From the north side of Antigo, at the intersection of USH-45/STH-47 with STH-64, take USH-45/STH47 north 13.0 mi. No safe parking anywhere along USH-45/STH-47 in the vicinity of the Trail. Use other parking options east and west of USH-45/STH-47.

Additional Parking: Roadside parking along CTH-B at Camp Susan's entrance drive. Access CTH-B from USH-45/STH-47 via Koepenick Rd., 0.7 mi south of the USH-45/STH-47 Trail access. At CTH-B turn right and go north 1.0 mi to Camp Susan's gated entrance drive. Parking permitted on the side of the access road. Do not block the gate!

THE HIKE

From its starting point on Forest Road the segment heads east on wide tread and quickly comes to a T-intersection (**LA11**) where hikers should turn right and head southeast. Hikers will soon see Alga Lake to the south.

Shortly after, the segment connects with the Camp Susan nature trails network with its many informational/educational signs. On this scenic part of the segment hikers follow a rolling ridge that divides the area's lakes and wetlands and highlights elevated views of Lake Susan through white birch and pine forests. The ridge was formed from rocky material that sloughed off the ice masses that formed the area kettle lakes and nearby Bogus Swamp, a large kettle now filled with peat.

The segment leaves the footpath (**LA10**) and drops down to connect with Camp Susan's entrance drive. The segment continues east on the drive for 1.8 miles through high-relief hummocky topography with erratics and some large conifers as it makes its way to CTH-B. There is a fine view of Alta Lake as the Trail skirts the north edge of a peat bog along the way.

Ice Age Trail Guidebook 2014

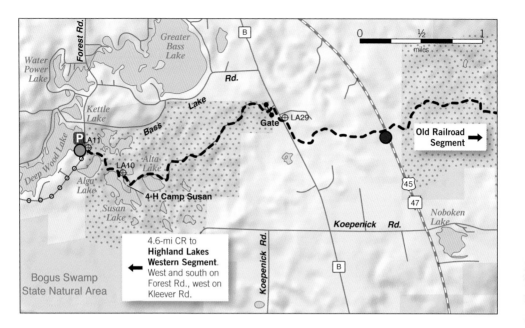

At CTH-B hikers should proceed south along the west side of CTH-B until a snowmobile trail crosses (**LA29**) the road. The segment follows the snowmobile trail across the road, turns south on an old railroad grade for 0.2 miles and then to the east through forested, relatively flat terrain. The segment is prone to flooding during wet periods and water may extend across the segment for several feet. A metal gate and sign mark the terminus of the segment at busy USH-45/STH-47. Hikers wishing to continue on to the next segment should cross the highway with caution.

AREA SERVICES

Summit Lake: Restaurant, convenience store, lodging. From the Camp Susan entrance road and CTH-B, take CTH-B north for 2.5 mi.

Elcho: Restaurant, grocery store, convenience store, lodging, medical care. From the USH-45/STH-47 Trail access go ~7 mi north on USH-45/STH-47. INN Style program lodging at the Elcho Victorian Rose B&B (715-275-4288, elchovictorianrose.com).

Antigo: Restaurant, grocery store, convenience store, general shopping, lodging, camping, library, medical care. From the USH-45/STH-47 Trail access go south 13.0 mi on USH-45/STH-47. Most services on USH-45/STH-47 and STH-64. Area info available from the Antigo Chamber of Commerce (888-526-4523, antigochamber.com).

Veterans Memorial Park: See Old Railroad Segment, p. 124. From the USH-45/STH-47 Trail access go south then east on CTH-J ~4 mi.

Local Area: Lodging at Koeppel's Cottages on Deep Wood Lake near Forest Rd. Trail access (715-350-2570). Overnight lodging available to hikers if there are vacant cottages. Meals at Bass Lake County Club–Grumpy's Inn on Waterpower Lake off Forest Rd. 1.0 mi north of Trail access.

Old Railroad Segment (Atlas Maps 33f, 34f)

9.2 miles: USH-45/STH-47 to CTH-A

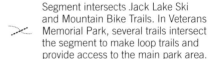 *This varied segment highlights former logging railways and scenic, remote lakes featuring some very nice primitive campsites.*

 At Veterans Memorial Park.

From Game and Jack lakes.

Primitive camping on county forest lands. Walk-to sites on Jack (**LA20**) and Game (**LA8**) lakes.

 Western portions of the segment crossing private land are closed during gun deer season.

 Portions overlap with logging/forest roads.

Segment intersects Jack Lake Ski and Mountain Bike Trails. In Veterans Memorial Park, several trails intersect the segment to make loop trails and provide access to the main park area.

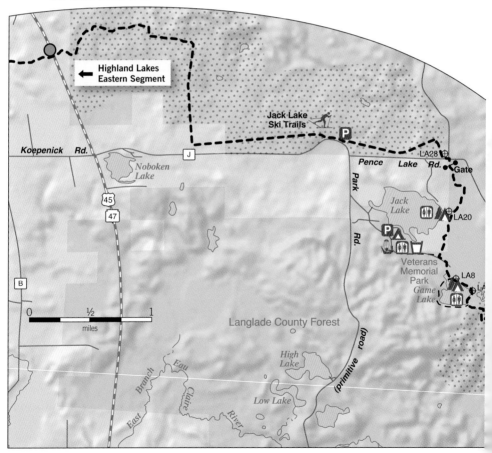

TRAIL ACCESS AND PARKING

USH-45/STH-47: From the north side of Antigo, at the intersection of USH-45/STH-47 with STH-64, take STH-45/47 north 13.0 mi. No parking.

CTH-A: From the north side of Antigo, at the intersection of USH-45/STH-47 with STH-64, take USH-45/STH-47 north 3.5 mi. At CTH-A turn right and go northeast 8.6 mi to the Trail access. Roadside parking on the west side of the road. Parking is also available in nearby parking areas of the Peters Marsh Wildlife Area located south on CTH-A within 0.5 mi of the Trail access.

Additional Parking: (i) CTH-B at Camp Susan's entrance drive. Access CTH-B from USH-45/STH-47 via Koepenick Rd. 0.7 mi south of the USH-45/STH-47 Trail access. At CTH-B turn right and go north 1.0 mi to Camp Susan's gated entrance drive. Parking permitted on the side of the access road. Do not block the gate! (ii) Jack Lake Cross Country Ski Area. From the north side of Antigo at the intersection of USH-45/STH-47 with STH-64, take USH-45/STH-47 north 12.1 mi. At CTH-J turn right and go east 2.0 mi to Jack Lake Cross Country Ski Area parking. (iii) Veterans Memorial Park.

THE HIKE

The segment is identified as "Old Railroad" because it incorporates a former railroad grade built in 1914 and active until 1941 that was used to haul logs from the area during the county's logging period in the early 1900s. Logs were hauled on the railroad grade from the extensive timber harvest areas to the main line at Koepenick Junction, just west of USH-45/STH-47. In addition, trains followed the current Ice Age Trail route carrying supplies and men to the lumber camps. Original wooden ties and iron spikes can be seen along the Trail. Hikers will pass through areas of yellow birch, tamarack and balsam in lowland bogs/wetlands and paper birch, maple and aspen in second growth hardwood forests which grew after the great white pines were logged.

From its starting point on USH-45/STH-47 the segment heads east and then south on mostly forested, relatively flat terrain. In spring or wet seasons watch for watery potholes and boggy areas. During the second mile, the segment passes through an aging red pine plantation. The segment bends east and continues along a railroad grade to the Jack Lake Cross-Country Ski Area parking lot. The lot serves the Ice Age Trail along with the Jack Lake Cross-Country Ski Trails, established in 1977, and the mountain bike trail, built in 1999. Beyond the parking lot the segment continues east along the railroad grade for a bit less than a mile.

The segment departs from the railroad grade and heads south for a quarter-mile to an intersection (**LA28**) with Pence Lake Road. Hikers should turn left and head east on the road for 300 feet, where the segment departs from the road and continues south. Hikers will soon encounter a primitive campsite (**LA20**) on Jack Lake, referred to as Loon Cry Outpost, that is part of Veterans Memorial Park. The site has room for up to four tents, a fire ring, a privy and a picnic table.

From the primitive camping site the segment continues south to a junction with a "You Are Here" locator sign. Here, hikers can turn right and go west to access the facilities of Veterans Memorial Park, including an arboretum, water, restrooms, showers, picnic areas, beach, campground and parking lot. A visit to the arboretum is worth it for those interested in seeing a collection of native plants suitable for landscaping. A marker recognizes Ray Webber, who designed and laid out the arboretum. A former Department of Natural Resources forester, Webber had a personal desire to foster a greater aesthetic appreciation for the natural landscape.

The segment continues south and intersects with the Game Lake Nature Trail. To stay on the Ice Age Trail hikers should turn left at the fork in the trail and continue along the northeast side of Game Lake, soon passing a spur trail to a second primitive campsite (**LA8**) with similar amenities to the first site. Game Lake is one of four lakes in the area (along with High, Low and Jack) reported to be named by card-playing loggers. Look for signs of beaver feeding and lodges and a floating bog that migrates over the surface of the lake depending on prevailing wind direction. Hikers should travel slowly across the bog-walk structure on the east side of the lake and take time to notice beaver lodges, birds, bog laurel, leatherleaf, Labrador tea, pitcher plants and other unique bog flora and fauna.

The segment departs from the Game Lake Nature Trail on the southeast side of Game Lake by heading up a steep hill to the left in a southeasterly direction, soon reaching a Leopold bench at an unmarked Trail junction (**LA7**). From this point, the segment continues south and then east to a second crossing of Pence Lake Road.

East of Pence Lake Road the segment continues through high-relief hummocky topography and second-growth forests on logging roads. Look for exposed multi-colored glacial drift stones and erratics, along with grouse, woodcock, deer and bear. Upper Ventor Lake is just visible from the route if there is little or no leaf cover. In an opening a giant white pine grows, a remnant of the forest cover that grew at the time of the earliest settlement. Openings like this one are developed and maintained by the Wisconsin Department of Natural Resources as a wildlife management measure. Swallowtail and mourning cloak butterflies, turkeys and other birds frequent these sunny areas. There are several openings on this portion of the segment. The segment parallels the west side of private Lower Ventor Lake as it makes its way to CTH-A.

AREA SERVICES

Veterans Memorial Park: Campground on Jack Lake, walk-in primitive campsites and cabin for rent. On Trail. From the north side of Antigo at the intersection of USH-45/STH-47 with STH-64, take USH-45/STH-47 north 12.1 mi to CTH-J. At CTH-J turn right and continue east for 2.3 mi then south 0.4 mi as CTH-J becomes Park Rd. to the park's entrance. For information and reservations call 715-623-6214.

Summit Lake: See Highland Lakes Eastern Segment, p. 122. From the USH-45/STH-47 Trail access go north 2.5 mi.

Elcho: See Highland Lakes Eastern Segment, p. 122. From the USH-45/STH-47 Trail access go north ~7 mi. Also see Trail Access and Parking directions, above.

Antigo: See Highland Lakes Eastern Segment, p. 122. From the USH-45/STH-47 Trail access go south ~13 mi. Also see Trail Access and Parking directions, above.

A bog to the east of Game Lake, Old Railroad Segment.

Langlade County

Lumbercamp Segment (Atlas Maps 34f, 35f)

SNAPSHOT

12.0 miles: CTH-A to STH-52

  This segment highlights the historic Norem Lumber Camp (and its modern-day "Hillybilly Hilton") and the dramatic Baker Lake basin.

No reliable sources of water.

Primitive camping on county forest lands and "Hillbilly Hilton" shelter (**LA5**) at the Norem Lumber Camp site.

 By law, dogs must be leashed April 15 to July 31 in the State Wildlife Area.

 A portion of the segment overlaps with snowmobile trails.

 Trails in the Peters Marsh State Wildlife Area.

TRAIL ACCESS AND PARKING

CTH-A: From the north side of Antigo, at the intersection of USH-45/STH-47 with STH-64, take USH-45/STH-47 north 3.5 mi. At CTH-A turn right and go northeast 8.6 mi to the Trail access. Roadside parking on the west side of the road. Parking is also available in nearby parking areas of the Peters Marsh Wildlife Area located south on CTH-A within 0.5 mi of the Trail access.

STH-52: From the north side of Antigo, at the intersection of USH45/STH-47 with STH-64, take STH-64 east 1.6 mi. At STH-52 turn left and go northeast 15.0 mi. At the Kettlebowl Ski Area turn right and park along the road between the gate for Kettlebowl Ski Area and STH-52. Please park vehicles on the side of the access road to allow authorized traffic beyond the gate.

THE HIKE

Heading east from the CTH-A Trail access, the western end of the segment passes through a portion of the 1687-acre Peters Marsh State Wildlife Area. The wildlife area has a network of other hiking trails and is made up of a variety of habitats home to numerous wildlife species. All lakes shown on the map are subject to seasonal groundwater fluctua-

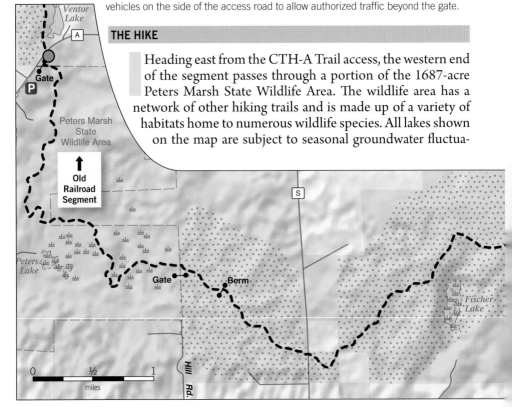

tions and hikers should not regard them as a dependable water source as they are known to go dry.

East of CTH-S the segment transitions from the more open landscape of the Peters Marsh State Wildlife Area to more forested land cover. For most of the remainder of the segment the route travels across the relatively flat surface of a pitted outwash plain deposited by streams flowing away from the Summit Lake Moraine. Logging can occur along this portion of the segment and there are several intersecting logging roads; hikers should pay close attention to signage in this area as some of the intersections can be confusing.

Just west of primitive Norem Camp Road/Otto Mauk Firelane, in a trailside clearing, are the remains of Norem Lumber Camp (**LA5**). From the 1920s until 1938, the camp contained several log structures, including a bunkhouse, hayshed, stable, community kitchen and mess hall. All that remain are the root cellar and several log foundations. The root cellar has been renovated and is affectionately called the "Hillbilly Hilton." Inside are sleeping platforms, a small table and shelving to welcome hikers out of the elements. Hikers who use the shelter should practice responsible stewardship by leaving the "Hilton" in as good condition or better than they found it.

The segment continues east from the primitive road and, a short distance west of Baker Lake, enters the high-relief hummocky topography representing the front of the Summit Lake Moraine. This portion of the segment is well marked but is rocky and can be a challenging hike. As hikers make their way through the Baker Lake basin toward the segment's endpoint on STH-52 they will see a dramatic exposure of massive boulders deposited by the ice on the north slope of the Summit Lake Moraine.

AREA SERVICES

Veterans Memorial Park: See Old Railroad Segment, p. 124. From the CTH-A Trail access go north and west ~7 mi.

Antigo: See Highland Lakes Eastern Segment, p. 122. From the STH-52 Trail access go south and west ~17 mi. Also see Trail Access and Parking directions, above.

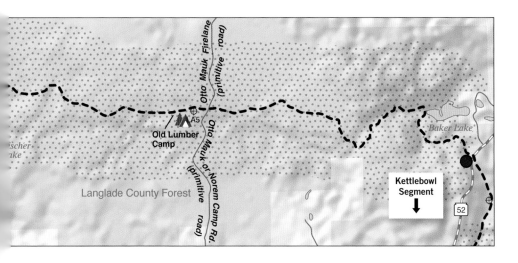

Kettlebowl Segment (Atlas Maps 35f, 36f)

9.9 miles: STH-52 to Oak Rd./Sherry Rd.

 This segment winds through hilly terrain dotted with huge granite erratics and has the most topographical relief of all segments in Langlade County.

  No reliable sources of water.

  Primitive camping on county forest lands.

 At the Kettlebowl Ski Area.

 Portions overlap with cross-country ski trails. A significant portion overlaps with logging/forest roads; some of these are frequently used by ATVs and snowmobiles.

 Spur trails to the Big Stone Hole, Kent Hill and Oak Rd./Sherry Rd. parking area.

TRAIL ACCESS AND PARKING

STH-52: From the north side of Antigo, at the intersection of USH45/STH-47 with STH-64, take STH-64 east 1.6 mi. At STH-52 turn left and go northeast 15.0 mi. At the Kettlebowl Ski Area turn right and park along the road between the gate for Kettlebowl Ski Area and STH-52. Please park vehicles on the side of the access road to allow authorized traffic beyond the gate.

Oak Rd./Sherry Rd.: From the north side of Antigo, at the intersection of USH-45/STH-47 with STH-64, take STH-64 east 9.0 mi. At Price-Polar Rd. turn left and go north 1.6 mi. At Oak Rd. turn right and go east 1.5 mi to where Sherry Rd. and Oak Rd. join. Continue on Oak Rd./Sherry Rd. south for 0.9 mi to the Trail access on the east side of the road. No parking. Alternatively, park in the parking area (**LA2**) where Oak Rd./Sherry Rd. turns south. The Trail is accessible from here on a short spur trail. No overnight parking.

THE HIKE

The Kettlebowl Segment generally follows a variety of logging and forest roads in various conditions that are used by and signed for multiple users, including Ice Age Trail hikers, snowmobilers, skiers and ATV users. There are numerous intersections with logging and forest roads. Segment signage can be obscured during growing seasons and can be sparse in some areas. Hikers should pay careful attention to Ice Age Trail signage, which can consist of yellow blazes, black block arrows on yellow signs and yellow and black signs with the Ice Age Trail logo. Hikers should carry (i) maps and (ii) a compass and/or a GPS unit.

From its starting point on STH-52 the segment follows the Kettlebowl Ski Area access road southeast, passing by pit toilets to the base of the ski slopes. Kettlebowl Ski Area is not actually located in a kettle; the ski runs are located on the north slope of the recessional Summit Lake Moraine. The segment departs from the ski area at a yellow marker near the bottom of the southernmost ski run (**LA25**).

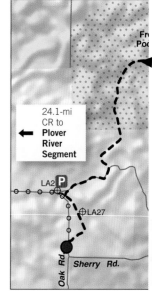

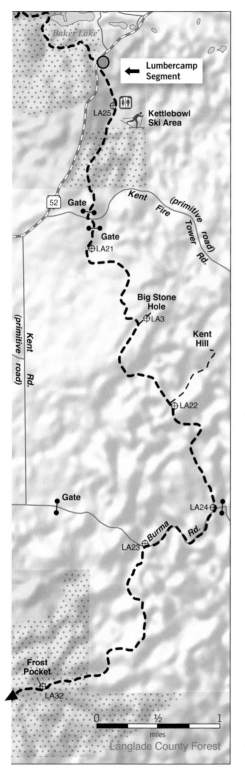

The segment highlights deep "frost pockets," a local expression for depressions with steep sloping sides. In some cases, they may represent "kettles," "kettle holes" or "kettlebowls" formed by remnants of huge blocks of ice, which broke from the ice sheet. The timber or tree line observed in the frost pockets is "inverted" or the reverse of the same phenomenon seen on many mountaintops. Because heavier, cooler air prevails at the lower elevations in the pocket, the lower levels are usually devoid of woody vegetation. These areas were more pronounced in years past. However, with warmer year-round temperatures, woody species have started to populate the once distinctive grassy bottoms. One such frost pocket (**LA21**) is found shortly after the crossing of primitive Kent Fire Tower Road, just off the Trail.

The area south of Kent Fire Tower Road is lined with large rocks, often Wolf River granite, on both sides of the Trail. About one mile south of the frost pocket the segment reaches a short spur trail that leads to "Big Stone Hole" (**LA3**), a large kettle loaded with granite erratics. Less than a mile south of the intersection with the spur trail to the Big Stone Hole, the segment reaches an intersection (**LA22**) with a logging lane marked by a yellow metal post without a sign that leads 0.8 miles east to Kent Hill, the highest point in Langlade County at 1903 feet above sea level. It is just 50 feet below Timm's Hill, the state's highest point, and 45 feet lower than the peak at Rib Mountain. The vista from Kent Hill is tremendous during leaf-off. Views to the southwest include distant Rib Mountain. Visible to the northeast, across the Wolf River valley, are McCaslin and Thunder mountains in Oconto and Marinette counties.

As the segment continues south and west it makes its way through the high-relief hummocky topography of the terminal Parrish Moraine, which in this area runs roughly parallel with the recessional Summit Lake Moraine. The segment reaches primitive Burma Road (**LA24**) in an active logging and ATV area. The segment bends west and follows Burma Road for approximately one mile before departing from the road (**LA23**) and continuing south.

Portions of the segment south of Burma Road are rough and can be overgrown due to a recent clear-cut. An early successional forest of young aspen, birch and cherry trees, as well as grasses, shrubs and other vegetation have started to recolonize the area, taking advantage of the lack of forest canopy. Deer, bear, grouse, turkey and porcupines inhabit the area. The segment skirts (**LA32**) another frost pocket shortly before it turns south and begins to make its way to Oak Road/Sherry Road. As the segment approaches Oak Road/Sherry Road, it intersects with a short spur trail leading to a parking area (**LA2**) and sharply turns south to follow a former railroad grade on the east side of Oak Road/Sherry Road. Hikers may notice some railroad ties underfoot. Besides the timber and lumber camp supplies this railroad grade carried, stock cars of sheep were also hauled over it in the 1920s and early 1930s. On the east side of the railroad grade in a clearing, about 0.2 miles south of where the Trail turned south, is the foundation of a huge barn (**LA27**), formerly part of a large sheep ranch owned by Endre Norem, one of the area's early settlers. The segment turns off the railroad grade and briefly cuts through woods to the segment terminus at Oak Road/Sherry Road.

AREA SERVICES

Antigo: See Highland Lakes Eastern Segment, p. 122. From the STH-52 Trail access go south and west ~17 mi or from the Oak Rd./Sherry Rd. Trail access go west and south ~12 mi. Also see Trail Access and Parking directions, above.

With the exception of the relatively small unglaciated portion, the entire surface of Wisconsin, the location of its rivers and lakes, its farmlands and marshes, its surface deposits of gravel, sand and till, is due principally to the Wisconsin Glacier. Nowhere else in the United States has glaciation left greater and more permanent marks on the face of the earth.

RAYMOND T. ZILLMER, FOUNDER,
ICE AGE TRAIL ALLIANCE

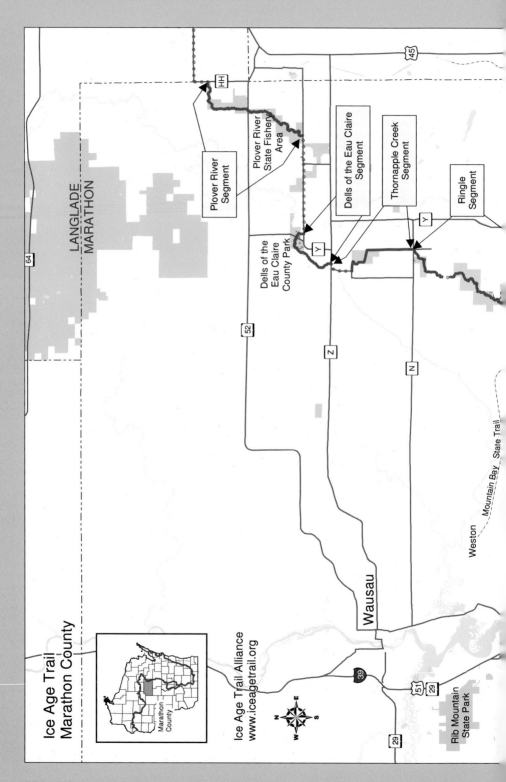

Ice Age Trail
Marathon County

Marathon County

Ice Age Trail Alliance
www.iceagetrail.org

LANGLADE
MARATHON

Plover River
Segment

Plover River
State Fishery
Area

Dells of the Eau Claire
Segment

Thornapple Creek
Segment

Ringle
Segment

Dells of the
Eau Claire
County Park

Wausau

Weston

Mountain Bay State Trail

Rib Mountain
State Park

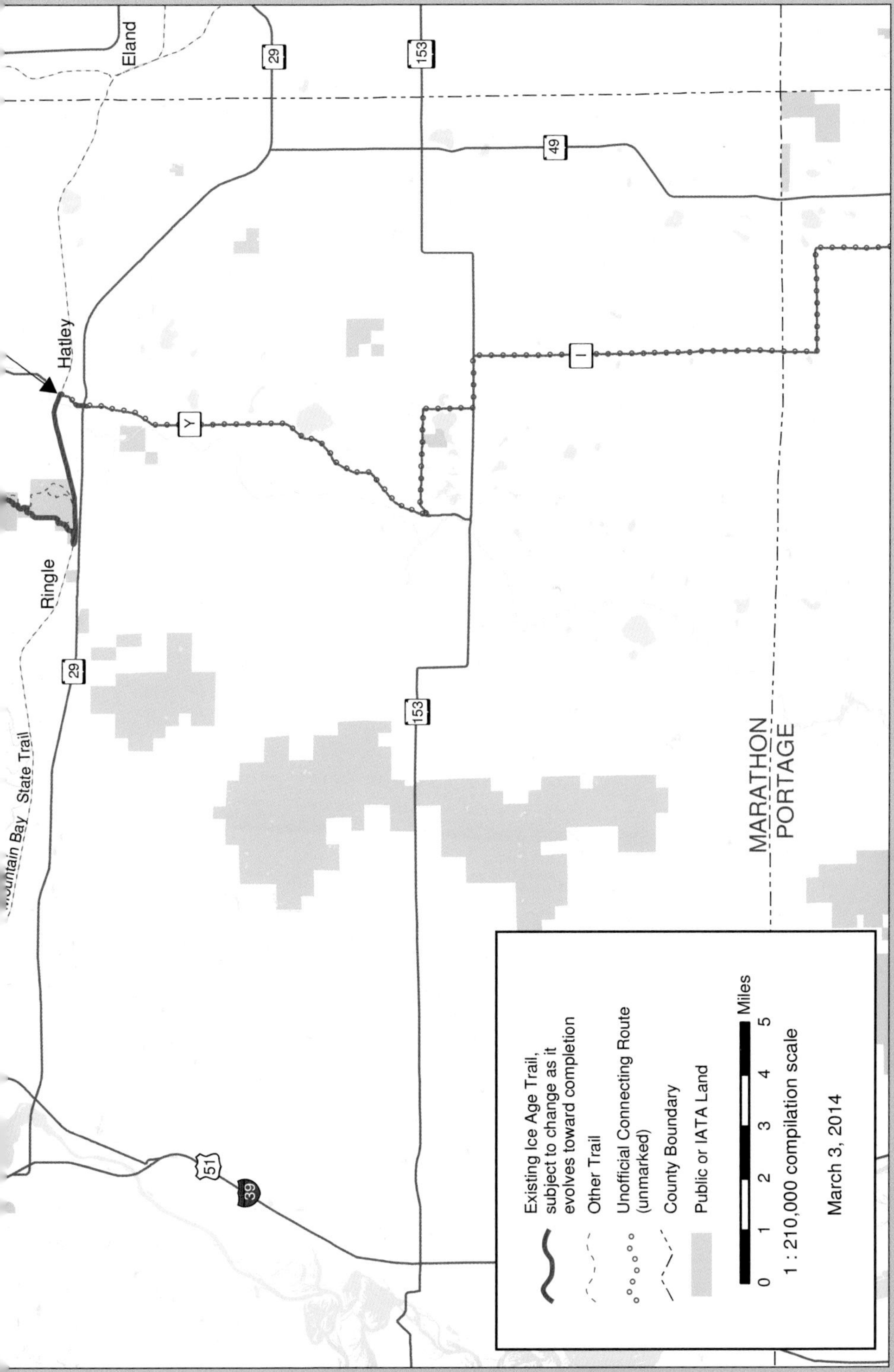

Eland

29

153

49

Hatley

Y

|—|

Ringle

Mountain Bay State Trail

29

153

MARATHON
PORTAGE

51

39

Existing Ice Age Trail,
subject to change as it
evolves toward completion

Other Trail

Unofficial Connecting Route
(unmarked)

County Boundary

Public or IATA Land

Miles

0 1 2 3 4 5

1 : 210,000 compilation scale

March 3, 2014

Marathon County

Trail miles: 20.4
Connecting route miles: 23.0

The glacial deposits in Marathon County vary in age and time periods. The eastern part of the county was the only portion covered by the Green Bay Lobe, where it abutted the Langlade Lobe. Glacial deposits in central and western Marathon County are from an earlier glaciation. The Ice Age Trail follows the Hancock Moraine, an end moraine of the Green Bay Lobe, for several miles north of the town of Ringle, before dipping into the previously glaciated landscape.

The main feature of the Trail west of the moraine is its walk along the Eau Claire River (French for "clear water") and the Dells of the Eau Claire. The Dells of the Eau Claire are mylonite rock bluffs carved when ice from the Green Bay and Langlade lobes thawed and the rush of a tremendous amount of meltwater found a fault in the bedrock. The mylonite bedrock is dated at about 1.8 billion years old and is similar in strength to granite, although it looks more like sandstone. This oldest type of exposed bedrock along the Ice Age Trail is also found along the Wisconsin River's Grandfather Falls in Lincoln County.

Today, the Dells of the Eau Claire County Park features the 65-foot-deep gorge with water cascading into a series of pools formed among the rock ledges. The county park contains several structures built by the Civilian Conservation Corps (CCC) in the 1930s.

CHAPTER INFORMATION

The Marathon County Chapter, originally named the Plover River Chapter, was formed in the early 1970s. Chapter volunteers built the first six miles of Ice Age Trail in the county, now known as the Ringle Segment, in 1973. Three years later, volunteers built six more miles of what are now the Thornapple Creek and Dells of the Eau Claire segments. Volunteers at six Mobile Skills Crew projects hosted by the chapter over four consecutive years (2010–2013) completed the Plover River Segment. There are plans for adding more new Trail in the area of the Plover River Segment and rerouting the Trail corridor in the Ringle Segment area. The chapter promotes use of the Trail for recreation and education. It hosts several workdays and hikes throughout the year, including an annual snowshoe hike in February, wildflower hike in May and fall colors hike in October.

COUNTY INFORMATION

Wausau/Central Wisconsin Convention & Visitors Bureau: 888-948-4748
or 715-355-8788, visitwausau.com

ERIC SHERMAN

Dells of the Eau Claire Segment.

Marathon County

Plover River Segment (Atlas Map 39f)

5.7 miles: CTH-HH to Sportsman Dr.

 This beautiful new segment highlights a dramatic traverse of the terminal moraine and the peaceful Plover River.

From the Plover River.

 A blue-blazed spur trail leads to a parking area on Highland Dr.

TRAIL ACCESS AND PARKING

CTH-HH: *From Wausau* on US-51 exit onto STH-52 and go east ~26 mi. At CTH-HH turn left and go north 1.5 mi to the Trail access on the west side of the road. No parking. *From Antigo* at the intersection of USH-45/STH-47 and STH-52/STH-64, take USH-45/STH-47/STH-52 south 11.0 mi. Continue on STH-52 west for 1.3 mi. At CTH-HH turn right and go 1.5 mi.

Sportsman Dr.: From Wausau take STH-29 east to Exit 185 for Hatley/CTH-Y. Take CTH-Y north 7.5 mi. At CTH-Z turn right and go east 2.0 mi. At North Pole Rd. turn left and go north 1.0 mi. At Sportsman Dr. turn right and go east 1.0 mi to the parking area on the north side of the road.

Additional Parking: (i) STH-52: From Wausau on US-51 exit onto STH-52 and go east ~25 mi to the parking area on north side of highway at the STH-52/Highland Dr. intersection. (ii) Highland Dr.: From the STH-52/Highland Dr. intersection, go south on Highland Dr. 0.7 mi to the DNR parking area at the junction with Village Rd. A blue-blazed spur trail leads 0.2 mi to the Ice Age Trail (**MR12**).

THE HIKE

The Plover River State Fishery Area includes hardwood and cedar forests, lowlands and spring ponds along the Plover River, a Class I, high-quality trout stream that has a naturally sustaining trout population.

From the CTH-HH Trail access head west across rolling, forested hills lined by mossy boulders and bright green ferns. Watch for wetlands, a boulder train, deep kettles and a stone hole as you cross the terminal moraine. Over 1,000 feet of volunteer-built boardwalk will keep boots high and dry through wetlands just north of STH-52. On the north section of boardwalk there is a welcoming observation deck adjacent to the boardwalk with comfortable benches (**MR14**).

The STH-52 Trail access has a handsome kiosk and ample parking. There is a good line of vision at the STH-52 crossing, but it still requires caution. Just south of STH-52 hikers will reach a stretch of puncheon and native timber bridge before continuing southward through a pine forest on the west side of the Plover River. Footing can be treacherous with rocks and roots in the path. After about one-third of a mile, hikers will reach a crossing of the river and can choose to either have their feet cooled by the river's waters or step across on boulders rising above the surface. Listen for the symphony of a "babbling brook" as the peaceful Plover River tumbles through the rocks at this crossing.

Now on the east side of the river, the segment continues southward through a riparian zone. In summer, ripe red raspberries line the segment just south of the Plover River crossing. Hop-scotch on roots and rocks as the segment travels alongside the river. The segment intersects with a blue-blazed spur trail that leads east 0.2 miles to the Highland Dr. Trail parking area (**MR12**).

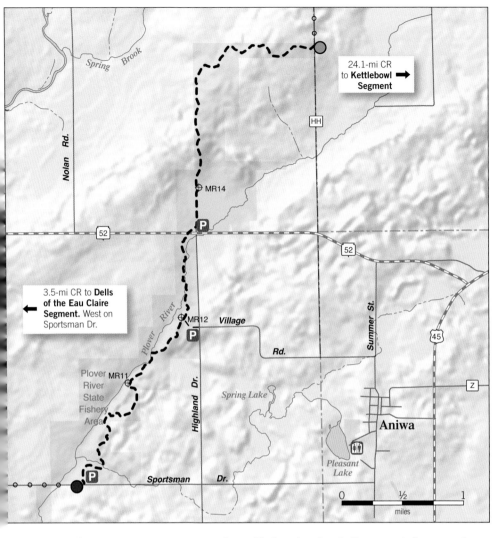

24.1-mi CR
to **Kettlebowl**
Segment ➡

HH

52

52

3.5-mi CR to **Dells
of the Eau Claire
Segment.** West on
Sportsman Dr.

MR14

P

MR12   *Village*

P

Rd.

Summer St.

45

Plover   MR11
River
State
Fishery
Area

Highland Dr.

Spring Lake

Z

Aniwa

*Pleasant
Lake*

P

Sportsman   Dr.

0   ½   1
miles

As the segment continues southward hikers head uphill to travel along a ridge through thick stands of balsam fir, northern white cedar and hemlock. At one point the segment traverses an interesting stone-lined glacial wash (**MR11**). The segment transitions to rolling, open grassland a short distance before reaching its endpoint at the Sportsman Drive parking area and informational kiosk.

Mobile Skills Crew project site, 2010, 2011, 2012, 2013

AREA SERVICES

Antigo: See Highland Lakes Eastern Segment, p. 122. From the STH-52 Trail access go east then north ~13 mi. Also see Trail Access and Parking directions, above.

Wausau: See Ringle Segment, p. 143. From the STH-52 Trail access go west ~25 mi. Also see Trail Access and Parking directions, above.

Dells of the Eau Claire Segment and Thornapple Creek Segment (Atlas Maps 40f, 41f)

SNAPSHOT

Dells of the Eau Claire Segment—2.6 miles: Sportsman Dr. to CTH-Z

Thornapple Creek Segment—3.9 miles (3.0 IAT, 0.9 CR): CTH-Z to CTH-N at Helf Rd.

 *The **Dells of the Eau Claire Segment** shows off one of the most dramatic sites on the entire Ice Age Trail.*

  At Dells of the Eau Claire County Park.

 From the Eau Claire River.

 The portion of the segment crossing private land between the Eau Claire River and CTH-Z is closed during gun deer season.

 Dells of the Eau Claire County Park trail network.

 *The **Thornapple Creek Segment** crosses a small creek in a quiet, primitive area.*

From Thornapple Creek.

 Portions of the segment crossing private land between Thornapple Creek Rd. and Partridge Rd. are closed for hunting Sept. 1 to Dec. 31.

Segment includes a connecting route roadwalk. Portions overlap with gravel Fire Lane Rd. and a snowmobile trail.

TRAIL ACCESS AND PARKING

Sportsman Dr.: From Wausau, take STH-29 east to Exit 185 for Hatley/CTH-Y. Take CTH-Y north 9.5 mi. At Sportsman Dr. (gravel road) turn right and travel east 0.3 mi to the Trail access on the north side of the road. Roadside parking.

CTH-N at Helf Rd.: From Wausau, take STH-29 east to Exit 185 for Hatley/CTH-Y. Take CTH-Y north 4.5 mi. At CTH-N turn left and go west 1.0 mi. At unsigned Helf Rd. (Fire Lane Rd.) turn south for roadside parking. Parking is also available 0.4 mi west in a parking area (**MR8**) on the south side of CTH-N.

Additional Parking: (i) Parking areas in Dells of the Eau Claire County Park. (ii) CTH-Z parking area. (iii) Partridge Rd. roadside parking.

THE HIKE

From the Trail access on Sportsman Drive the **Dells of the Eau Claire Segment** heads north along a mowed path for a quarter-mile then bends west near a trail junction where a Dells of the Eau Claire County Park trail continues straight ahead to CTH-Y. Hikers should turn right and cross the Eau Claire River on a walkway above a dam that makes a small lake for the park's campground. Above the dam are the safe swimming and beach area, ample parking, rest rooms and a picnic ground.

After crossing the dam the segment heads west, past the Park Manager's office, on the park's North River Trail. Hikers will find several places to step out on ancient volcanic rock palisades for a closer view and feel of the river's roaring rapids before reaching CTH-Y. The road crosses the river on a massive stone-arch bridge that was built in 1927. Nearby is the county park's main picnic shelter (constructed by the Civilian Conservation Corps [CCC]) and picnic tables scattered beneath large shade trees.

The segment continues westward along the north bank on the bluff high above the river. There are multiple scenic overlooks with stone walls at the edge. The area is quite spectacular in spring and after rainy periods when water levels are up. The cascading river winds through a series of ledges and pools in the mylonite bedrock gorge formed thousands of years ago from the glacial meltwater of the Green Bay Lobe. In addition, potholes carved up to five feet in diameter are found along the river.

The segment crosses 30 feet above the river on the Dells High Bridge that was built by the CCC in the 1930s and spans 120 ft. South of the bridge hikers will encounter a trail junction; the Ice Age Trail heads southwest along the river while county park trails head south into Dells of the Eau Claire River State Natural Area.

The segment continues southwest along the quiet and peaceful east bank of the river past many trailside benches that were an Eagle Scout service project and eventually encounters large Sandberg Island, the southern foot of which marks the boundary of the county park. Just south of the park boundary, after a roped area, steps lead down to the river. This is the point at which the Ice Age Trail crosses the 45th parallel (**MR4**) marking the halfway point between the North Pole and Equator.

Continuing south, the pine forest along the river gives way to deciduous woods as the segment makes its way to its terminus at CTH-Z.

The **Thornapple Creek Segment** starts with a 0.9-mile connecting route west along CTH-Z and then south on Thornapple Creek Road. The segment leaves the road (**MR9**) along a farm field and continues east and south toward the Partridge Road/Fire Lane Road intersection. (Note: This rough and rugged stretch is often wet and may be difficult to pass. Hikers may bypass this area— and must bypass it from Sept. 1 to Dec. 31 for hunting seasons—by continuing south on Thornapple Creek Road and then heading east on Partridge Road.)

After departing from Thornapple Creek Road and then crossing Thornapple Creek, the segment emerges from a wooded area onto a powerline right-of-way for a short stretch. The Trail re-enters the woods to the east on a snowmobile trail and eventually intersects with a wide, grassy two-track logging road where the segment turns to the south. When the logging road goes around a gate and intersects with Partridge Road, it becomes Fire Lane Road and gradually transitions from grassy two-track to gravel as it makes its way south. Moderate-size erratics are strewn off the edge of the path among spring-blooming trilliums. Hikers may note a fire tower perched atop a hill just east of the road before reaching the segment's endpoint at the intersection of CTH-N and Helf Road.

Mobile Skills Crew project site, 2005

AREA SERVICES

Dells of the Eau Claire County Park: Camping. On Trail. For information contact Marathon County Park and Recreation Department (715-261-1550; reservations: 715-261-1566).

Wausau: See Ringle Segment, p. 143. From the CTH-N at Heft Rd. Trail access go west ~13 mi. Also see Trail Access and Parking directions, above.

Ringle Segment (Atlas Map 41f)

SNAPSHOT

9.4 miles (9.1 IAT, 0.3 CR): CTH-N at Helf Rd. to Curtis Ave. (CTH-Y)

 This segment traverses the terminal moraine of the Green Bay Lobe and prominently features kames, kettles and erratics.

 At the Hatley library.

 From the Plover River.

 The first half-mile west of Helf Rd. is closed Sept. 1 to Dec. 31 for hunting season. A blue-blazed spur from CTH-N (**MR8**) is available as an alternative. Portion of segment crossing private land northeast of Meadowlark Ln. is closed during gun deer season. A small portion south of Meadowlark Ln. is also closed during gun deer season. Therefore, hikers may NOT access the Trail from Meadowlark Ln. during gun deer season.

 Portions overlap with Meadowlark Ln., snowmobile trails, a cross-country ski trail and the multi-use Mountain-Bay State Trail (MBST).

 The MBST continues west and east.

Portions of this segment may be suitable for those using wheelchairs or similar devices.

TRAIL ACCESS AND PARKING

CTH-N at Helf Rd.: From Wausau, take STH-29 east to Exit 185 for Hatley/CTH-Y. Take CTH-Y north 4.5 mi. At CTH-N turn left and go west 1.0 mi. At unsigned Helf Rd. (Fire Lane Rd.) turn south for roadside parking. Parking is also available 0.4 mi west in a parking area (**MR8**) on the south side of CTH-N.

Curtis Ave. (CTH-Y): From Wausau, take STH-29 14.0 mi east to Exit 185 for Hatley/CTH-Y. On Curtis Ave. (CTH-Y) go north 0.5 mi to the intersection with the Mountain-Bay State Trail and Ice Age Trail access. Parking area at the village library directly adjacent to the Trail.

Additional Parking: (i) Poplar Ln. parking areas (north and south sides of road). (ii) 2nd Ave. parking area along Mountain-Bay State Trail.

THE HIKE

From the intersection of CTH-N and Helf Road the segment heads south for a short stretch along Helf Road and then departs the road heading southwest. The Trail passes through beautiful, heavily wooded country with maples, oaks and pines. After 0.5 miles the segment intersects (**MR7**) with a blue-blazed spur trail (which provides Ice Age Trail access during hunting seasons) that leads north 0.25 miles to the CTH-N parking area (**MR8**). From this intersection the segment continues southward toward Mole Brook Road.

Upon reaching the intersection of Mole Brook Road and Meadowlark Lane, hikers will continue south for 0.3 miles on Meadowlark Lane, then onto a private driveway. At the southern end of the driveway (**MR6**) the segment continues off-road. Hikers should watch carefully for Trail signage as it may be sparse in this area.

South of Meadowlark Lane, the segment passes by a large open meadow that

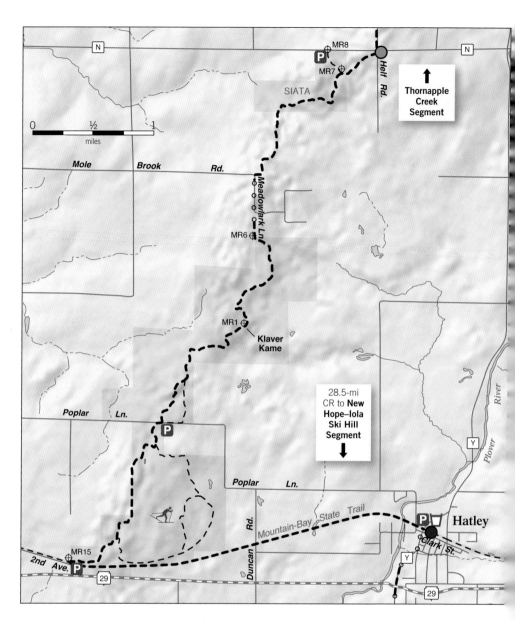

is covered in wildflowers in summer and then climbs over Klaver Kame, which features a bench (**MR1**) at the top. Klaver Kame was named after an early settler. The segment crosses Poplar Lane and continues southward, twice intersecting a cross-country ski trail that loops around the Marathon County landfill.

Near the 2nd Avenue Trail access the segment intersects (**MR15**) with the 83.4-mile-long Mountain-Bay State Trail (MBST) that occupies the former Chicago and Northwestern Railroad right-of-way between Wausau and Green Bay. Hikers will turn left and head east toward Hatley on the MBST's crushed limestone surface. The segment ends in Hatley at Curtis Avenue (CTH-Y) at the site of an Ice Age Trail/MBST kiosk.

AREA SERVICES

Ringle: Restaurant. From the 2nd Ave. parking area go west 1.5 mi on 2nd Ave.

Hatley: Restaurant, convenience store, library. On Curtis Ave. (CTH-Y) and on STH-29 frontage road.

Wausau Area: Restaurant, grocery store, convenience store, general shopping, lodging, camping, library, medical care. From the CTH-Y/STH-29 intersection go west 14.5 mi on STH-29. INN Style program lodging at the Everest Inn (888-848-5651, www.everestinn.com). For area info, contact Wausau Region Chamber of Commerce (715-845-6231, wausauchamber.com).

Mountain-Bay State Trail: On Trail (920-448-4466, dnr.wi.gov/topic/parks/name/mountainbay).

Plover River Segment.

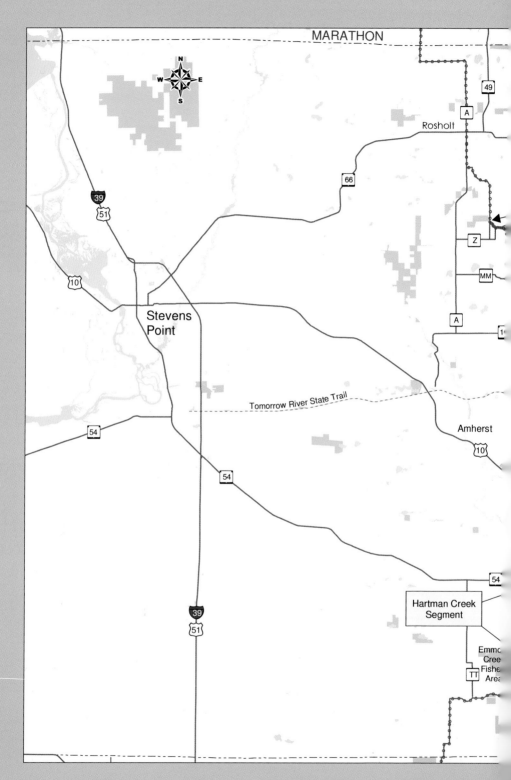

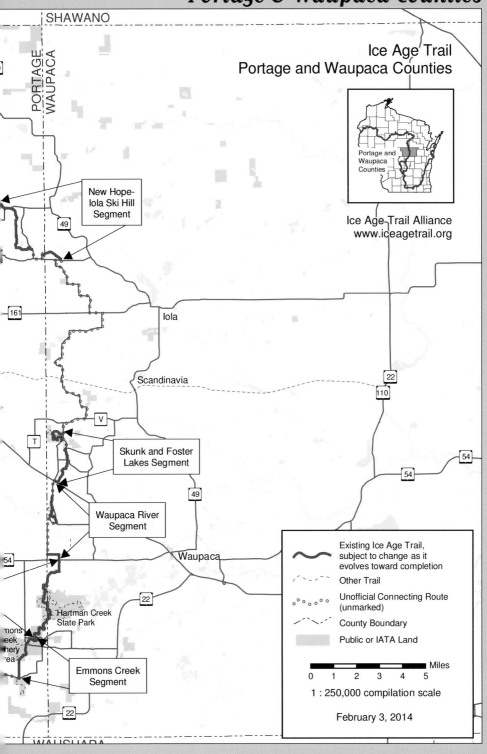

SHAWANO

PORTAGE
WAUPACA

Ice Age Trail
Portage and Waupaca Counties

Portage and
Waupaca
Counties

Ice Age Trail Alliance
www.iceagetrail.org

New Hope-
Iola Ski Hill
Segment

49

161

Iola

Scandinavia

22

110

V

T

54

Skunk and Foster
Lakes Segment

49

Waupaca River
Segment

54

Waupaca

22

Hartman Creek
State Park

nons
eek
hery
ea

Emmons Creek
Segment

22

Existing Ice Age Trail,
subject to change as it
evolves toward completion

Other Trail

Unofficial Connecting Route
(unmarked)

County Boundary

Public or IATA Land

Miles
0   1   2   3   4   5

1 : 250,000 compilation scale

February 3, 2014

WAUSHARA

Portage & Waupaca Counties

Trail miles: 19.0
Connecting route miles: 32.9

Several glacial advances formed the landscape of eastern Portage County and all of Waupaca County. The Green Bay Lobe moved from the east, with its farthest advance extending a few miles east of Stevens Point. Successive glacial advances often stopped short of previous ones, each leaving their own set of moraines. The Ice Age Trail along the county border passes over several Elderon Moraines, deposited approximately 13,000 years ago. These moraines, like several others to the west, are narrow and noncontiguous, broken by channels cut by westward torrents of glacial meltwater and pitted outwash. The meltwater drainageways flushed glacial debris of sand and gravel onto stagnant ice fields. After the buried ice melted, the deposited glacial debris collapsed onto the underlying ground forming the undulating and irregular landscape of ridged hills and knobs interspersed with steep-sided depressions that later filled and became lakes. The geological formation known as the Farmington Drumlins is the largest swarm of drumlins along the entire Ice Age Trail. Miles from the terminal moraine the drumlins were formed beneath a continental glacier through the sculpting of sand, pebbles and other glacial debris. Found in clusters called swarms, drumlins have a distinctive shape that has been described as a teardrop, oval or cigar-shaped.

These counties have many plant communities, including oak barrens, prairie and northern hardwood forests. The Ice Age Trail passes through several state fishery areas, state natural areas and Hartman Creek State Park. In addition to camping at Hartman Creek State Park, the Portage County Parks Department offers camping near the Ice Age Trail at Collins and Lake Emily county parks.

CHAPTER INFORMATION

The Portage County Chapter (**portagecoiat.org**) and Waupaca County Chapter were formed in 1986 and 1987, respectively. The two chapters share the care of the Ice Age Trail that crosses back and forth into each county. The chapters get assistance from the county parks departments, Fox Valley Sierra Club, Hartman Creek State Park and local landowners. Both chapters offer special hikes and work closely with landowners to obtain and maintain Trail privileges. Every fall the two chapters join for their annual Fall Hike-A-Thon.

COUNTY INFORMATION

Portage County Information: co.portage.wi.us

Waupaca County Visitor and Promotional Council: visitwaupacacounty. com

Stevens Point Area Convention and Visitors Bureau: 715-344-2556, stevenspointarea.com

Portage County Parks Department: 715-346-1433, co.portage.wi.us/parks

Group Camps and Cabins: There are several places near the Trail route that offer camping or log cabin lodging for larger groups. (i) Camp Helen Brachman: Seasonal group lodging (9341 Asbury Dr., Almond, 715-366-2234, campbrachman.org). (ii) Central Wisconsin Environmental Station: Log cabins (10186 CTH-MM, Amherst Junction, 715-824-2428, uwsp.edu/cnr/cwes). (iii) Wisconsin Lion's Camp: Limited camping (3834 CTH-A, Rosholt, 715-366-4761, wisconsinlionscamp.com).

ERIC SHERMAN

Sunset over Skunk Lake on the Skunk and Foster Lakes Segment.

New Hope-Iola Ski Hill Segment (Atlas Map 45f)

SNAPSHOT

5.7 miles (4.7 IAT, 1.0 CR): Sunset Lake Rd. to CTH-MM at Iola Winter Sports Club

This segment traverses areas of high-relief hummocky topography and has a strong Northwoodsy character.

 At Iola Winter Sports Club lodge (winter only).

 From Severson Lake.

 Walk-to shelter (**PW21**) just off the segment on Iola Winter Sports Club property.

 At Iola Pines Campground ~6 mi east and Collins County Park ~9 mi west (see Area Services).

 At Sunset Lake County Park.

 Segment is closed during gun deer season.

 Portions overlap with Iola Winter Sports Club ski trails. Hike well off to the side when groomed.

 Network of Iola Winter Sports Club ski trails.

TRAIL ACCESS AND PARKING

Sunset Lake Rd.: *From Stevens Point* at the intersection of I-39 and USH-10, take USH-10 east 8.0 mi. At STH-161 turn left and go east 3.8 mi. At CTH-A turn left and go north 4.0 mi. At CTH-Z turn right and go east 1.5 mi. At Sunset Lake Rd. turn left and go north 0.9 mi to the Trail access on the east side of the road. No parking. There is a parking area on the east side of Sunset Lake Rd. a short distance north of the Trail access and a parking area on the west side of Sunset Lake Rd. 0.1 mi north of the Trail access at New Hope Pines State Natural Area. *From Waupaca* at the intersection of STH-49 and USH-10, take STH-49 north 23.5 mi. At CTH-Z turn left and go west 2.8 mi. At Sunset Lake Rd. turn right and go north 0.9 mi.

CTH-MM at Iola Winter Sports Club: *From Stevens Point* at the intersection of I-39 and USH-10, take USH-10 east 8.0 mi. At STH-161 turn left and go east 3.8 mi. At CTH-A turn left and go north 2.3 mi. At CTH-MM turn right and go east 4.0 mi to the Iola Winter Sports Club parking area. *From Waupaca* at the intersection of STH-49 and USH-10, take STH-49 north 19.5 mi. At CTH-MM turn left and go west 1.6 mi.

Additional Parking: CTH-Z parking area (**PW15**).

THE HIKE

Before starting off on this segment, hikers looking for an extra adventure should walk 0.1 miles north from the segment's starting point on Sunset Lake Road to pay a visit to New Hope Pines State Natural Area. It features one of the largest and least disturbed northern dry-mesic forests remaining in central Wisconsin and is reminiscent of the vast "pineries" found in this region prior to European settlement. A primitive yet easily navigable path winds through the SNA, which is likely to one day host a segment of the Ice Age Trail.

From Sunset Lake Road the segment heads southeast through dense forest, dropping down into a low area and then climbing out as the route approaches CTH-Z. Upon arriving at CTH-Z hikers should cross to the opposite side of the road, turn left and follow the road around to the east for 0.2 miles to the CTH-Z parking area (**PW15**). From here, the segment then reenters the woods and continues south then southeast.

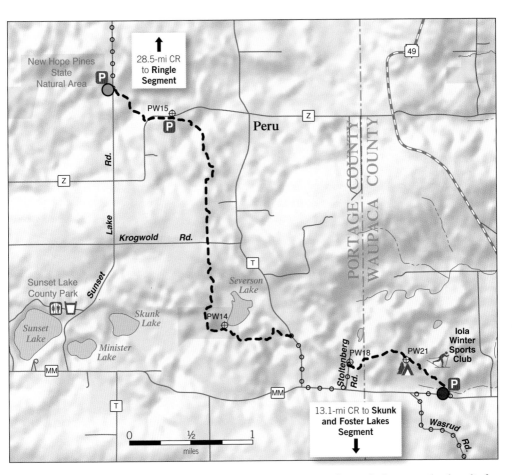

Between CTH-Z and CTH-T the segment moves through dramatic high-relief hummocky topography. The area's high water table and clay-laden soil produce marshes in the small depressions that harbor nesting ducks. A few larger kettles contain lakes, including Severson (Budsberg) Lake (**PW14**). This portion of the segment traverses open meadows and climbs in and out of three steep wooded ravines. Short bridges cross low wet marshy areas. Northwoods red and white pine and birches mix with Hill's oak; several of the oaks and pines are assumed to be well over 100 years old.

Upon reaching CTH-T hikers should turn right and follow the road south for 0.4 miles, then head east on CTH-MM for 0.4 miles, then head north on Stoltenberg Road for 0.2 miles watching carefully for the Trail access (**PW18**) on the right. From Stoltenberg Road the segment resumes its off-road course eastward and soon enters the grounds of the Iola Winter Sports Club, a full service winter sports area that also includes a shelter (**PW21**) for overnight use by Ice Age Trail hikers. There are a number of intersecting trails in this area; pay close attention and look carefully for yellow blazes and directional arrows. The club's ski jump is located on the top of Norseman Hill and uses the relief and steep slopes of a deep kettle. The total relief is approximately 100 feet suggesting the ice block buried here was at least 100 feet thick.

Rosholt: Restaurant, grocery store, lodging, camping, library. From the Sunset Lake Rd. access go north to CTH-T. Continue north on CTH-T then CTH-A to STH-66. Go west 1.0 mi on STH-66. Camping at Collins County Park (715-346-1433), 3.5 mi south and west of town. The library has limited hours.

Iola: Restaurant, grocery store, lodging, camping, library. From the CTH-MM access go east on CTH-MM to STH-49. Turn right and follow STH-49 for 3.5 mi. Camping at Iola Pines Campground (715-445-3489, iolapines.com).

Stevens Point: See Skunk and Foster Lakes Segment and Waupaca River Segment, p. 154. From the CTH-MM Trail access go west then south ~18 mi. Also see Trail Access and Parking directions, above.

Waupaca: See Skunk and Foster Lakes Segment and Waupaca River Segment, p. 154. From the CTH-MM Trail access go east then south ~21 mi. Also see Trail Access and Parking directions, above.

DAVE CALIEBE

The Ice Age Trail is largely built and maintained by volunteers. More help is always welcome...from volunteers of all ages and talents.

Waupaca River Segment.

Portage & Waupaca Counties

ERIC SHERMAN

Skunk and Foster Lakes Segment and Waupaca River Segment (Atlas Map 47f)

SNAPSHOT

Skunk and Foster Lakes Segment—4.4 miles (3.9 miles IAT, 0.5 miles CR): N. Foley Dr. Northern Trail Access to USH-10

Waupaca River Segment—4.9 miles (2.2 miles IAT, 2.7 miles CR): USH-10 to STH-54

 *The **Skunk and Foster Lakes Segment** passes through a beautiful State Natural Area, highlights a drumlin swarm and features clear, undeveloped kettle lakes, hilly topography and huge trailside erratics.*

 From trailside lakes and streams.

 Segment includes a connecting route roadwalk.

 A white-blazed loop on northwest end, a blue-blazed spur to a parking area and several DNR access trails.

 Portion of the segment crossing private land between Indian Valley Rd. and USH-10 is closed during gun deer season.

 *The varied **Waupaca River Segment** highlights a steep ridge with a trailside ridgetop cabin and the scenic Waupaca River.*

 From the Waupaca River.

 A trailside cabin (first-come, first serve) just west of Foley Dr. (**PW7**).

Portions of the segment crossing private lands both north and south of the Waupaca River State Fishery Area are closed during gun deer season.

 Segment includes two connecting route roadwalks.

 A blazed loop trail west of the segment near the Waupaca River and a blazed spur trail to the Foley Dr. parking area.

TRAIL ACCESS AND PARKING

N. Foley Dr. Northern Trail Access: *From Waupaca* at the intersection of highways STH-49 and USH-10, take USH-10 west 5.5 mi. At Foley Dr. turn right and go north 2.1 mi. (Please note that Foley Dr. becomes N. Foley Dr. at Floistad Rd.) No parking at the Trail access. Instead park at the Skunk and Foster Lakes SNA parking area 0.1 mi south of the N. Foley Dr. northern Trail access on the west side of the road. A blue-blazed spur trail leads to the Trail. *From Stevens Point* at the intersection of I-39 and USH-10, take USH-10 east 18.0 mi. At Foley Dr. turn left and go north 2.1 mi.

STH-54: *From Waupaca* at USH-10 and STH-54, take STH-54 west 5.0 mi to the parking area on the north side of the road. *From Stevens Point* at the intersection of I-39 and USH-10, take I-39 south 6.5 mi. Exit STH-54 and go east 17.0 mi.

Additional Parking: (i) Indian Valley Rd.; roadside parking. (ii) Foley Dr. Waupaca River State Fishery Area parking area, 1.4 mi south of USH-10. A blazed spur trail leads to the Trail.

THE HIKE

The first half of the **Skunk and Foster Lakes Segment** is a horseshoe-shaped route in the Skunk and Foster Lakes State Natural Area (SNA) with several undeveloped kettle lakes and loop and side trail options. From its starting point at the North Foley Drive northern Trail access the segment heads west and parallels Sannes Creek, which flows through the ancient meltwater channel that surrounds the SNA. As the segment bends south through white and red pines, it approaches the north shore of 11-acre spring-fed Skunk Lake and arrives at an intersection (**PW12**) with a white-blazed loop trail and a DNR access forest road. Hikers looking for additional adventures can head west on the 0.8-mile loop trail which explores a scenic, mature maple forest set in more rolling topography.

From the junction with the loop trail, the segment continues southeast, crossing another access path that leads to the shore of Skunk Lake, which is surrounded by a wetland dominated by cattails and bulrush. The Trail continues into hummocky terrain east of Skunk Lake. Numerous impressive-sized Wolf River granite boulders are scattered throughout the area. The route descends through second growth forest for a brief view of 7-acre shallow, hard water Foster Lake, then circles east toward Grenlie Lake, a clear lake fed by seepage and springs.

On the southwest corner of Grenlie Lake, the segment passes a hillside filled with large ferns then follows along the north shore of the lake. The blue-blazed spur trail that leads to the parking area on North Foley Drive intersects the segment near the east end of the lake. From here the segment heads south across the lake's outlet on a bridge. Continuing along, the Trail follows the shoreline with views of popular waterfowl habitat and then soon ascends

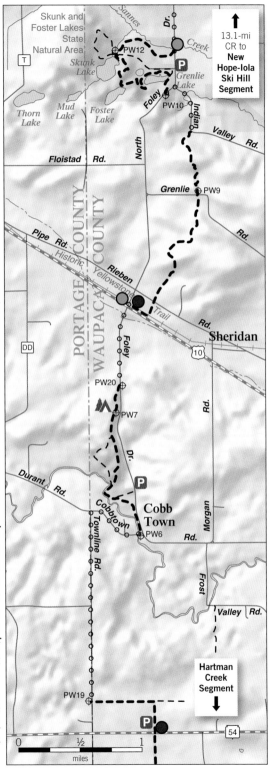

through a glacial erratic field, fern garden and pine forest on the way to the North Foley Drive southern Trail access (**PW10**).

From here, hikers should follow a 0.5-mile connecting route roadwalk: northeast on North Foley Drive and then southeast and south on Indian Valley Road to the spot where Indian Valley Road turns sharply east.

The segment goes off-road and continues south under the cover of woods on an uneven forest road and climbs steadily to a cattle pasture. The canopy opens up to the fenced pasture with a large cell/transmission tower in the middle of the field. A second tower is also visible a little farther south. The Trail hugs the tree line along the field, then descends through woods and open prairie where sumac turns flaming red in the fall. As the segment reaches Grenlie Road, hikers will notice huge erratics lined along the road.

The segment crosses Grenlie Road (**PW9**) and immediately enters woods and passes through the western side of a drumlin swarm. This area is one of the few along the Ice Age Trail where hikers have a close encounter with drumlins. Drumlins are elevated tear-shaped land formations that indicate the flow of the glaciers. The steep end faced the flow of the ice and the tail end tapers to the ground like a ramp. Drumlins are never individual and are always found in groups called a drumlin field or swarm. The segment in this area crosses several private dirt access roads. Hikers should pay close attention to signage at intersections.

As the Trail continues, it slips out of the woods alongside an agricultural field then returns to the woods crossing up and over the westernmost drumlin about halfway toward USH-10. Coming down off the drumlin, the segment follows field edges as it makes its way to cross Rieben Road. The segment continues briefly south on the perimeter of a field and pasture and then bends northwest to parallel the Canadian National Railroad and USH-10. Footing can be rough along this section of Trail and tends to become overgrown. The segment ends on the north side of USH-10 where the Trail reaches Foley Drive and turns south to cross the Canadian National Railroad.

Mobile Skills Crew project site, 2005, 2009, 2012

The **Waupaca River Segment** begins with a 0.7-mile connecting route roadwalk south on Foley Drive. From the Canadian National Railroad track crossing, hikers should head south and cross four-lane USH-10 with extreme caution. USH-10 is on the route of the historic Yellowstone Trail, the first transcontinental highway in the northern tier of the United States. It was conceived in 1912 and impacted communities from Massachusetts to Washington State economically, politically and socially. Hikers should follow Foley Drive south to where the off-road portion of the segment heads west (**PW20**) from the road.

The segment's topography is mainly pitted outwash made up of glacial debris left behind when the glaciers retreated. The steep slope just east of the first part of the segment resulted from buried ice melting and the outwash surface collapsing. The Trail ascends steeply from the road and after 0.3 miles arrives at a small, simple trailside cabin (**PW7**) built on private land by the Wisconsin Conservation Corps in the 1990s that is open to the public for overnight stays. South of the cabin the segment reaches the northern junction with a blazed scenic loop trail that splits off to the west. The Trail continues through rolling terrain with steep slopes on the sides of the Trail in mixed oak woodland and pine forest. South of the southern junction with the scenic loop trail, the segment flattens out to follow along near the placid Waupaca River. Native Americans living in this area named the river "Waupaca," which translates to "tomorrow" because it took them 24 hours to paddle the river's length. The segment leaves the river bank briefly, intersects a blue-blazed spur trail leading to the parking area on Foley Drive, then returns to the river before emerging at the Cobbtown Road/Foley Drive intersection (**PW6**).

From this point hikers follow a 2.0-mile connecting route roadwalk. Hikers should cross over the river on the bridge and head west following Cobbtown Road, then turn left and follow Townline Road south until the segment heads east (**PW19**) from the road. Here the segment crosses a pitted outwash landscape along a field edge, then heads south to the segment terminus at STH-54. A prominent field of drumlins sits about a half mile east of the parking area.

Mobile Skills Crew project site, 2009, 2012

AREA SERVICES

Waupaca: Restaurant, grocery store, convenience store, general shopping, lodging, camping, library, medical care. From the USH-10 Trail access, go ~6 mi east on USH-10. Most services in the area of USH-10 and STH-54/49. INN Style program lodging at the Apple Tree Lane B&B (877-277-5316, appletreelanebb.com), Cleghorn B&B (715-258-5235, cleghornbandb.com) and Crystal River Inn (715-258-5333, crystalriver-inn.com). Area info available from the Waupaca Area Chamber of Commerce (888-417-4040, WaupacaAreaChamber.com).

Amherst: Restaurant, grocery store, lodging, camping, library, medical services. From the USH-10 Trail access go ~5 mi northwest on USH-10. The library has limited hours. INN Style program lodging at Artha Sustainable Living Center B&B (715-824-3463, arthaonline.com). Additional lodging at The Amherst Inn B&B (888-211-3555, amherstinn.com).

Amherst Junction: Convenience store, lodging, camping. From the USH-10 Trail access go ~7 mi northwest on USH-10. Camping at Lake Emily County Park (715-346-1433).

Stevens Point: Restaurant, grocery store, convenience store, general shopping, lodging, library, medical care. From the USH-10 Trail access go ~19 mi northwest on USH-10. INN Style program lodging at A Victorian Swan on Water (715-345-0595, victorianswan.com) and Dreams of Yesteryear B&B (715-341-4525, dreamsofyesteryear.com). Area info available from the Stevens Point Area Convention and Visitor Bureau (715-344-2556, stevenspointarea.com).

Hartman Creek State Park: See Hartman Creek Segment, p. 158. From the STH-54 Trail access go east then south 2.5 mi.

Turner's Fresh Market & Greenhouses: See Hartman Creek Segment, p. 158. From the STH-54 Trail access go west 0.2 mi.

Hartman Creek Segment (Atlas Map 48f)

5.6 miles: STH-54 to Emmons Creek Rd.

 This segment features the forested, hilly terrain of Hartman Creek State Park and one of the largest erratics on the entire Ice Age Trail.

At various locations throughout Hartman Creek State Park (HCSP).

From Allen Creek and Allen Lake.

 Portion of segment crossing private land between STH-54 and HCSP is closed during gun deer season.

 Portions overlap with bike and ski trails. Hike well off to the side when ski trails are groomed.

 Several unmarked side trails and the extensive HCSP trail network.

TRAIL ACCESS AND PARKING

STH-54: *From Waupaca* at USH-10 and STH-54, take STH-54 west 5.0 mi to the parking area on the north side of the road. *From Stevens Point* at the intersection of I-39 and USH-10, take I-39 south 6.5 mi. Exit STH-54 and go east 17.0 mi.

Emmons Creek Rd.: *From Stevens Point* at the intersection of I-39 and USH-10, take I-39 south. Exit STH-54 and go east 15.0 mi. At CTH-D turn right and go south 2.5 mi. Continue south on Stratton Lake Rd. 0.8 mi. At Emmons Creek Rd. turn left and go east 0.5 mi to the Trail access. Watch carefully for Trail signage on the north side of the road. No parking at the Trail access; continue 0.25 mi east of the Ice Age Trail to a DNR parking area on the north side of the road. *From Waupaca*, at USH-10 and STH-54, take STH-54 west 6.6 mi to CTH-D. Follow the directions described above from CTH-D to the Trail access.

Additional Parking: (i) Edminster Ln. parking area at Trail access. (ii) Hartman Creek State Park parking areas on Windfeldt Ln.

THE HIKE

From its starting point on STH-54 the segment heads south and then west along field edges, enters a hilly wooded area, crosses Allen Creek and then passes through a pine plantation before emerging onto Edminster Road. In this initial portion the segment intersects several unmarked side trails.

South of Edminster Road the segment enters Hartman Creek State Park, which has a long history. The Wisconsin Conservation Department, the precursor to the Wisconsin Department of Natural Resources (DNR), bought 309 acres from the Allen and Hartman family estates in 1939 for $8,500. The Conservation Department dammed a creek and created Allen Lake, in honor of George W. Allen, and named the property "Hartman Creek State Fish Hatchery" in honor of the Hartman family. Today, the park consists of approximately 1,400 acres.

The park is located on terrain formed as the Wisconsin glacier retreated down a regional slope. The eastern part of the park lies on gently rolling ground moraine and pitted outwash where flowing rivers from the melting glacier deposited layers of gravel and sand. The resulting topography is pitted outwash to the west; as the glacier melted back from this position it left a substantially lower land surface to the east.

The segment makes its way south through the park sharing portions of the park's extensive trail network. Just south of a huge erratic, hikers can depart from the Ice Age Trail at a waypoint (**PW17**) to access Hartman Creek State Park's facilities and campground. In the summer, a large tepee, which can be reserved for camping, is visible next to the Trail and is part of the campground.

Nearly the entire portion of the segment through the northern part of the park (north of Winfeldt Lane) is on rolling, forested terrain. A kiosk explaining the geological landscape of the Elderon Moraine and the outwash plain is a short distance east of the segment's route at a parking area on Windfeldt Lane.

South of Windfeldt Lane the segment goes through a large, open prairie on the edge of an old orchard, where bluebirds and other songbirds thrive. The segment then intersects with several mountain bike paths. As the segment enters Emmons Creek Barrens State Natural Area, the most hilly portion of the segment, the forest clears away and hikers can see a large clearing and long views across the treetops. The segment narrows and descends into the clearing as it approaches its endpoint on Emmons Creek Road.

Mobile Skills Crew project site, 2012

AREA SERVICES

Turner's Fresh Market & Greenhouses: Snacks. From STH-54 parking area go 0.2 mi west on STH-54. Farmer's market with fresh fruits, vegetables, snacks and drinks; 715-258-3355, turnersfreshmarket.com.

Hartman Creek State Park: Camping, water, restrooms, seasonal concession stand and recreational rentals. On Trail (715-258-2372, dnr.wi.gov/topic/parks/name/hartman; reservations: 888-947-2757, reserveamerica.com).

Stevens Point: See Skunk and Foster Lakes Segment and Waupaca River Segment, p. 154. From the STH-54 Trail access go west ~23.5 mi. Also see Trail Access and Parking directions, above.

Waupaca: See Skunk and Foster Lakes Segment and Waupaca River Segment, p. 154. From the STH-54 Trail access go east ~5 mi. Also see Trail Access and Parking directions, above.

Emmons Creek Segment (Atlas Map 48f)

2.6 miles: Emmons Creek Rd. to 2nd Ave.

 This segment and its accompanying *Faraway Valley Loop* highlight charming Emmons Creek and oak woodland and savanna areas.

From Emmons Creek.

 Green-blazed Faraway Valley loop and white-blazed loop south of 2nd Ave.

TRAIL ACCESS AND PARKING

Emmons Creek Rd.: *From Stevens Point* at the intersection of I-39 and USH-10, take I-39 south. Exit STH-54 and go east 15.0 mi. At CTH-D turn right and go south 2.5 mi. Continue south on Stratton Lake Rd. 0.8 mi. At Emmons Creek Rd. turn left and go east 0.5 mi to the Trail access. Watch carefully for Trail signage on the north side of the road. No parking at the Trail access; continue 0.25 mi east of the Ice Age Trail to a DNR parking area on the north side of the road. *From Waupaca*, at USH-10 and STH-54, take STH-54 west 6.6 mi to CTH-D. Follow the directions described above from CTH-D to the Trail access.

2nd Ave.: *From Stevens Point* at the intersection of I-39 and USH-10, take I-39 south. Exit STH-54 and go east 12.0 mi. At CTH-TT turn right and go south 2.5 mi. Join CTH-D south for another 0.5 mi. Where CTH-D turns west, continue south on 16th Rd. for another 2.2 mi. At 2nd Ave. turn left and go east 1.5 mi to the Trail access on the north side of the road. No parking. Instead, continue east on 2nd Ave. for 50 yards to the parking area for the Murry Creek loop trail. *From Waupaca*, at USH-10 and STH-54, take STH-54 west 8.6 mi. At CTH-TT turn left. Follow the directions described above from CTH-TT to the Trail access.

Additional Parking: Stratton Lake Rd. parking area with informational kiosk.

THE HIKE

From its starting point on Emmons Creek Road, the segment heads south through the Emmons Creek State Fishery Area, traversing along a dramatic ridge through oak woodlands. The river valley below is revealed when leaves are off trees. Leopold benches along the Trail provide convenient resting places. The segment descends from the ridge through a pine plantation to Stratton Lake Road and the segment's main parking area. The green-blazed Faraway Valley Loop leaves the segment from the parking area and heads west through a meadow, crosses Emmons Creek on the 3rd Avenue road bridge, returns to the woods and heads south to rejoin the segment south of Emmons Creek.

Back on the Trail, south of Stratton Lake Road, the segment passes through a large meadow before crossing Emmons Creek at a scenic footbridge (**PW2**). Boardwalks take the segment through a seasonally wet area noted for skunk cabbage and marsh marigolds. The segment overlooks the Emmons Creek valley, reaches the southern junction with the Faraway Valley Loop and heads south on a straight line toward its endpoint on 2nd Avenue.

Upon arriving at 2nd Avenue, hikers may explore a white-blazed lollipop loop (with a total distance of 2.7 miles) that heads south from 2nd Avenue, crosses narrow Murry Creek (usually hoppable with a single step) and then winds through pine plantations. Small meadows here sometimes yield sightings of the rare and endangered Karner blue butterfly.

Mobile Skills Crew project site, 2012

AREA SERVICES

Almond: Restaurant, library. From the 2nd Ave. Trail access go west ~9 mi. The library has limited hours.

Hartman Creek State Park: See Hartman Creek Segment, p. 158. From the 2nd Ave. Trail access go east then north ~7 mi.

Stevens Point: See Skunk and Foster Lakes Segment and Waupaca River Segment, p. 154. From the 2nd Ave. Trail access go west then north ~28 mi. Also see Trail Access and Parking directions, above.

Waupaca: See Skunk and Foster Lakes Segment and Waupaca River Segment, p. 154. From the 2nd Ave. Trail access go east then north ~12 mi. Also see Trail Access and Parking directions, above.

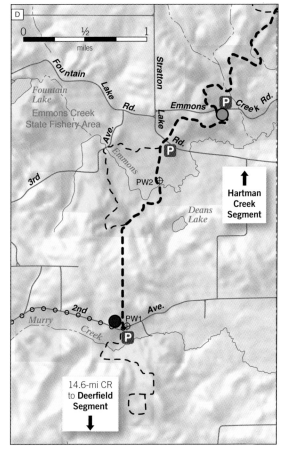

The first time I saw a bear on the Trail I was filled with so much joy and fear; all I could do was look for another for days. Every time I saw a shadow in the woods I got a shiver of anticipation. Being this close to nature was the ultimate high; the woods seemed to accept me as a part of its family. Animals stopped running away from me and instead just looked to see what I was, or minded their own business. Even an elusive bobcat took a few minutes to check me out as it crossed the street. He did not run; instead he slowly sulked away back into the woods without much concern. Truly amazing.

ADAM HINZ, ICE AGE TRAIL THOUSAND-MILER

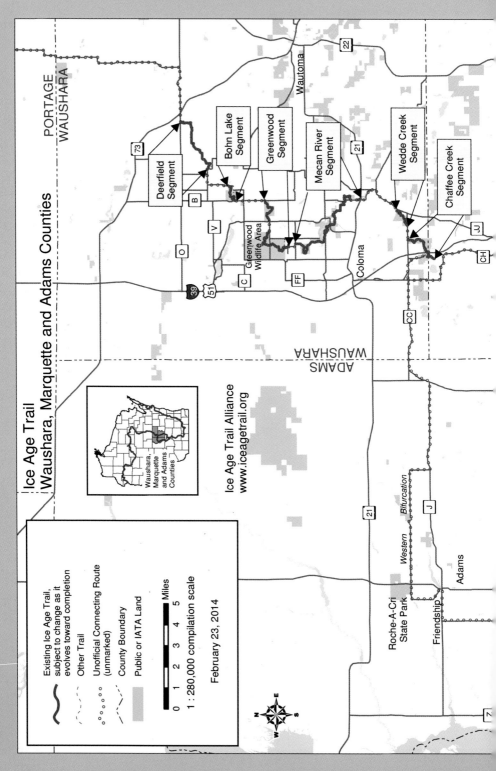

Ice Age Trail
Waushara, Marquette and Adams Counties

Deerfield Segment

Bohn Lake Segment

Greenwood Segment

Mecan River Segment

Wedde Creek Segment

Chaffee Creek Segment

Greenwood Wildlife Area

Wautoma

Coloma

PORTAGE
WAUSHARA

ADAMS WAUSHARA

Roche-A-Cri State Park

Western   Bifurcation

Friendship

Adams

Ice Age Trail Alliance
www.iceagetrail.org

Waushara,
Marquette
and Adams
Counties

Existing Ice Age Trail,
subject to change as it
evolves toward completion

Other Trail

Unofficial Connecting Route
(unmarked)

County Boundary

Public or IATA Land

Miles

0 1 2 3 4 5

1 : 280,000 compilation scale

February 23, 2014

Waushara & Marquette Counties

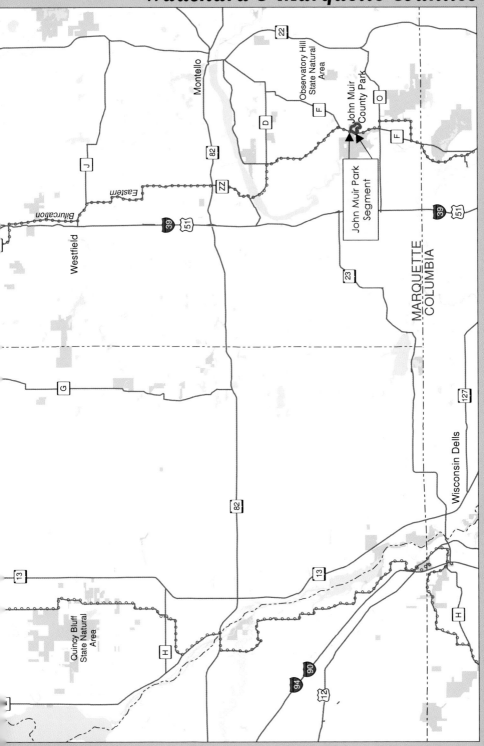

John Muir Park Segment

John Muir County Park

Observatory Hill State Natural Area

Montello

Westfield

Bifurcation

Eastern

Quincy Bluff State Natural Area

MARQUETTE
COLUMBIA

Wisconsin Dells

Waushara County

Trail miles: 19.6
Connecting route miles: 20.2

Within the Central Sand Hills region, the Ice Age Trail corridor in Waushara County courses through a complex terminal moraine zone of the westward-flowing Green Bay Lobe. The moraines along the Trail were deposited during the late Wisconsin Glaciation. Most of these moraines were deposited after the Green Bay Lobe reached its maximum extent about 15,000 years ago. As the ice sheet retreated and advanced, it deposited a series of moraines. When the westward torrents of glacial meltwater flowed through the region, the moraines became pitted and meltwater channels sliced through them. The moraines were also partially covered by the glacial outwash debris.

A mixture of farmland, woodlots, wetlands, small kettle lakes, cold-water streams and rural communities characterizes the county. The Ice Age Trail passes through land managed by the Wisconsin Department of Natural Resources (DNR), including Bohn Lake State Ice Age Trail Area/State Natural Area, Greenwood State Wildlife Area and Mecan River, Wedde Creek and Chaffee Creek State Fishery Areas. These public lands protect a wide range of plant communities, including wetlands, restored prairie and rare oak and pine barrens. Private landowners host Trail segments through handshake agreements or easements providing permanent Trail protection.

In southern Waushara County the eastern and western routes of the Ice Age National Scenic Trail "bifurcation" split (or rejoin, depending on hike direction). Currently, there are more Ice Age Trail segments completed along the eastern branch. The only completed segment on the western bifurcation route is in the city of Baraboo in Sauk County. Contact the Ice Age Trail Alliance for more information on the bifurcation.

Navigation note: hikers should be aware that many of the roads in Waushara County share the same name and differ only in the road "suffix" paired with the road name (e.g., Beechnut Dr., Beechnut Rd.; 7th Ave., 7th Ln., 7th Dr.).

CHAPTER INFORMATION

The Waushara County Chapter works to maintain current and build new Ice Age Trail segments. The chapter hosts several popular gatherings each year including a fall colors hike and a winter candlelight snowshoe hike.

COUNTY INFORMATION

Waushara County: www.co.waushara.wi.us

Overlooking Mecan Springs on the Mecan River Segment.

Waushara County

Deerfield Segment (Atlas Map 50f)

SNAPSHOT

3.7 miles: CTH-O to Beechnut Dr.

  This segment features well-managed oak woodlands, a trek along the crest of the Almond Moraine and a descent into a dramatic tunnel channel.

From a small kettle lake reachable via a blue-blazed spur trail.

Entire segment closed during gun deer season.

 Short blue-blazed spur trail to small kettle pond, white-blazed loop trail to additional parking area and other types of trails.

TRAIL ACCESS AND PARKING

CTH-O: *From I-39* take Exit 131 (Hancock) and follow CTH-V east 4.3 mi. Join CTH-B and go north 0.2 mi. Continue north on CTH-B for 1.3 mi (where CTH-V turns east) to CTH-O. At CTH-O turn right and go east 3.6 mi. *From Wautoma* take STH-73 north 6.7 mi to CTH-O. At CTH-O turn left and go west 0.4 mi. Roadside parking on the south side of the road.

Beechnut Dr: From I-39 take Exit 131 (Hancock) and follow CTH-V east 4.3 mi. Join CTH-B and go north 0.2 mi. At Beechnut Dr. (CTH-V) turn right and go east 0.5 mi. Where CTH-V turns north continue straight (east) on Beechnut Dr. for 0.2 mi. A Trail access kiosk and roadside parking are on the northeast corner. Be cautious of soft sand on the west side of the road and a sharp drop-off in front of the kiosk.

Additional Parking: Beechnut Dr. (**WS16**), 0.25 mi south then east on Beechnut Dr. from the Beechnut Dr.Trail access listed above. A white-blazed loop trail leads from the parking area to the segment.

THE HIKE

Private landowners are vital partners in the development and maintenance of this segment. The sustainable forestry practiced by the landowners who host this segment is on display in several red pine plantations that landowners have thinned to enable white pines to regenerate naturally in the forest understory. Landowners are also working to restore prairies along the route and have erected numerous bluebird houses. Hikers will also find many beautiful wildflowers and ripe blackberries in summer months.

From its starting point on CTH-O, the segment heads south and then west through hummocky, pitted outwash to 12th Avenue. After crossing the road, the segment ascends to the crest of the Almond Moraine. The segment intersects a variety of trails, including the Wagon Trail (**WS12**), a track laid down by stage-coaches that traveled regularly between Wautoma and Plainfield in the 19th century.

As it makes its way to its endpoint on Beechnut Drive, the segment descends dramatically into a tunnel channel with a deep kettle at the bottom. A 0.1-mile blue-blazed spur trail (**WS11**) leads to the kettle. Also, a half-mile white-blazed loop trail departs from the segment route and heads south to an alternative parking area on Beechnut Drive (**WS16**), then returns to the main segment a bit farther west. The main segment route continues northwest, ascending out of the tunnel channel to reach the Trail access on Beechnut Drive.

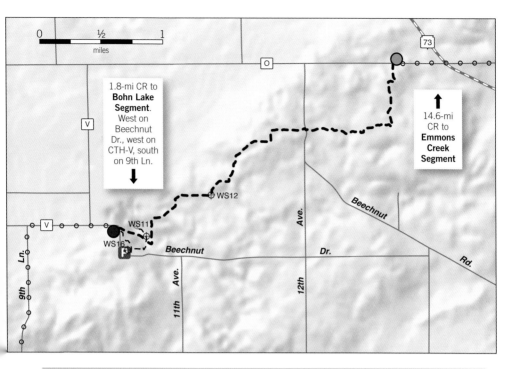

AREA SERVICES

Wild Rose: Restaurant, grocery store, convenience store, lodging, camping, library, medical care. From the CTH-O Trail access go west 5.7 mi to STH-22, then head north on STH-22 for 1.7 mi.

Hancock: See Bohn Lake Segment and Greenwood Segment, p. 167. From the CTH-O Trail access go west ~9 mi. Also see Trail Access and Parking directions, above.

Wautoma: See Mecan River Segment, p. 171. From the CTH-O Trail access go east then south 7.1 mi. Also see Trail Access and Parking directions, above.

Bohn Lake Segment and Greenwood Segment (Atlas Map 51f)

SNAPSHOT

Bohn Lake Segment—1.2 miles: 9th Ln. to CTH-B (9th Ave.)

1.5 mile Connecting Route

Greenwood Segment—4.7 miles (4.2 IAT, 0.5 CR): 9th Ave. to Bow String Dr.

  The **Bohn Lake Segment** explores a State Ice Age Trail Area featuring scenic, undeveloped Bohn Lake.

From Bohn Lake.

 At Hancock-area campgrounds 4.0 mi west (see Area Services).

Nearby Bohn Lake Accessible Hiking Trail.

The **Greenwood Segment** and its accompanying loop and spur trails feature deep kettles, restored prairies and oak savannas.

No reliable sources of water.

At Hancock-area campgrounds ~4 mi west (see Area Services).

By law, dogs must be leashed April 15 to July 31 in the State Wildlife Area.

 Road walk along Brown Deer Ct.

 Two blue-blazed spur trails and the white-blazed kettle loop.

TRAIL ACCESS AND PARKING

9th Ln.: From I-39 take Exit 131 (Hancock) and follow CTH-V east 4.4 mi. At CTH-B turn left and continue north on CTH-V/CTH-B 0.2 mi. Turn right and continue on CTH-V east 0.8 mi. At 9th Ln. turn right and go south 1.0 mi. The Trail access (no parking) is on the west side of the road.

Bow String Dr.: From I-39 take Exit 124 (Coloma) and follow STH-21 east 1.4 mi. At 6th Ave. turn left and go north 2.6 mi. At Buttercup Dr. turn right and go east 0.6 mi. At 6th Lane turn left and go north 0.4 mi. At Bow String Dr. turn left to the Trail access on the north side of the road. Roadside parking.

Additional Parking: (i) Bohn Lake Segment Accessible Hiking Trail parking area on the west side of 9th Dr., 0.4 mi. north of CTH-B/CTH-C. (ii) CTH-B (9th Ave.) parking area. (iii) CTH-GG Trail access; roadside parking. (iv) 7th Dr./Brown Deer Ct. Trail access (**WS10**); roadside parking. (v) Brown Deer Ct. parking area on the north side of the road. (vi) 7th Ave. Greenwood Wildlife Area parking area.

THE HIKE

The **Bohn Lake Segment** traverses the Bohn Lake State Ice Age Trail Area (SIATA) and features a wild lake that is part of a 14-mile-long glacial tunnel channel. The tunnel channel was created by a meltwater river flowing beneath glacial ice whose outlet was where the village of Hancock stands today. The lake basins along and within the tunnel, such as Bohn Lake and Fish Lake, were created from buried blocks of ice left behind when the tunnel collapsed. The northwest part of the property contains a portion of an end moraine. The property is designated as Bohn Lake State Natural Area due to natural values that include an undeveloped 13-acre hard water seepage lake, mature oak forest and an unbroken lake edge that varies considerably in width due to water levels that fluctuate with seasonal low and high water events and from varying water table depths. The land is a mix of wetland, oak forest and open fields.

Mobile Skills Crew project site, 2007

In 2009, Waushara County Chapter volunteers, the Operating Engineers Local 139, local high school students and community volunteers contributed their time, labor and equipment to create the Bohn Lake Accessible Hiking Trail. The "all access" quarter-mile route offers a compacted crushed-stone surface with minimal grade to a scenic view of Bohn Lake. Those who explore the trail will meander through wildflowers and woods to relax on a handsomely crafted log bench at the lookout point which includes an interpretive panel explaining the creation of kettle lakes.

The Bohn Lake Segment ends at CTH-B (9th Avenue). From here hikers should turn left and hike 1.5 miles south on CTH-B (9th Avenue) to the Greenwood Segment.

The **Greenwood Segment** is located between two major meltwater tunnel channels. To the south of the segment is the Mecan River tunnel channel. To

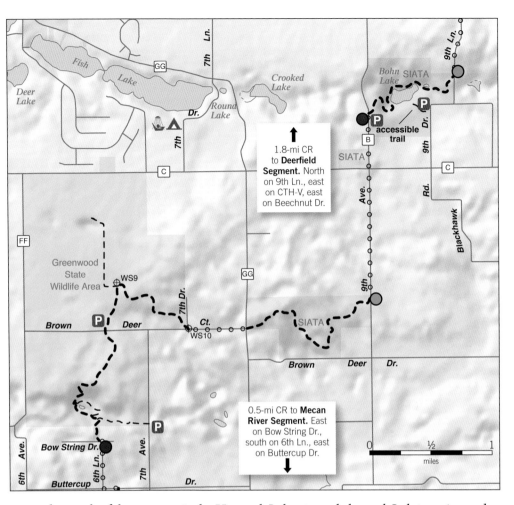

1.8-mi CR to **Deerfield Segment.** North on 9th Ln., east on CTH-V, east on Beechnut Dr.

accessible trail

0.5-mi CR to **Mecan River Segment.** East on Bow String Dr., south on 6th Ln., east on Buttercup Dr.

0   ½   1
miles

the north of the segment is the Hancock Lakes tunnel channel. In late spring and early summer, many of the grassy openings throughout the segment are carpeted in blue lupine creating a welcome environment for the endangered Karner blue butterfly.

From its starting point at 9th Avenue, the segment heads west through pitted outwash of the Almond Moraine. A mixed forest of stately oaks and various other woodland species keeps this portion of the segment shaded. The segment meanders along rolling hills and ridges with views of deep kettles. George and Lois Siler and family generously gifted 80 acres of land over which this portion of the segment passes.

Upon reaching CTH-GG hikers will cross the road and head west on a connecting route, following Brown Deer Court west for 0.5 miles. At 7th Drive hikers should turn right and head north for a few yards to re-connect with the Trail (**WS10**). Here the segment leaves the road and continues northwest into the rolling terrain of the Greenwood State Wildlife Area.

Soon the segment arrives at Pine Tree Point (**WS9**) where hikers can enjoy a panoramic view of an open prairie edged by oak savanna while putting up their feet on the beautifully crafted (and very comfortable) log couch and ottoman tucked under the shady pines. The restored prairie is one square mile (the largest in Waushara County) and features bottle gentian, blazing star, leadplant and prairie willow.

From Pine Tree Point, the Kettle Trail, a blue-blazed spur trail, heads west then north through the prairie for 0.7 miles (one-way) to an impressive, open view of an entire 78-foot dry glacial kettle.

The segment continues southwest from Pine Tree Point along the edge of the Almond Moraine. During the spring of 2011 a tornado touched down here uprooting hundreds of trees, temporarily closing the Trail. A hiker can observe how the area is now naturally regenerating. South of Brown Deer Court the segment heads southeast, taking hikers a short distance back from the moraine's outer edge. The segment continues southwest and then west before dropping down toward a 200-foot-deep glacial kettle that was likely part of a tunnel channel running out to the Hancock Moraine several miles west. The narrow banana-shaped kettle is almost a mile long and has four separate ponds in the bottom. A white-blazed loop trail weaves along the north and east ridge overlooking the ponds at the bottom of the kettle and rejoins the segment on the south side of the kettle. A short distance farther from where the white-blazed loop reconnects, a blue-blazed spur trail heads east to the 7th Avenue parking area. From the junction with the blue-blazed spur, the segment heads south to its endpoint on Bow String Drive.

Mobile Skills Crew project site, 2010, 2011, 2013

AREA SERVICES

Hancock: Restaurant, convenience store, lodging, camping, library. From the CTH-B Trail access, go north on CTH-B for 1.1 mi. At CTH-V turn left and go west 3.9 mi. Trail supporter at Samsel's Sawshop, Millwork and Tree Farm (800-699-3793, samselsawmill.com). INN Style program lodging at the Walker House (715-249-3100, walkerhousewi.com). Camping at Hancock Village Campground (715-249-5521) and Tomorrow Wood Campground (715-249-5954, tomorrowwood.com). Library has limited hours.

Coloma: See Mecan River Segment, p. 171. From the Bow String Dr. Trail access go south then west 5.6 mi. Also see Trail Access and Parking directions, above.

Wautoma: See Mecan River Segment, p. 171. From the Bow String Dr. Trail access go south then east ~14 mi.

Mecan River Segment (Atlas Map 52f)

SNAPSHOT

7.2 miles (6.8 IAT, 0.4 CR: Buttercup Dr. to STH-21

> **Note:** It is anticipated that volunteers will build a new section of Trail in 2014 south of STH-21. The new route is shown as "Future Trail" on the accompanying map. Check with the Ice Age Trail Alliance (800-227-0046, iceagetrail.org) for more details.

 This segment traverses a variety of natural communities from wetland to grassland to forest and includes outstanding views of the Mecan Springs and Mecan River.

 From the Mecan River.

 A Dispersed Camping Area (**WS14**) south of Buttercup Dr.

Portion of the segment crossing private land between CTH-GG and 9th Ave. is closed during gun deer season.

 Road walk along 9th Ave.

 Blue-blazed spur trail (**WS6**) to Mecan River vista.

TRAIL ACCESS AND PARKING

Buttercup Dr.: From I-39 take Exit 124 (Coloma) and follow STH-21 east 1.4 mi. At 6th Ave. turn left and go north 2.6 mi. At Buttercup Dr. turn right and go east 0.8 mi to the parking area on the south side of the road.

STH-21: From I-39 Exit 124 at Coloma, take STH-21 east 4.0 mi to the parking area on the north side of STH-21 between 9th Ave. and the Mecan River.

Additional Parking: (i) 6th Ln. parking area. (ii) CTH-GG roadside parking. (iii) 9th Ave. DNR parking areas located 0.6 and 0.8 mi north of STH-21.

THE HIKE

From its starting point at the parking area on Buttercup Drive, the segment heads south on a grass-and-dirt access road. The segment then heads west through a pine plantation, where one of the Waushara County Chapter's signature log benches (**WS14**) offers a shady respite. A signed spur trail leads to a nearby Dispersed Camping Area for long-distance hikers. The segment continues through a State Ice Age Trail Area property that contains rolling hills with steep slopes and scenic panoramas of the rural farm countryside. The property is a mix of pine plantations, upland woods and grasslands. As the segment makes its way south toward Chicago Road, it passes through a large, open field where whitetail deer are often spotted at dawn and dusk.

South of Chicago Road the segment heads into the Mecan River headwaters area and intersects an outstanding example of a tunnel channel. The channel extends west several miles through the Almond Moraine to the edge of the Hancock Moraine. As it bends around the western edge and then southern edge the segment offers outstanding views of the Mecan Springs more than a hundred feet below. Many migratory and wetland birds visit the area including sandhill cranes, northern bobwhite quail, red-shouldered hawks and bald eagles.

The segment bends south away from the springs, crosses CTH-GG and con-

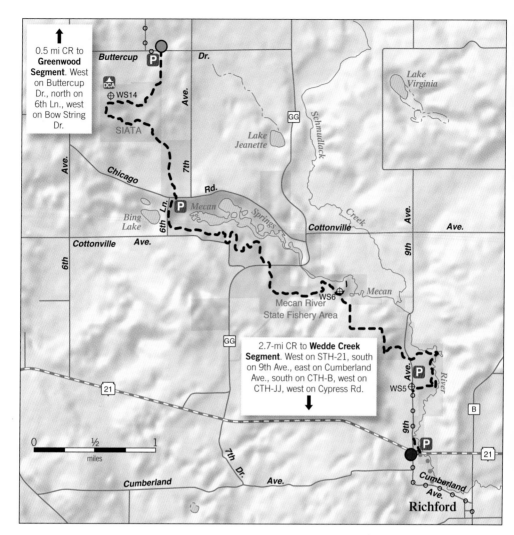

0.5 mi CR to **Greenwood Segment**. West on Buttercup Dr., north on 6th Ln., west on Bow String Dr.

2.7-mi CR to **Wedde Creek Segment**. West on STH-21, south on 9th Ave., east on Cumberland Ave., south on CTH-B, west on CTH-JJ, west on Cypress Rd.

tinues south and east for a short distance before arriving at a spot above the banks of the Mecan River, renowned as one of the finest trout streams in central Wisconsin. A little farther on, a rewarding side trip on the blue-blazed Mecan Vista Trail (**WS6**) offers views of the Mecan River.

The segment departs from the Mecan River State Fishery Area briefly and passes over the Wisconsin Operating Engineer training grounds. For safety's sake, hikers should stay on the Trail to avoid the heavy equipment operated on the grounds.

As it approaches 9th Avenue, the segment re-enters the fishery area property. Hikers will cross through a recent timber harvest area, part of an oak regeneration project. East of 9th Avenue the segment hits another recent pine timber harvest area. Pay close attention to Trail signage in these logged areas.

From 9th Avenue the segment continues past rock piles cleared from pioneer farmers' fields and through deciduous forest and openings of prairie and wetlands along the river. The segment bends back to the west and passes through a pine plantation before emerging back onto 9th Avenue (**WS5**). Here, hikers should turn left and walk south 0.4 miles along the road. The segment then leaves the road again, heading southeast along the river for a short distance before reaching the segment's terminus at the STH-21 parking area.

Volunteers are planning to build a new section of Trail in 2014 between STH-21 and Cumberland Avenue. Included in this new section will be a 32-foot-long bridge and 70-foot-long boardwalk to span wet areas.

Mobile Skills Crew project site, 2003, 2010, 2014

AREA SERVICES

Richford: Restaurant, lodging. From the intersection of STH-21 and 9th Ave., go south on 9th Ave. 0.2 mi then south and east on Cumberland Ave. for 0.6 mi. INN Style program lodging at Mecan River House B&B (call first, 715-228-3283). Lodging at Mecan River Inn (N1264 CTH-B, Coloma, 866-322-6466 or 715-228-2555, mecanriverinn.net). Meals at Johann's Bar & Grill across from the Mecan River Inn.

Coloma: Restaurant, grocery store, convenience store, lodging, camping, library. From the STH-21 Trail access go west 4.0 mi on STH-21. Lodging at the Coloma Hotel (715-228-2401, colomahotel.com) and Caribou Bay Retreat (920-716-5918, cariboubayretreat.com).

Wautoma: Restaurant, grocery store, convenience store, lodging, camping, library, medical care. From the STH-21 Trail access go east ~10 mi on STH-21.

Hancock: See Bohn Lake Segment and Greenwood Segment, p. 167. From Buttercup Dr. Trail access go west then north ~6 mi.

Students from Coloma Elementary School enjoying the Bohn Lake Segment.

Wedde Creek Segment and Chaffee Creek Segment (Atlas Map 52f)

SNAPSHOT

Wedde Creek Segment—1.2 miles: Cypress Rd. to Czech Ave.

0.7 mi Connecting Route

Chaffee Creek Segment—2.5 miles: Czech Ave. to I-39 Southbound Wayside

  *The short **Wedde Creek Segment** passes through oak woodlands and highlights quiet Wedde Creek.*

 From Wedde Creek.

Portion of the segment overlaps with a snowmobile trail.

Short spur trail to parking area.

  *The **Chaffee Creek Segment** highlights savannas, meadows and a charming creek and offers highway travelers a good spot to stretch their legs.*

At the Interstate 39 wayside.

From Chaffee Creek.

Short blue-blazed spur trail (**WS1**) to 6th Ave. parking area.

TRAIL ACCESS AND PARKING

Cypress Rd.: From I-39 take Exit 124 (Coloma) and follow STH-21 east 4.9 mi. At CTH-B turn right and go south 0.7 mi. At CTH-JJ turn right and go southwest 1.5 mi. At Cypress Rd. turn right and go west 0.1 mi. Roadside parking.

I-39 Southbound Wayside: From Coloma on I-39, go south 3.5 mi and exit at the highway wayside at Mile Marker 120. The Trail access is at the kiosk on the west end of the wayside.

Additional Parking: (i) Czech Ave. parking area 0.3 mi east of the Wedde Creek Segment Czech Ave. Trail access. A short spur trail leads north to the Ice Age Trail. (ii) 6th Ave. cul-de-sac. A blue-blazed spur trail leads 0.2 mi south to the Ice Age Trail.

THE HIKE

From its starting point on Cypress Road the **Wedde Creek Segment** heads south through hardwood forest and a prairie restoration area to a crossing on a wooden bridge of the South Branch of Wedde Creek. Shortly before crossing the creek, the segment intersects with a snowmobile trail and shares this trail for about 0.4 miles. The segment follows a ridge above the south side of the creek for a short distance before heading south and then west along the crest of a small end moraine. As the segment continues, hikers should look for a large erratic in an oak opening south of the Trail. The segment intersects with a spur trail that leads south to a parking area on Czech Avenue, then continues west through conifer forests and oak barrens to the segment's endpoint on Czech Avenue, a short distance west of the parking area.

To reach the next segment, hikers should head 0.7 mi west on a connecting route along Czech Avenue.

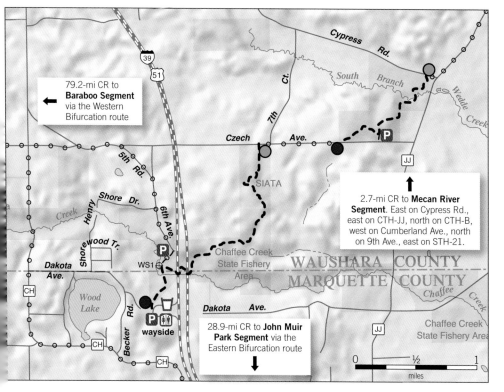

79.2-mi CR to **Baraboo Segment** via the Western Bifurcation route

2.7-mi CR to **Mecan River** Segment. East on Cypress Rd., east on CTH-JJ, north on CTH-B, west on Cumberland Ave., north on 9th Ave., east on STH-21.

28.9-mi CR to **John Muir** Park Segment via the Eastern Bifurcation route

WAUSHARA COUNTY
MARQUETTE COUNTY

From Czech Avenue, the **Chaffee Creek Segment** heads south on a narrow strip between two agricultural fields. As it makes its way southwest toward the Chaffee Creek valley the segment passes several trailside kettles while passing through grassy meadows and savanna woodlands.

The segment arrives at Chaffee Creek and continues west under I-39. A short distance west of the I-39 underpass the segment arrives at a T-intersection (**WS1**). A blue-blazed spur trail heads north from the intersection 0.2 miles to the 6th Avenue cul-de-sac.

The segment heads south from the intersection, crosses Chaffee Creek and passes through Upper Chaffee Creek Meadow, one of three units of the Upper Fox Headwaters State Natural Area. The unit recognizes the unique flora that grow in the Chaffee Creek valley including wet-mesic prairie, wetland fen complex and sedge meadow. The area boasts over 100 native plants species. Prairie grasses include big and little bluestem, blue-joint grass and slender wheat grass.

Continuing south beyond the meadow the segment reaches its endpoint at an Ice Age Trail kiosk in the I-39 southbound wayside.

AREA SERVICES

Coloma: See Mecan River Segment, p. 171. From the Cypress Rd. Trail access go northwest ~7 mi. Also see Trail Access and Parking directions, above.

Richford: See Mecan River Segment, p. 171. From the Cypress Rd. Trail access go east and north ~2 mi.

Wautoma: See Mecan River Segment, p. 171. From the Cypress Rd. Trail access go east and north ~12 mi.

Marquette County

Trail miles: 1.7
Connecting route miles: 30.8

Marquette County was entirely covered by the Green Bay Lobe. The region is often referred to as the central sands of Wisconsin. The county is mostly undeveloped, with pine and oak forests and extensive grass marshes. The mucky-peat soils of these marshes owe their origin to two major geologic events. The glacier ice, advancing across east central Wisconsin, gouged out the original basins. Then water from the melting glaciers transformed them into lake basins. The lake basins were sandy along the beach areas, but the deep-water areas had fine water-sorted deposits. As the climate warmed, vegetation started to encroach upon the water areas. Over the last 10,000 years, sedges and marsh grasses slowly replaced the water areas. The wet environment of the marsh inhibits the decomposition of these plant remains, so it accumulates. The organic soils we see today are simply centuries of decayed plant residues. Each winter, another layer of dead plants is added. Research on bogs in Wisconsin shows that these organic soils form at a rate of one inch every 40 years. One marsh in the area has an organic layer up to nine feet thick.

John Muir, known as the father of America's National Parks, grew up on a farm near Fountain Lake, now called Ennis Lake and the site of a national historic landmark, state natural area and county park. Although the county has few off-road Ice Age Trail miles on the ground, it has plenty of places of interest to explore, such as Page Creek Marsh State Natural Area and Observatory Hill State Natural Area.

The National Park Service, Wisconsin Department of Natural Resources and Marquette County have started the planning process for determining the future Ice Age Trail corridor through the county. It will be several years before the Ice Age Trail corridor will be determined.

CHAPTER INFORMATION

The Marquette County Chapter focuses on (i) supporting IATA activities, Trail maintenance and advocacy for the Ice Age Trail corridor planning process; (ii) building outdoor family traditions by planning a variety of Trail-related events and (iii) developing relationships with community organizations with interests in health, conservation and preservation. The chapter has created the *John Muir Park Ice Age Trail Guide* that enhances a hiker's experience in the park. It is available from the Marquette County Chapter's home page on the IATA website.

Marquette County Visitor Information: 888-318-0362, www.co.marquette.
wi.us

John Muir Park Segment.

John Muir Park Segment (Atlas Map 56f)

SNAPSHOT

1.7 miles: Within John Muir Memorial County Park

 This segment highlights the boyhood playground of John Muir, "Father of the National Parks."

From Ennis Lake.

In John Muir Memorial County Park. Restrooms are seasonal.

Numerous side trails leading to the lake or the tops of small hills.

TRAIL ACCESS AND PARKING

John Muir Memorial County Park: From Portage, take STH-33 north. At CTH-F turn left and continue north 9.5 mi. The park is located on the east side of the road and has a large parking area.

THE HIKE

This segment is a short loop that features views of picturesque Ennis Lake and passes through prairie and meadows that fill with wildflowers in the summer, bogs crossed by boardwalks, open oak forests and fens bordered by tamarack and bog birch. On this segment hikers will explore and experience the land that made such a positive and lifelong impression on John Muir. Trailside benches offer hikers the chance to enjoy views of the lake and contemplate the rich history of the area.

The segment can be hiked by heading either north or south from the park's parking area. The segment encircles the lake passing through the 150-acre Muir Park State Natural Area. The 30-acre lake is a spring-fed kettle occupying a marshy pocket in ground moraine. The park includes land that was homesteaded in 1849 by the Ennis and Muir families and was the boyhood home of John Muir, eminent naturalist and founder of the Sierra Club. The lake was then known as Fountain Lake and the Muirs lived on the northeast side of the lake from 1849 to 1856. Although he traveled all over the world, John Muir never forgot this land and tried several times to buy and preserve it. He said, "Even if I should never see it again, the beauty of its lilies and orchids is so pressed into my mind, I shall always enjoy looking back at them in imagination, even across the seas and continents and perhaps after I am dead."

Many unusual and rare plants can be found in the park; a guide showing plant communities along the loop is available on the Marquette County Chapter's home page on the IATA website (**marquette.iceagetrail.org**). On the south end of the lake, the segment crosses a low prairie which grades into a spongy sedge meadow and tall scrub community. Present here are big bluestem, Indian grass, blazing-star and prairie phlox. The bog near the lake's southeast corner offers the right environs for the northern wet forest dominated by tamarack, poison sumac and bog birch, with numerous pitcher plants beneath. Along the segment are a wet-mesic prairie, oak openings and a southern dry forest. Several side trails lead

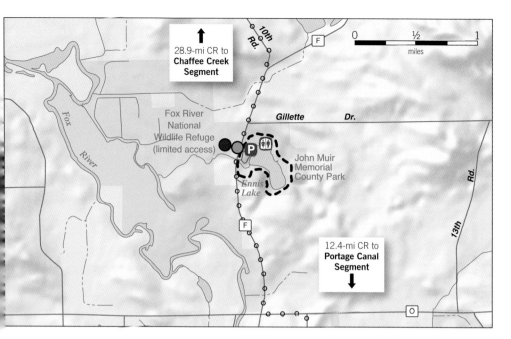

to the lakeside or to the tops of small hills. Board bridges cross rich fens that surround the lake's eastern inlet and western outlet. The calcareous fen and prairie contain a diversity of unusual and rare species such as grass-of-Parnassus, Kalm's lobelia, bottle gentian and nodding lady's-tresses orchid. Rare plants include small fringed gentian, low nut-sedge, prairie flameflower and false asphodel.

Several memorials to John Muir exist in the Park: a granite monument, a wooden sign and an extensive informational display near the parking area. There is also an exhibit on his life at the Montello Museum (55 West Montello Street). But the park itself is likely the best memorial to the man; hikers can literally walk in Muir's footsteps and see a landscape that has changed little since he lived here more than a century and a half ago.

POINTS OF INTEREST

Observatory Hill State Natural Area: From John Muir Memorial Park, head north on CTH-F for 0.1 mi. Turn right on Gillette Dr. and go east 2.0 mi. Turn left on 13th Rd. and go north 1.0 mi. Turn right on Gillette Ave. and go east 0.6 mi to the parking area (dnr.wi.gov/topic/lands/naturalareas/index. asp?sna=223).

The highest point in Marquette County, Observatory Hill rises 300 feet above the surrounding landscape. On the exposed rocks at the summit are polished rock surfaces with grooves, striations, and chatter marks created by the passage of the glacial ice 12,000 years ago. The hill was a favorite childhood haunt of John Muir.

AREA SERVICES

Montello: Restaurant, grocery store, convenience store, lodging, library, medical care. From John Muir Memorial County Park, go north on CTH-F 7.8 mi. At STH-22 (Main St.) turn left and continue north for 0.8 mi. Area info available from the Montello Area Chamber of Commerce (888-318-0362, montellowi.com).

Portage: See Portage Canal Segment, p. 184. From John Muir Memorial County Park go south ~10 mi. Also see Trail Access and Parking directions, above.

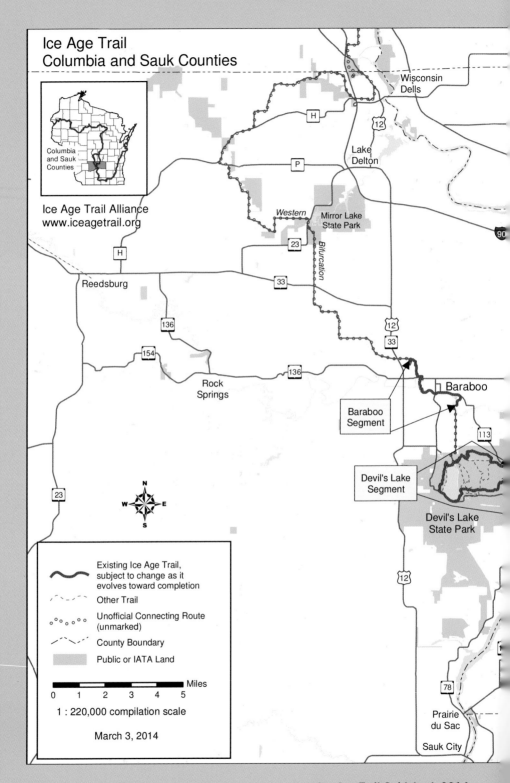

Ice Age Trail
Columbia and Sauk Counties

Columbia
and Sauk
Counties

Ice Age Trail Alliance
www.iceagetrail.org

Wisconsin
Dells

Lake
Delton

Western

Mirror Lake
State Park

Bifurcation

Reedsburg

Rock
Springs

Baraboo

Baraboo
Segment

Devil's Lake
Segment

Devil's Lake
State Park

Prairie
du Sac

Sauk City

Existing Ice Age Trail,
subject to change as it
evolves toward completion

Other Trail

Unofficial Connecting Route
(unmarked)

County Boundary

Public or IATA Land

Miles
0   1   2   3   4   5

1 : 220,000 compilation scale

March 3, 2014

Sauk & Columbia Counties

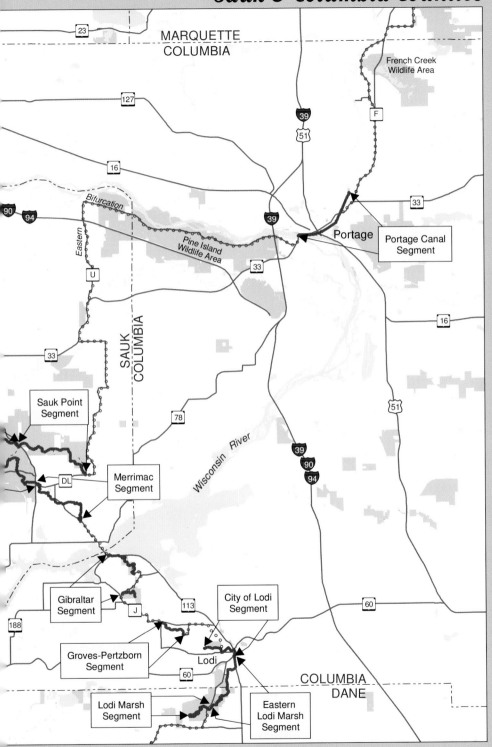

French Creek
Wildlife Area

Portage

Portage Canal
Segment

MARQUETTE
COLUMBIA

Bifurcation

Eastern

Pine Island
Wildlife Area

SAUK
COLUMBIA

Wisconsin River

Sauk Point
Segment

Merrimac
Segment

DL

Gibraltar
Segment

City of Lodi
Segment

Groves-Pertzborn
Segment

Lodi

COLUMBIA
DANE

Lodi Marsh
Segment

Eastern
Lodi Marsh
Segment

Sauk & Columbia Counties

Northern Columbia County

Trail miles: 2.9
Connecting route miles: 14.7

The Green Bay Lobe covered nearly all of Columbia County during the Wisconsin Glaciation. When the ice sheet receded, the Green Bay Lobe left behind the Fox River, one of the few rivers in Wisconsin that flows northward. The Fox River empties into Lake Winnebago and then Green Bay. From there the waters eventually flow through the Great Lakes and out the St. Lawrence River to the north Atlantic. North of the Wisconsin River, the Ice Age Trail traverses low, rolling topography with large, open wetlands, grasslands and forested woodlots. Portage lies on a large outwash plain deposited by the Wisconsin River. The Ice Age Trail winds its way through the city of Portage, highlighting the history of the area and the Portage Canal. The Portage Canal Segment is dotted with historical sites including the Portage Canal and locks and the Historic Indian Agency House.

The Ice Age Trail route in the northern part of the county is yet to be determined. Currently the connecting route (see map on p. 181) highlights the Fox River and French Creek State Wildlife Area.

CHAPTER INFORMATION

The Heritage Trail Chapter works with the City of Portage, Boy Scouts and local agencies to build and maintain the Trail. It is called the "Heritage" Trail Chapter because the Ice Age Trail blends and highlights the area's cultural, natural and glacial history.

COUNTY INFORMATION

Columbia County Visitor Bureau: 608-742-6161, travelcolumbiacounty.net

Portage Canal Segment.

Northern Columbia County

Portage Canal Segment (Atlas Map 57f)

2.9 miles: Agency House Rd. to STH-33 Wisconsin River Bridge

 This segment takes hikers through one of Wisconsin's most historically significant communities.

 At the Historic Indian Agency House (when open), nearby Veteran's Memorial Fields/Columbia County Fairgrounds and Pauquette Park (seasonal).

 At the Historic Indian Agency House (when open), Veteran's Memorial Fields/Columbia County Fairgrounds, Riverside Park (seasonal) and Pauquette Park (seasonal).

 From the Fox River.

 Hikers will not have any interaction with hunting on this segment.

At nearby Veteran's Memorial Fields/Columbia County Fairgrounds.

Segment overlaps Portage Canal Bike Path.

 At Pauquette Park and Riverside Park.

 Wisconsin River Levee Trail.

 At Pauquette Park and Veteran's Memorial Fields/Columbia County Fairgrounds.

 Portions of this segment may be suitable for those using wheelchairs or similar devices.

TRAIL ACCESS AND PARKING

Agency House Rd.: From I-39 exit onto STH-33 and follow it east through Portage to the east side of town. Turn left and follow Agency House Rd. north to the parking area.

STH-33 Wisconsin River Bridge: From I-39 exit onto STH-33 east and cross the Wisconsin River. Trail access is in a grassy area on the east side of the road right after crossing the bridge. No parking. Park at Pauquette Park on the west side of STH-33.

Additional Parking: (i) Parking area on the east bank of the Portage Canal. Entrance located on the north side of STH-33. (ii) Veteran's Memorial Fields/Columbia County Fairgrounds. (iii) Riverside Park.

THE HIKE

This segment's name is inspired by the area's compelling history. The City of Portage is located between the Wisconsin River flowing toward the Mississippi and eventually the Gulf of Mexico and the Fox River flowing toward Lake Michigan and ultimately the Atlantic Ocean. The easy canoe portage here between the rivers was an important transportation route to Native Americans, French explorers and fur trappers moving between the Great Lakes and the Mississippi basin with access up the Missouri River to the northern plains. Construction on the now historic Portage canal began in 1838. Although boats used the canal from the early 1850s, the canal was not finished until 1876 when the Army Corps of Engineers completed construction. Boats used the canal until 1951 when the locks were permanently closed. The peak use of the Canal occurred in 1908 for recreational boat traffic.

The segment starts on the west side of the Portage Canal at the Agency House Rd. Trail access parking area. The Historic Indian Agency House (**agencyhouse. org**), listed on the National Historic Registry, is just to the southwest of the parking area on Agency House Road. Built in 1832, it is one of Wisconsin's earliest homes built for European settlers. The U.S. government constructed it as a residence for John Kinzie, the first Indian agent to the Ho-Chunk tribe. Over the years, the Agency House has also been used as a tavern, trading post and boarding house. The Kinzies' granddaughter was Juliette Gordon Low, founder of the Girl Scouts.

From the Trail access parking area, hikers will cross a footbridge and walk on a flat, wide, packed-gravel path that follows along the east bank of the Portage Canal for about three-quarters of a mile to another Trail parking area, just north of STH-33, that includes benches and a kiosk. From this parking area, the Fort Winnebago Surgeon's Quarters (**fortwinnebagosurgeonsquarters.org**) is a 0.5-mile side trip northeast on STH-33. The Surgeon's Quarters is the only remaining building of Fort Winnebago, a National Historic Landmark (1828–1845). Among other functions, the fort protected traffic crossing the Fox–Wisconsin portage.

Hikers should head south under the STH-33 bridge and continue along the canal to another underpass, this one of an active railway. The boardwalk under this second underpass can be very slippery when wet. The segment continues briefly through woods bordering the canal and then emerges onto a mowed area. After passing behind a large yellow metal building, hikers should immediately turn left out to Mullett Street (**NC2**).

The segment follows Mullett Street southwest to a 3-way intersection with Dodge and Thompson Streets. Hikers should turn right on Thompson Street and shortly rejoin the now-restored Portage Canal, turning left along a bike trail

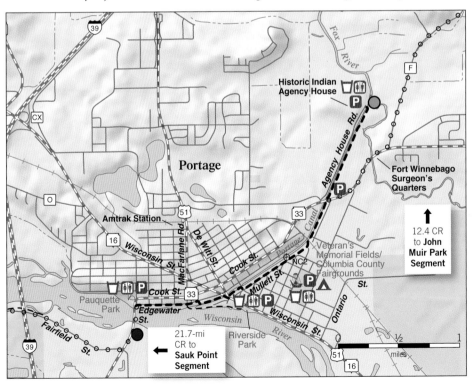

beside the canal that passes by the historic wooden feed mill which was initially constructed in 1862. Upon reaching busy Wisconsin Avenue (USH-51), hikers should cross using the marked crosswalks and then rejoin the bike path next to the canal. The segment passes the Wisconsin River lock, jogs to the right on Lock Street and then follows Edgewater Street to the left.

Along the way the segment passes 506 Edgewater Street, a large white Greek Revival style house built in 1906 by Pulitzer Prize winning author Zona Gale. Her study and other exhibits on local history can be seen nearby at the Museum at the Portage (**portagemuseum.org**) located about half a mile off the Trail at 804 MacFarlane Road in a house where the author lived after her marriage. Historian Fredrick Jackson Turner also called Portage home.

The segment ends at a Trail access sign in a grassy area near the STH-33 Wisconsin River bridge. Across STH-33 is Pauquette Park. The park is named after Pierre Pauquette, an agent for the American Fur Company, who operated a ferry and trading post at the site between the mid-1820s and 1834.

AREA SERVICES

Portage: Restaurant, grocery store, convenience store, general shopping, lodging, camping, library and medical care. On Trail. Most services on USH-51/STH-16/Wisconsin St. and on STH-33. Camping, water, restrooms and showers at Veteran's Memorial Fields/Columbia County Fairgrounds (608-742-2178, portagewi.gov; available during nonevent weekends and weekdays). From the Trail route on Mullett St. take Griffith St. 3 blocks southeast. It is located between Superior St. and Wauona Trail. For area info, contact the Portage Area Chamber of Commerce (608-742-6242 or 800-474-2525, portagewi.com). Train service at the Portage Amtrak Station (400 W. Oneida St., 800-872-7245, amtrak. com), an unstaffed station consisting of a small waiting room with no station services.

The great memories and amazing people that combine to make
the numerous highs of my trip are far too many to name. I believe
the only way to truly understand the magnitude of the peaks and
valleys during the trip is to embark on a journey of your own.

PAUL BIRRITTELLA, ICE AGE TRAIL THOUSAND-MILER

Northern Columbia County

Sauk County

Trail miles: 22.3
Connecting route miles: 19.1

The Baraboo Hills are the dominant feature of the Ice Age Trail in Sauk County. Formed 1.6 billion years ago, the hills rise 500 feet above the surrounding landscape. The Green Bay Lobe covered the eastern half of the Baraboo Hills and deposited the end moraine to create Devil's Lake. To the north and south of the Baraboo Hills, the Ice Age Trail crosses glacial outwash plains and small moraines.

Devil's Lake State Park is one of the Ice Age National Scientific Reserve units and the Ice Age Trail winds through the park and around the lake. A combination of interesting geology, diverse fauna, prehistoric effigy mounds, historic Civilian Conservation Corps (CCC) buildings and spectacular scenery make Devil's Lake a popular destination. Parfrey's Glen State Natural Area (SNA 1) anchors the current Ice Age Trail route in the county to the east of Devil's Lake State Park. The state recognizes several other designated State Natural Areas within in the park, including East Bluff (SNA 98), Devil's Lake Oak Forest (SNA 27) and South Bluff/Devil's Nose (SNA 97). The name "Devil's Lake" is a mistranslation from several different Native American names for the lake, which was believed to be the abode of good and evil spirits.

In Devil's Lake State Park the two branches of Ice Age Trail's bifurcation, which had split in Waushara County, reunite (or split depending on hike direction). The western branch arrives after passing through the lakebed of Glacial Lake Wisconsin, the Wisconsin Dells, Mirror Lake and Baraboo. The eastern branch, with more established segments of the Ice Age Trail at this time, arrives after passing through Marquette County, the city of Portage and Pine Island State Wildlife Area. Contact the Ice Age Trail Alliance for more information on the bifurcation.

CHAPTER INFORMATION

The Baraboo Hills Chapter works to develop, maintain and protect the Ice Age Trail in Sauk County. The chapter also promotes the use of the Trail for education and recreation. Throughout the year, it hosts monthly outings, including hiking, biking, cross-country skiing and canoeing. The Lodi Valley and Baraboo Hills chapters of the Ice Age Trail Alliance have partnered to create the "Glacial Drifters" hiking award program. Participants in the program will earn an award for hiking all of the approximately 50 miles of the Ice Age Trail and connecting route roadwalks within these two chapters' areas, with the hiking to be done on each individual's own timetable. Registered participants will be sent maps and information about each of the various segments along with a hiking log for tracking progress.

COUNTY INFORMATION

Sauk County Tourism Information: co.sauk.wi.us (click on "Community" then "Visiting" for tourist info)

Prairie on the Merrimac Segment, with the bluffs of Devil's Lake State Park on the horizon.

Sauk County

Baraboo Segment (Atlas Map 60f)

4.0 miles: UW-Baraboo/Sauk County to Effinger Rd. at Manchester St.

 This "Trail Town" segment shows off the Baraboo River along a network of city parks and includes a stop at Circus World Museum.

 On the UW-Baraboo/Sauk County Campus, and seasonally at Ochsner Park and Zoo, Attridge Park, Mary Roundtree Park and Broadway Park.

 From the Baraboo River.

At several of the city parks. Restroom also available at UW-Baraboo/Sauk County Campus.

 Segment is entirely in the city of Baraboo.

 By law, dogs must be leashed in city parks.

 Portions follow sidewalks or roads and the Baraboo Riverwalk. The Riverwalk is also open to bikes.

 Other trails in some city parks.

 Portions of this segment may be suitable for those using wheelchairs or similar devices.

TRAIL ACCESS AND PARKING

UW-Baraboo/Sauk County: From I-90/94 take Exit 92 and follow USH-12E south 6.0 mi. At Terrytown Rd. turn left and go east 0.4 mi. At Fox Hills Rd./Connie Rd. turn right and go south 0.2 mi. Enter UW-Baraboo/Sauk County parking area on east side of road. Trail access is at the north end of the parking area at a kiosk.

Effinger Rd. at Manchester St.: From I-90/94 Exit 106 for STH-33 Baraboo/Portage. Take STH-33 west 11.9 mi. At Washington St. turn left and go south 0.6 mi. At Water St. (STH-113) turn left and go east less than 0.1 mi. At Effinger Rd. turn right and go south 0.4 mi to its intersection with Manchester St. The Trail access is on the northwest corner of the intersection. No parking.

Additional Parking: (i) Ochsner Park and Zoo. (ii) Attridge Park. (iii) Lower Ochsner Park. (iv) Mary Roundtree Park. (v) Broadway Park.

THE HIKE

From its starting point at the UW-Baraboo/Sauk County parking area the segment follows a ridge with fine views toward the Baraboo Range and passes through campus property featuring mixed hardwoods, remnant prairie and oak savanna. The segment passes through the campus's disc golf course and then bends south, skirting athletic fields for area schools, passing through Baraboo High School's Parking area and then intersecting with Berkeley Boulevard.

The segment heads east then south a short distance on Berkeley Boulevard, then continues east on 9th Avenue for 0.2 miles. At Draper Street the segment turns south, crosses 8th Avenue (Ringling Boulevard/STH-33) and continues through a wooded area in Ochsner Park and Zoo, then down steep stone stairs to an intersection with the Baraboo Riverwalk. The Riverwalk parallels the Baraboo River for most of its route as it goes through or connects to several city parks.

Once on the Riverwalk route, the segment heads south through Lower Ochsner Park, passing an old bridge crossing the Baraboo River to Attridge Park. The Trail bends east on 2nd Avenue a short distance to skirt private property along

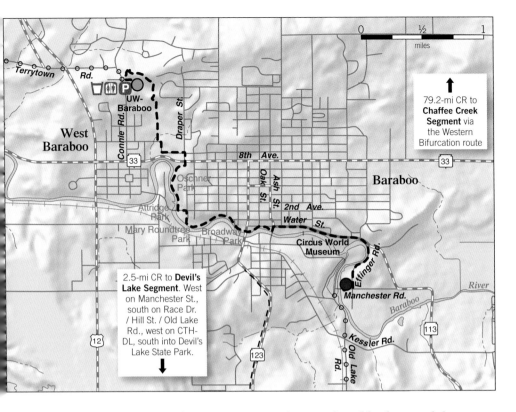

On the map:

Terrytown Rd.

UW-Baraboo

West Baraboo

Connie Rd.

Draper St.

33

8th Ave.

Oschner Park

Oak St.

Ash St.

2nd Ave.

Water St.

Attridge Park

Mary Roundtree Park

Broadway Park

Circus World Museum

Baraboo

Effinger Rd.

Manchester Rd.

Baraboo

River

113

79.2-mi CR to **Chaffee Creek Segment** via the Western Bifurcation route

2.5-mi CR to **Devil's Lake Segment**. West on Manchester St., south on Race Dr. / Hill St. / Old Lake Rd., west on CTH-DL, south into Devil's Lake State Park.

12

123

Kessler Rd.

Old Lake Rd.

0   ½   1
miles

the river, then heads south into Mary Roundtree Park and back toward the river before resuming an eastward course into Broadway Park. The segment crosses underneath South Boulevard (STH-123) and continues to follow the Baraboo Riverwalk to Water Street (STH-113).

On Water Street (STH-113) the segment passes the Circus World Museum. This National and State Historic Landmark was the site of Ringlingville, the Ringling Bros. Circus winter quarters from 1884 to 1918. It is home to 200 preserved circus wagons and has extensive historical circus exhibits on display.

The segment departs from Water Street at Effinger Road and heads south for 0.4 miles to its terminus at Manchester Street.

Mobile Skills Crew project site, 2008

AREA SERVICES

Baraboo: Restaurant, grocery store, convenience store, general shopping, lodging, camping, library, medical care. On Trail. INN Style lodging at Pinehaven (608-356-3489, pinehavenbnb.com) and Inn at Wawanissee Point (608-355-9899, innatwawanisseepoint.com). Baraboo area info available from the Baraboo Chamber of Commerce (800-227-2266, baraboo.com).

Devil's Lake State Park: See Devil's Lake Segment, p. 194. From the UW-Baraboo/Sauk County campus go south ~5 mi.

Sauk Point Segment (Atlas Map 61f)

3.8 miles: CTH-DL to STH-113

 This segment covers a very quiet corner of Devil's Lake State Park and offers access to spectacular Parfrey's Glen.

 At Parfey's Glen parking area.

 Dogs are not allowed in Parfrey's Glen State Natural Area (SNA) except on the IAT. By law, dogs must be leashed when hiking on the IAT in Parfrey's Glen SNA and Devil's Lake State Park.

Trail into Parfrey's Glen State Natural Area and blue-blazed spur trail (**SA7**) to Solumn Ln. parking area.

TRAIL ACCESS AND PARKING

CTH-DL: From Baraboo at the intersection of STH-123 and STH-113, take STH-113 south 6.5 mi. At CTH-DL turn left and go east 2.0 mi to the parking area for Parfrey's Glen State Natural Area on the north side of the road.

STH-113: From Baraboo at the intersection of STH-123 and STH-113, take STH-113 south 5.0 mi to the parking area on the west side of the road.

Additional Parking: (i) Solum Ln. parking area. A blue-blazed spur trail leads to the Ice Age Trail (**SA7**).

THE HIKE

The segment starts at the information kiosk and parking area for Parfrey's Glen State Natural Area, Wisconsin's first State Natural Area. From the parking area, the segment climbs gently but consistently uphill on a narrow single track trail through a thickly shaded young forest. Occasional large "wolf trees," surrounded by mostly younger trees, indicate this area was probably used as farmland or open pasture before being allowed to transition back to forest a few decades ago. After a mile the segment passes into Devil's Lake State Park and a more mature forest of maples and oaks, some reaching 90 feet tall. Hikers may note oak trees with double trunks, indicating harvested trees from 50 to 60 years ago that have regenerated multiple trunks.

The segment passes through a number of openings in the forest and a hiker may catch a glimpse of a nearby cell tower. This tower marks Sauk Point, the highest point in Sauk County, which is only 0.5 miles from the Trail but on private land and inaccessible to the public. The segment heads west and soon reaches a junction (**SA7**) with a blue-blazed spur trail that leads 0.25 miles south to a parking area on Solum Lane.

West of the spur trail, the segment reaches its highest elevation at the "Blue Mounds Vista" (**SA8**), with a bench in a grassy area offering spectacular views of the lower Wisconsin River valley and (about 30 miles away) Blue Mounds. On a clear day when leaves are down, hikers can look southeast and see the state capitol's dome in Madison.

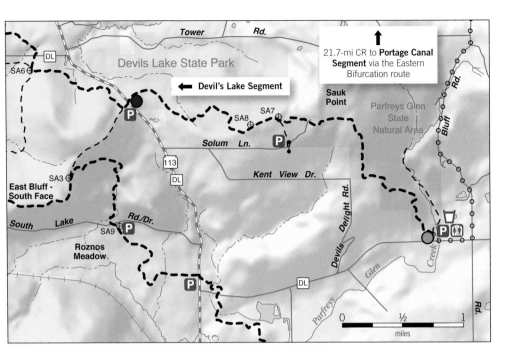

From here the Trail moves slowly downhill amongst hummocky ridges, rocky downhill stretches and a few dry stream crossings. Hikers reach a farm and briefly cross a farm field before following a rolling ridge to the segment's endpoint on STH-113.

Mobile Skills Crew project site, 2009

POINTS OF INTEREST

Parfrey's Glen State Natural Area: On Trail (dnr.wi.gov/topic/Lands/naturalareas/index.asp?SNA=1).

Designated in 1952 as Wisconsin's first State Natural Area, Parfrey's Glen offers a 0.7-mile nature trail that passes through a spectacular deep gorge carved into the sandstone conglomerate of embedded quartzite pebbles and boulders on the south flank of the Baraboo Hills. The uppermost part of the Glen, with its jumble of huge fallen rocks, is nearly 100 feet deep. Hikers will pass moss-covered walls moist from seepage before the trail ends at a small waterfall. The Glen's unique microclimate grows northern flora, including white pine, yellow birch, mountain maple and rare cliff plants. An unusual aquatic ecosystem flourishes in the fast, cold, hardwater stream that flows through the gorge and the Glen harbors a diverse insect fauna with a few rare and threatened species. Pets are not allowed in Parfrey's Glen SNA except along the Ice Age Trail.

AREA SERVICES

Devil's Lake State Park: See Devil's Lake Segment, p. 194. From the STH-113 Trail access go west ~3 mi.

Baraboo: See Baraboo Segment, p. 190. From the STH-113 Trail access go north ~5 mi. Also see Trail Access and Parking directions, above.

Devil's Lake Segment (Atlas Map 61f)

SNAPSHOT

10.9 miles: STH-113 Northern Trail Access to STH-113 Southern Trail Access

 This is arguably the most dramatic Ice Age Trail segment of all, exploring Wisconsin's largest and most-visited state park and offering magnificent views from 500-foot quartzite bluffs overlooking a 360-acre lake.

At various locations throughout Devil's Lake State Park (DLSP).

From Devil's Lake.

At DLSP campgrounds and several nearby private campgrounds.

 By law, dogs must be leashed in DLSP.

 Portions overlap with DLSP roads, bike and ski trails. Hike well off to the side when ski trails are groomed.

 Extensive DLSP trail network.

TRAIL ACCESS AND PARKING

STH-113 Northern Trail Access: From Baraboo at the intersection of STH-123 and STH-113, take STH-113 south 5.0 mi to the parking area on the west side of the road.

STH-113 Southern Trail Access: From Merrimac at the intersection of Baraboo St. and STH-113/78, take STH-113/78 west for 2.5 mi. Continue on STH-113 north for 2.3 mi to the Devil's Lake State Park Roznos Meadow parking area on the west side of the road.

Additional Parking: Parking areas throughout Devil's Lake State Park.

THE HIKE

Devil's Lake State Park is a place of striking contrasts. The purple rock, called Baraboo quartzite, in the walls of Devil's Lake gorge is more than 1.6 billion years old. The glacially deposited ridges or moraines that block both ends of the gorge are only about 16,000 years old. A geologic map of the park, found at the park's Nature Center, shows that the moraines wrap around high points in the landscape. Ice filled the lowlands in the eastern part of the park and flowed into both ends of the gorge but did not advance onto the higher western parts of the landscape. The ice left behind two prominent moraines that plugged both ends of the ancient gorge, now occupied by Devil's Lake.

These two moraine "plugs" and the way they create the lake are unique in the entire world. Breathtaking views of the western part of the park, part of the unglaciated Driftless Area, can be had from the many rock ledges the Ice Age Trail passes along the rim of the East Bluff. Cold airflow from the bluffs provides habitat for unusual northern plant species. Areas of dry prairie, red oak and maple forest are found atop the bluffs.

From the northern Trail access parking area on STH-113, the segment heads southwest and quickly intersects with Devil's Lake State Park's Upland Trail Loop. Hikers should turn right and hike northwest (following the loop counterclockwise) for about a mile to a junction (**SA6**) with the park's Johnson Moraine Loop. At the junction, hikers should turn right and head north across CTH-DL.

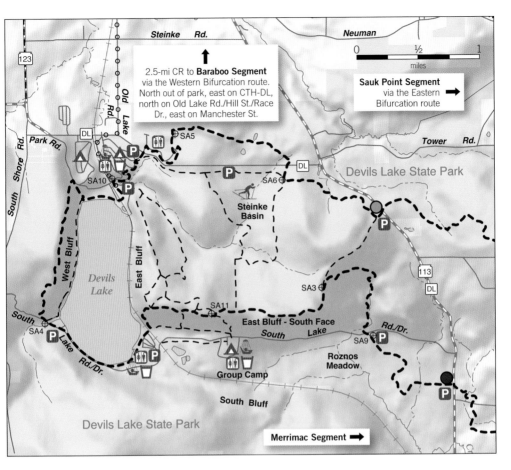

The segment makes its way west through a mix of meadows and woodlands, then drops down to the park's Ice Age Campground, intersecting with the campground road between sites 419 and 420 (SA5). The segment follows the campground road south and then west, then follows a park road out of the campground and under CTH-DL. The segment continues southwest along the park road and through woods, passing by the Northern Lights campground and the park's amphitheater along the way.

Upon reaching the intersection (SA10) with the park's main exit road, hikers have arrived at the spot where the two branches of the Ice Age Trail bifurcation reunite. The connecting route from the western branch arrives from the Baraboo Segment down the park's exit road.

From the bifurcation intersection, the segment crosses a set of railroad tracks and passes through the North Shore Picnic Area with a seasonal concession stand and continues west paralleling the north shore of Devil's Lake on an asphalt path. The segment then makes its way northward from the lakeshore to connect with the park's West Bluff Trail.

The portion following the West Bluff Trail climbs steeply to the top of the West Bluff, 500 feet above lake level. Because it is in the Driftless Area, there are no erratics on the West Bluff. This is a popular rock climbing area that is said to have more than 2000 possible climbing routes. The segment here passes through mixed woodlands with hardwoods and pine and features many woodland wild-flowers such as jack-in-the-pulpit, Solomon's seal, wild geranium, tinkers weed, tick trefoil and woodland milkweed.

The segment descends gradually down the West Bluff to the South Lake Road (South Lake Drive) western Trail access (**SA4**). Hikers should stay left to head east along the south shore of Devil's Lake and eventually pass through the South Shore Picnic Area, with a seasonal concession stand, water and restrooms. Here the Trail passes by Bird Mound, an impressive Indian effigy mound in the shape of a bird, which has a wingspread of 240 ft. One of a number of mounds in the park, this is the only one in which a human skeleton was found.

The segment crosses railroad tracks and follows the park's Balanced Rock Trail up steep stone steps to an intersection with the park's East Bluff Trail. This short section of Ice Age Trail can be a strenuous and challenging climb. Use caution when climbing on the rocks and pay close attention to Trail signage. At the inter-section with the East Bluff Trail, hikers should turn right and head east along the East Bluff Trail, which offers spectacular views of the South Bluff, Baraboo Hills and the terminal moraine below. This portion of the segment is shaded in places by small oaks and gnarled red cedars. There are remnants of dry prairie here with flora including blazing star, leadplant, yellow false foxglove, shooting star, sun-flower, goldenrod, aster and big bluestem grass. From the many rock ledges along the south face of the East Bluff, hikers can watch for turkey vultures and raptors soaring, sometimes at eye level.

Continuing east the segment departs (**SA11**) from the park's East Bluff Trail by the Moldy Buttress cliffside rock formation via a connector trail heading north then east about 0.25 miles to reconnect with the park's Upland Trail Loop. The segment follows the Upland Trail Loop east through woodlands and at another trail intersection (**SA3**) departs from the Upland Trail Loop and continues east, dropping down the south face of the East Bluff. Hikers may catch views of the largest unbroken sandstone escarpment in the park, a rare hanging sedge meadow and many rock outcrops. The segment passes a babbling brook in a diverse wood-land with several species of fern and wildflowers such as mayapple, milkweed, goldenrod, aster and tick trefoil.

The segment crosses South Lake Road (South Lake Drive) and enters Roz-nos Meadow. Here the segment traverses open prairie and grassland, giving 360-degree views of the surrounding Baraboo Hills towering above. A National Park Service interpretive sign (**SA9**) explains the moraine dam, an important gla-cial feature that had a major influence on the creation of the surrounding land-scape. The segment ends at the STH-113 southern Trail access parking area.

Mobile Skills Crew project site, 2002, 2003, 2004, 2008, 2009, 2012

POINTS OF INTEREST

Aldo Leopold Legacy Center: From the park's north entrance head north on STH-123 to Baraboo. At the intersection of STH-123 (Gollmar Blvd.) and STH-33 (Ringling Blvd.) in Baraboo take STH-33 east then north 6.9 mi. At CTH-U, veer left and continue north then west for 2.6 mi. At Schepp Rd. turn right and go north 1.2 mi. At Levee Rd. turn left and go 0.1 mi (E13701 Levee Rd., Baraboo, 608-355-0279, aldoleopold.org).

The Aldo Leopold Foundation operates the Aldo Leopold Legacy Center, which is an educational and interpretive facility near the Leopold "Shack." Here Aldo Leopold converted a chicken coop on his farm and wrote part of his conservation classic masterpiece on land ethics, A Sand County Almanac. This is also the very same land where Aldo Leopold died in 1948 fighting a brush fire. The Legacy Center is an excellent place to learn more about this famous American naturalist and see how the Leopold Foundation is carrying out his message of land ethics today. The Aldo Leopold Legacy Center is open to the public with limited hours. The Aldo Leopold Shack and Farm are not open to the public, except with special permission on a guided tour. Visit the website or contact the Aldo Leopold Foundation and Legacy Center for more information.

AREA SERVICES

Devil's Lake State Park: Concession stand (seasonal), camping. On Trail (608-356-8301, dnr.wi.gov/topic/parks/name/devilslake; reservations: 888-947-2757, reserveamerica.com).

Baraboo: See Baraboo Segment, p. 190. From the STH-113 northern Trail access go north ~5 mi. Also see Trail Access and Parking directions, above.

DAVE CALIEBE

Devil's Lake Segment.

Sauk County

Merrimac Segment (Atlas Map 61f)

3.6 miles: STH-113 to Marsh Rd. Southern Trail Access

  This segment highlights the diverse landscape of Riverland Conservancy's Merrimac Preserve and offers a quiet break from the crowds at Devil's Lake.

From creeks and wetland areas.

At nearby private campground (see Area Services) and Devil's Lake State Park.

 The portion of the segment crossing the Merrimac Preserve is closed early October for gun deer hunt for persons with disabilities and the first Saturday of November for Youth Outdoor Education Day.

 Briefly overlaps with snowmobile trails.

 Riverland Conservancy trail network.

TRAIL ACCESS AND PARKING

STH-113: From Merrimac at the intersection of Baraboo St. and STH-113/78, take STH-113/78 west for 2.5 mi. Continue on STH-113 north for 2.3 mi to Devil's Lake State Park's Roznos Meadow parking area on west side of road.

Marsh Rd. Southern Trail Access: From STH-113/78 at Merrimac turn north on Baraboo St. and go 0.3 mi. At Cemetery Rd., which becomes Marsh Rd., turn left and go west then north 0.9 mi to parking area on the northeast side of the road.

THE HIKE

This segment passes through the Merrimac Preserve, which is owned and managed by the Riverland Conservancy and encompasses more than 1,800 acres of forest, prairie, savanna, wetlands and streams. The preserve provides an integral wildlife corridor between the Baraboo Bluffs and the Wisconsin River. Riverland Conservancy began in 1997 as Wisconsin Power and Light Stewardship Trust through the generous donation of lands and equipment by Wisconsin Power and Light Co. Due to the variety of terrain, the segment contains a diverse array of flora, especially prevalent during warmer months.

The segment heads east from STH-113 and quickly enters a wooded area, passes by a hidden stream in an intimate setting and enters a prairie opening that leads to CTH-DL. Across the road, the segment continues south through a diverse prairie before descending toward a wetland and boardwalk crossing. The segment climbs gently and enters a savanna area with informational signs about groundwater and invasive species. Through this savanna area, views to the west feature the bluffs of Devil's Lake State Park and the terminal moraine between them. The segment returns to the woods then crosses another wetland area on a long boardwalk protecting fragile soils underneath. The segment continues alongside a meadow and briefly joins a snowmobile trail before reaching the northern Trail access on Marsh Road. Views to the west feature the bluffs of Devil's Lake State Park and the terminal moraine between them.

East of Marsh Road the segment winds through a mix of wooded areas, recent timber harvest areas and restored oak savannas and prairies. At one point the seg-

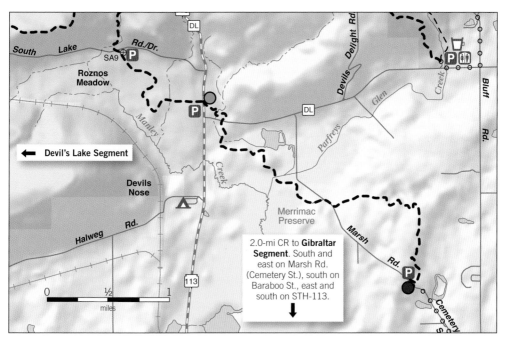

Devil's Lake Segment

Roznos Meadow

Devils Nose

2.0-mi CR to **Gibraltar Segment**. South and east on Marsh Rd. (Cemetery St.), south on Baraboo St., east and south on STH-113.

Merrimac Preserve

ment skirts the edge of a farm field with a primitive mowed airstrip. Toward the end, the segment drops down and out of a wooded kettle. At this point the Trail turns sharply east then south through a recently logged area before gently curving through the woods to the segment's terminus at the southern Trail access on Marsh Road.

Mobile Skills Crew project site, 2012

POINTS OF INTEREST

Merrimac Ferry: STH-113 across Lake Wisconsin (608-246-3872, dot.wisconsin.gov/travel/water /merrimac).

Listed in the National Register of Historic Places, the *Colsac III* ferry (commonly referred to as the Merrimac Ferry) is the lone survivor of about 500 ferries that used to operate in the 19th century across Wisconsin. The name "Colsac" is the phonetic rendering of the two counties the ferry connects, Columbia and Sauk. The ferry crosses the Wisconsin River at a wider part of the river known as Lake Wisconsin, which is a reservoir produced by a dam downstream. At that spot, it is both the Wisconsin River and Lake Wisconsin. The ferry takes seven minutes to cross approximately 0.45 miles. State-operated, the service is free to all, including cars, bikes and pedestrians, and runs 24 hours, 7 days a week April 15 through November 30. The ferry is closed December 1 through April 14. There is a separate lane for pedestrians and bicycles, boarding from the sidewalk on the east (upriver) side of the ferry. Contact the IATA (800-227-0046, iceagetrail.org) for an alternative pedestrian route when the ferry is closed.

AREA SERVICES

Merrimac: Restaurant, convenience store. From the Marsh Rd. southern Trail access go south and east 0.9 mi on Marsh Rd., which becomes Cemetery Rd. At Baraboo St. turn right and go south 0.3 mi. For area info, contact Merrimac Visitor Information (www.tn.merrimac.wi.gov).

Merry Mac's Campground: Camping. 0.7 mi south of Roznos Meadow lot on STH-113 (608-493-2367, merrymacscampground.com).

Devil's Lake State Park: See Devil's Lake Segment, p. 194. From the STH-113 Trail access go north and west ~5 mi.

Baraboo: See Baraboo Segment, p. 190. From the STH-113 Trail access go north ~6 mi.

Southern Columbia County

Trail miles: 11.8
Connecting route miles: 5.6

Southern Columbia County is home to iconic Gibraltar Rock and the Lodi Marsh State Wildlife Area. The Ice Age Trail in this region passes through some unique geological features and diverse ecological habitats, giving hikers an excellent experience of glacially shaped valleys, bluffs and drumlins while passing through prairies, savannas and woodlands. The Trail also wanders through the historic city of Lodi, where a hiker may be tempted off the Trail by restaurants, taverns, a Swiss bakery and specialty shops.

Following recent land acquisitions volunteers have built several more miles of the Ice Age Trail in the area over the past few years, giving hikers the opportunity to walk from the Merrimac Ferry on Lake Wisconsin, over several glacial bluffs, including Gibraltar Rock, and out to Lodi Marsh with much less road walking along the way.

CHAPTER INFORMATION

Lodi Valley Chapter volunteers construct and maintain trails, lead hikes and field trips, educate and assist in land stewardship. They are visible in their community, participating in and hosting local events. The chapter's hiking program, "The Glacial Drifters," recognizes those who have walked all Ice Age Trail segment and connecting route miles in the Lodi Valley and Baraboo Hills areas, approximately 50 miles.

COUNTY INFORMATION

Columbia County Visitor Bureau: 608-742-6161, travelcolumbiacounty.net

Gibraltar Rock Segment.

Southern Columbia County

JO ELLARSON

Gibraltar Segment (Atlas Map 62f)

SNAPSHOT

4.8 miles (3.9 IAT, 0.9 CR): STH-113 Ferry Wayside to CTH-V

 *This segment is a rolling ramble through mixed woodlands, prairies and fields. It features dramatic climbs and wide ranging views of Lake Wisconsin, a pastoral valley and the Baraboo Hills.*

 At nearby Merrimac Ferry north ramp on STH-113 (seasonal).

From Lake Wisconsin.

At a Dispersed Camping Area (**SC9**).

At STH-113 Ferry Wayside (seasonal).

 Segment includes a connecting route roadwalk.

 Two white-blazed loop trails, a spur trail to the DCA and Gibraltar Rock State Natural Area trails and road.

TRAIL ACCESS AND PARKING

STH-113 Ferry Wayside: In Lodi, from the intersection of STH-113 and STH-60, take STH-113 north 6.0 mi to the Ferry Wayside parking area. Closed in winter.

CTH-V: In Lodi, from the intersection of STH-113 and STH-60, take STH-113 north 4.0 mi. At CTH-V turn left and go west 1.7 mi. to the parking area on the east side of the road.

Additional Parking: (i) Slack Rd. parking area. (ii) CTH-VA (Gibraltar Rock Rd.) parking area.

THE HIKE

The segment starts at a grassy picnic area with a kiosk and benches near the Merrimac Ferry south ramp. Posts with Ice Age Trail yellow blazes guide hikers through the STH-113 wayside area. The Trail then passes through a woods of white oak, shagbark hickory and maple before crossing (**SC6**) busy STH-113 (cross with caution) near Northern Cross Arm Road.

The segment then ascends the north face of a 200-foot hill, taking in fine views of Lake Wisconsin through a screen of large oaks. Limestone outcroppings dot the hill, but the granite erratics scattered throughout the area remind hikers this area was covered by the Wisconsin Glaciation.

The Trail continues southeast through red cedar and existing remnant prairie areas with big bluestem, Indian grass, little bluestem and other native grass species. Prairie restoration is an ongoing priority in this area. More scenic views of Lake Wisconsin and the surrounding landscape are offered from different points along the route. This portion of the segment also includes a white-blazed trail that makes a short loop to the west of the main route.

Shortly after the white-blazed trail reconnects with the main route, hikers will reach a spur trail (**SC9**) with signage pointing west to a Dispersed Camping Area (DCA) for long distance hikers. Continuing on the main segment route, after a steady climb in open prairie for about a quarter-mile, the Trail reaches a stunning panoramic vista (**SC8**) of the Wisconsin River and Baraboo Hills.

Continuing on, hikers will arrive at a junction with another white-blazed trail

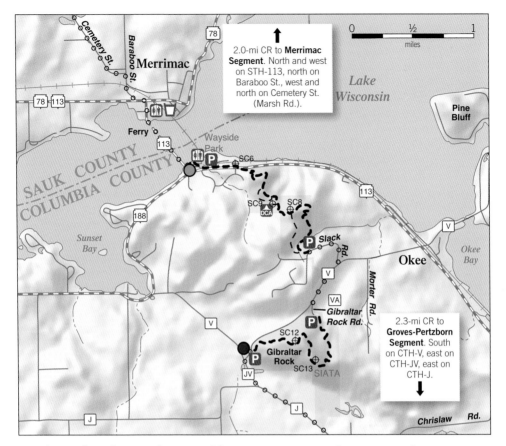

2.0-mi CR to **Merrimac Segment**. North and west on STH-113, north on Baraboo St., west and north on Cemetery St. (Marsh Rd.).

2.3-mi CR to **Groves-Pertzborn Segment**. South on CTH-V, east on CTH-JV, east on CTH-J.

that makes a loop to the west of the main route. From the junction, the main segment route soon reaches a viewpoint that offers great views during the leaf-off season of the surrounding hills and Wisconsin River Valley. From here, the segment drops almost 200 feet on a series of switchbacks through a woods of white pine and oaks, eventually reaching a boulder studded dry ravine. The segment crosses the ravine and ascends to the Slack Road parking area and rejoins with the white-blazed loop.

From the parking area, hikers should follow a 0.9-mile connecting route. From the Slack Road parking area go east and south 0.4 miles. At CTH-V turn right and continue southwest 0.4 miles to CTH-VA (Gibraltar Rock Road). Hikers should turn left on CTH-VA (Gibraltar Rock Road) and walk through the parking area for the Gibraltar Rock Area State Ice Age Trail Area to a gated access road and the start of the next portion of the segment.

Hikers should walk around the gate for the DNR access road and look for Ice Age Trail signage directing hikers east off the road and into the second-growth forest of white pine, hickory, and oak. The DNR access road of mixed gravel and crumbling blacktop steeply leads to the top of Gibraltar Rock. The Ice Age Trail route instead winds its way through the forest and gradually brings the hiker to the top.

Rising 1,234 feet above sea level, Gibraltar Rock is a flat-topped butte, an outlier of the Magnesian escarpment, with a thin dolomite cap over St. Peter sandstone. Its 200-foot sheer cliffs offer spectacular panoramic views of the Wisconsin River valley and Lake Wisconsin. On the south side of the butte is a rock face bluff overlooking a large leather-leaf bog and a bucolic valley.

At the top of Gibraltar Rock there are no safety guardrails and hikers should use extreme caution when hiking near or along the bluff. A memorial plaque (SC13) commemorating the Richmond Memorial Park of the Rock of Gibraltar, a park dedicated in 1929 in memory of James and Emma F. Richmond and other early pioneers, sits at a high point near where the DNR access road emerges.

The segment meanders along the top offering several views of the countryside below from rock outcrops framed by weathered red cedars. A loop trail, stretching along the "backside" of Gibraltar Rock, provides hikers with another option to pass across the top.

The segment leaves the big views and begins its gradual descent, first through a maple forest and then a white-pine-dominated woods as the Trail winds around the base of the bluff. Black locust and stone retaining walls line much of the route.

The segment emerges from the woods to the full panoramic "Horton Vista" (SC12). This vantage point offers outstanding long views of the field opening, the valley below and the Baraboo Hills in the distance. At this spot in the mid-20th century, Gaylord Nelson, founder of Earth Day, principal architect of the National Trails System Act and a Wisconsin governor and senator, descended from the woods one afternoon in a white dress shirt and slacks and found Don Horton, who the state purchased the land from in 2008, taking a break from field work. Nelson said, "You've got a beautiful piece of land here." Horton offered the stranger a drink of water and they went their separate ways.

Hikers will continue through the former farm field to the mulberry tree growing prominently along the Trail and can pause to further take in the views. The segment returns to a wooded canopy as the descent continues along the edge of the field opening until it reaches an intersection of two old farming roads. The blazed route, now on an old road, soon reaches the parking area on the former site of the Horton family homestead.

Mobile Skills Crew project site 2005, 2009, 2010, 2013, 2014

POINTS OF INTEREST

Merrimac Ferry: See Merrimac Segment, p. 198

AREA SERVICES

Merrimac: See Merrimac Segment, p. 198. From the ferry wayside Trail access take the ferry across to the north side of Lake Wisconsin. On STH-113 go north then east 1.0 mi.

Devil's Lake State Park: See Devil's Lake Segment, p. 194. From the ferry wayside Trail access take the ferry across to the north side of Lake Wisconsin. Take STH-113 north and west ~10 mi.

Baraboo: See Baraboo Segment, p. 190. From the ferry wayside Trail access take the ferry across to the north side of Lake Wisconsin. Take STH-113 north ~12 mi.

Lodi: See Groves-Pertzborn Segment and the City of Lodi Segment, p. 205. From the ferry wayside Trail access take STH-113 south 6.0 mi. Also see Trail Access and Parking directions, above.

Groves-Pertzborn Segment and City of Lodi Segment (Atlas Map 63f)

Groves-Pertzborn Segment—1.3 miles: CTH-J to Bilkey Rd.

2.4 mile Connecting Route

City of Lodi Segment—1.8 miles: Lodi School Complex to Pleasant St.

 The quiet, hilly **Groves-Pertzborn Segment** features dense woods, diverse vegetation and a steep climb.

 No reliable sources of water.

 Segment is closed during gun deer season.

 The **City of Lodi Segment** saunters through a charming "Trail Town" and highlights the impressive Rainbow Bridge.

 At town public buildings.

From Spring Creek.

At Strangeway Playlot and Veterans Memorial Park and at nearby Goeres Park and Pool (175 Fair St.).

 Hikers will not have any interaction with hunting on this segment.

 Most of the segment follows town roads and sidewalks.

 Portions of this segment may be suitable for those using wheelchairs or similar devices.

TRAIL ACCESS AND PARKING

CTH-J: In Lodi, from the intersection of STH-113 and STH-60, take STH-113 north. At CTH-J turn left and go west 2.0 mi to the parking area on the south side of the road just before the intersection with Lovering Rd.

Pleasant St.: In Lodi, from the intersection of STH-113 and STH-60, take STH-113 south 0.3 mi to Pleasant St. Turn right and go over a bridge for roadside parking on Water St.

Additional Parking: (i) Bilkey Rd.: In Lodi from the intersection of STH-113 and STH-60, take STH-113 north. At CTH-J turn left and go west 1.0 mi. At Bilkey Rd. turn left and go south then west 0.5 mi. Roadside parking. (ii) Lodi Middle and High School Complex on Sauk St. Parking is available at the high school on the northeast side in the pool parking area. Walk north behind the high school toward the bridge to reach the Ice Age Trail. Additional parking reserved for Ice Age Trail hikers is located at Lodi Middle School on the east side of the school. Walk north through the prairie to reach the Ice Age Trail. (iii) City of Lodi public parking area. From the intersection of STH-113 and STH-60, take STH-113 south 0.1 mi, follow the right bend on STH-113 and immediately turn right into the public parking area.

THE HIKE

The **Groves–Pertzborn Segment** is in an area of rounded hills covered with a thin layer of glacial till supporting area fields and woods. The Ice Age Trail travels through dense woods filled with oak, basswood, aspen and other woodland species and climbs up and down a steep hill. Several species of fern as well as wild geraniums, wood anemone, Solomon's seal, jack-in-the-pulpit and mayapple highlight the segment. The diverse vegetation, steep ravine and dense forest

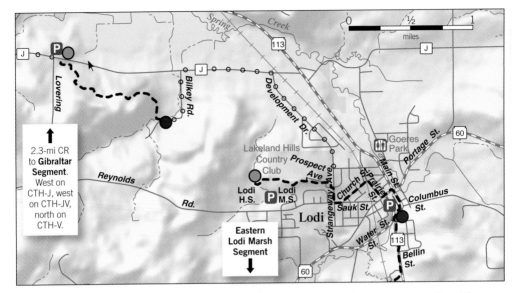

canopy make this section feel like a rain forest. Be wary of poison ivy and wild parsnip along the segment, which ends at a Trail access point on Bilkey Road.

From the Bilkey Road Trail access, hikers can reach the next segment via the following 2.4-mile connecting route: hike northeast on Bilkey Road for 0.5 miles. Turn right and hike east on CTH-J for 0.8 miles. Turn right and hike south on Development Drive (which turns into Strangeway Avenue) for 1.1 miles to the intersection of Strangeway Avenue and Prospect Avenue.

From the intersection of Strangeway Avenue and Prospect Avenue, the first order of business for those wanting to explore the full **City of Lodi Segment** is to hike a short out-and-back stretch of Ice Age Trail to the west of Strangeway Avenue. Head west on Prospect Avenue and go 100 feet to Strangeway Playlot. The segment leaves the pavement here. Follow the posts with blazes through the playlot, across the street and into the woods paralleling Lakeland Hills Country Club.

The segment passes prairie restoration efforts behind Lodi Middle School before crossing the largest human-made structure on the Ice Age Trail, a 150-foot-long footbridge spanning a ravine between Lodi's middle and high schools. Based on a 16th century Chinese Rainbow Bridge, the bridge was designed by U.S. Forest Products Lab forester and IATA Lodi Valley Chapter member Ron Wolfe. The twin arches, decking and railing are constructed of black locust and demonstrate the economical use of small-diameter invasive species. It is handicap accessible. Hundreds of volunteer hours of Ice Age Trail Alliance members, students and community members have gone into this collaborative project. This bridge is a dynamic symbol and traditional centerpiece in Lodi High School's senior graduation ceremony.

From the western end of the bridge, the Trail continues another 200 feet to the end-of-segment sign. From here, backtrack 0.6 miles to Strangeway Avenue to resume hiking the remainder of the City of Lodi Segment.

For the remainder of the City of Lodi Segment, the Trail is well-marked with yellow blazes on light poles and street signs throughout this "Trail Town." From the intersection of Prospect Avenue and Strangeway Avenue, hike south on

Strangeway Avenue for 0.1 miles. Turn left and hike east on Sauk Street for 0.1 miles. Turn left and hike northeast on Church Street for 0.3 miles. Turn right and hike southeast on Prairie Avenue for 0.2 miles. Turn left and hike northeast on Lodi Street (STH-60) for 0.2 miles. Turn right and hike southeast on Main Street (STH-113) for 0.1 miles.

The segment then departs from Main Street and turns southwest, passing through Country Doctor Park to a parking area, then on to a footbridge over Spring Creek. The segment then follows a grassy path southward along the creek through Veterans Memorial Park. It then turns southeast and recrosses Spring Creek on the Pleasant Street road bridge. Continuing eastward, the segment ends where Pleasant Street meets Corner Street (STH-113).

Mobile Skills Crew project site, 2009

AREA SERVICES

Lodi: Restaurant, grocery store, convenience store, lodging, medical care. On Trail. Services along Main St. or on STH-60 and STH-113. Meals at Lodi Coffee Roasters (107 S. Main St., 608-592-3325). INN Style program lodging at Victorian Dreams B&B (608-592-0362, victoriandreamsbnb.com). For area info, contact the Lodi and Lake Wisconsin Chamber of Commerce (608-592-4412, lodilakewisconsin.org).

Eastern Lodi Marsh Segment and Lodi Marsh Segment (Atlas Map 63f)

SNAPSHOT

Eastern Lodi Marsh Segment—3.2 miles: Pleasant St. to Lodi-Springfield Rd. (Robertson Trailhead)

Lodi Marsh Segment—1.6 miles: Lollipop trail on west side of Lodi-Springfield Rd. (Robertson Trailhead)

The **Eastern Lodi Marsh Segment** *transitions from a Trail Town to a beautiful ridgetop natural area with outstanding restored prairies and stunning views.*

 No reliable sources of water.

 Portion of segment crossing private land between STH-113 parking area and Lodi Marsh State Wildlife Area is closed during gun deer season.

 By law, dogs must be leashed April 15 to July 31 in the State Wildlife Area.

 A short portion parallels STH-113.

Spur trail leading to additional parking area.

The **Lodi Marsh Segment** *is a quiet lollipop hike that highlights a remarkable prairie in a quintessential rural setting.*

 From Spring Creek and numerous springs.

 By law, dogs must be leashed as much of this segment traverses a State Natural Area.

TRAIL ACCESS AND PARKING

Pleasant St.: In Lodi, from the intersection of STH-113 and STH-60, take STH-113 south 0.3 mi. to Pleasant St. Turn right and go over a bridge for roadside parking on Water St.

Lodi-Springfield Rd. (Robertson Trailhead): In Lodi, from the intersection of STH-113 and STH-60, take STH-60 west 0.6 mi. At Riddle Rd. (Lodi-Springfield Rd. in Dane Co.), just past the railroad trestle, turn left and go south 2.0 mi to the Robertson Trailhead parking area with a kiosk on the west side of road.

Additional Parking: (i) City of Lodi public parking area. In Lodi, from the intersection of STH-113 and STH-60, take STH-113 south 0.1 mi, follow the right bend on STH-113 and immediately turn right into the public parking area. (ii) STH-113. In Lodi, from the intersection of STH-113 and STH-60, take STH-113 south 0.7 mi to the parking area on the west side of STH-113. (iii) Twin Pines Trailhead on Lodi-Springfield Rd. (**SC1**). This parking area is 0.5 mi. north of the Robertson Trailhead on the east side of the road. A short spur trail leads to the Ice Age Trail.

THE HIKE

The **Eastern Lodi Marsh Segment** follows several dolomite ridges that are outliers of the Magnesian Cuesta, a sister escarpment of the more famous Niagara escarpment to the east. These ridges were sculpted, not obliterated, by glacial ice. It incorporates outstanding views of a glacial tunnel channel, Central Bluff, Gibraltar Rock, the Baraboo Hills and the marsh below. Hikers will pass through areas of stately oak, shagbark hickory, walnut and other hardwoods.

The segment starts by heading south 0.4 miles on a sidewalk and path along Corner St. (STH-113) to a parking area on the west side of the road. Be wary of poison ivy and wild parsnip along this part of the segment. Hike west across lands owned by Lodi Canning Company, crossing under a railroad trestle and then traversing a field edge before entering a narrow, wooded easement with large erratics and cleared field stones between agricultural fields.

The segment begins a steady climb through a classic southern Wisconsin woods consisting of white oak, hackberry, black cherry and short-lived elm, intermixed with a few dolomite outcrops, and enters the Lodi Marsh State Wildlife Area.

After crossing under some power lines, hikers will leave the woods for open prairie. Countless hours and ongoing efforts of local volunteers have restored and maintained several hundred acres of prairie and oak savanna. Bring a wildflower guide to identify the immense variety of prairie flowers in the goat prairie and restored prairie near "Dave's View" (**SC7**). Look for whitetail deer, wild turkeys, pheasants, eastern meadowlarks, red tail hawks and bluebirds.

From "Dave's View," looking straight west, one can see the striking U-shaped cut between Center Bluff and the bluff to the north. It is believed this was formed by a large under-glacier river draining meltwater toward the ice margin near the Sauk City area. Farther to the northwest one can see the prominent bulge of Gibraltar Rock and beyond that the Baraboo Hills.

After the big prairie and the magnificent view, hikers will drop back into the hardwoods. In about 0.3 miles a spur trail (**SC10**) to the Twin Pines Trailhead (**SC1**) forks to the right. Bear left to stay on the Ice Age Trail. Continue through alternating woods and prairie before reaching Lodi-Springfield Road and the Robertson Trailhead.

The **Lodi Marsh Segment** consists of a lollipop loop to the west side of Lodi-Springfield Rd. The segment, located near the Dane/Columbia county border, winds through glacially sculpted landscape of dolomite hills and deep valleys in the Lodi Marsh State Natural Area.

The segment travels along the edge of a marsh, through a lowland prairie and over limestone bedrock ridges and drumlins that were shaped by the Green Bay Lobe. Lodi Marsh is a large, mostly open wetland complex located in a valley partially filled with glacial till and contains diverse community types and over 160 native plant species. The wetland borders the headwaters and upper two miles of Spring Creek, which runs through the natural area and includes numerous springs and spring runs, a southern sedge meadow and cattail marsh.

After the first dip, the segment passes through a beautifully restored oak savanna with large open-growth bur oaks and hickory. Local Boy Scout troops and others have worked to keep this area brush free and "oak-friendly."

The segment then drops into a wet prairie that is frequently saturated, especially in the spring or after heavy rains. From here the segment climbs a drumlin and crosses the least disturbed dry-mesic prairie in the state (**DA19**). Located at the lower hill slopes, the interesting prairie contains such plants as big and little bluestem, Indian grass, showy goldenrod, sky-blue aster and the state-threatened prairie thistle. On the north-facing slope is a dry-mesic forest of sugar maples and basswoods. Indicators of the area's high-quality prairie and wetland habitat, fourteen species of Papaipema moths and significant wetland-restricted moths have been found here. Birders have reported seeing great blue heron, sandhill cranes, common snipe, willow and alder flycatcher, sedge wren and blue-winged warbler.

AREA SERVICES

Lodi: See Groves-Pertzborn Segment and the City of Lodi Segment, p. 205. From the Lodi-Springfield Rd. Robertson Trailhead go north ~3 mi. Also see Trail Access and Parking directions, above.

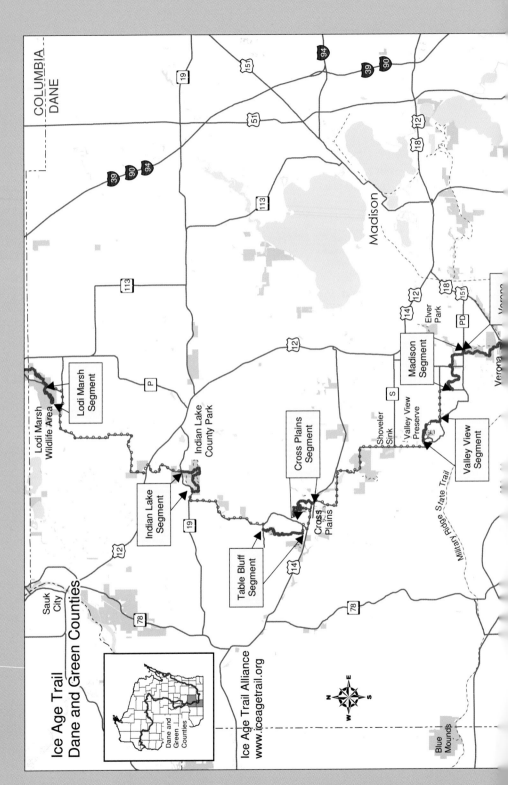

Ice Age Trail
Dane and Green Counties

Dane and Green Counties

Ice Age Trail Alliance
www.iceagetrail.org

COLUMBIA
DANE

Madison

Lodi Marsh
Wildlife Area

Lodi Marsh
Segment

Indian Lake
County Park

Indian Lake
Segment

Cross Plains
Segment

Cross
Plains

Table Bluff
Segment

Sauk
City

Elver
Park

Madison
Segment

Valley View
Preserve

Shoveler
Sink

Valley View
Segment

Military Ridge State Trail

Verona

Blue
Mounds

N E W S

Dane & Green Counties

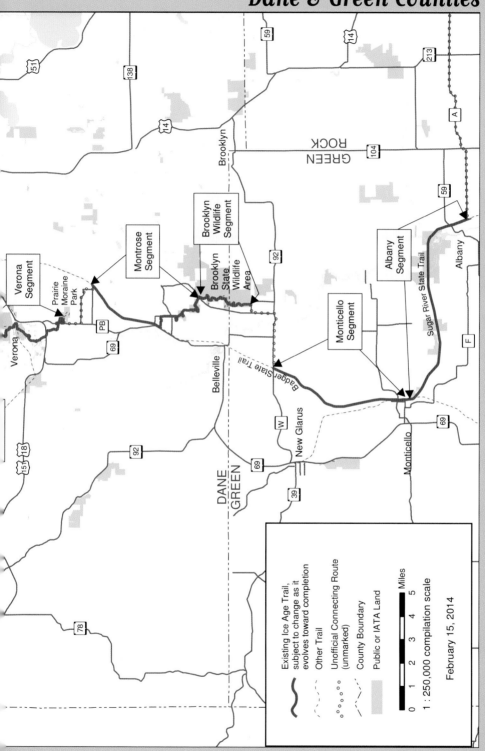

Dane County

Trail miles: 30.3
Connecting route miles: 30.3

Dane County straddles two distinct physical landscapes. Western Dane County is an unglaciated area of narrow, stream-cut valleys and angular ridges of exposed sandstone and dolomite, part of the Driftless Area. The eastern two-thirds of the county is covered with layers of sand, clay and gravel left by a series of glacial advances. The Green Bay Lobe covered most of this eastern portion 15,000 years ago. The Ice Age Trail weaves back and forth between the two landscapes. Prairie Moraine County Park, near Verona, is a great place to see the Johnstown End Moraine that marks the farthest advance of the Green Bay Lobe. A string of public lands protects portions of the Ice Age Trail in Dane County. These include, from north to south, Lodi Marsh State Wildlife Area; Indian Lake County Park; the Cross Plains National Scientific Reserve; Ice Age Junction Area, Badger Prairie and Prairie Moraine County Parks and Brooklyn State Wildlife Area. Increase Lapham wrote in 1846 that Dane County was "almost entirely oak openings or prairie."

CHAPTER INFORMATION

One of the original IATA chapters, the Dane County Chapter sponsors many events each year such as trail-building and maintenance outings, hikes and interpretive walks and prairie and woodland restoration projects. The chapter promotes public awareness of the Ice Age Trail through displays at community functions, annual outdoor shows and restoration events. Their chapter newsletter, the *Ice Age Drift*, is available on the chapter's home page on the IATA website.

COUNTY INFORMATION

Greater Madison Convention and Visitors Bureau: 800-373-6376, visitmadison.com.

Dane County Parks: 608-242-4576, countyofdane.com/lwrd/parks.

Camping in Dane County Parks: 608- 224-3730, reservedane.com

A maiden voyage on the Montrose Segment.

Dane County

Lodi Marsh Segment

This segment is located in Dane County just south of the Dane/Columbia county line. It is linked with the Eastern Lodi Marsh Segment and described in the Southern Columbia County chapter of this book (see p. 207).

Indian Lake Segment (Atlas Map 64f)

THE HIKE

Indian Lake fills a shallow depression formed by a melting ice block in a broad east–west oriented valley walled by bedrock hills. As the Green Bay Lobe melted, a large river of meltwater spread across this valley on its way to the Wisconsin River. The Ho-Chunk people frequented the lake for hunting and fishing before European Americans arrived in the area.

Indian Lake County Park is a popular destination for outdoor activities. Eight miles of cross-country ski and hiking trails lace through the 450-acre park. While the segment overlaps with some the park's ski trails, which have their own color-coded makings, the Ice Age Trail is well marked and not difficult to follow. The park has a warming hut/cabin (**DA24**) that is open during the ski season; thru-hikers looking for a place to spend the night can contact the Dane County Parks

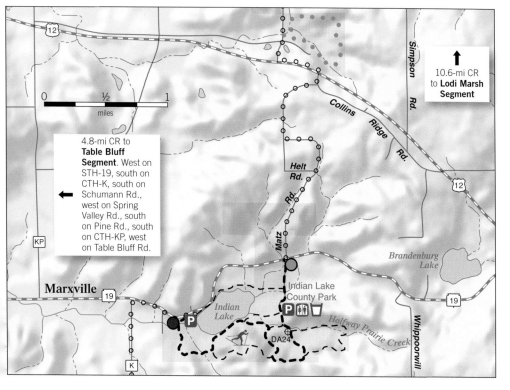

Department (**608-246-3896**) to request permission to access the hut.

From its starting point at STH-19 at the Indian Lake County Park entrance the segment follows the park entrance road to the main parking area. A side trail leads about 0.5 miles uphill to St. Mary of the Oaks Chapel (look for signage behind and to the right of the main parking area restrooms). The small stone chapel was built in 1857 by a German immigrant, John Enders, to thank God for sparing his family from a deadly epidemic. It was constructed based on building methods common in Germany at the time and contains statues and religious icons. An overlook near the chapel offers beautiful views of Indian Lake and the surrounding valley.

Back on the Trail, hikers will enter and travel through an oak and maple woods as the segment climbs up and down steep hills and then briefly follows along the south side of Indian Lake. Leaving the woods, the segment crosses meadows, passes by a marsh and skirts around a dog exercise area before ending at Indian Lake County Park's dog exercise/lake access parking area on STH-19.

AREA SERVICES

Sauk City: Restaurant, grocery store, convenience store, lodging, library, medical care. From the STH-19 eastern Trail access go north 1.9 mi on Matz Rd. At Collins Rd. turn left and go 0.1 mi. At USH-12 turn left and go northwest for 7.1 mi. For area info contact the Sauk Prairie Area Chamber of Commerce (608-643-4168, saukprairie.com).

Cross Plains: See Table Bluff Segment and Cross Plains Segment, p. 216. From the STH-19 western Trail access go west then south ~10 mi.

Middleton: See Valley View Segment and Madison Segment, p. 220. From the STH-19 eastern Trail access go east then south ~13 mi. Also see Trail Access and Parking directions, above.

Table Bluff Segment
and Cross Plains Segment (Atlas Map 65f)

SNAPSHOT

Table Bluff Segment—2.5 miles: Table Bluff Rd. to Scheele Rd.

1.9 mile Connecting Route

Cross Plains Segment—2.8 miles: Hickory Hill St. to Bourbon Rd.

 The **Table Bluff Segment** *offers long ridgetop views and showcases the results of some remarkable land stewardship efforts.*

 No reliable sources of water.

The southern two-thirds of the segment crossing private land are closed during gun deer season.

 Dogs must be leashed.

 Two white-blazed loop trails and additional informal trails.

 The diverse **Cross Plains Segment** *highlights a Trail Town, the Ice Age Trail Alliance headquarters and the surprisingly remote-feeling bluffs, prairies and woodlands north of town.*

At the public library, public pool and IATA headquarters.

From Black Earth Creek.

At Legion Park, 1 block west of the Trail on American Legion Dr.

At Legion Park and town pool.

 Portions follow town streets and sidewalks.

 Additional informal trail in Hickory Hill Conservation Area.

 Portions of this segment may be suitable for those using wheelchairs or similar devices.

TRAIL ACCESS AND PARKING

Table Bluff Rd.: From the Ice Age Trail Alliance headquarters in Cross Plains, take USH-14 west 1.2 mi At CTH-KP turn right and go north 2.4 mi. At Table Bluff Rd. turn left and go west 0.3 mi to the parking area on the south side of the road.

Bourbon Rd.: From west of Madison on the Beltline Highway (USH-12/14) near Middleton, take Exit 251 for University Ave. (USH-14) and go west on University Ave. (USH-14) for 7.2 mi to Cross Plains. At CTH-P turn left and go south across Black Earth Creek then immediately turn right at Bourbon Rd. The segment begins a short distance west where a paved path intersects the road. Roadside parking.

Additional Parking: (i) Roadside parking at Hickory Hill St. near the gated access road for Hickory Hill Conservation Park. (ii) Roadside parking at Lewis St. Trail access. (iii) Parking area at Village of Cross Plains Municipal Park pool at 2106 Lewis St. (behind the library). (iv) Parking area behind IATA headquarters (**DA26**), 2110 Main St.

Note: USH-14 will be rebuilt through Cross Plains in 2015. Hikers should expect delays when accessing the Trail in this area during construction.

THE HIKE

Located in the Driftless Area of southwestern Wisconsin, the **Table Bluff Segment** traverses restored prairie as well as steep, rocky slopes. There is approximately 200 feet of total vertical relief and several vistas from the heads of two valleys and two prominent goat prairies that offer great views of the Driftless Area. Meltwater from the Laurentide ice sheet poured through a preglacial valley depositing sand and gravel and partially filling the lower valley floors, which now hold extensive wetlands and a tributary stream of Black Earth Creek, a Class I trout stream. The area is home to various types of wetland, prairie oak opening and forest plants.

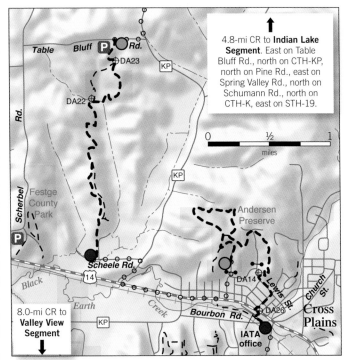

From the Trail access on Table Bluff Rd., the segment heads south across a 73-acre IATA-owned property. After passing through a prairie and then an old orchard area hikers will come to an intersection (**DA23**) with a white-blazed loop trail that offers a 0.5-mile "bubble" to the west of the main Ice Age Trail route. The loop trail traverses up a ridge through a mixed hardwood forest containing a grove of several large oak trees and offers views of the valley floor to the east.

Back on the main segment, from its initial encounter with the white-blazed loop trail the segment continues south across a large prairie restored to its natural state. A thriving population of the rare pale purple coneflower can be found here. Hikers will find this area to be a wildflower treasure trove—shooting star, rattlesnake master, stiff gentian, hoary vervain, pasque flower, prairie smoke, leadplant, bird's-foot violet, compass plant, harebell, cream gentian and cream baptisia have all been identified here. The segment then enters a wooded area and dips down onto a valley floor. After crossing an open area the segment makes its second connection with the white-blazed loop trail (**DA22**).

The remainder of the segment traverses the privately owned Swamplovers property. From the valley floor, the segment climbs up a ridge and traverses nearly a mile of woodlands of oak and hickory before entering a prairie/oak savanna area that is being faithfully restored to its native state by owners of the Swamplovers property. This area, including a second white-blazed loop, features dramatic rock outcroppings of Ordovician dolomite and views southwest to the Blue Mounds. At the top of the bluff area is a shelter with picnic tables that is available to hikers when not already in use by the property owners. From the top of the bluff the segment drops precipitously on a series of switchbacks to the segment's endpoint on the Swamplovers property access road.

To reach the Cross Plains Segment, hikers should follow the 1.9-mile connecting route by heading south on the access road to its intersection with gravel Scheele Road. From there, hikers should turn left and head east on Scheele Road, turn right and head south on CTH-KP, turn left and head west on USH-14 (Main Street in Cross Plains), turn left and head north on Hickory Street which jogs slightly to the right, then turn left and head north on Hickory Hill Street.

The **Cross Plains Segment** shows off the village of Cross Plains, which is situated along Black Earth Creek in a valley between tall bluffs. It sits at the boundary of the most recent glaciation to the east and north and the Driftless Area to the west and south. Meltwater from the receding glacier eroded and carried the terminal moraine downstream from the site of the village. Cross Plains is named for the intersection of two early roads: the military road from Fort Crawford (Prairie du Chien) to Fort Howard (Green Bay) and the lowland road from Arena to Madison.

The segment starts at the end of Hickory Hill Street, where a gate crosses an access road that leads north uphill into to the Hickory Hill Conservation Park. Departing from the access road, the segment enters a former agricultural field being restored to native prairie which shows great variations and color over the seasons. Shortly after entering the former agricultural field, hikers will encounter signage for a "cut-off" path that heads east. To continue with the full segment hikers should veer northwest at this junction. The segment continues across the former agricultural field and soon enters a woodland that features not only native flora such as jack-in-the-pulpit, shooting stars and wild ginger but also the glacial drainage network known as "Three Gorges."

The segment exits the forest and once more crosses the former agricultural field. After passing by the cut-off path, hikers will continue southeast through an oak savanna in the midst of a restoration. The segment continues southeast, gaining elevation up the side of a dolomite ridge. At the head of the ridge hikers will find a Leopold bench and views to the south and east displaying what conservationist Increase Lapham described as the "Great Dividing Ridge." On the distant ridge to the south hikers may see a lone majestic white pine, marking the approximate location of a future Ice Age Trail segment through the Cross Plains National Scientific Reserve. The Blue Mounds are also clearly visible to the west.

At this point the segment drops steeply 150 feet down a series of switchbacks to emerge at Lewis Street (**DA14**) between two houses. From here, the segment continues on sidewalks and roads through residential Cross Plains.

The segment heads east 0.2 miles on Lewis Street to its intersection with Caesar Street, where hikers should turn right and head southwest on the east side of Caesar Street, passing the Rosemary Garfoot Public Library and Village of Cross Plains Municipal Park and Pool.

At the intersection of Caesar Street and Julius Street signage directs hikers to continue southwest on Caesar Street but first to cross to the opposite (west) side of the street.

The segment reaches busy Main St. (USH-14), which hikers should cross cautiously and then turn left to head east down Main Street.

Hikers will soon encounter the Ice Age Trail Alliance's headquarters building (**DA26**) on the south side of the road at 2110 Main Street. The headquarters building is open 8 p.m. to 5 p.m. weekdays except in the case of special events. Though not a true "Visitor Center" hikers are urged to stop in—IATA staff love to chat with Trail users! Restrooms and drinking water are available for all, as are shower and laundry facilities for thru-hikers. Ice Age Trail merchandise can be purchased here as well.

The segment leaves Main Street and turns southwest to cross the IATA headquarters property, which features a rain garden, lawn with native prairie plants and boulders along the segment route bearing the names of the IATA's 21 volunteer chapters and the organization's key partners—the Wisconsin Department of Natural Resources and the National Park Service.

The segment exits the IATA headquarters property and crosses Black Earth Creek on a bridge then heads east on a paved path through H.M. Zander Community Nature Park to the segment's terminus on Bourbon Road.

Mobile Skills Crew project site, 2004, 2006, 2009

POINTS OF INTEREST

Cross Plains National Scientific Reserve and Future National Park Service Interpretive Area: From the IATA Headquarters in Cross Plains: Take Main St. (USH-14) east 2.6 mi. At Cleveland Rd. turn right and go south 0.9 mi. At Old Sauk Pass Rd. turn right and go west 0.5 mi to entrance gate. Roadside parking. Do not block the gate with vehicles. From west of Madison on the Beltline Highway (USH-12/14) near Middleton: Take Old Sauk Rd. exit and go west 4.0 mi. At Timber Ln. turn right and go north 0.5 mi. At a bend in the road, continue west on Old Sauk Pass Rd. 0.7 mi. Additional parking: Shoveler Sink, a U.S. Fish and Wildlife Service Waterfowl Production Area, on Timber Ln.

This area features a complex of lands owned by Dane County, the Wisconsin Department of Natural Resources and the National Park Service and includes the Cross Plains Unit of Ice Age National Scientific Reserve, one of nine such units. The area represents a world-renowned example of the interface of glaciated and unglaciated terrain. The relationship between moraine and glaciated landscapes on one side of the moraine and unglaciated bedrock landscapes on the other side is strikingly exhibited. Rugged ridges of the moraine formed during the Wisconsin Glaciation meet the eroded Driftless Area to the south and west. Oak savanna, oak forest, wetlands and prairies cover the area.

Unmarked hiking trails penetrate both the DNR land north of Old Sauk Pass and the NPS-owned land south of the road. Dogs are welcome on leash. There are no public restrooms or other visitor facilities available at this time. The National Park Service is in the process of developing a general management plan for the area. This area will be home to a segment of the Ice Age Trail in the future. Details are available at parkplanning.nps.gov/projectHome.cfm?projectID=21764.

AREA SERVICES

Cross Plains: Restaurants, grocery store, convenience store, general shopping, lodging, library, medical care. On Trail. Most services on Main St. (USH-14). Meals at Crossroads Coffeehouse (2020 Main St., 608-798-2080, crossroadscoffeehouse.net) and Coach's Club (1200 Main St., 608-413-0400, coachsclub.com). Area info available from the Cross Plains Chamber of Commerce (608-843-3166, crossplainschamber.net).

Mendota County Park: Camping. From the IATA headquarters go east 7.0 mi on USH-14. Pass under the Beltline Highway and continue east on University Ave. for 1.0 mi. At Branch St. turn left and go north 0.6 mi. At CTH-M/Century Ave. turn right and go east 1.3 mi to the park entrance (5133 CTH-M, Middleton, 608-224-3730, reservedane.com).

Cedar Hills Campground: Camping. From the IATA headquarters go ~8 mi west on USH-14. At STH-78 go 3.0 mi north to the campground entrance (seasonal; 6406 STH-78, Mazomanie, 608-795-2606).

Middleton: See Valley View Segment and Madison Segment, p. 220. From the IATA headquarters on USH-14 go east ~8 mi. Also see Trail Access and Parking directions, above.

Madison: See Valley View Segment and Madison Segment, p. 220. From the IATA headquarters on USH-14 go east ~13 mi.

Valley View Segment and Madison Segment (Atlas Map 66f)

SNAPSHOT

Valley View Segment—1.8 miles (1.5 IAT, 0.3 CR): Ice Age Ln. to Shady Oak Ln. at Mid Town Rd.

1.8 mile Connecting Route

Madison Segment—3.2 miles: Woods Rd. to CTH-PD (McKee Rd.)

  The **Valley View Segment** is a delightful suburban jaunt through a restored prairie with good interpretive signage and views west to the Blue Mounds

 No reliable sources of water.

 Hikers will not have any interaction with hunting on this segment.

 Dogs must be leashed.

 Portions overlap with roads and sidewalks.

 An extensive, color-coded trail network through the prairie area.

  For being on the outskirts of town, the **Madison Segment** retains a surprisingly remote feel as it passes unobtrusively through a scenic golf course and residential neighborhoods.

At the University Ridge Golf Course clubhouse (seasonal).

Hikers will not have any interaction with hunting on this segment.

Dogs are not allowed between Woods Rd. and CTH-M.

Portions overlap with golf course paths, city roads (including dangerous CTH-M), a driveway and sidewalks and a multi-use recreation path.

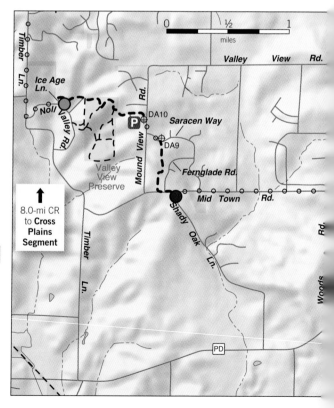

TRAIL ACCESS AND PARKING

Ice Age Ln.: From west of Madison on the Beltline Highway (USH-12/14), take Exit 254 for Mineral Point Rd. (CTH-S) and go west on Mineral Point Rd. (CTH-S) for 4.0 mi. At Timber Ln. turn left and go south 1.3 mi. At Noll Valley Rd. turn left and go east 0.3 mi. At Ice Age Ln. turn left and go north 0.1

mi. Roadside parking on the right side of the road by the gate.

CTH-PD (McKee Rd.): From Verona, at the intersection of Verona Ave. (Bus. Rt. USH-18/151) and CTH-M (Main St./Pleasant View Rd.), take CTH-M (Main St./Pleasant View Rd.) north 1.7 mi. At CTH-PD (McKee Rd.) turn right and go east 0.6 mi to the parking area on the south side of CTH-PD.

Additional Parking: (i) Parking area at Middleton Ice Age Trail Access park (**DA10**) on Mound View Rd. (ii) Roadside parking on Woods Rd. (iii) University Ridge Golf Course lower parking area, open seasonally during golf course hours. Accessed by car from the main golf course entrance along CTH-PD (McKee Rd.). Gate is sometimes locked. (iv) O.J. Noer Turfgrass Research and Education Center parking area on the west side of CTH-M (Pleasant View Rd.). Available only on weekends and after 4:00 p.m. on weekdays. (v) Roadside parking on Flagstone Dr.; see safety note below. (vi) Roadside parking on Raymond Rd./Oakview Rd.

THE HIKE

The **Valley View Segment** starts at the Ice Age Lane Trail access along the brown fence to the right of the gate. After passing through a patch of woods, the segment crosses a residential driveway at a white lantern post. From there it enters the highlight of the segment, an open prairie with a series of looped side trails and trailside benches. Hikers should be very alert and watch for each Ice Age Trail post when hiking through the prairie. This portion of the segment is on the terminal moraine and is a fine example of prairie and oak savanna restoration. Driven by area landowners, with a collaboration of various community volunteer groups, 14 acres spanning parts of three properties were returned to their native habitat. In part this project removed aggressive invasive plants and scrubs and reintroduced native prairie seeds representing 105 species. The project was possible through a lot of hard physical work, grants and the support from Dane County Parks, DNR and IATA.

On a clear day, hikers can see the Blue Mounds from the prairie. Increase Lapham wrote that the Blue Mounds "were very important landmarks to guide the traveler in his course through the boundless prairies." Their Indian name is Mucha-wa-ku-nin or "Smoky Mountains."

After exiting the prairie the segment passes through a residential area featuring prairie-style homes drawing their inspiration from Wisconsin-born architect Frank Lloyd Wright. Please respect private property by staying on the Trail. The segment then arrives at the Ice Age Trail Access parking area (**DA10**), a Town of Middleton park. From this spot hikers will continue on the following 0.3-mile connecting route to reach the next off-road portion of the segment: Hike east on Moraine Ridge Road, turn right and hike south on Mound View Road, turn left and hike east on Saracen Way.

From the Saracen Way access (**DA9**) the segment works its way south through a wooded area. Emerging from the woods, hikers should continue walking south on the grassy path between the residential area and the farm fields. The segment then bends east and parallels Mid Town Road. Hikers will pass a residential sign for Glacier's End and cross Fernglade Road before reaching the segment terminus at a yellow-blazed Trail post on the northeast side of the intersection of Shady Oak Lane and Mid Town Road.

To reach the Madison Segment, hikers should follow a 1.8-mile connecting route by heading east on Mid Town Road and then turning right and heading south on Woods Road.

From the access point on Woods Road the **Madison Segment** makes its way eastward through woods located between the 10th and 11th holes of University Ridge, the University of Wisconsin-Madison's golf course. Please respect the Trail host by walking quietly when passing by those enjoying a round of golf.

The segment emerges briefly from the woods and crosses the cart path that leads to the 10th-hole tee before continuing southwest through another wooded area. The segment emerges again from the woods and intersects with another paved path; hikers can turn left and access the golf course's clubhouse, which features water, restrooms and a snack bar. Ice Age Trail hikers are welcome to use the clubhouse.

Shortly after crossing the road to the clubhouse hikers will come to another path, this one leading to the golf course's lower parking area. Hikers parking in the lower parking area can use this path to access the Trail.

The segment continues southeast through a grassland area located west of the golf course's 1st hole, bends east and passes between the tee boxes for the 2nd and 9th holes and then intersects and follows the cart path that passes behind the 8th hole green. The segment travels through a small wooded area and again crosses the cart path between the 7th and 8th holes. It makes its way up a moraine and continues north through grassland before bending east and cutting through woods adjacent to the golf course's practice area.

The segment exits the woods, reaches a large grassy field and climbs to the top of another glacial moraine with expansive views. The segment passes through one last small patch of woods before intersecting with a path that leads northeast to the University's Noer Turfgrass Research Center. Hikers should follow the center's driveway to CTH-M (Pleasant View Road), turn left and briefly walk north along CTH-M (Pleasant View Road) to Flagstone Drive.

Note: CTH-M (Pleasant View Road) is a very busy road with high-speed traffic despite a 35 mph speed limit. Those hiking the full segment should exercise extreme caution when making the ⅛-mile connection along CTH-M between the Noer Center's driveway and Flagstone Drive to the north. Those hiking only a portion of the segment either east or west of CTH-M are strongly advised to park vehicles west (in the Noer Center lot) or east (on Flagstone Drive) of CTH-M, depending on which portion will be hiked.

The segment continues east from CTH-M on Flagstone Drive. After a short distance the segment departs from Flagstone Drive and heads southeast through a field full of tall grasses and wildflowers and then a small wooded area. The segment crosses Raymond Road, passes along the west side of a large drainage basin and makes its way due south into a small aspen and oak grove that gives way to prairie. *Note: Along the north/south stretch between Raymond Road and CTH-PD, a multi-use paved path separate from the Ice Age Trail parallels the segment a short distance to the west.*

Passing through an area of native grasses and wildflowers that is part of a restoration project begun by Veridian Homes, the segment bends east and joins a paved multi-use walkway. The segment parallels CTH-PD (McKee Road) to reach South High Point Road for a safer crossing of CTH-PD (McKee Road) at the stoplight. After crossing to the south side of CTH-PD (McKee Road), hikers should continue south a short distance on the Ice Age Junction Bicycle Pedestrian Trail. The segment leaves the main paved pathway and makes a right to go west on the paved access pathway to the parking area for the Ice Age Junction Area and the segment's endpoint.

AREA SERVICES

University Ridge Golf Course: Restaurant. On Trail. Open seasonally (9002 CTH-PD, Madison, 608-845-7700 or 800-897-4343, universityridge.com).

Madison: Restaurant, grocery store, convenience store, general shopping, lodging, camping, library, medical care. INN Style program lodging at the Arbor House, Ltd. (608-238-2981, arbor-house.com). Outfitter/camping supplies at REI (608-833-6680, rei.com/stores/madison) behind West Towne Mall. Area info available from the Greater Madison Chamber of Commerce (608-256-8348, greatermadisonchamber.com).

Mendota County Park: See Table Bluff and Cross Plains Segment, p. 216. From the CTH-PD (McKee Rd.) Trail access go west then north ~10 mil.

Middleton: Restaurant, grocery store, convenience store, general shopping, lodging, camping, library, medical care. From the CTH-M Trail access, go north on CTH-M 2.5 mi. At CTH-S (Mineral Point Rd.) turn right and go east 0.3 mi. At USH-12 go north 2.6 mi to the USH-14 Exit. Area info available from the Middleton Chamber of Commerce (608-827-5797, middletonchamber.com).

Verona: See Verona Segment, p. 224. From the CTH-PD (McKee Rd.) Trail access go west then south ~3 mi. Also see Trail Access and Parking directions, above.

Prairie on the Valley View Segment, with Blue Mound on the horizon.

Verona Segment (Atlas Map 66f)

6.4 miles: CTH-PD (McKee Rd.) to Prairie Moraine County Park at Wesner Rd.

This suburban segment makes good use of three county parks and links up to a variety of additional hiking and biking trails.

  At Reddan Soccer Park parking area (seasonal), Verona Public Library, Badger Prairie County Park main shelter (seasonal) and Ceniti Park Baseball Complex (seasonal).

 At the Dispersed Camping Area (**DA21**) in Badger Prairie County Park.

In Badger Prairie County Park.

 At Reddan Soccer Park, Badger Prairie County Park and Ceniti Park Baseball Complex.

 Portions overlap with multi-use paths, town sidewalks and roads and the Military Ridge State Trail (MRST).

 MRST continues east and west from IAT; also numerous bike trails and spur trails.

TRAIL ACCESS AND PARKING

CTH-PD (McKee Rd.): From Verona, at the intersection of Verona Ave. (Bus. Rt. USH-18/151) and CTH-M (Main St./Pleasant View Rd.), take CTH-M (Main St./Pleasant View Rd.) north 1.7 mi. At CTH-PD (McKee Rd.) turn right and go east 0.6 mi to the parking area on the south side of CTH-PD.

Prairie Moraine County Park at Wesner Rd.: From USH-18/151 south of Verona take Exit 79 onto CTH-PB and drive south 1.0 mi. At Wesner Rd. turn left to enter the Prairie Moraine County Park parking area.

Additional Parking: (i) Reddan Soccer Park parking area on Cross Country Rd. (No parking during tournaments.) (ii) Verona Public Library. (iii) Badger Prairie County Park (Exit 81 from USH 18/151). (iv) Military Ridge State Trail/Ice Age Trail access on Old PB Rd. just south of Verona Ave. (Exit 81 from USH 18/151). (v) Ceniti Park Sports Complex on the south side of E. Verona Ave. (vi) Lincoln St. foot/bike bridge parking at end of street.

THE HIKE

The Verona Segment travels through several park areas including the Ice Age Junction Area, Badger Prairie County Park and Prairie Moraine County Park. Hikers will encounter a number of spur/side trails and bike trails in these parks and therefore should pay close attention to Trail signage as only some of these trails are noted below.

The segment starts from the Ice Age Junction Area Trail access parking area on the south side of CTH-PD and makes its way west parallel to the road before bending south and traversing a prairie. The green space from CTH-PD south to Cross Country Road is the Ice Age Junction Area, an open space managed by the Dane County Parks Department that visually and physically separates Verona from southwest Madison. It hosts the Ice Age Trail and a paved bike trail. About 200 acres is restored prairie.

As the segment makes its way south through the prairie, it begins a slight descent toward a wooded area. A look to the south offers a fine overview of features hikers will encounter—the old water tower at Badger Prairie and the moraine on the horizon at the end of the segment, with CTH-PB's cut through it.

The segment enters the wooded area and follows to the left at a fork. The segment travels south through another prairie before reaching a short spur trail (near a maintenance shed) that leads west to picnic tables and a kiosk display explaining the Dane County Parks Department's prairie restoration and seed collection program. Additional displays about the Upper Sugar River Valley and the Ice Age Trail are located on the kiosk or nearby. Just beyond the kiosk is the northeast corner of the Reddan Soccer Park parking area.

The segment continues south and reaches Cross Country Road. The Trail runs west along a fence on the north side of Cross County Road to the entrance of the soccer park and crosses the road at a marked pedestrian crossing. Hikers can find several restaurants 0.3 miles west on Cross Country Road. After crossing the road the segment enters Badger Prairie County Park and continues southward. The Trail quickly intersects with a mowed park path and briefly follows it west before turning south and ascending a ridge. Hikers can look to the southwest to see the prominent red-orange roof of the Verona Public Library, which is accessible via a spur trail that runs south to the park road or by a mowed bike path.

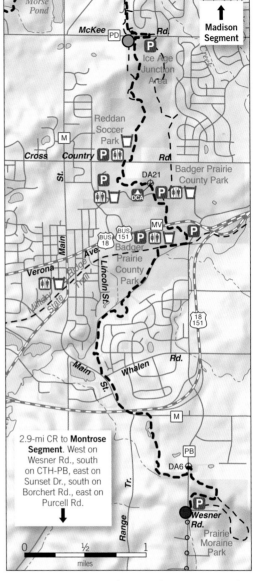

2.9-mi CR to **Montrose Segment**. West on Wesner Rd., south on CTH-PB, east on Sunset Dr., south on Borchert Rd., east on Purcell Rd.

The segment crosses the top of the ridge and begins its descent first on a gravel road then on a mowed path. Just before reaching the park's main shelter, the segment passes by a Dispersed Camping Area (**DA21**) in the restored prairie that dominates the park. Here multi-day long-distance hikers can camp legally in a minimally developed area. The site is NOT intended for those doing a one-night out-and-back hike.

After passing by the DCA and the main park shelter and parking area, the segment continues south, hooking up with a bike trail as it makes its way to Verona Avenue (CTH-MV). To access town services, hikers can head west on Verona Avenue 0.4 miles to a motel and another 0.5 miles to the town center.

The segment goes under Verona Avenue (CTH-MV) via a tunnel and continues southeast on the bike path to the Military Ridge State Trail (MRST) Park & Ride parking area. The multi-use MRST, connecting Madison to Dodgeville, is located on a railroad grade abandoned in the 1970s that once extended to Galena, IL.

The segment heads west on the MRST for approximately a quarter-mile, then just past the "3 Mile" marker departs from the MRST and makes its way south along the west side of Badger Mill Creek, which flows through a meltwater gap in the moraine. The segment passes a spur trail with a bike/pedestrian bridge over the creek with trails heading east and south to a residential neighborhood.

Continuing southwest the segment passes through a wetland area, running on top of a berm for part of the route. After dropping off the berm, the Trail meanders through a wooded creek bottom and a pine grove to a bridge where it crosses over to the east side of the creek, crosses a swampy area on a 275-foot boardwalk/puncheon span and eventually intersects with a paved spur trail that connects two residential neighborhoods. To the west, the spur trail leads across the creek on the Lincoln Street footbridge and connects with the street's dead end. Lincoln Street provides access to Verona's city center less than a mile away. To reach several restaurants, a supermarket and a hardware store, hikers can walk northwest via Lincoln Street, left on Valley View Street and right on South Main Street.

The segment moves south through woods in the meltwater gap, makes a steep ascent from the creek and heads around the east side of a quarry before reaching CTH-M. The Trail then continues southeast near or along CTH-M, crosses US Highway 18/151 and soon departs CTH-M making its way south along the edge of a field before entering woods and passing by several kettle ponds. The Trail continues eastward mostly through woods to CTH-PB. Hikers will see an oak and hickory restoration in progress. At the intersection with CTH-PB, hikers will need to briefly walk north to cautiously cross the road at the end of a median (**DA6**). Hikers can continue less than a quarter mile north on CTH-PB to a convenience store.

Upon crossing CTH-PB the segment enters a wooded area of the 160-acre Prairie Moraine County Park, which features a 0.8-mile-long stretch of the terminal moraine on St. Peter sandstone bedrock. The segment briefly makes its way south before heading southeastward, gently ascending along the north-northeast side of the terminal moraine through restored prairie and savanna. At the top of the moraine, a spur trail heads east to a viewing platform that offers views of a ravine cut in the moraine by meltwater and of the upper Sugar River Valley in the Driftless Area to the south.

From a saddle on the moraine, the segment descends westward using several short switchbacks, then curls southward to reach the Trail access at a gate in the northwestern corner of the park's parking area near CTH-PB. The moraine and the Ice Age Trail are fenced off from a heavily used dog exercise area located in the southeastern area of Prairie Moraine Park.

Verona: Restaurant, grocery store, convenience store, general shopping, lodging, camping, library, medical care. From the E. Verona Ave. (CTH-MV) Trail crossing go west 0.9 mi on E. Verona Ave. Dispersed Camping Area site at Badger Prairie County Park on Trail for long-distance hikers only. Area information available from the Verona Chamber of Commerce (608-845-5777, veronawi.com).

Military Ridge State Trail: On Trail (608-437-7393, dnr.wi.gov/topic/parks/name/militaryridge).

Madison: See Valley View Segment and Madison Segment, p. 220. From the CTH-PD (McKee Rd.) Trail access go east and north ~5 mi to the West Towne Mall area.

Montrose Segment (Atlas Map 67f)

SNAPSHOT

7.5 miles: Purcell Rd. to CTH-D

3 2 *This segment has two distinct experiences: a jaunt down a quiet multi-use rail trail and a beautiful new off-road trek featuring bedrock outcroppings, restored prairies and long views.*

 No reliable sources of water.

 A Dispersed Camping Area (**DA26**) north of CTH-D.

 In nearby Paoli (see Area Services).

 Portions overlap with the multi-use Badger State Trail (BST) and Piller Rd.

 BST continues north and south. Also, prairie spur trails and blue-blazed spur trail to DCA.

 Portions of this segment may be suitable for those using wheelchairs or similar devices.

TRAIL ACCESS AND PARKING

Purcell Rd.: From USH-18/151 south of Verona, take CTH-PB south 2.2 mi. At Purcell Rd. turn left and go east 1.7 mi. At Sayles Trail turn right and immediately turn right again into the Badger State Trail/Ice Age Trail parking area with kiosk.

CTH-D: From Madison, take Fish Hatchery Rd. (CTH-D) ~15 mi south. No parking. Alternatively, park at the CTH-DD parking area just west and south of the CTH-D endpoint. Access the segment via the Brooklyn Wildlife Segment.

Additional Parking: (i) CTH-A (**DA5**) roadside parking near the intersection where CTH-A heads west from STH-69. The Ice Age Trail/Badger State Trail is 100 ft to the east across STH-69. (ii) Frenchtown Rd./Piller Rd. parking area on the south side of the road.

THE HIKE

The segment starts out from Purcell Road by heading southwest along the Badger State Trail (BST), which opened in 2007 and extends north to Madison's Capital City Trail and south to the Illinois border. The BST is called a "well-connected trail," with links to the Capital City, Military Ridge and Sugar River state trails; Capital Springs and New Glarus Woods state parks; the Albany State Wildlife Area; numerous local parks and the Jane Addams State Trail in Illinois. Just south of the Purcell Road Trail access the segment crosses the Johnstown Moraine (**DA20**) before traversing several refurbished trestle bridges spanning

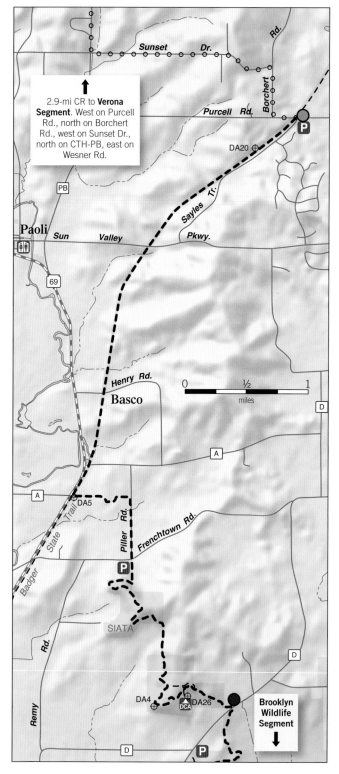

2.9-mi CR to **Verona Segment**. West on Purcell Rd., north on Borchert Rd., west on Sunset Dr., north on CTH-PB, east on Wesner Rd.

intermittent creeks.

The segment departs from the BST near the southern intersection of CTH-A and STH-69 at a point (**DA5**) where CTH-A heads west and the Ice Age Trail heads due east. The segment makes its way between two agricultural fields, crosses a 40-foot-long bridge over a ditch and meanders through a small wooded area before making its way to Piller Road, where the segment turns south and follows a field edge and then the road itself.

From the intersection of Piller Road and Frenchtown Road, site of a large parking area, the segment continues due south and climbs gradually up a slope between two agricultural fields before entering a wooded area. Once in the wooded area the segment bends west, then south, then back east as it climbs up to a former agricultural field, passing along the way an impressive bedrock outcropping dotted with ferns. The segment heads southeast through the open fields to a high plateau from which hikers can enjoy long views, especially in leaf-off seasons. On this high plateau volunteers are hard at work with prairie restoration activities.

The segment turns east when entering another wooded area and drops down a ridge, then continues south across a farm field and re-enters the woods. From this point the segment climbs gradually up the west side of a sandstone ridge, eventually making its way to a fine restored goat prairie and trailside bench (**DA4**) where hikers will enjoy outstanding views across a glacial outwash plain to the Sugar River watershed and the city of Belleville.

The segment takes a turn northeast and crosses a high prairie plateau. Right before the segment re-enters the woods, hikers will reach a junction with a blue-blazed spur trail and a sign indicating directions to a Dispersed Camping Area (DCA) for long-distance hikers. The spur trail leads 0.1 miles to the DCA (**DA26**). From the junction with the spur, the segment enters the woods and turns southeast to reach its terminus on CTH-D.

Mobile Skills Crew project site, 2009, 2011, 2012

AREA SERVICES

Badger State Trail: On Trail (608-527-2335, dnr.wi.gov/topic/parks/name/badger).

Paoli: Restaurant, grocery store. From Purcell Rd. go west 1.6 mi, then south 1.1 mi on CTH-PB, then west on Sun Valley Pkwy. Note: There is no access to Sun Valley Parkway from the Ice Age Trail/BST.

Belleville: See Brooklyn Wildlife Segment, p. 230. From the CTH-D Trail access go west then south ~3 mi.

Verona: See Verona Segment, p. 224. From the Purcell Rd. Trail access go west then north ~4 mi. Also see Trail Access and Parking directions, above.

DAVE CALIEBE

Montrose Segment.

Brooklyn Wildlife Segment (Atlas Map 68f)

3.5 miles: CTH-D to Hughes Rd.

  This segment follows a rolling course over glacial outwash and bedrock hills through the Brooklyn State Wildlife Area.

From a hand pump south of the southern CTH-DD parking area (**DA2**).

 By law, dogs must be leashed April 15 to July 31 in the State Wildlife Area.

Two blue-blazed spur trails to parking areas.

CTH-D: From Madison, take Fish Hatchery Rd. (CTH- D) ~15 mi south. No parking.

Hughes Rd.: From Belleville at the intersection of STH-92 and STH-69, take STH-92 east then south 3.0 mi to Dayton. At Dayton take Green County's CTH-D north 1.0 mi. At Hughes Rd. turn right and go east 0.3 mi to a parking area on the north side of the road.

Additional Parking: There are two parking area on CTH-DD that have blue-blazed spur trails to access the Ice Age Trail. (i) "North" CTH-DD parking area is just south of the intersection of Dane County's CTH-D and CTH-DD. Be careful of ruts. (ii) "South" CTH-DD parking area is 1.2 mi north of the Green County CTH-D and Hughes Rd. intersection or 0.75 mi south of the "North" CTH-DD parking area.

Note: A potential source of confusion in the area is the naming of county roads. In Dane County, the county's CTH-D crosses the Ice Age Trail as the road is making its way southwest toward Belleville. In Green County, the county's CTH-D runs north/south, passing through the town of Dayton on its way to the Green/Dane county line. Upon reaching the county line, Green County's CTH-D becomes CTH-DD, which in turn connects up a mile north with Dane County's CTH-D.

Brooklyn Wildlife Segment traverses an area featuring highly eroded glacial deposits from an earlier glacial advance more than 60,000 years ago. The segment highlights meadows, woodlands, oak savannas and colorful prairies. The variety of habitat in the area results in great bird-watching opportunities. Herons and cranes fish in the Story Creek wetlands and plenty of turkeys resting with their young can be stirred up on sandy portions of the segment. Volunteers from the Friends of Brooklyn Wildlife Area and the Ice Age Trail Alliance's Dane County Chapter have worked extensively on prairie restoration and removal of invasive species throughout the Brooklyn Wildlife Area.

From its starting point at the CTH-D Trail access the segment heads south. Several side trails make loops with the Ice Age Trail and give access to Story Creek. Two blue-blazed spur trails lead to the parking areas on CTH-DD. Hikers should pay attention to signage as some of the side-trail intersections can be confusing. About 1.8 miles south of CTH-D hikers will encounter a particularly impressive overlook (**DA27**) and view from the Trail of the Story Creek wetlands and the Johnstown Moraine. Another 0.6 miles farther on hikers will find a trailside hand water pump (**DA2**). From the site of the hand water pump the segment bends briefly northwest then continues its southern course to the Hughes Road Trail access.

AREA SERVICES

Belleville: Restaurant, grocery store, convenience store, lodging, library, medical care. From the Dane County CTH-D Trail access go west 2.6 mi on CTH-D and then south 0.3 mi on STH-69. INN Style program lodging at the Cameo Rose Victorian County Inn (866-424-6340, cameorose.com). The city park has a public swimming pool with showers.

Cooksville: INN Style program lodging at Cooksville Farmhouse Inn (608-335-8375, cooksvillefarmhouseinn.com).

New Glarus: See Monticello Segment, p. 234. From the CTH-D Trail access go west then south ~11 mi.

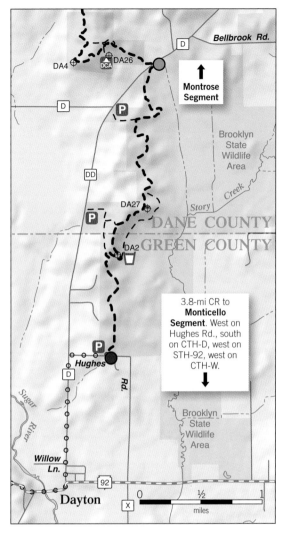

At first, my husband, Gene, thought I was crazy. But then he got so into it he became my coach, encouraging and supporting me with shuttles. While I hiked, he'd drive the rustic roads. He loved the rustic roads and sometimes after my day of hiking, he would drive them again with me.

SYLVIA OBERLE, ICE AGE TRAIL THOUSAND-MILER

Green County

Trail miles: 15.9
Connecting route miles: 6.9

Green County was largely untouched by the Green Bay Lobe of the late Wisconsin Glaciation. At its maximum extent, roughly 15,000 years ago, this lobe crept as far south as the village of Brooklyn. Earlier glacial advances covered most of the county, except a portion to the northwest that is part of the Driftless Area. The county has a rich history of European settlers. French explorers, traders and trappers were the first wave of Europeans in the region. Miners seeking lead ore came later.

Describing Green County in 1846, Increase Lapham wrote, "The mineral country extends nearly to the eastern part of this county, where the lead bearing rock crops out...There are already several very valuable discoveries of lead, and many flattering prospects of more. These mines are nearer Lake Michigan than any other in the mining country."

In the northern part of the county the Ice Age Trail follows the Badger State Trail (BST). A 2007 addition to the State's rail-trail system, the Badger State Trail runs on the former Illinois Central Railroad corridor from Madison's Capital City Trail across the state line to Orangeville, IL, joining the Grand Illinois Trail system. Near the town of Exeter, the BST goes through the historic Stewart Tunnel, the 27th longest rail tunnel in the country. Of note, old Ice Age Trail segment signs dot the countryside in the Exeter and Dayton area. These segments are no longer open for public use.

In Monticello the Ice Age Trail switches over to the Sugar River State Trail (SRST). On the former Milwaukee Road ("Limburger Special"), the SRST was created in 1974 after the Wisconsin Department of Natural Resources purchased the abandoned rail bed. The crushed limestone rail-trail stretches 23.1 miles from New Glarus to Brodhead, and with its 1% grade, it is perhaps one of the few flat surfaces in the county. It follows the Sugar River and crosses it 14 times on various trestle bridges. The Ice Age Trail shares the SRST as it passes over rushing streams and through picturesque rolling hills, dairy farms, verdant meadows and state wildlife refuges. Wild edible plants can be found along this wildlife corridor during warmer months. The SRST is a popular weekend destination for bicyclists.

Hiking on these two rail-trails is free; bike use requires a pass and fee payable at trailheads. Snowmobiles use the SRST in winter. There is no camping allowed along either rail trail.

CHAPTER INFORMATION

The Green County Chapter is currently inactive. Contact the IATA for more information.

COUNTY INFORMATION

Green County Visitor Information: 888-222-9111, greencounty.org

Sugar River State Trail: 608-527-2334, dnr.wi.gov/topic/parks/name/sugarriver

Badger State Trail: 608-527-2335, dnr.wi.gov/topic/parks/name/badger

Inside the 1,260-foot-long Stewart Tunnel on the Monticello Segment.

Monticello Segment (Atlas Maps 68f, 69f)

SNAPSHOT

6.5 miles: CTH-W to Monticello's Old Train Depot

  This segment follows multi-use rail-trails and offers the unique experience of hiking through the long, dark Stewart Tunnel.

 At Monticello's Old Train Depot (seasonal).

From the Little Sugar River.

At nearby New Glarus Woods State Park ~3 mi west of the Trail (see Area Services).

 By law, dogs must be leashed on the Badger State Trail (BST) and Sugar River State Trail (SRST)

 The BST and SRST are open to bicycles and snowmobiles.

 The BST and SRST both continue north and south.

 Portions of this segment may be suitable for those using wheelchairs or similar devices.

TRAIL ACCESS AND PARKING

CTH-W: From Belleville take STH-92 south 3.0 mi. At CTH-W turn left and go west 1.3 mi. No parking available. Roadside parking at CTH-CC crossing located another 0.2 mi west on CTH-W and then south on CTH-CC 0.3 mi.

Monticello's Old Train Depot: From STH-69 at Monticello, turn east on Lake Ave. and go 1.0 mi. At Pratt Rd. turn right and go 1 block south to parking area at Old Trail Depot, just north of CTH-EE.

Additional Parking: Tunnel Rd. northern Trail access (**GR6**). Roadside parking.

THE HIKE

This segment starts off from CTH-W in a southwesterly direction on the wide, crushed-gravel-surfaced Badger State Trail. After crossing CTH-CC and then Tunnel Road (**GR6**) the route reaches the northern end of the Stewart Tunnel (**GR3**). Completed in 1887, the 1,260-foot-long train tunnel is named after James Stewart of Pennsylvania, the contractor for the railroad construction. In 1886, he was killed nearby when he was thrown from his buggy while driving the proposed rail route. Blasted through limestone, the tunnel's opening is 14 by 22 feet. Hiking through the cool, dark, damp tunnel is quite an experience. It is lightless due to the curve midway through it. Hikers should have a flashlight ready! Springs above the tunnel trickle water down along the sides and onto the trail floor. Like a cave, it maintains a steady temperature. In summer it offers a cool retreat with temperatures staying between 50 and 60 degrees.

After exiting the tunnel at its south end the segment crosses Tunnel Road a second time and then Exeter Crossing Road (**GR2**). Shortly after crossing the scenic Little Sugar River on a long wooden bridge, the Ice Age Trail leaves the Badger State Trail and switches to the Sugar River State Trail at the signed crossover (**GR5**). The Ice Age Trail continues south on the Sugar River State Trail to Monticello. (*Heading north opposite the Ice Age Trail's route, the Sugar River State Trail takes users first to New Glarus Woods State Park and then to the Swiss-style village of New Glarus, known as "America's Little Switzerland."*)

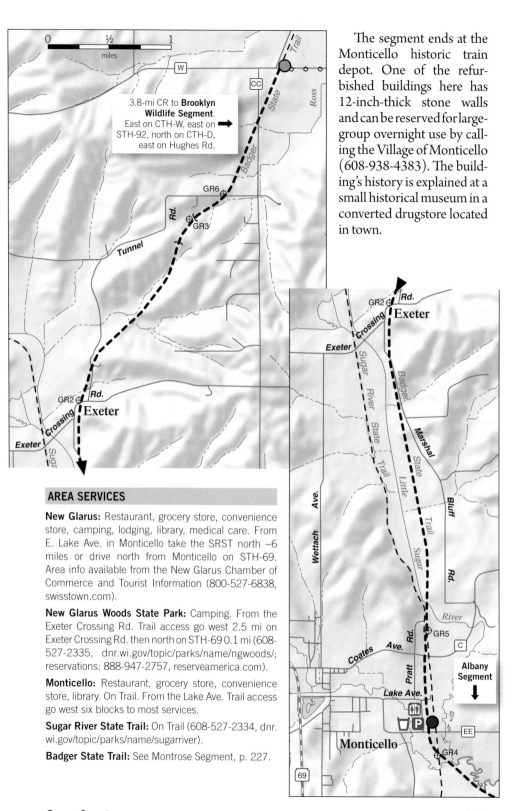

The segment ends at the Monticello historic train depot. One of the refurbished buildings here has 12-inch-thick stone walls and can be reserved for large-group overnight use by calling the Village of Monticello (608-938-4383). The building's history is explained at a small historical museum in a converted drugstore located in town.

3.8-mi CR to **Brooklyn Wildlife Segment**. East on CTH-W, east on STH-92, north on CTH-D, east on Hughes Rd.

AREA SERVICES

New Glarus: Restaurant, grocery store, convenience store, camping, lodging, library, medical care. From E. Lake Ave. in Monticello take the SRST north ~6 miles or drive north from Monticello on STH-69. Area info available from the New Glarus Chamber of Commerce and Tourist Information (800-527-6838, swisstown.com).

New Glarus Woods State Park: Camping. From the Exeter Crossing Rd. Trail access go west 2.5 mi on Exeter Crossing Rd. then north on STH-69 0.1 mi (608-527-2335, dnr.wi.gov/topic/parks/name/ngwoods/; reservations: 888-947-2757, reserveamerica.com).

Monticello: Restaurant, grocery store, convenience store, library. On Trail. From the Lake Ave. Trail access go west six blocks to most services.

Sugar River State Trail: On Trail (608-527-2334, dnr. wi.gov/topic/parks/name/sugarriver).

Badger State Trail: See Montrose Segment, p. 227.

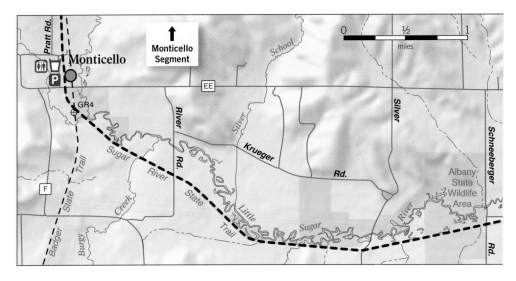

Albany Segment (Atlas Maps 69f, 70f)

9.4 miles: Monticello's Old Train Depot to Bump Rd.

 1 This very straight and flat segment highlights the quiet, twisty Little Sugar and Sugar rivers.

 At Monticello's Old Train Depot (seasonal) and Sugar River State Trail (SRST) parking area in Albany (seasonal).

 From the Little Sugar and Sugar rivers.

Private campground south of Bump Rd. (see Area Services).

By law, dogs must be leashed on the SRST.

 The SRST is open to bicycles and snowmobiles.

 The SRST continues north and south. The Badger State Trail continues south.

 Portions of this segment may be suitable for those using wheelchairs or similar devices.

TRAIL ACCESS AND PARKING

Monticello's Old Train Depot: From STH-69 at Monticello, turn east on Lake Ave. and go 1.0 mi. At Pratt Rd. turn right and go 1 block south to parking area at Old Trail Depot, just north of CTH-EE.

Bump Rd.: From STH-59 in Albany, turn south on Cincinnati St. and go 0.8 mi. At Bump Rd. turn left and go 0.1 mi to the Trail access. No parking. Alternatively, park at the Sugar River State Trail parking area on 4th St. From STH-59 in Albany, turn south on Cincinnati St. and go 0.4 mi. At 4th St. turn left and go 0.1 mi; parking area on left.

THE HIKE

This segment shares the wide, crushed-gravel-surfaced Sugar River State Trail for the segment's full length. It begins and ends in small towns and is filled with long stretches of pastoral views. The segment meanders along the Little Sugar River and through the Albany Wildlife Area and features rustic wooden bridges, frequent wildlife sightings and seasonal sounds of bullfrogs and dairy cows.

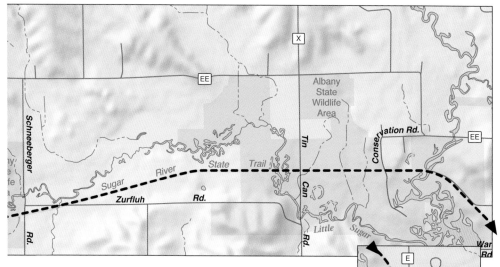

From the historic train depot in Monticello the segment heads in a southeasterly direction; just after the crossing of CTH-EE, the Sugar River State Trail intersects (**GR4**) the Badger State Trail, which is heading south toward the Illinois border.

After leaving the Badger State Trail behind, the segment heads east, paralleling the Little Sugar River. Watch for wild turkeys, pheasant, deer, sandhill cranes, snakes and turtles, who cross the path to lay their eggs.

As it nears the village of Albany, the segment crosses the Little Sugar River and then, on a long curving bridge with a picturesque view, the Sugar River. The latter crossing is just upstream from where the two rivers converge.

Upon reaching Albany, hikers can walk a few blocks off-Trail to the town's historical museum, which offers a nice slice of area history. It explains that the Ho-Chunk people called the river "Tonasookarah," meaning sugar, referring to the maple trees along the riverbank. They set up camps along the river in spring, cultivated gardens and fished in the Sugar River. As Europeans migrated west, the first settlers came to the area from New York State and New England and later Norway, Germany, Ireland, Wales and Switzerland. At the end of the 19th century, the Sugar River was called "River of Pearls," due to its abundance of oysters and clams, which are now protected.

AREA SERVICES

Albany: Restaurant, grocery store, convenience store, lodging, library, medical care. On Trail. From the Trail access, the business district is a few blocks west. INN Style program lodging at the Albany House B&B (866-977-7000, albanyhouse.com). At the Trail's junction with STH-59 is a moderate-size grocery with a deli. Camping is available 2.4 mi south of Bump Rd. on CTH-E at Sweet Minihaha Campground (608-862-3769, sweetminihaha.com).

Sugar River State Trail: See Monticello Segment, p. 234.

Monticello: See Monticello Segment, p. 234. From the Monticello Old Train Depot go north then west 7 blocks. Also see Trail Access and Parking directions, above.

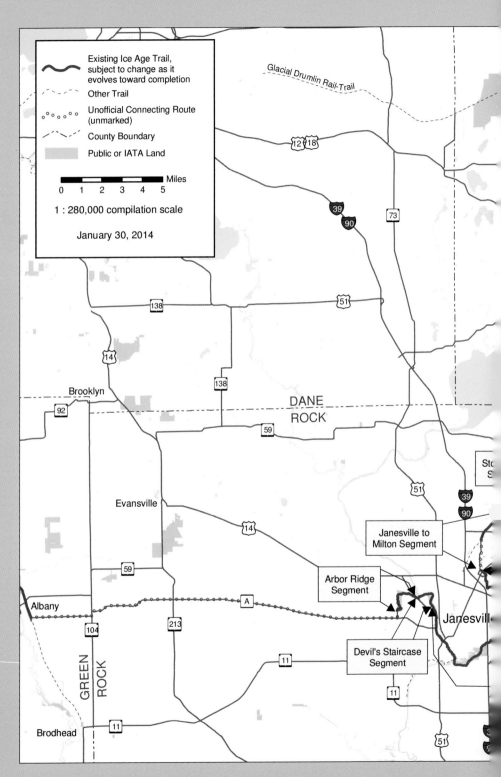

Existing Ice Age Trail,
subject to change as it
evolves toward completion

Other Trail

Unofficial Connecting Route
(unmarked)

County Boundary

Public or IATA Land

Miles

0 1 2 3 4 5

1 : 280,000 compilation scale

January 30, 2014

Glacial Drumlin Rail-Trail

12 18

39
90

73

138

14

138

Brooklyn

92

DANE
ROCK

59

Evansville

Sto
S

51

39
90

14

Janesville to
Milton Segment

59

Arbor Ridge
Segment

Albany

104

A

213

GREEN
ROCK

11

Devil's Staircase
Segment

Janesvill

11

11

Brodhead

11

51

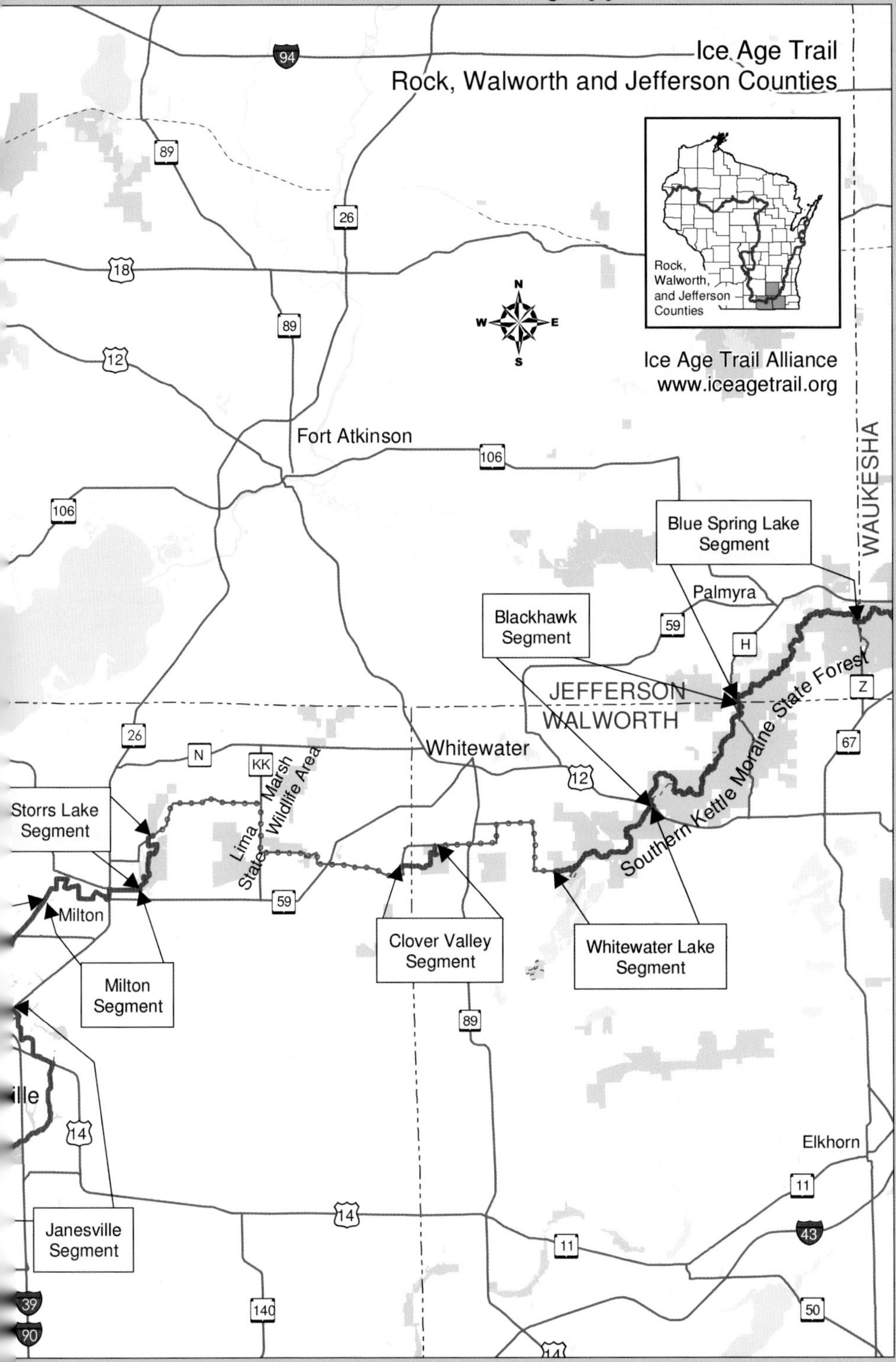

Rock, Walworth & Jefferson Counties

Rock,
Walworth,
and Jefferson
Counties

Ice Age Trail Alliance
www.iceagetrail.org

94

89

26

18

89

12

Fort Atkinson

106

106

Blue Spring Lake
Segment

WAUKESHA

Palmyra

Blackhawk
Segment

59

H

Z

JEFFERSON
WALWORTH

26

N

KK

Lima Marsh State Wildlife Area

Whitewater

12

67

Southern Kettle Moraine State Forest

Storrs Lake
Segment

59

Milton

Clover Valley
Segment

Whitewater Lake
Segment

Milton
Segment

89

14

Elkhorn

Janesville
Segment

11

43

14

39

90

140

11

50

Rock County

Trail miles: 22.1
Connecting route miles: 26.8

In Rock County, home to the southernmost segments of the Ice Age Trail, the Green Bay Lobe lost power and faded away 15,000 years ago. The northern third of the county has hills, kettles and other landforms left behind when the ice sheet came to a stop. The Johnstown Moraine can be seen along the Ice Age Trail route between Janesville and Milton. The terminal moraine was formed when the Green Bay Lobe worked like a conveyor to drop glacial material between the two cities. The Johnstown Moraine is named after a town in eastern Rock County and extends north to Waushara County. The remainder of Rock County was glaciated more than 25,000 years ago and is part of an area that stretches south beyond the Illinois border as prairie flatlands. The Ice Age Trail crosses the Rock River, which was a massive glacial meltwater channel during the last glacial advance and retreat. Today the river carries a smaller volume of water and can trace its origin north to Horicon Marsh in Dodge and Fond du Lac counties.

The Sauk, Fox, Illinois, Potawatomi and Ho-Chunk nations all were in this area at one time. They named the Rock River after the rocks that caused the rapids at the mouth of the river where it empties into the Mississippi. Historical sites significant to Blackhawk War events are located throughout the county, including a few noted along the Ice Age Trail route. The Trail winds through the cities of Janesville and Milton, highlighting their Ice Age and cultural history. Trail users are urged to check out the chapter's page on the IATA website. Among other things, the page has information to connect hikers with volunteers interested in lending a hand with shuttling and other support.

CHAPTER INFORMATION

The Rock County Chapter hosts workdays and special events throughout the year. Chapter members work in collaboration with the Rock Trail Coalition in developing trails in the county for hiking and biking. The chapter's "Walk Across Rock County" program rewards hikers who have walked all Ice Age Trail segments in the chapter's territory. Trail users are urged to check out the chapter's page on the IATA website. Among other things, the page has information to connect hikers with volunteers interested in lending a hand with shuttling and other support.

COUNTY INFORMATION

Rock County Tourism Council: 866-376-8767, rockcounty.org
Rock County Parks Department: 608-757-5451

Devil's Staircase Segment.

Rock County

Arbor Ridge Segment and Devil's Staircase Segment (Atlas Map 74f)

Arbor Ridge Segment—2.1 miles: Upper Parking Area of the Robert Cook Memorial Arboretum to Washington St. (CTH-E)

Devil's Staircase Segment—1.7 miles: Washington St. (CTH-E) to Riverside Park South Pavilion

 The scenic **Arbor Ridge Segment** through the Robert Cook Memorial Arboretum is handy to Janesville but feels miles away.

 At the arboretum shelter (seasonal).

 From Marsh Creek.

Hikers will not have any interaction with hunting on this segment.

 By law, dogs not permitted in Janesville Parks May 15 to Sept. 15; must be leashed at other times.

 Small portion overlaps with asphalt walkway in the arboretum.

 Robert Cook Memorial Arboretum trail network.

 Like the Arbor Ridge Segment, the remarkable, remote-feeling **Devil's Staircase Segment** will make hikers forget they are in a city.

 At Riverside Park North and South pavilions. Restrooms and drinking water are seasonal.

 From the Rock River.

Hikers will not have any interaction with hunting on this segment.

 By law, dogs not permitted in Janesville Parks May 15 to Sept. 15; must be leashed at other times.

 Small portions overlap with golf course paths.

TRAIL ACCESS AND PARKING

Upper Parking Area of the Robert Cook Memorial Arboretum: From Janesville at the intersection of Washington St. and Memorial Dr., take W. Memorial Dr. west 1.4 mi. Memorial Dr. becomes CTH-A. Continue west on CTH-A 0.4 mi to the gravel entrance drive for the Arboretum on the right shortly after passing the Arbor Ridge subdivision entrance. The Ice Age Trail is accessed from the upper parking area. Additional parking in the lower parking area.

Riverside Park South Pavilion: From I-39/90 at Janesville, take Exit 171B onto USH-14 and go west 4.0 mi. At N. Washington St. (CTH-E) turn left and go south 2.5 mi. At Parkside Dr. turn left and go northeast for 0.4 mi to the pavilion. Roadside parking.

Additional Parking: (i) Roadside parking in Arbor Ridge subdivision. (ii) N. Washington St. (CTH-E) parking area on the east side of the road across from the entrance to the Arbor Ridge subdivision. (iii) Riverside Park parking areas on Parkside Dr.; one is located along the road between the pavilions and another is located at the end of the road near the North Pavilion.

THE HIKE

The **Arbor Ridge Segment** traverses through an area of bedrock hills covered with till from glacial advances much older than those explored by most of the Ice Age Trail. From its starting point at the upper parking area for the Robert Cook Memorial Arboretum–Janesville Schools

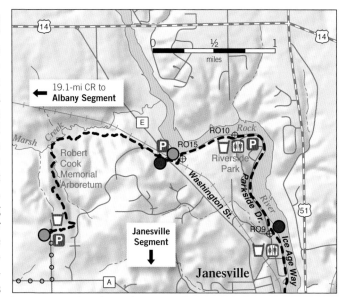

Outdoor Laboratory, the segment heads under an archway and into the heart of the arboretum property. Trailside signage provides educational information on trees and local flora. The arboretum is a 166-acre City of Janesville park (managed by the Janesville school district) that is open to the public sunrise to sunset.

The segment route heads east from the parking area and then turns north, descending down a long bedrock ridge to Marsh Creek. Upon reaching the creek the segment turns east and follows along the base of the bedrock ridges and valleys. Some of Marsh Creek's intermittent tributaries line the bottom of valleys in the hilly terrain, with elevation gain and loss of 200 feet. Volunteers have worked hard to remove invasive species in the area and open the mixed hardwood forest to views of magnificent oaks.

The segment bends away from Marsh Creek and parallels an active railway within a thirty-foot-wide wooded easement granted to the IATA for foot traffic only. The segment then intersects with an Arbor Ridge subdivision road, Northridge Drive, where hikers should turn left and follow Trail signage east a short distance to the segment's endpoint at the Ice Age Trail parking area across Washington Street (CTH-E).

Mobile Skills Crew project site, 2011

From its starting point at the parking area on the east side of of Washington Street (CTH-E), the **Devil's Staircase Segment** heads southeast a short distance parallel to the road, then emerges onto the City of Janesville's Riverside Golf Course property. As the segment continues, hikers will walk past a couple of the golf course's tee and green areas, crossing a set of railroad tracks in the process. Hikers are asked to be respectful of golfers when passing through this area; keep voices low and yield to those in the process of teeing off, hitting approach shots or putting. Hikers should stay on the mulched pathway and off the grass.

The segment parallels a high-tension power line and then enters a wooded area. For the next half-mile, hikers will traverse one of the more unique portions of the entire Ice Age Trail and may have a hard time remembering they are in the city of Janesville. The Civilian Conservation Corps built trail here in the early 1930s; however, it deteriorated to the point where it became impassible. The Ice Age Trail Alliance, along with great cooperation from the city, golf course, environmental groups, local businesses and dozens of local and statewide volunteers, rebuilt the Trail with an emphasis on keeping the area as natural as possible. As a result, when hiking the segment hikers will not see the golf course but will enjoy outstanding views of the Rock River. Skillfully placed rock steps that blend into the landscape take the hiker up and down steep hills. A portion of the route incorporates and preserves stonework attributed to the Civilian Conservation Corps.

As hikers begin this unique section of the Ice Age Trail, the segment descends a steep switchback into the natural feature known as the Devil's Staircase (**RO15**). This area features a huge gully (usually dry) descending from the golf course down across the Trail to the river. Lining the gully are large rocks that appear as though purposely placed as steps, thus leading to the name "Devil's Staircase."

The segment departs from the Devil's Staircase gully and continues along to the shore of the Rock River. The route then ascends from the river's shore up into the wooded area between the golf course and the river. On the uphill (south) side of the segment hikers will soon encounter carbonate calcareous rock faces, some of which rise up to 50 feet above the Trail. Numerous cliff-dwelling plants and woodland wildflowers highlight this portion of the segment.

Continuing east the segment arrives at a hand-crafted stone bench, where hikers will leave the wooded area by descending a steep set of manmade steps (**RO10**) and arrive at Riverside Park's North Pavilion area. From here to its endpoint at the park's South Pavilion the segment hugs the shoreline, generally sticking to the thin strip of land between the Rock River and Parkside Drive.

Mobile Skills Crew project site, 2007, 2009, 2011

AREA SERVICES

Janesville: See Janesville Segment, p. 246. From the Washington St. (CTH-E) Trail access go south into the city. Also see Trail Access and Parking directions, above.

DEAN PAYNTER

Devil's Staircase Segment.

Rock County

Janesville Segment (Atlas Map74f)

10.4 miles: Riverside Park South Pavilion to West Rotamer Ct.

 This segment uses the City of Janesville's extensive paved trail system that links parks to create an urban greenbelt.

 At the Riverside Park South Pavilion and the many other parks (seasonal) along the segment's route.

 From the Rock River.

 Hikers will not have any interaction with hunting on this segment.

 By law, dogs not permitted in Janesville Parks May 15 to Sept. 15; must be leashed at other times.

 Portions overlap with multi-use recreational paths, sidewalks and roads.

 Side trails in city parks.

Portions of this segment may be suitable for those using wheelchairs or similar devices.

TRAIL ACCESS AND PARKING

Riverside Park South Pavilion: From I-39/90 at Janesville, take Exit 171B onto USH-14 and go west 4.3 mi. At N. Washington St. (CTH-E) turn left and go south 2.5 mi. At Parkside Dr. turn left and go northeast for 0.4 mi to the pavilion. Roadside parking.

W. Rotamer Ct.: From I-39/I-90 take Exit 171A and go north on STH-26 (Milton Ave.). At Kettering Rd. turn left and go 0.1 mi. Turn right and go northeast on Whitney St. for 0.2 mi. Turn right at W. Rotamer Ct. Roadside parking.

Additional Parking: (i) Ashland Ave. at N. Washington St. parking area. A 0.2-mi spur leads to the Trail. (ii) N. River Rd. parking area (2 hour parking) just north of Mineral Point Ave. (iii) W. Milwaukee St. at the Rock River. (iv) S. River St. parking areas. (v) Dawson Ball Field. (vi) Rotary Botanical Gardens. (vii) Palmer Park. (viii) Blackhawk Meadows Park. (ix) N. Wright Rd. roadside parking. (x) Amhurst Rd. roadside parking. A short spur from the cul-de-sac leads to the Trail. (xi) Deerfield Dr. parking area between Home Depot and theaters. A short spur leads to the Trail.

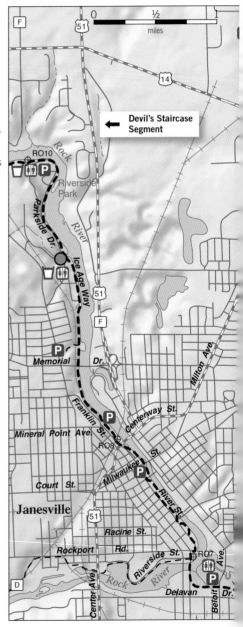

THE HIKE

From its starting point at Riverside Park's South Pavilion, the Janesville Segment exits the park and follows Ice Age Way for two blocks and then continues south along the Rock River on the Kiwanis Bike Trail. The segment passes by a portion of the Rock River opposite Traxler Park, where in summer the Rock Aqua Jays water ski team performs free world-class shows on the river every Sunday and Wednesday evening. A bench allows viewing the shows across the river.

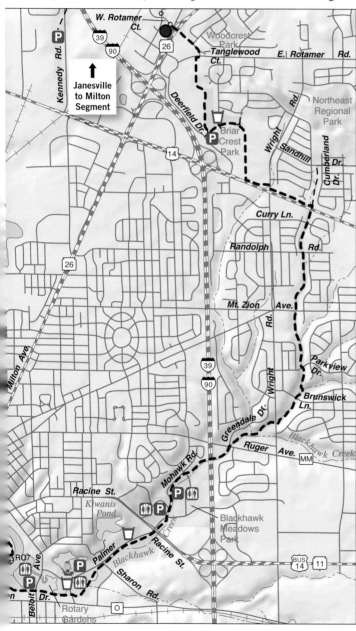

This section of Trail can flood in spring or after periods of heavy rain.

The segment intersects with North River Street and briefly follows it south underneath a railroad bridge (RO8) and across Centerway Street. The segment then continues south and southeast on the Kiwanis Trail along the Rock River and River Street on a mix of sidewalks and bike trail.

At the end of River Street the segment heads west for a short distance on Rockport Road sidewalks, turns south on the City of Janesville's Spring Brook Bike Trail, passes by the City of Janesville's trail hub (RO7) and then crosses the Rock River on an old railroad bridge. This bridge has a section where you can enjoy the river passing by without being in the flow of traffic.

After heading a short distance south from the railroad bridge the segment bends east and follows an intermittent stream that was once a large glacial melt-water river. For portions of the Spring Brook Trail hikers may forget they are in a city as they walk through sections of forest and restored prairies. The segment passes a historical marker near Dawson Field that commemorates the site of the winter and eventual year-round grounds of the Burr Robins Circus. In the 1870s, the circus was the third largest in the world and had a significant economic impact on Janesville.

The segment then bends north to intersect with Palmer Drive. Just a bit west down Palmer Drive hikers can explore the Rotary Botanical Gardens and Lions Beach (details below in Points of Interest section).

The segment continues northeast along Palmer Drive and passes by the Black-hawk Golf Course; the Black Hawk War Grove historical marker that indicates where men, women and children of the Sac, Fox and Kickapoo Nations camped during the Black Hawk War; Palmer Park; and Black Hawk Meadows Park.

The segment heads north and eventually crosses under USH-14. From here the Trail turns northwest along USH-14, north along the backside of a big-box retail shopping area, west to skirt Briar Crest Park and north again, passing behind a Walmart and Sam's Club on the way to the south side of East Rotamer Road. Cross East Rotamer Road at Tanglewood Drive and continue north and west on Tanglewood Drive 0.1 miles, picking up the multi-use path and crossing the STH-26 pedestrian bridge to the end of the segment at West Rotamer Court.

POINTS OF INTEREST

Lincoln-Tallman House: Just west of waypoint **RO8** at 426 N. Jackson St. (608-756-4509, rchs.us/lincoln-tallman-house).

The Lincoln-Tallman House is Rock County's most iconic historical structure. Constructed between 1855 and 1857, this six-floor mansion is an excellent example of Italianate-style architecture. From the basement to the cupola, each floor offers visitors a unique glimpse of daily life in 19th century Rock County. Over seventy percent of the furniture is original, making it one of the most complete historic houses in the Midwest. In October of 1859, Abraham Lincoln stayed at the house after a series of speeches in Beloit, forever cementing the reputation of the Lincoln-Tallman House as "where Lincoln slept."

Rotary Botanical Gardens and Lions Beach: Just west of the Trail's western intersection with Palmer Drive (608-752-3885, rotarybotanicalgardens.org).

The 20-acre Rotary Botanical Gardens, dedicated to international peace and friendship, showcase 18 different thematic gardens, many with an international theme, along with award-winning roses, unusual plant combinations, special collections of annuals and more. There is an admission fee. Just west of the Gardens is Lions Pond and Beach, with its large swimming area and changing rooms.

AREA SERVICES

Janesville: Restaurant, grocery store, convenience store, general shopping, lodging, library, medical care. Area info available from the Janesville Area Convention and Visitors Bureau (seasonal visitor center located on the Trail in Palmer Park; 800-487-2702, janesvillecvb.com), City of Janesville Parks Department (608-755-3025) and City of Janesville Leisure Services (608-755-3030, www.ci.janesville.wi.us/index.aspx?page=100). Recommended services: (i) From the Trail at Washington St. (CTH-E) go east to Bogg Trotters (2006 N. CTH-E, 608-757-1444) for meals. (ii) From the Trail through the downtown area along the river find meals, convenience store, library and medical care. (iii) From the Trail at Mt. Zion Ave. go west 0.25 mi for meals and convenience store. (iv) From the segment endpoint find meals, groceries, convenience store, general shopping and lodging in the Deerfield Drive/USH-14 area.

Janesville to Milton Segment (Atlas Map 75f)

SNAPSHOT

3.2 miles (1.7 IAT, 1.5 CR): W. Rotamer Ct. to Manogue Rd.

 This segment links two suburban areas via a portion of a pleasant, tree-lined converted railway path.

 No reliable sources of water.

 By law, dogs must be leashed on the multi-use path.

Segment shares a multi-use recreational path and includes a portion of road walk.

The multi-use path on the abandoned railroad bed extends southwest from the segment into Janesville.

 Portions of this segment may be suitable for those using wheelchairs or similar devices.

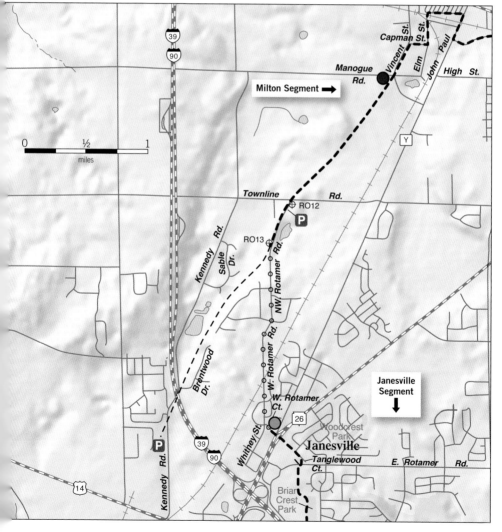

TRAIL ACCESS AND PARKING

W. Rotamer Ct.: From I-39/I-90 take Exit 171A and go north on STH-26 (Milton Ave.). At Kettering Rd. turn left and go 0.1 mi. Turn right and go northeast on Whitney St. for 0.2 mi. Turn right at W. Rotamer Ct. Roadside parking.

Manogue Rd.: From I-39/90 north of Janesville, take Exit 163 and go east then south on STH-59 for 5.9 mi to Milton. In Milton, where STH-59 turns east, continue straight (south) on S. Clear Lake Ave. for 0.1 mi. At Ansley Ave. turn right and go west 0.1 mi. At Vincent St. turn left and go south 0.6 mi to Manogue Rd. (High St.). The Trail access is on the southwest corner. Roadside parking.

Additional Parking: NW Rotamer Rd. parking area, just south of Townline Rd. (**RO12**).

THE HIKE

From its starting point on West Rotamer Court the segment heads northwest 0.1 miles. At West Rotamer Road/Whitney Street hikers should turn right and continue north on West Rotamer Road (which transitions to NW Rotamer Road) for 1.4 miles. As the segment approaches Townline Road hikers will depart from the road and merge (**RO13**) onto an abandoned railroad bed that has been converted for public use as a multi-use recreational path. The segment continues northeast on the railroad bed, crossing Townline Road and then continuing through a tree-lined corridor in agricultural landscape to the segment's endpoint at the intersection of Vincent Street and Manogue Road (High Street).

AREA SERVICES

Janesville: See Janesville Segment, p. 246. From the West Rotamer Court Trail access go west then south 1.0 mi to a large commercial area. Also see Trail Access and Parking directions, above.

Milton: See Milton Segment and Storrs Lake Segment, p. 251. From Manogue Rd. Trail access go north and east into town. Also see Trail Access and Parking directions, above.

I have read and heard from people who have hiked the entire Ice Age Trail, what they have seen and felt along its thousand-plus miles of rural roads and wooded paths. And now, having completed the journey myself, I find that my only regret is that those earlier hikers have used up all the best words in describing the Trail's beauty. I would have to be another Robert Frost to touch it with any justice.

TOM TEEPLES (AKA "LRRP"), ICE AGE TRAIL THOUSAND-MILER

Milton Segment and
Storrs Lake Segment (Atlas Map 75f)

Milton Segment—4.3 miles: Manogue Rd. to Storrs Lake Rd.

Storrs Lake Segment—1.9 miles: Storrs Lake Rd. to Bowers Lake Rd.

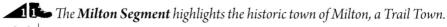 The **Milton Segment** highlights the historic town of Milton, a Trail Town.

 At South Goodrich Park.

  At a private campground located 2.0 miles north of Milton.

 Hikers will not have any interaction with hunting on this segment.

 By law, dogs must be leashed on the entire segment.

 Almost entirely on sidewalks and roads.

 Portions of this segment may be suitable for those using wheelchairs or similar devices.

 The **Storrs Lake Segment** passes through woods where Abraham Lincoln camped and features wetlands and mixed forest teeming with songbirds and waterfowl.

From Storrs Lake and Bowers Lake.

By law, dogs must be leashed April 15 to July 31 in the State Wildlife Area.

 Portion of the segment crossing private land south of Bowers Lake Rd. is closed during gun deer season.

Hunting/social trails in the State Wildlife Area.

Manogue Rd.: From I-39/90 north of Janesville, take Exit 163 and go east then south on STH-59 for 5.9 mi to Milton. In Milton, where STH-59 turns east, continue straight (south) on S. Clear Lake Ave. for 0.1 mi. At Ansley Ave. turn right and go west 0.1 mi. At Vincent St. turn left and go south 0.6 mi to Manogue Rd. (High St.). The Trail access is on the northeast corner. Roadside parking.

Bowers Lake Rd.: From I-39/90 at Janesville, take Exit 171A and go north on STH-26 for 4.7 mi. Take Exit 8 and go east on STH-59 for 0.6 mi. At Janesville St. turn right and go north for 1.3 mi. At Bowers Lake Rd. turn right and go east 1.5 mi to the parking area on the north side of the road.

Additional Parking: Storrs Lake State Wildlife Area Ice Age Trail parking area on Storrs Lake Rd. The Trail access is on the north side of the parking area.

From its starting point on Manogue Road (High Street) the **Milton Segment** heads north on a grassy path just east of Vincent Street. At Capman Street hikers should turn right and go east two blocks. This area used to be a separate community called Milton Junction and was linked with Milton through its 19th century railroad history. The old railroad depot area, Milton's "second main street," now houses restaurants and specialty shops. Hikers should follow the yellow blazes on utility poles and street signs along Elm Street, Vernal Avenue, John Paul Road (CTH-Y) and Municipal Drive to reach the Milton Senior High School

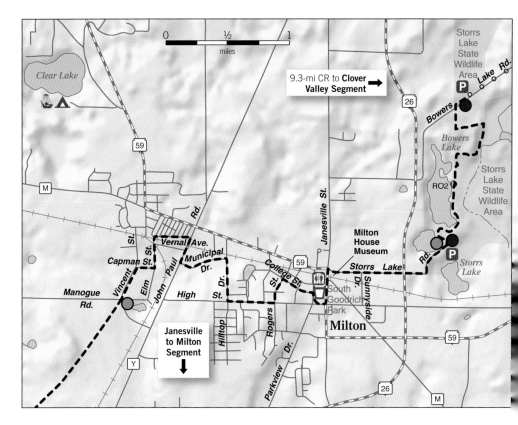

and the school's outdoor laboratory, which exhibits a restored prairie project.

Continue following the yellow blazes on Hilltop Drive, High Street and Rogers Street to go past old Milton College, which sits atop the terminal moraine of the Green Bay Lobe. Milton College closed in 1982 and is now an office building with antique shops.

At College Street hikers should turn right and go east three blocks through the Milton historic area. Upon reaching Parkview Drive hikers should cross the road and continue southeast through South Goodrich Park to High Street and on to Janesville Street. Turn left on Janesville Street and go north 0.3 miles past the historic Milton House (see Points of Interest) to Storrs Lake Road.

The route heads east on Storrs Lake Road for 1.1 miles before reaching the segment's end point at the large parking area for the Storrs Lake State Wildlife Area.

The 950-acre Storrs Lake State Wildlife Area traversed by the **Storrs Lake Segment** is a rich brocade of old oak trees, tall prairie grasses, dry kettles, wildflowers and lakes teeming with northern pike, walleye and sunfish. It is home to sandhill cranes, deer, wood ducks, mallards, turkey, egrets, pheasants and barred and great horned owls. On July 1, 1832, young Abraham Lincoln camped beside Storrs Lake as one of 4,500 soldiers commanded by brigadier General Henry Atkinson. They were in pursuit of Sauk Chief Black Hawk, who was fleeing north and west along the Rock River with 400 warriors and 1,200 women and children.

From its starting point on the north side of the parking area for the Storrs Lake

State Wildlife Area the segment heads north and winds through tranquil forest of old bur and white oaks, mixed hardwoods and grasslands. The route offers delightful views of Bowers Lake along an upland terrace before emerging from the forest at a signed intersection (**RO2**). *During periods of heavy rain or high water, the portion of the segment north of the signed intersection can become swampy to the point of being impassable. Check with the Ice Age Trail Alliance (**800-227-0046, iceagetrail.org**) for current conditions and bypass options.*

The segment continues north, east and then north again, meandering between wetlands and forest and overlooking a meltwater channel. The segment then heads west and north past an old apple orchard and along the edge of a cornfield before reaching Bowers Lake Road. Hikers should cross the road and follow the segment to the right to reach its endpoint at the parking area on Bowers Lake Road.

Mobile Skills Crew project site, 2004

POINTS OF INTEREST

Milton House Museum: On Trail at 18 S. Janesville St. in Milton (608-868-7772, miltonhouse.org).

The Milton House is one of twelve Underground Railroad National Historic Landmarks. In 1844, the Milton House was a stagecoach inn and station on the Underground Railroad for runaway slaves from the south. Fugitive slaves would have traveled through Illinois and Wisconsin with the goal of reaching Lake Michigan and boarding a ship with a sympathetic captain to travel the Great Lakes and escape into Canada. Visitors can tour the tunnel that was used to transport fugitive slaves. Seasonal hours; please call first.

AREA SERVICES

Milton: Restaurant, grocery store, convenience store, lodging, camping, library, medical care. On Trail. Most services located on or near Janesville St. in Milton and south of STH-59 and at the old railroad depot area at Capman St. and Vincent St. Area info available from the Milton Chamber of Commerce (608-868-6222, maccit.com). Camping is available 2.0 mi north of Milton (north on STH-59 and west on Clear Lake Rd. and Blackhawk Dr.) at Blackhawk Camping Resort (866-652-2586, blackhawkcampingresort.com).

Janesville: See Janesville Segment, p. 246. From the Storrs Lake Rd. Trail access go south ~5 mi. Also see Trail Access and Parking directions, above.

Determined to see more of our scenic Wisconsin and to find a "sport" we could do together, hiking the Ice Age Trail was a likely candidate. Originally we didn't start with a plan nor did we set out to hike the entire Ice Age Trail. However, as miles were completed, we made it our 10-year goal. We saw it as an opportunity to do several of our favorite things: visit new and familiar places in Wisconsin, do something active, then replenish ourselves with good beer and great food.

RICK (AKA "BUZZ") AND ROBERTA (AKA "FREIDA") BIE,
ICE AGE TRAIL THOUSAND-MILERS

Walworth & Jefferson Counties

Trail miles: 20.3
Connecting route miles: 4.9

In 1846, famed conservationist Increase Lapham wrote of Walworth County: "It is one of the richest and most important agricultural counties in the Territory; possessing a rich soil, with about the proper proportion of timber and prairie land to suit the convenience and fancy of the first settlers of a new country."

The Kettle Moraine reaches its southern end near Richmond in Walworth County. Here, the Green Bay and Lake Michigan lobes parted to extend west and south. The Ice Age Trail in this section is mostly in the Southern Unit of the Kettle Moraine State Forest (KMSF). It features many forests of white, black and bur oak, oak savannas, prairies, lakes, eskers and kettles. One highlight is the trip to the top of Bald Bluff, which showcases a thriving prairie and offers panoramic views to the west. Controlled burns by the Wisconsin Department of Natural Resources have rejuvenated the original prairie landscape and have encouraged the return of native prairie flowers. See the Waukesha County section for further information about the KMSF.

CHAPTER INFORMATION

Since 1993, the Walworth/Jefferson County Chapter has reached out to residents of communities such as Whitewater, Elkhorn, Lake Geneva, East Troy and Palmyra. Chapter leaders conduct popular weekly walks, along with special-interest hikes such as full moon, prairie flower, National Trails Day and Fall Colors. Other chapter activities include an Adopt-a-Segment program, monthly Trail maintenance days, family events and potlucks. Contact the chapter on for more details on their "Kettle Trekkers" hiking program.

COUNTY INFORMATION

KMSF Southern Unit headquarters: 262-594-6200, dnr.wi.gov/topic/parks/
   name/kms/

Jefferson County Tourism Council: 920-674-4511, enjoyjeffersoncounty.com

Walworth County Tourism Council: 800-395-8687, visitwalworthcounty.
   com

The "Stone Elephant" on the Blue Spring Lake Segment.

Walworth & Jefferson Counties

Clover Valley Segment (Atlas Map 77f)

1.6 miles: County Line Rd. to Island Rd.

  This short and quiet segment crossing the Clover Valley State Wildlife Area features wet meadow habitat and Spring Brook.

From Spring Brook.

By law, dogs must be leashed April 15 to July 31 in the State Wildlife Area.

TRAIL ACCESS AND PARKING

County Line Rd.: From the south edge of Whitewater at the bypass intersection of USH-12, STH-59 and STH-89, take STH-89 south 2.0 mi. At Island Rd. turn right and go west 1.6 mi. At East Spring Brook Rd. (Converse Rd.) veer left and go southwest 0.1 mi. At County Line Rd. turn left and go south 0.4 mi. The segment starts at a tree line on the east side of the road. No parking.

Island Rd.: From the south edge of Whitewater at the bypass intersection of USH-12, STH-59 and STH-89, take STH-89 south 2.0 mi. At Island Rd., turn right and go west 0.9 mi to the parking area on the south side of the road. (Note: At the corner of STH-89 and Island Rd., the street sign is mismarked as Island Dr.)

THE HIKE

The Clover Valley State Wildlife Area is a part of a vast wetland that was previously drained for agricultural use. It has been managed as hunting and trapping areas for waterfowl, deer, pheasant, woodcock and small game. Other recreational activities available are hiking, berry picking, fishing and bird and wildlife viewing. Sandhill cranes frequent the area. Portions of this segment can be seasonally flooded or extremely wet after heavy rainfall.

The segment starts at a trail access point just west of the Rock/Walworth county line and follows the edge of a farm field through woods of silver maple, box elder and willow before crossing a bridge over a small stream and then a few

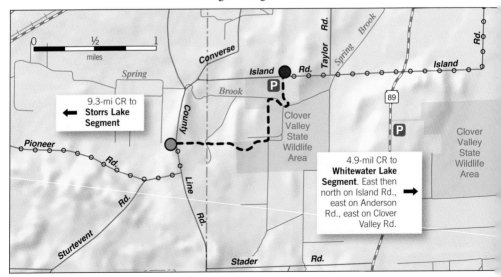

boardwalks. The segment then passes through a meadow area where big blue-stem, Indian grass and assorted coneflowers commingle with invasive reed canary grass and Queen Anne's lace.

After passing through the meadow the segment enters mature woodlands of slightly higher elevation. Hikers can easily find wild geraniums, jack-in-the-pulpit, mayapple and wild raspberry colonies. The segment passes a large white oak on the southeast edge of these woods. Continuing east, the segment follows a fencerow through a field containing many summer-blooming bottle gentians. Hikers will then turn north and hike through shrub carr (a wetland community dominated by tall shrubs such as red-osier dogwood, silky dogwood, meadow-sweet and various willows) and an area of old drainage ditches. Upon reaching Spring Brook, the segment follows it east for a quarter mile before crossing the brook on a wooden bridge.

From the bridge the segment winds 0.2 miles north through shrub carr, meadow and prairie to the segment's terminus at the Island Road parking area.

AREA SERVICES

Whitewater: See Whitewater Lake Segment, p. 257. From the Island Rd. Trail access go east then north ~3 mi. Also see Trail Access and Parking directions, above.

Whitewater Lake Segment (Atlas Map 78f)

SNAPSHOT

4.6 miles: Clover Valley Rd. to USH-12

◢3 2➤ *This hilly segment features wooded moraines, kettles and outstanding views of Rice and Whitewater lakes from atop a steep rise.*

 At the Rice Lake Nature Trail, DNR contact station and State Rec Area/Campground.

 From Whitewater Creek.

 At Whitewater Lake Rec Area/Campground.

 At Whitewater Lake Rec Area/Campground and USH-12 Trail access parking area.

 A small portion of the Trail overlaps with a bridle/snowmobile trail.

 Connects with Rice Lake Nature Trail and Whitewater Lake Recreation Area and DNR Contact Station spur trails.

TRAIL ACCESS AND PARKING

Clover Valley Rd.: From the south edge of Whitewater at the bypass intersection of USH-12 and STH-89, take STH-89 south 1.4 mi. At Anderson Rd. turn left and go east 0.8 mi. At the T-intersection, the road becomes Clover Valley Rd. Continue straight (east) following what is now Clover Valley Rd. for 2.6 mi. The road turns south and passes the artesian flowing well and Kiwanis International Wayside Park (**JW8**), before turning east again. Access the Trail on the northeast side of the road. Roadside parking. Park with tires off pavement.

USH-12: *From La Grange* take USH-12 west 3.0 mi to the parking area. *From Whitewater* at the bypass intersection of USH-12 and STH-89, take USH-12 east 5.0 mi.

Additional Parking: (i) Rice Lake Nature Trail parking area on State Park Rd. To access the Ice Age Trail from the parking area, take the Rice Lake Nature Trail loop northwest for 0.4 mi. Continue on the blue-blazed spur trail 0.1 mi across Kettle Moraine Dr. to its junction with the Ice Age Trail near Hi-Lo Rd. (ii) Whitewater Lake DNR Contact Station parking area on Kettle Moraine Dr. A 0.2-mi spur trail leads from the parking area to the Ice Age Trail. (iii) Esterly Rd. Trail access, roadside parking.

THE HIKE

From the Trail access on Clover Valley Road, the segment starts off by passing through a shady pine plantation before crossing Whitewater Creek, the outlet stream from Rice Lake, on a series of puncheons and a 30-foot bridge. These structures protect the sensitive wetland bordering Whitewater Creek and offer tranquil views of the surrounding wetlands and valley. Many spring wildflowers, such as blue-flag iris and marsh marigold, along with skunk cabbage, line the creek valley.

After crossing Whitewater Creek the segment then skirts the Whitewater Lake Recreation Area's walk-in campsites before reaching a junction (**JW6**) with a blue-blazed spur trail. The spur trail heads south across Kettle Moraine Drive to a self-guided 0.6-mile nature trail loop along the shore of Rice Lake. A large parking area is located off the loop trail.

From the junction with the spur trail the segment continues east, crossing Hi-Lo Road before reaching another spur trail, this one labeled "Office," which heads southeast 0.2 miles to the Whitewater Lake DNR Contact Station parking area. After the path to the office, the segment encounters yet another side trail, this one to the entrance of the Whitewater Lake Recreation Area (**JW5**).

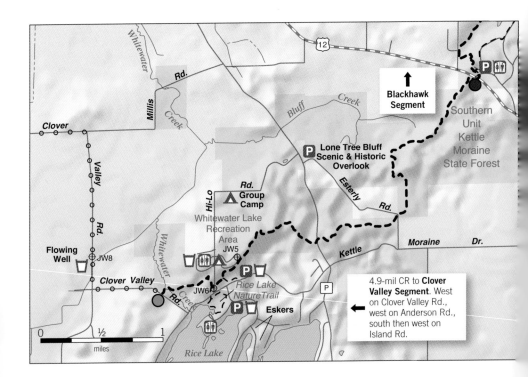

Ice Age Trail Guidebook 2014

The segment continues east through rugged, rolling terrain past many trail-side kettles. After passing behind several Whitewater Lake Campground drive-in campsites the segment climbs a steep rise to a bench and lookout offering views of Rice and Whitewater lakes. The segment crosses CTH-P and rises steeply to another secluded pine plantation before crossing Esterly Road. The segment briefly joins a bridle/snowmobile trail before branching off and eventually crossing a cleared area beneath a power line. The headwaters of Bluff Creek lie below to the west and can be viewed off the segment by hiking north in the cleared area to the utility poles on top of the hill. A bench is located to the west of these poles. Just beyond the power line the segment passes through Bluff Creek State Natural Area. Here the segment travels across cavernous kettles with ancient oaks providing the canopy. This area is particularly beautiful after a wet-heavy snowfall. Shortly before the segment's end at USH-12, a clearing offers views to the west of the glacial outwash plain and the city of Whitewater from a trailside bench.

Mobile Skills Crew project site, 2007

AREA SERVICES

KMSF Southern Unit Whitewater Lake Recreational Area (seasonal): Camping Memorial Day to Labor Day. On Trail (262-473-7501, dnr.wi.gov/topic/parks/name/kms/camping.html; reservations: 888-947-2757, reserveamerica.com).

Elkhorn: INN Style program lodging at Ye Olde Manor House B&B (262-742-2450, yeoldemanorhouse.com).

La Grange: Meals. From the USH-12 Trail access parking area go 3.0 mi east on USH-12 to the La Grange General Store (262-495-8600).

Whitewater: Restaurant, grocery store, convenience store, general shopping, lodging, library, medical care. From the USH-12 Trail access parking area, go 5.0 mi west on USH-12, follow Business USH-12. INN Style program lodging at the Hamilton House B&B (262-473-1900, bandbhamiltonhouse.com). Lodging at the Super 8 Motel (262-472-0400). Meals at Randy's Restaurant and Funhunters Brew Pub (262-473-8000). Area info available from the Whitewater Chamber of Commerce (262-473-4005, whitewaterchamber.com).

Blackhawk Segment (Atlas Map 79f)

SNAPSHOT

7.0 miles: USH-12 to Young Rd.

This segment highlights scenic Lake La Grange, hardwood forests and the historic Ole Oleson Homestead.

 At nearby Nordic Trails parking area south of CTH-H Trail access.

 From Lake La Grange.

 At a walk-to trailside shelter (**JW3**) (reservations required).

 At the USH-12 Trail access parking area and Backpack Shelter 3 (please respect those who have reserved the shelter) and parking areas for nearby John Muir and Nordic trails.

 A small portion overlaps with a snowmobile trail.

 White-blazed loop trail and several KMSF spur trails.

TRAIL ACCESS AND PARKING

USH-12: *From La Grange* take USH-12 west 3.0 mi to the parking area. *From Whitewater* at the bypass intersection of USH-12 and STH-89, take USH-12 east 5.0 mi.

Young Rd.: From the intersection of STH-59 and CTH-H in Palmyra take CTH-H southwest 3.0 mi. At Young Rd. turn left and go east 0.1 mi. Roadside parking.

Additional Parking: (i) Duffin Rd. Trail access (**JW12**) 0.4 mi south of the Oleson Cabin; roadside parking. (ii) Oleson Cabin Historic site on Duffin Rd.; roadside parking. (iii) John Muir Hiking and Biking Trails parking area on CTH-H. (iv) Nordic Hiking and Ski Trails parking area on CTH-H. (v) Bald Bluff Scenic Overlook parking area. From the intersection of STH-59 and CTH-H in Palmyra, take CTH-H southwest 2.8 mi. Parking area on east side of road. The trail to Bald Bluff serves as a spur to the Ice Age Trail.

THE HIKE

The segment begins at the USH-12 Trail access information kiosk and parking area, a popular meeting point for events sponsored by the Ice Age Trail Alliance's local Walworth/Jefferson County Chapter. The segment crosses

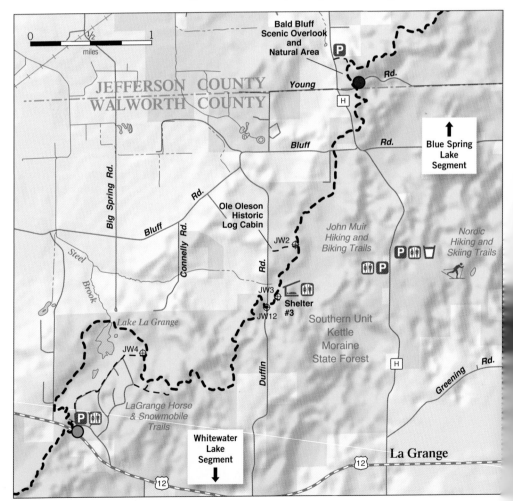

through excellent bird habitat and many species can be seen.

From the USH-12 parking area, the segment briefly climbs a hill, offering long views of deciduous forests and a nice view toward Whitewater from a bench. The Trail descends on a serpentine course and then meanders north and east around Lake La Grange past marshes bordering the lake and through woods and open tall-grass prairies. Along the way a couple of benches offer scenic views of Lake La Grange.

The segment reaches an intersection (**JW4**) with a white-blazed path that heads south along the eastern shore of Lake La Grange back toward the USH-12 Trail access. From this junction, the Ice Age Trail continues eastward, passing through hardwood forest before descending 200 feet to Duffin Road (**JW12**).

Shortly after the Duffin Road crossing the segment intersects with a spur trail that leads 0.1 miles to Backpack Shelter 3 (**JW3**), situated atop a steep hill surrounded by dense forest.

A bit farther north from the shelter spur, the segment intersects with another spur trail (**JW2**), this one to the historic Ole Oleson Homestead, where an early Norwegian pioneer built a two-story tamarack log cabin. On display outside the cabin is an old sleigh similar to the one used by Ole Oleson to transport the logs for the house. Another spur trail leads east 0.6 miles to a pioneer limekiln with a descriptive plaque. This spur trail is not always maintained.

Continuing from the Ole Olson spur trail, the segment leads through dense forest, frequently passing along the rims of large kettle depressions, among a diverse and undisturbed quantity of flora and fauna. The Trail passes a small lake and then enters dense pine plantations.

After crossing Bluff Road, the segment goes through a section of red, black and jack pine before crossing CTH-H and climbing steeply through a savanna-like open forest of hardwoods, pockmarked by kettle depressions and scattered boulders. At the top there is a beautiful view to the horizon overlooking forests and the surrounding terrain. A short downhill trek takes hikers to the segment terminus on Young Road.

AREA SERVICES

KMSF Southern Unit Backpack Shelter 3: Camping. On Trail. Reservations (available only by calling 888-947-2757) are required to use the shelter and only one group per shelter per night is allowed. No potable water is available at the shelter.

La Grange: See Whitewater Lake Segment, p. 257. From the USH-12 Trail access go east 3.0 mi. Also see Trail Access and Parking directions, above.

Whitewater: See Whitewater Lake Segment, p. 257. From the USH-12 Trail access go west ~5 mi. Also see Trail Access and Parking directions, above.

Palmyra: See Blue Spring Lake Segment, p. 262. From the Young Rd. Trail access go west then north ~3 mi. Also see Trail Access and Parking directions, above.

Blue Spring Lake Segment (Atlas Map 79f)

SNAPSHOT

7.1 miles: Young Rd. to CTH-Z

  This up-and-down segment features panoramic views from the top of Bald Bluff and the Stone Elephant, a massive granite erratic.

 At Horserider's Camp on Little Prairie Rd. and Emma Carlin Trails parking area.

From small ponds and springs near the segment.

Bald Bluff trails, Stone Elephant spur trail and Emma Carlin bike/hike trail system.

TRAIL ACCESS AND PARKING

Young Rd.: From the intersection of STH-59 and CTH-H in Palmyra take CTH-H southwest 3.0 mi. At Young Rd. turn left and go east 0.1 mi. Roadside parking.

CTH-Z: From the intersection of STH-59 and STH-67 in Eagle, take STH-59 west 3.7 mi. At CTH-Z turn left and go south 0.6 mi. No parking. Use nearby Emma Carlin Trails parking area on CTH-Z south of the Ice Age Trail access. A short blue-blazed spur trail leads to the Ice Age Trail.

Additional Parking: (i) Bald Bluff Scenic Overlook parking area. From the intersection of STH-59 and CTH-H in Palmyra, take CTH-H southwest 2.8 mi. Parking area on east side of road. The trail to Bald Bluff serves as a spur to the Ice Age Trail. (ii) Tamarack Rd. Trail access; roadside parking. (iii) Horserider's Camp parking area on Little Prairie Rd.

THE HIKE

From the trail access point on Young Road the segment heads north and quickly intersects (0.3 miles) with a spur trail that leads west to the CTH-H Bald Bluff parking area. From this intersection the segment makes its way up Bald Bluff on a series of switchbacks. Bald Bluff is the largest and most diverse of the area's dry native prairie openings, which are often found on gravel knobs and steep south-and west-facing ridges. Here grow prairie flowers and grasses such as little bluestem, sideoats grama, prairie dropseed, silky aster, pasqueflower, grooved yellow flax and rough blazing star. Trailside benches encourage hikers to soak in the panoramic view. Bald Bluff is one of the highest points in Jefferson County at 1,050 feet above sea level and 200 feet above the surrounding area. Native Americans used the prominence as a lookout and for ceremonial dancing. Twice in July 1832, General Henry Atkinson camped with troops to the northwest of the bluff as he pursued the Sauk Chief Black Hawk in the Black Hawk War. A brochure for the self-guided nature trail is available at the KMSF's Southern Unit headquarters or at the Bald Bluff trailhead on CTH-H.

The segment descends down Bald Bluff and after a mile comes to a small clearing. Past the clearing the segment intersects with a short spur trail that leads downhill to the massive granite erratic known as the Stone Elephant (**JW1**). Prairie Potawatomi Native Americans visited the rock frequently and probably considered it a sacred area. Early settlers named the rock the Stone Elephant because of its color, size and general elephant-like shape. In the 1920s it was a popular day

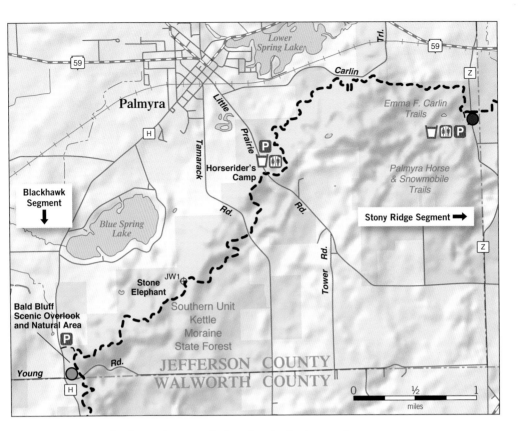

outing, in which tourists traveled to the site by horse-drawn surrey.

Almost all of the portion of this segment between Young Road and Tamarack Road traverses the Kettle Moraine Oak Opening State Natural Area. This area is a mixture of oak openings and oak woodland dominated by open-grown bur and black oaks. The Trail also passes a few native dry prairie remnants along the way. The first is located 0.2 miles past the Stone Elephant spur intersection and is located in a field on the north side of the Trail. The showy rough blazing star, a dry prairie species, is found here; the best time to see this plant is late August. The second remnant is found about 0.3 miles east of the first remnant (or about 0.5 miles southwest of Tamarack Road) on a south-facing slope. Here are found flora such as silky aster, leadplant, goldenrod, purple prairie clover, flowering spurge, sunflowers, arrow-leaf aster and a number of prairie grasses. A trailside bench provides a rest stop with a view.

The segment leaves the State Natural Area, crosses Tamarack Road and then Little Prairie Road before climbing to the top of a steep, narrow ridge, where a clearing with a bench offers views to the northwest. From this bench, Horse-rider's Camp is 0.2 miles farther on.

The segment crosses through the Horserider's Camp and 0.2 miles east of the camp passes a small trailside pond. The segment continues east past a few more small ponds and small springs and eventually comes to an opening with a trail-side map and a view of a barn across Carlin Trail (a road). From here hikers will travel up and down some hills and be rewarded with nice views down into the forest on both sides of the segment. In early spring hikers should watch for fields of mayapples in this area.

In the final mile a careful observer may notice a rock seat embedded in a tree and discover an old foundation with day lilies. Just south of the segment's end point on CTH-Z a short spur trail leads to the Emma Carlin Trails parking area.

Mobile Skills Crew project site, 2003

AREA SERVICES

Palmyra: Restaurant, grocery store, convenience store, library, medical care. From the Little Prairie Rd. Trail access go 1.0 mi northwest on Little Prairie Rd. The library has limited hours.

Eagle: See Eagle Segment, p. 272. From the CTH-Z Trail access go north then east ~4 mi. Also see Trail Access and Parking directions, above.

I came to feel as though the Trail was my home. I walked along it by day and slept along it by night. I met people whose homes are established along it as well as animals living and dying there. Shelter could mean an empty culvert or an established campsite, a house or a hotel. I loved being with those who sheltered me for the night or hiked with me for a day or days. I left my warm and dry, comfortable "normal" home for a wider concept of home as being the state of Wisconsin. I fell in love with my state!

CHRIS MILLER (AKA "DANCING DOVE"), ICE AGE TRAIL THOUSAND-MILER

Blue Spring Lake Segment.

Walworth & Jefferson Counties

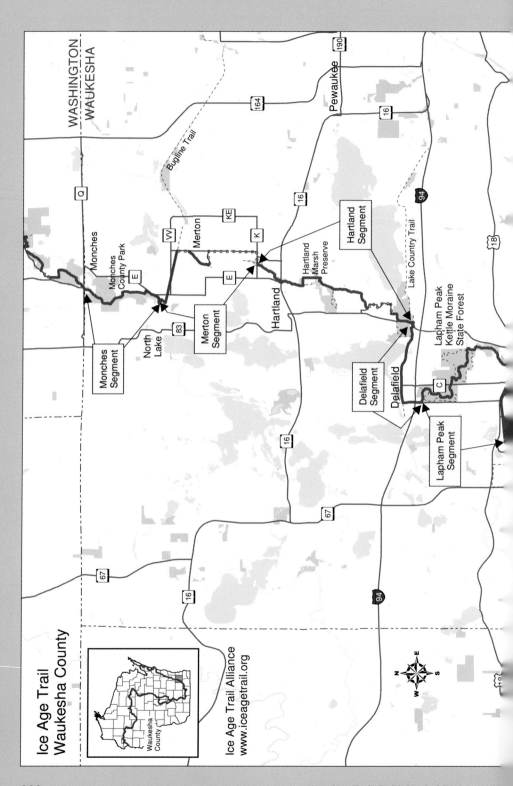

Ice Age Trail
Waukesha County

Ice Age Trail Alliance
www.iceagetrail.org

Waukesha
County

WASHINGTON
WAUKESHA

Pewaukee

Bugline Trail

Monches

Monches
County Park

Monches
Segment

North
Lake

Merton
Segment

Merton

Hartland

Hartland
Marsh
Preserve

Hartland
Segment

Lake Country Trail

Lapham Peak
Kettle Moraine
State Forest

Delafield
Segment

Delafield

Lapham Peak
Segment

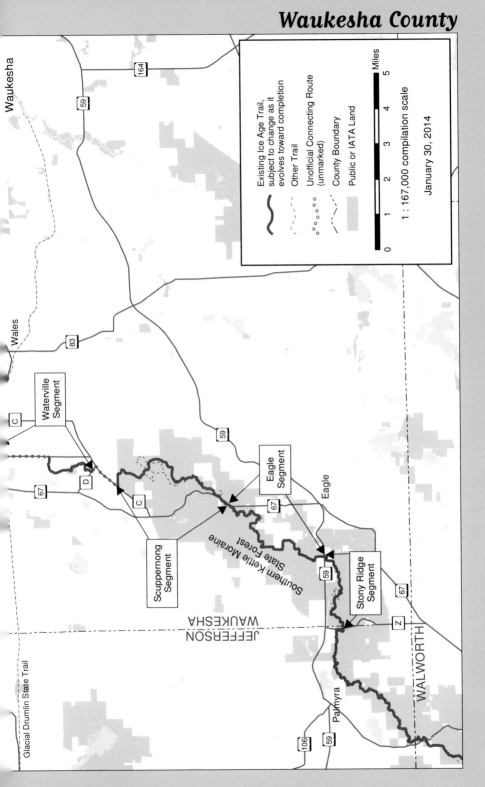

Waukesha County

Trail miles: 38.7
Connecting route miles: 6.0

The Ice Age Trail is within the Kettle Moraine for most of Waukesha County but does occasionally veer to the west onto an outwash plain where small areas of the Niagara Escarpment protrude from the soil. The Ice Age Trail crosses major glacial meltwater spillways near the villages of Wales and Hartland. Many types of glacial formations can be seen along the Trail such as kettles, erratics, eskers, drained lake plains, drumlins and kames. Vegetation includes oak forest, oak openings and wet and dry prairie.

Seasonal wildflowers punctuate all these areas. The Trail highlights area city and county parks, multi-use recreation trails and the Kettle Moraine State Forest's Southern Unit and Lapham Peak Unit.

The Southern Unit contains 20,000 undeveloped acres of forest. It has numerous hiking, nature, mountain biking, equestrian, snowmobile and cross-country ski trails. Also within the unit are recreational sites for camping, picnic areas, boating and swimming. The Southern Unit's headquarters features natural and historical exhibits about the surrounding area.

CHAPTER INFORMATION

The Waukesha/Milwaukee County Chapter was established in 1984 and has one of the largest chapter memberships. The chapter regularly sponsors Ice Age Trail workdays, hikes and campouts. The chapter's "Walk the Wauk" program rewards hikers who have walked all Ice Age Trail segments in the chapter's territory.

COUNTY INFORMATION

Waukesha Area Convention and Visitors Bureau: 262-542-0330 or 800-366-8474, visitwaukesha.org

Waukesha County Parks and Land Use Department: 262-548-7801, waukeshacounty.gov

Kettle Moraine State Forest Lapham Peak Unit: 262-646-3025, dnr.wi.gov/topic/parks/name/lapham

Kettle Moraine State Forest Southern Unit: 262-594-6200, dnr.wi.gov/topic/parks/name/kms

Wisconsin Conservationists' Hall of Fame: Several of our country's foremost conservationists called Wisconsin home. In 2001, the Ice Age Trail Alliance formally recognized these environmental immortals by creating the Wisconsin Conservationists' Hall of Fame. Conceived and funded by former U.S. Congressman Henry S. Reuss, five sites within Waukesha County honor Increase Lapham, Aldo Leopold, John Muir, John Wesley Powell and Carl Schurz. Each site is marked with an informative sign. Visitors have the opportunity to learn about the history of conservation in Wisconsin while enjoying a hike through the woods and wetlands of the Kettle Moraine.

Hikers snake away from the Lapham Peak tower during a hike organized by the IATA's Waukesha/Milwaukee County Chapter.

Stony Ridge Segment (Atlas Map 80f)

3.1 miles: CTH-Z to STH-59

 This segment winds through a pine plantation, oak forest and sections of dry prairie and passes by the Kettle Moraine State Forest's Southern Unit headquarters.

 At Emma Carlin Trails parking area and at Forest HQ and Visitor Center.

 At a walk-to trailside shelter (**WK18**, reservations required).

At Emma Carlin Trails parking area, Forest HQ and Visitor Center and Backpack Shelter 2 (please respect those who have reserved the shelter).

 Portion of segment crossing private land between CTH-S and STH-59 is closed during gun deer season.

 Dogs must be leashed.

 A short portion overlaps with roads.

 Stony Ridge Nature Trail and other spur and horse trails.

TRAIL ACCESS AND PARKING

CTH-Z: From the intersection of STH-59 and STH-67 in Eagle, take STH-59 west 3.7 mi. At CTH-Z turn left and go south 0.6 mi. No parking. Use nearby Emma Carlin Trails parking area on CTH-Z south of the Ice Age Trail access. A short blue-blazed spur trail leads to the Ice Age Trail.

STH-59: From the intersection of STH-59 and STH-67 in Eagle, take STH-59 west 1.6 mi. No parking. Instead, head north on the gravel road a short distance east of the STH-59/CTH-S intersection. This DNR road leads to two large parking areas and provides access to the Ice Age Trail and a dog training area.

Additional Parking: Southern Unit Kettle Moraine State Forest Headquarters on STH-59, 2.6 mi west of Eagle. A spur trail leads to the Ice Age Trail.

THE HIKE

Before starting out on this segment, hikers looking for an interesting side trip can follow CTH-Z south 0.2 miles to Stute Springs and Homestead Trail. A self-guided loop takes hikers around early 20th-century farm buildings, past natural springs, through ancient woods and up to the top of Big Hill at 1050 feet.

From its starting point on CTH-Z, the segment heads east through a relatively flat stretch of woods and meadow, emerging into open prairie on the bed of Glacial Lake Scuppernong. The segment crosses a bridge over a small stream filling in with plant growth, rises gradually across a grassy savanna and climbs a wooded esker on rocky outwash. Less than 2 miles east of CTH-Z the segment reaches a spur trail leading to the Kettle Moraine State Forest's Southern Unit Headquarters. Its natural history museum has displays and videos on glacial geology, Native American and pioneer history and animal and plant life throughout the Southern Unit and surrounding areas. Self-guided brochures are available in the gift shop for the many nature trails found near the Ice Age Trail, including Stute Springs and Homestead Trail. The self-guided Stony Ridge Nature Trail also starts at the headquarters.

Near the spur trail to the headquarters the segment intersects (**WK18**) with another spur, this one heading 0.2 miles south to Backpack Shelter 2. Continu-

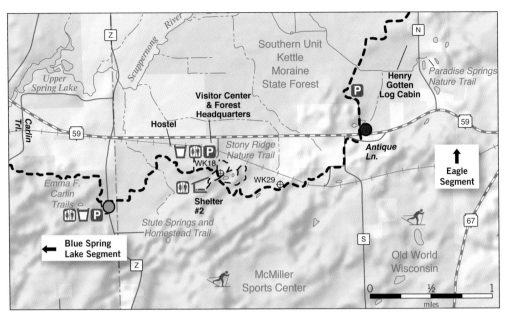

ing east from this junction, the segment climbs between a long pond and a deep water-filled kettle, descends into an open field and winds on a sandy track through a fire-scarred forest. It then climbs atop a long, steep sided esker (**WK29**) with kettles and marshes at the bottom of the slopes. After descending the esker, the segment crosses railroad tracks and travels through a pine plantation en route to CTH-S. The segment ends with a short walk north along CTH-S and east paralleling Antique Lane before reaching its endpoint on STH-59.

POINTS OF INTEREST

Old World Wisconsin: From the STH-59 Trail access, go east on STH-59 for 1.6 mi. At STH-67 turn right and go south 1.4 mi (262-594-6301, oldworldwisconsin.wisconsinhistory.org).

Old World Wisconsin is America's largest outdoor museum of rural life. Live characters recreate daily historical scenes of farm and village life from a century ago. Farmsteads and settlements representing German, Finnish, Polish, Norwegian, African American, Danish and Yankee pioneers dot nearly 600 acres. Open every day during spring, summer and fall. There is an admission fee.

AREA SERVICES

Southern Unit Kettle Moraine State Forest Headquarters: Information. From the STH-59 Trail access, go west on STH-59 1.1 mi (262-594-6200, dnr.wi.gov/topic/parks/name/kms).

KMSF Southern Unit Backpack Shelter 2: Camping. On Trail. Reservations (available only by calling 888-947-2757) are required to use the shelter and only one group per shelter per night is allowed. No potable water is available at the shelter. Hikers should obtain water from the Forest HQ, 0.2 mi north of the shelter.

Eagle Home Hostel: Lodging. From the CTH-Z Trail access go 1.0 mi north on CTH-Z then east on STH-59. An unmarked side trail off the Ice Age Trail leads to the hostel. Please call ahead for dates of operation and reservations (262-495-8794 or 262-442-6360). No walk-ins.

Eagle: See Eagle Segment, p. 272. From the SKMSF Headquarters on STH-59 go east ~3 mi. Also see Trail Access and Parking directions, above.

Palmyra: See Blue Spring Lake Segment, p. 262. From the SKMSF Headquarters on STH-59 go west ~4 mi.

Eagle Segment (Atlas Map 80f)

5.6 miles: STH-59 to STH-67 Wayside

 This segment passes through extensive prairie restoration areas, oak savannas and wetland areas with springs and features Brady's Rocks, a portion of the Niagara Escarpment.

At the STH-67 wayside.

From small ponds and springs.

Dogs must be leashed.

 A short portion overlaps with a road.

Brady's Rock white-blazed loop trail and two short spur trails. Paradise Springs Nature Trail is nearby.

TRAIL ACCESS AND PARKING

STH-59: From the intersection of STH-59 and STH-67 in Eagle, take STH-59 west 1.6 mi. No parking. Instead, head north on the gravel road a short distance east of the STH-59/CTH-S intersection. This DNR road leads to two large parking areas and provides access to the Ice Age Trail and a dog training area.

STH-67 Wayside: From I-94 at Oconomowoc, take Exit 282 onto STH-67 and go south 11.2 mi to the parking area.

Additional Parking: (i) CTH-N small parking area. (ii) Wilton Rd. roadside parking. (iii) STH-67 parking area northeast of Brady's Rocks.

THE HIKE

From its starting point on STH-59 the segment heads a short distance up a gravel drive and then northeast across a prairie toward CTH-N. The openness of the landscape provides hikers with views of the expansive natural prairie seasonally filled with blooming wildflowers. The segment crosses a small stream coming from Paradise Springs. About 0.4 miles west of CTH-N hikers will find a bench and a nearby Scuppernong River Habitat Area map.

North of the CTH-N crossing the segment skirts the Scuppernong Prairie State Natural Area, one of the oldest of Wisconsin's State Natural Areas and part of Scuppernong River Habitat Area that highlights the largest native wet prairie east of the Mississippi. The prairie is growing in the bed of the former Glacial Lake Scuppernong.

After passing by Scuppernong Prairie the segment reaches Wilton Road. Hikers should turn right and head east 0.1 miles, where the segment leaves Wilton Road and continues due north. In this area the segment skirts the edges of the Kettle Moraine Low Prairie State Natural Area. The low prairie has been the site of controlled burns and tree removal since 1999. The entire area has returned to its original condition and long-dormant plant species specific to the low prairie have dramatically reappeared. It's often a wet area in spring, and ground-nesting birds can be observed among the many types of flowers in bloom.

The segment bends south and leads to a white-blazed loop trail (**WK17**) weaving between the 8-foot-high outcroppings of Brady's Rocks, named for Irish immigrants Michael and Kathleen Brady who settled here in 1855. These outcroppings are a portion of the Niagara Escarpment, a thick layer of dolomite that extends through Door County, dips under Lake Michigan and the state of Michigan and reemerges at the end of Lake Erie at Niagara Falls. The cool, shaded area of Brady's Rocks has a unique fern population, including the walking fern, fragile fern and cliff brake fern, found growing out of cracks in the dolomite bedrock.

Past the Brady's Rocks loop trail, the segment passes remnants of a rubble stone fence from the Bradys' farm and climbs to the top of a grassy knoll and, at a Leopold bench dedicated to David P. Moritz, offers nice views to the north of the prairie and drained Glacial Lake Scuppernong. A spur trail shortly beyond the bench leads to a scenic overlook.

After crossing a gravel road, another short spur trail leads to some springs and the segment crosses over an intermittent spring-fed creek in the shadows of a cluster of inspiring old oaks. Continuing north the segment passes over a series of three puncheons and a small bridge, totaling close to 400 feet in length, built during a 2007 Mobile Skills Crew project hosted by the IATA's Waukesha/Milwaukee County Chapter. The segment ends at a wayside on STH-67.

Mobile Skills Crew project site, 2007

AREA SERVICES

Eagle: Restaurant, grocery store, convenience store, lodging, library, medical care. From the STH-59 Trail access go 1.6 mi east on STH-59. INN Style program lodging at the Eagle Centre House B&B (262-363-4700, eagle-house.com).

North Prairie: See Scuppernong Segment, p. 274. From the STH-59 Trail access go northeast ~7 mi.

Palmyra: See Blue Spring Lake Segment, p. 262. From the STH-59 Trail access go west 4.5 mi.

Southern Unit Kettle Moraine State Forest Headquarters: See Stony Ridge Segment, p. 270. From the STH-59 Trail access go west less than 1 mi.

Scuppernong Segment (Atlas Maps 80f, 81f)

SNAPSHOT

5.6 miles: STH-67 Wayside to CTH-C

  This segment courses over hilly terrain, through hardwood forests and past many trailside kettles.

 At STH-67 wayside, CTH-ZZ Scuppernong Trails trailhead and Pinewoods Campground.

 From McKeawn Springs.

 At a walk-to trailside shelter (reservations required).

 At Pinewoods Campground and nearby Ottawa Lake Campground.

 At nearby Ottawa Lake Campground.

 At Backpack Shelter 1 (please respect those who have reserved the shelter), CTH-ZZ Scuppernong Trails trailhead and Pinewoods Campground.

 Dogs must be leashed.

 A small portion of the segment overlaps with a campground road..

 Spurs to McKeawn Springs, Backpack Shelter 1, two blue-blazed spur trails to parking areas and the Scuppernong ski/hike trail network.

TRAIL ACCESS AND PARKING

STH-67 Wayside: From I-94 at Ononomowoc, take Exit 282 onto STH-67 and go south 11.2 mi to the parking area.

CTH-C: From I-94 at Oconomowoc, take Exit 282 STH-67 and go south 8.5 mi. At CTH-C turn left and go east 0.8 mi to the Trail access on the south side of road. Roadside parking.

Additional Parking: (i) Piper Rd. roadside. (ii) CTH-ZZ Scuppernong Hiking and Ski Trail parking areas. There is a parking area on each side of CTH-ZZ. Each parking area has a blue-blazed spur trail leading to the IAT. (iii) Pinewoods Campground on G Rd. off Waterville Rd. Enter campground and go to the group camp loop. Park near restrooms.

THE HIKE

From its starting point at the STH-67 wayside, the segment continues along the west side of STH-67 for less than half a mile before crossing over to the east side of the road and then intersecting with a spur trail (**WK16**) leading up to Backpack Shelter 1. Perched atop Spy Glass Hill, the vista from the shelter area is of a flat plain left behind after water drained from Glacial Lake Scuppernong. Just past the spur to the shelter a second spur trail leads to McKeawn Springs, which flow into a trout pond and Scuppernong Creek.

The segment crosses Piper Road and travels through hilly terrain. A short distance south of CTH-ZZ, the segment intersects with a blue-blazed spur trail. Hikers can follow the spur to the Scuppernong Trail network's southside parking area. Shortly after crossing CTH-ZZ hikers will encounter another blue-blazed spur trail leading to the Scuppernong Trail network's northside parking area and trailhead, with restrooms and water. The segment heads east and then north, skirting around the Mackie Group Picnic Area.

North of CTH-ZZ the segment traverses a roller coaster of hills set in hardwood forests among numerous trailside kettles. The segment reaches its highest point (1066 feet) at a location (**WK28**) marked with a bench and crosses the Scuppernong skiing/hiking trail several times as it continues north and west. The segment passes through the Southern Unit's Pinewoods Campground, then bends to the west and makes its way to its endpoint on CTH-C.

AREA SERVICES

North Prairie: Restaurant, convenience store. From the Piper Rd. Trail access go 3.5 miles east on Piper Rd. to State Rd.

KMSF Southern Unit Backpack Shelter 1: Camping. On Trail. Reservations (available only by calling 888-947-2757) are required to use the shelter and only one group per shelter per night is allowed. No potable water is available at the shelter. Hikers should obtain water from the STH-67 wayside, 0.4 mi south of the shelter's spur trail intersection with the Trail.

KMSF Southern Unit Pinewoods Campground: Camping (seasonal). On Trail (262-594-6220; dnr.wi.gov/topic/parks/name/kms; reservations: 888-947-2757, reserveamerica.com).

KMSF Southern Unit Ottawa Lake Recreation Area: Camping. From the STH-67 wayside go north on STH-67 1.7 mi. Where CTH-ZZ heads west from STH-67, turn left on to CTH-ZZ and go 0.2 mi (262-594-6220, dnr.wi.gov/topic/parks/name/kms; reservations: 888-947-2757, reserveamerica.com).

1.1-mi CR to **Waterville Segment**. North on CTH-C, west on CTH-D.

Reagons Lake

Group Camp

Pinewoods Campground

Southern Unit Kettle Moraine State Forest

Ottawa Lake Recreation Area

Scuppernong Hiking and Skiing Trails

WK28

ZZ

Ottawa Lake

Scuppernong Springs Nature Trail

ZZ

67

Scuppernong River

Piper Rd.

WK16

Shelter #1

Road X

Eagle Segment

0   ½   1
miles

Eagle: See Eagle Segment, p. 272. From the STH-67 wayside go south ~3 mi.

Dousman: See Waterville Segment, p. 276. From the STH-67 wayside go north ~8 mi.

I spend every Sunday from October to April in the Kettle Moraine, irrespective of weather.

RAYMOND T. ZILLMER, FOUNDER, ICE AGE TRAIL ALLIANCE

Waterville Segment (Atlas Map 81f)

SNAPSHOT

3.8 miles (2.6 IAT, 1.2 CR): CTH-D to UW-Waukesha Field Station at Glacial Drumlin State Trail

  This varied segment includes portions through a woods and the UW-Waukesha Field Station.

💧 From small intermittent streams.

 Segment includes a connecting route roadwalk.

🐕! Dogs must be leashed.

TRAIL ACCESS AND PARKING

CTH-D: From I-94 at Oconomowoc, take Exit 282 STH-67 and go south 5.8 mi. At CTH-D turn left and go east 0.7 mi to the Trail access on the north side of the road. Roadside parking.

UW-Waukesha Field Station at Glacial Drumlin State Trail: From I-94 near Delafield, take Exit 285 onto CTH-C (Kettle Moraine Dr.) and go south 2.8 mi. At STH-18 turn right and go west 2.0 mi. At Waterville Rd. turn left and go south 0.5 mi to the UW-Waukesha Field Station. On the east side of the road, look for the gravel drive entrance. Parking is along the drive and at the main parking area near the buildings. No overnight parking allowed.

Additional Parking: Manor House Rd. From UW-Waukesha Field Station, drive south on Waterville Rd. 1.3 mi. At Manor House Rd. turn right. Roadside parking.

THE HIKE

The Waterville Segment is an exception to most of the Ice Age Trail route in Waukesha County because it lies slightly west of the Kettle Moraine. The land rolls gently in contrast to the steep hills and kettles of other area segments and showcases remnants of pre-settlement vegetation: oak forest, oak openings, prairie and wetland.

From its starting point on CTH-D the segment heads north through a low lying area that may be wet, especially after periods of rain. After 0.5 miles hikers may see a small exposed section of Niagara Escarpment dolomite bedrock (**WK13**). The segment gradually moves uphill through mostly forested terrain with occasional breaks into prairies as it makes its way northeast to Waterville Road.

After crossing Tallgrass Court the segment turns east and then intersects (**WK12**) with Waterville Road. At this point hikers should turn left and head north on a connecting route for 1.2 miles along Waterville Road. The segment leaves Waterville Road near the UW-Waukesha Field Station, heading east and then north through the Field Station property to the segment's endpoint at a junction with the Glacial Drumlin State Trail.

POINTS OF INTEREST

UW-Waukesha Field Station: On Trail (262-965-2227, waukesha.uwc.edu and search "Field Station").
Modeled after UW-Madison's Arboretum, the Field Station hosts plant communities that can be found throughout the entire state. Currently there is an 8-acre prairie restoration and oak savanna area, pine plantation and hardwood forest in development. Call for information about educational classes open to the public. Also located here is the Wildlife In Need Center (262-965-3090, helpingwildlife.

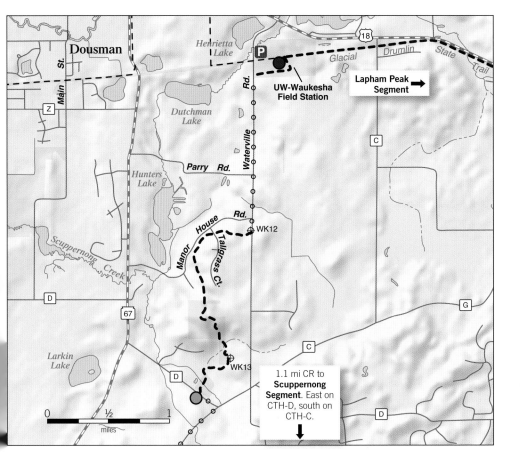

org). The center is focused on the treatment and care of injured, diseased, or orphaned indigenous wildlife and the return of healthy wildlife to the wild. The Center is primarily run by volunteers.

AREA SERVICES

Dousman: Restaurant, convenience store. From the UW-Waukesha Field Station, take Waterville Rd. north 0.5 mi to USH-18, turn left and go west 1.7 mi to Main St., turn left and go south 0.4 mi.

Wales: See Lapham Peak Segment and Delafield Segment, p. 278. From the CTH-D Trail access go east then north ~5 mi.

KMSF Southern Unit Pinewoods Campground: See Scuppernong Segment, p. 274. From the CTH-D Trail access go south ~2 mi.

KMSF Southern Unit Ottawa Lake Campground: See Scuppernong Segment, p. 274. From the CTH-D Trail access go south ~2 mi.

Lapham Peak Segment and Delafield Segment (Atlas Maps 81f, 82f)

Lapham Peak Segment—7.6 miles: UW-Waukesha Field Station at Glacial Drumlin State Trail to Cushing Park Rd.

Delafield Segment—2.8 miles: Cushing Park Rd. to STH-83

 The hilly **Lapham Peak Segment** *winds through woods and prairie restoration sites and includes outstanding views from the Lapham Peak observation tower.*

At various locations in the Lapham Peak Unit (LPU).

From Scuppernong Creek, a couple of small ponds and Nemahbin Springs (**WK8**).

At a walk-to site (**WK30**, reservations required) in the LPU.

 Dogs must be leashed.

 A portion of the segment overlaps with the multi-use Glacial Drumlin State Trail (GDST).

The GDST extends west and east from the segment. The LPU has an extensive network of trails.

 The **Delafield Segment** *highlights the "Trail Town" of Delafield and includes a trek along part of the Lake Country Recreational Trail.*

At Cushing Memorial Park and Naga-Waukee County Park.

 At Naga-Waukee County Park Campground.

 Hikers will not have any interaction with hunting on this segment.

 Dogs must be leashed.

 The entire segment overlaps with the Lake Country Recreational Trail (LCRT), city sidewalks and roads.

 The LCRT extends west and east from the segment. Also, a spur trail to Naga-Waukee County Park.

 Portions of this segment may be suitable for those using wheelchairs or similar devices.

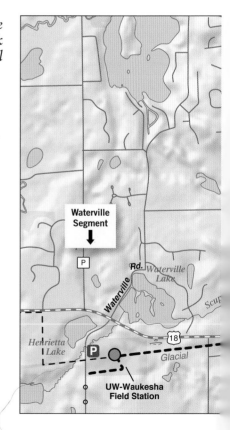

TRAIL ACCESS AND PARKING

UW-Waukesha Field Station at Glacial Drumlin State Trail: From I-94 near Delafield, take Exit 285 onto CTH-C (Kettle Moraine Dr.) and go south 2.8 mi. At STH-18 turn right and go west 2.0 mi. At Waterville Rd. turn left and go south 0.5 mi to the UW-Waukesha Field Station. On the east side of the road, look for the gravel drive entrance. Parking is along the drive and at the main parking area near the buildings. No overnight parking allowed.

STH-83: From I-94 near Delafield, take Exit 287 onto STH-83 and go north 0.3 mi to the Nagawaukee Park-and-Ride on the west side of the highway.

Additional Parking: (i) STH-18 Trail access (**WK10**); roadside parking. (ii) Lapham Peak Unit parking areas. (iii) Cushing Park Rd. Trail access. (iv) Cushing Memorial Park on Cushing Park Rd., 0.1 miles north of Main St. (v) Fish Hatchery Park, on the north side of Main St. at Wells St. (vi) Naga-Waukee County Park.

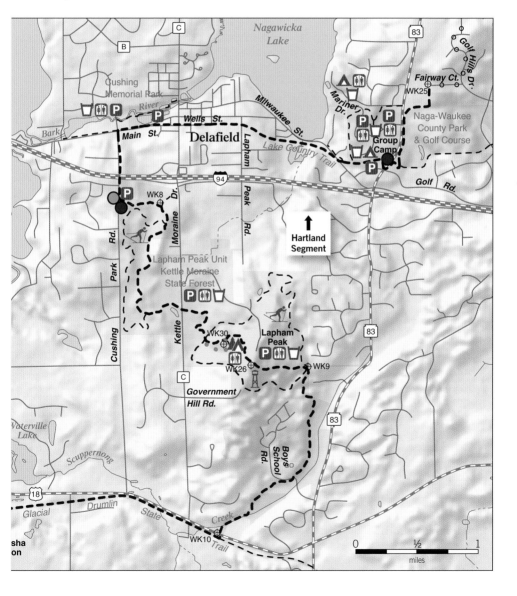

The **Lapham Peak Segment** starts by heading east on the Glacial Drumlin State Trail, a multi-use paved rail-trail that spans 52.0 miles between Cottage Grove to the west and Waukesha to the east. The segment departs from the Glacial Drumlin State Trail after 2.0 miles, crosses (**WK10**) busy STH-18 and makes its way northeast near Scuppernong Creek, eventually following the west bank of an ancient glacial meltwater spillway (river) that once carried water from the east side of the Kettle Moraine to the west.

The segment then enters the Lapham Peak Unit of the Kettle Moraine State Forest. The unit is named after conservationist and geographer Increase Lapham, who spent his lifetime researching and documenting regional geography, botany, biology, conservation, forestry, geology and archeology. Lapham's work in meteorology led to the creation of the United States National Weather Service and modern weather forecasts.

The Lapham Peak Unit is 1,000 acres and has numerous hiking, mountain bike and groomed cross-country ski trails. In the spring, the white and bur oak savannas teem with native woodland wildflowers like Dutchman's breeches, toothwort, columbine, Jacob's ladder and wild geranium. Summer prairie flowers include prairie dock, rattlesnake master, cup plant, common evening and pale Indian primrose, lupine and purple coneflower. The restored prairies offer a haven for a variety of butterflies and are lined with eastern bluebird boxes. Wild turkey and pileated woodpecker live among white oaks more than 100 years old.

Not long after entering the Lapham Peak Unit the segment comes to a spur trail that leads down into a kettle with a nice pond. Shortly after, the Trail arrives at a point where there is a confluence of trails (**WK9**). Paths head off in various directions creating popular loops for walkers and cross-country skiers. Hikers should pay close attention to signage to continue on the Ice Age Trail route.

From the trail junction, the segment heads up Lapham Peak. At 1,223 feet above sea level, the glacial-formed kame is the county's highest point and site of the original National Weather Service signal station. Atop it is a 45-foot observation tower (**WK26**) that offers 360-degree views. To the north are views of Hartland, Holy Hill and Kettle Moraine ridges. To the east are views of downtown Milwaukee. To the south are Dousman and the wooded rolling hills of the southern Kettle Moraine. To the west, near Oconomowoc, is a large flat area that was once covered by an ancient glacial lake. The tower area has water (seasonal), restrooms, picnic areas and parking.

After passing by the tower area the segment meanders down the side of the kame through open woods. The Trail soon intersects (**WK30**) with another short spur trail that leads to a backcountry campsite with a table and a privy. Continuing on, the segment makes its way east to CTH-C (Kettle Moraine Drive) passing a small pond with an observation deck on the way.

West of CTH-C the segment passes another pond and begins to weave through the Lapham Peak Unit's Prairie Path as it heads toward Cushing Park Road. The Trail offers some nice long views of the prairies and surrounding areas. Less than half a mile from the segment's endpoint a spur trail (**WK8**) leads to Nemahbin Springs, home to a flourishing frog population and many aquatic plants.

From the terminus of the Lapham Peak Segment on Cushing Park Road, the **Delafield Segment** starts by heading north alongside Cushing Park Road on a paved path for a half-mile to its intersection with Main Street. Worth a side trip is Cushing Memorial Park and the Wisconsin Veterans Memorial Riverwalk (see Points of Interest, below).

From the intersection of Cushing Park Road and Main Street, the segment heads east along Main Street, passing by the fire station and Fish Hatchery Park to the intersection with Wells Street. The segment shifts from Main Street to Wells Street and continues eastward. At the intersection of Wells Street and Bleeker Street, the segment continues due east, transitioning onto the Lake Country Recreational Trail, a multi-use rail-trail running through a subdivision and offering views of 981-acre Nagawicka Lake. The lake lies in a preglacial valley, blocked in on the east and west by glacial drift.

The segment continues eastward along the Lake Country Recreational Trail and skirts the southern edge of Naga-Waukee County Park. The segment ends on the west side of STH-83 next to the Nagawaukee Park-and-Ride.

POINTS OF INTEREST

Cushing Memorial Park and Wisconsin Veterans Memorial Riverwalk: From the intersection of Cushing Park Rd. and Main St., go north on Cushing Park Rd. 0.1 mi to Cushing Memorial Park and the west end of the Wisconsin Veterans Memorial Riverwalk (cityofdelafield.com/parks_and_recreation.html, 262-646-6220).

Cushing Memorial Park honors the Civil War hero brothers Navy Commander William Cushing, Army 1st Lieutenant Howard Cushing and Medal of Honor recipient Army 1st Lieutenant Alonzo Cushing. A 50-foot Barre granite monument stands on part of the original Cushing homestead. The Wisconsin Veterans Memorial Riverwalk links nine separate U.S. war memorials with educational displays about each war. The 0.75-mile walk winds along the Bark River on a boardwalk and gravel path from Cushing Memorial Park's Peace Garden and Spring (west end), a historic Potawatomi meeting site, to St. John's Pond (east end) on Genesee Street. The Riverwalk's main entry plaza and bridge are just north of the Ice Age Trail route at Main Street and Dopkins Street.

AREA SERVICES

Glacial Drumlin State Trail: On Trail (262-646-3025, dnr.wi.gov/topic/parks/name/glacialdrumlin).

Kettle Moraine State Forest Lapham Peak Unit: Hike-to camping. On Trail (262-646-3025, dnr.wi.gov/topic/parks/name/lapham). Call or stop by to reserve the campsite; there is a fee and the maximum group size is 10. Information about the Lapham Peak Unit is also available from the KMSF headquarters office (262-594-6200).

Wales: Restaurant, grocery store, convenience store, lodging, library, medical care. From the STH-18 Trail access go 1.4 mi east using the Glacial Drumlin Trail or 0.8 mi east on STH-18, then south 0.5 mi on STH-83. INN Style program lodging at the Pedal'rs Inn (262-968-4700, pedalrsinn.com).

Waukesha: Restaurant, grocery store, convenience store, general shopping, lodging, camping, library, medical care. From the STH-18 Trail access go ~8 mi east on STH-18.

Delafield: Restaurant, grocery store, convenience store, general shopping, lodging, camping, library, medical care. On Trail. Services available in the area of STH-83 at Golf Rd. and in the city of Delafield. Camping at Naga-Waukee County Park (262-646-3555). Meals at the Delafield Brewhaus Brewery and Restaurant, 1.3 mi east of STH-83 at I-94 (3832 Hillside Dr., 262-646-7821). Area info available from the Delafield Chamber of Commerce and Tourism Council (262-646-8100, visitdelafield.org).

Dousman: See Waterville Segment, p. 276. From the UW-Waukesha Field Station go north then west ~3 mi.

Hartland: See Hartland Segment, p. 282. From the STH-83 Trail access go north ~5 mi.

Hartland Segment (Atlas Map 82f)

SNAPSHOT

6.8 miles (5.6 IAT, 1.2 CR): STH-83 to CTH-K at Centennial Park

This segment winds through another "Trail Town," Hartland, and highlights three Conservationists' Hall of Fame commemorative sites.

 At nearby Naga-Waukee County Park, Nixon Park and Hartbrook Park.

 From the Bark River, which the segment route crosses six times.

 At Naga-Waukee County Park Campground.

 At nearby Naga-Waukee County Park, Hartland Marsh-John Muir Overlook and Hartbrook Park.

 At nearby Naga-Waukee County Park, Hartbrook Park and Centennial Park.

 At nearby Naga-Waukee County Park, Nixon Park, Bark River Park, Hartbrook Park and Centennial Park.

 Dogs must be leashed and are not allowed on portion between Hartbrook Park and Centennial Park.

 Segment includes a connecting route roadwalk. Portions overlap with multiuse rec trails and town sidewalks.

 Hartland Marsh lollipop trail and Aldo Leopold Overlook trails.

 Portions of this segment may be suitable for those using wheelchairs or similar devices.

TRAIL ACCESS AND PARKING

STH-83: From I-94 near Delafield, take Exit 287 onto STH-83 and go north 0.3 mi to the Nagawaukee Park-and-Ride on the west side of the highway.

CTH-K at Centennial Park: Near Hartland heading west on STH-16, take Exit 183 for Merton Ave. (CTH-KC). From the exit ramp turn right on Merton Ave. (CTH-KC) and go north 0.7 mi. At CTH-K (Lisbon Rd.) turn left and go west 0.2 mi to Centennial Park. If heading east on STH-16, take Exit 182 for North Ave. (CTH-E). From the exit ramp turn left and go north 1.0 mi. At CTH-K (Lisbon Rd.) turn right and go east 0.5 mi to the parking area for Centennial Park. Open sunrise to sunset.

Additional Parking: (i) Naga-Waukee County Park. (ii) Hartland Marsh-John Muir Overlook on Cottonwood Ave. (**WK24**). (iii) Aldo Leopold Overlook on Maple Ave. (CTH-E) (**WK22**). (iv) Nixon Park. (v) Bark River Park. (vi) Hartbrook Park.

THE HIKE

The segment starts from the west side of STH-83 by heading east on the Lake Country Recreational Trail, crossing busy STH-83 at the Golf Road stoplight. Shortly after crossing STH-83 the segment departs from the Lake Country Recreational Trail and heads north, skirting the west side of Naga-Waukee Golf Course. The segment bends east briefly before resuming a northward course, passing behind Westbrook Church before reaching Fairway Court (**WK25**). At Fairway Court hikers will begin following a 1.2-mile unmarked connecting route: east on Fairway Court, left turn to head north on Golf Hills Drive, turn left to head north on Fieldwood Drive (which transitions into Streff Drive), turn left to head northwest on Foxwood Drive.

From Foxwood Drive (**WK5**), near the Foxwood Estates entrance, the segment continues off-road to the northeast over wooded, hilly topography to a crossing of CTH-KE (North Shore Drive) (**WK4**). From here, most of the remainder of the segment is paved. The segment continues north and links up with Cottonwood Avenue. Just south of the Cottonwood Avenue/Lindenwood Drive intersection, hikers will discover the Hartland Marsh–John Muir Overlook (**WK24**), a loop trail to the west of the segment route that includes two islands, oak savanna openings, boardwalks and a picnic shelter. This area is the first of three Conservationists' Hall of Fame commemorative sites along or near the segment route. Muir was an early leader in the conservation movement. He led the advocacy efforts to establish Yosemite National Park, founded the Sierra Club in 1892 and was a leading proponent for the national park system.

The John Wesley Powell commemorative site (**WK23**) is located off-route 0.4 miles north of the Hartland Marsh loop trail access on Cottonwood Avenue and south of the Bark

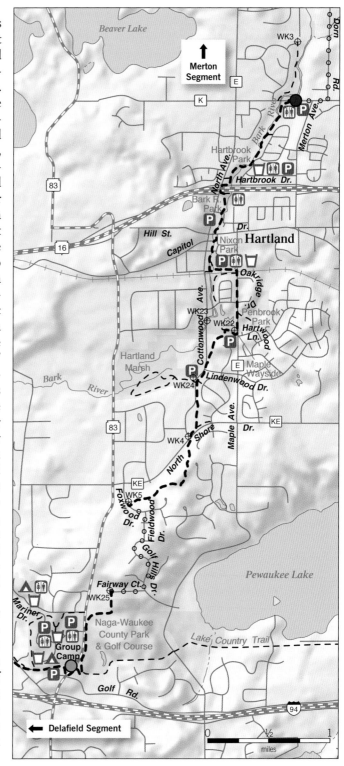

River Bridge. This roadside wetland is part of an ancient glacial meltwater spillway of the Kettle Moraine. Powell was an explorer, geologist and conservationist, one of the first to introduce science to natural resource management. While serving as Director of the United States Geological Survey from 1880–1894, he worked to implement prudent land and water policies.

From the Hartland Marsh loop trail access, the segment continues briefly on Cottonwood Avenue then heads northeast through the Aldo Leopold Overlook (**WK22**) in an area bounded by Cottonwood Avenue, Cardinal Lane, Maple Avenue (CTH-E) and Lindenwood Drive. The Leopold site offers trails with a boardwalk, two ponds and a view from atop a 45-foot glacial hill. Aldo Leopold is honored as an ecology pioneer who wrote "Ecology tells that no animal—not even man—can be regarded as independent of his environment. Plants, animals, men and soil are a community of interdependent parts."

At Maple Avenue (CTH-E) the segment turns north and follows the road 0.5 miles. After crossing railroad tracks, hikers should turn west into Nixon Park. From here most of the remainder of the segment travels close to the Bark River. The segment leaves Nixon Park, takes a quick route through "downtown" Hartland and goes into Bark River Park before reaching STH-16. North of STH-16 the segment continues briefly on Hartbrook Drive before leaving the road and entering Hartbrook Park. Between Hartbrook Park and the its endpoint at Centennial Park the segment follows a particularly scenic section of the Bark River adjacent to a housing development.

AREA SERVICES

Hartland: Restaurant, grocery store, convenience store, library, medical care. On Trail. Most services located on Cottonwood Ave and Cardinal Ave. Area info available from the Hartland Area Chamber of Commerce (262-367-7059, hartland-wi.org).

Brookfield: General shopping. ~15 mi east of Hartland. Outfitter/camping supplies at REI (262-783-6150, rei.com/stores/brookfield).

Delafield: See Lapham Peak Segment and Delafield Segment, p. 278. Many services in the vicinity of the STH-83 Trail access at Golf Rd.

Merton: See Merton Segment and Monches Segment, p. 285. From the CTH-K at Centennial Park Trail access go east then north ~3 mi.

Merton Segment and Monches Segment (Atlas Map 83f)

SNAPSHOT

Merton Segment—5.2 miles (2.7 IAT, 2.5 CR): CTH-K at Centennial Park to East Kilbourne Rd.

Monches Segment—3.1 miles: East Kilbourne Rd. to CTH-Q

  *The **Merton Segment** courses along the Bark River and the abandoned Kettle Moraine Railway bed.*

 At nearby Fireman's Park in North Lake (seasonal).

 From the Bark River.

 At Centennial Park and nearby Fireman's Park in North Lake.

 At Centennial Park (seasonal) and nearby community park on south side of CTH-VV a short distance east of North Lake.

 By law, dogs must be leashed at all times.

 Segment includes connecting route roadwalks. Portions follow an abandoned rail bed.

 A paved spur trail along the west bank of the Bark River.

  *Much of the **Monches Segment** traverses a mature maple forest and parallels the Oconomowoc River; of particular interest are the spring and early summer woodland wildflowers.*

At nearby Monches County Park (seasonal) on CTH-E. (There is no spur from the park's parking/services area to the Ice Age Trail.)

From the Oconomowoc River.

By law, dogs must be leashed at all times.

A blue-blazed spur trail leading to a parking area.

Note: Trail users should be aware that portions of the Monches Segment have been opened up to hunting in recent years. As with all Ice Age Trail segments, if you choose to hike here during hunting seasons, wear blaze-orange clothing.

TRAIL ACCESS AND PARKING

CTH-K at Centennial Park: Near Hartland heading west on STH-16, take Exit 183 for Merton Ave. (CTH-KC). From the exit ramp turn right on Merton Ave. (CTH-KC) and go north 0.7 mi. At CTH-K (LisbonRd.) turn left and go west 0.2 mi to Centennial Park. If heading east on STH-16, take Exit 182 for North Ave. (CTH-E). From the exit ramp turn left and go north 1.0 mi. At CTH-K (Lisbon Rd.) turn right and go east 0.5 mi to the parking area for Centennial Park, which is open sunrise to sunset.

CTH-Q: From Menomonee Falls take USH-41/45 north. Exit onto County Line Rd. (CTH-Q) and go west 11.3 mi. Roadside parking south of County Line Rd. (CTH-Q) on CTH-E (**WK20**). NO PARKING north of County Line Rd. (CTH-Q) on CTH-K. An off-road parking area is available 0.5 mi east in a DNR parking lot on the north side of County Line Rd. (CTH-Q).

Additional Parking: (i) Community park on south side of CTH-VV a short distance east of North Lake. (ii) E. Kilbourne Rd. (formerly Funk Rd.) 0.1 mi west of the Trail. A blue-blazed spur trail leads to the Ice Age Trail from the parking area.

THE HIKE

At the **Merton Segment** starting point on CTH-K at Centennial Park, hikers can first explore a paved spur trail that extends 0.5 miles north of CTH-K along the west bank of the Bark River in the Four Winds subdivision. A rather large prairie is planted on either side of the spur trail as it winds between the residential development and the Bark River. This trail may become part of the Ice Age Trail in the future pending land acquisition to enable public access north of its current dead-end at a cul-de-sac (**WK3**).

The segment starts with a lengthy connecting route that heads east on CTH-K for 0.3 miles to Dorn Road, then heads north on Dorn Road for 1.4 miles and then west on Richter Road for 0.4 miles. Hikers should use caution when walking along these roads as they have narrow gravel shoulders and moderate traffic. At the end of Richter Road continue west into the woods over the short boardwalk. The seg-

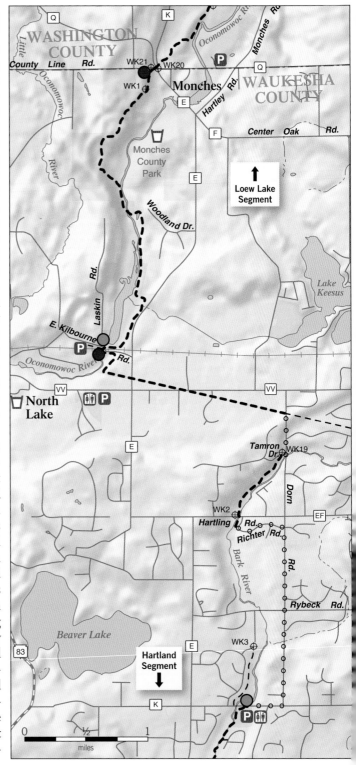

ment immediately turns north along the Bark River to Hartling Road (CTH-EF) where hikers should turn left and cross the bridge. The segment departs from the road (**WK2**) and meanders northeast along the west bank of the Bark River. The segment emerges onto Tamron Drive (**WK19**), where hikers should turn right and hike east to Dorn Road.

The segment heads north on Dorn Road for 0.4 miles, then leaves the road and travels west onto the old Kettle Moraine Railway right-of way. Plans call for the development of the right-of-way into a multi-use trail. Hikers not wishing to hike on the actual rail bed can parallel the rail bed for 1.9 miles west along the hedgerow, crossing CTH-VV and CTH-E along the way. The segment departs from the rail bed and heads north to East Kilbourne Road. After a brief road walk west then north on East Kilbourne Road, hikers will pass under a railroad trestle and arrive at the end of the segment. A blue-blazed spur trail leads west to a parking area.

A mature maple forest is the setting for much of the **Monches Segment**. The forest here is named in honor of conservationist Carl Schurz, United States Secretary of the Interior from 1877–1881. He established the first U.S. Forest Reserves and helped lay the groundwork for establishment of the U.S. Forest Service and the National Park Service.

The segment departs from East Kilbourne Road and heads north, soon arriving at a bridge over a picturesque cascading brook. Skunk cabbage and marsh marigolds inhabit the natural, spring-fed environment. Continuing north hikers will enjoy glimpses of the Oconomowoc River. In spring and early summer, expect to see ephemeral flowers like Dutchman's breeches, spring beauty, shooting star, marsh marigold, trillium and jack-in-the-pulpit. The segment soon reaches a boardwalk and crosses a second bridge to the west side of the river. In early May, trout lilies carpet the steep hillside just north of the bridge.

As it makes its way through the forest to its endpoint on County Line Road (CTH-Q), the segment climbs the bank remnants of a glacial meltwater spillway (river) (**WK1**). On top, the view across the meadow offers a nice example of forest progression. Just west of the segment's endpoint is a large sign (**WK21**) memorializing Carl Schurz.

AREA SERVICES

Merton: Restaurant. From the CTH-EF (Hartling Rd.) Trail access go 1.0 mi east and 0.5 mi north on CTH-VV.

North Lake: Restaurant, convenience store, library. From the CTH-VV Trail access go 1.5 mi west.

Monches: Restaurant. From the CTH-Q Trail access go east 0.5 mi to CTH-E.

Hartland: See Hartland Segment, p. 282. From the CTH-K at Centennial Park Trail access go east then south ~2 mi. Also see Trail Access and Parking directions, above.

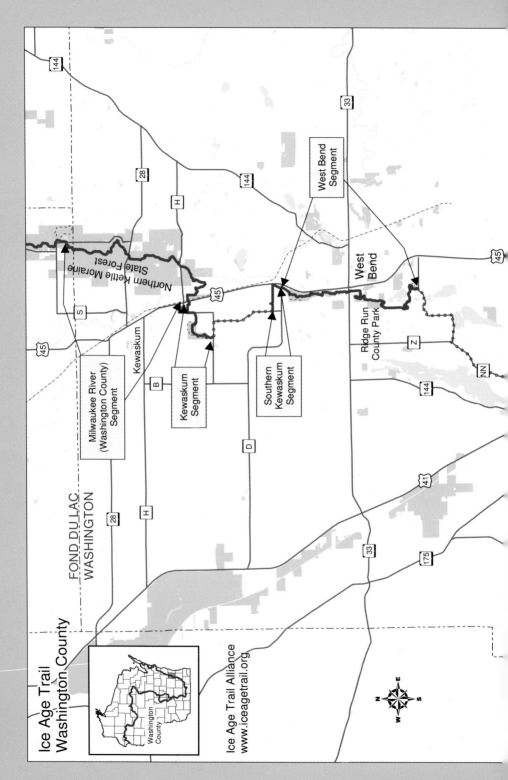

Ice Age Trail
Washington County

FOND DU LAC
WASHINGTON

Northern Kettle Moraine
State Forest

Milwaukee River
(Washington County)
Segment

Kewaskum

Kewaskum
Segment

Southern
Kewaskum
Segment

West Bend
Segment

West
Bend

Ridge Run
County Park

Ice Age Trail Alliance
www.iceagetrail.org

Washington
County

288

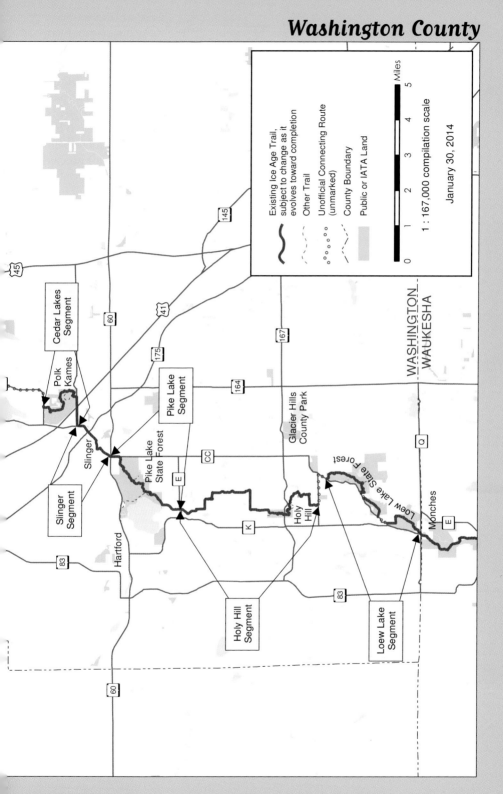

Washington County

Existing Ice Age Trail,
subject to change as it
evolves toward completion

Other Trail

Unofficial Connecting Route
(unmarked)

County Boundary

Public or IATA Land

1 : 167,000 compilation scale

January 30, 2014

Miles

0 1 2 3 4 5

145

45

Cedar Lakes
Segment

60

41

Polk
Kames

175

Pike Lake
Segment

167

164

Slinger

Pike Lake
State Forest

CC

Slinger
Segment

E

Glacier Hills
County Park

WASHINGTON
WAUKESHA

Q

Loew Lake State Forest

Hartford

83

K

Holy
Hill

Monches

E

Holy Hill
Segment

83

Loew Lake
Segment

60

Washington County

Trail miles: 35.2
Connecting route miles: 9.4

The Ice Age Trail's entire route through the county is within the margins of the Kettle Moraine. These ridges formed from rock debris deposited where the Green Bay and Lake Michigan lobes butted up against each other, often atop the Niagara Escarpment. To either side of the Kettle Moraine are drumlins and till plains left behind by each of the lobes. Wisconsin's most distinctive geological landform is the glacier-formed kame. Kames are the result of glacial streams that flowed down through cracks or shafts in the ice sheets that rose thousands of feet above our modern landscape. Several prominent kames, such as Holy Hill, Powder Hill and a cluster known as the Polk Kames, dominate this narrow landscape and offer panoramic hilltop views.

The Trail route in Washington County winds through the Kettle Moraine State Forest's Loew Lake and Pike Lake units, with a trek to Holy Hill sandwiched between. Further north the route highlights the village of Slinger, Ridge Run County Park, the city of West Bend and Glacial Blue Hills Recreation Area. Toward the northern end of the county the Trail begins its traverse of the Northern Unit of the Kettle Moraine State Forest near the Milwaukee River.

CHAPTER INFORMATION

Volunteers formed the Washington/Ozaukee County Chapter in 1987, though they had developed the first Washington County segment of the Ice Age Trail ten years prior. The chapter works to permanently protect Ice Age Trail segments in its territory and seeks routes to connect the existing Trail segments. The chapter promotes the Ice Age Trail with local news articles and service club memberships and sponsors regular hikes and workdays. The chapter hosts annual events for National Trails Day and a Fall Colors Hike. The chapter's "Meander the Mid-Moraine" hiking program recognizes hikers who have walked all 45 miles of the chapter's Ice Age Trail segments and connecting routes.

COUNTY INFORMATION

Kettle Moraine State Forest Northern Unit: 262-626-2116, dnr.wi.gov/
topic/parks/name/kmn

Kettle Moraine State Forest Pike Lake Unit: 262-670-3400, dnr.wi.gov/
topic/parks/name/pikelake

Washington County Convention & Visitors Bureau: 888-974-8687 or 262-677-5069, visitwashingtoncounty.com

PHILIA HAYES

Enjoying a break during a trek on the Slinger Segment.

Washington County

Loew Lake Segment (Atlas Maps 83f, 84f)

4.8 miles (4.3 IAT, 0.5 CR): CTH-Q to Emerald Dr. Northern Trail Access.

 This segment highlights the Oconomowoc River valley and Loew Lake while passing through wooded terrain and a large, scenic meadow.

 From the Oconomowoc River.

 Two short spur trails.

 Segment includes connecting-route roadwalks.

By law, dogs must be leashed April 15 to July 31 when crossing the KMSF Loew Lake Unit.

CTH-Q: From Menomonee Falls take USH-41/45 north. Exit onto County Line Rd. (CTH-Q) and go west 11.3 mi. Roadside parking south of County Line Rd. (CTH-Q) on CTH-E (**WK20**). NO PARKING north of County Line Rd. (CTH-Q) on CTH-K. An off-road parking area is available 0.5 mi east in a DNR parking lot on the north side of County Line Rd. (CTH-Q).

Emerald Dr. Northern Trail Access: From Hartford at the intersection of STH-83 and STH-60, take STH-83 south 4.7 mi. At STH-167 turn left and go east 1.5 mi. At CTH-K turn right and go south 1.0 mi. At Donegal Rd. turn left and go east 1.5 mi. At Emerald Dr. turn right and go south 0.3 mi. No parking.

Additional Parking: Emerald Dr. parking area (**WA18**) 0.5 mi south of segment's northern terminus. A blue-blazed spur trail from the parking area leads to the Ice Age Trail.

This segment is a key link in the green belt between Washington and Waukesha counties and generally follows the rim of the Oconomowoc River valley winding along the Oconomowoc River and 23-acre Loew Lake. The valley served as a glacial spillway where meltwater flowed south between the Green Bay and Lake Michigan glacial lobes. The segment highlights the Loew Lake Unit of the Kettle Moraine State Forest, an area that offers a variety of habitats for wildlife and is extremely popular with hunters and fishermen in all seasons.

From its starting point near the CTH-K/CTH-Q intersection at the Washington/Waukesha county line, the segment passes through a conifer plantation before dropping down to briefly parallel the Oconomowoc River. The segment departs from the riverbank and continues north, crossing a boardwalk bridge at the edge of a marsh filled with skunk cabbage and tall cow parsnips. Hikers will pass by a natural spring off to the right (**WA20**) shortly before the end of the boardwalk. The segment follows several field hedgerows before intersecting with Emerald Drive.

Upon reaching Emerald Drive hikers should turn right and head northeast along the road for 0.4 miles before heading east onto a short off-road section that features not-so-distant views of the Holy Hill Shrine to the north. After an additional 0.1-mile walk along Emerald Drive, the segment again departs the road heading east and weaves in and out of woods, alongside meadows and atop a steep-sided ridge (**WA19**). The segment intersects a horse trail that heads east

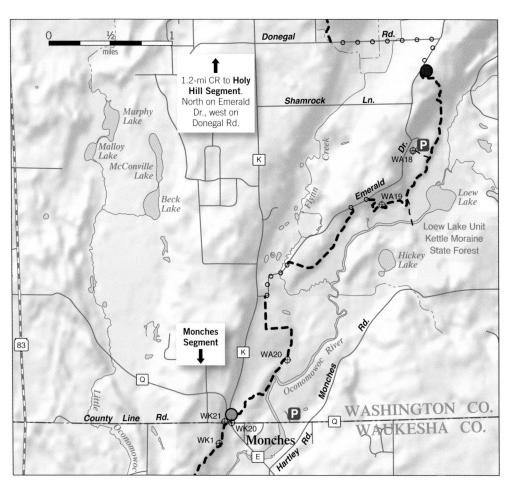

to cross the Oconomowoc River; a short distance later the segment intersects with a blue-blazed spur trail that heads west to the DNR's Emerald Drive parking area (**WA18**). From this last junction, the segment continues north through a large meadow before climbing out of the river valley on a series of switchbacks to reach the segment's endpoint on Emerald Drive.

AREA SERVICES

Kettle Moraine State Forest Loew Lake Unit: Recreation. On Trail. Access on Emerald Dr. (262-670-3400, dnr.wi.gov/topic/parks/name/loewlake).

Hartland: See Hartland Segment, p. 282. From the CTH-K at CTH-Q Trail access go south ~7 mi.

Monches: See Merton Segment and Monches Segment, p. 285. From the CTH-K at CTH-Q Trail access go east 0.3 mi.

Hartford: See Pike Lake Segment, Slinger Segment and Cedar Lakes Segment, p. 296. From the Emerald Dr. northern Trail access go west and north ~9 mi. Also see Trail Access and Parking directions, above.

Holy Hill Segment (Atlas Map 84f)

SNAPSHOT

6.9 miles: Donegal Rd. to CTH-E

  Especially popular during fall color season, this segment showcases the Holy Hill kame, wooded, hilly terrain and deep kettles.

 At the Station Way Rd. picnic area (seasonal) and the Basilica complex.

Portion of segment crossing private land between Pleasant Hill Rd. and CTH-E is closed during gun deer season.

Dogs must not stray from the Trail.

Portions of the segment overlap with Pleasant Hill Rd. and Glassgo Dr.

Several short spur trails.

TRAIL ACCESS AND PARKING

Donegal Rd.: From the Menomonee Falls area take USH-41/45 north. Exit onto STH-167 and go west 6.0 mi. At CTH-CC turn left and go south 0.8 mi. At Emerald Rd. turn right and go west, curving south 0.7 mi. At Donegal Rd. turn right and go west 0.8 mi. No parking.

CTH-E: From USH-41 exit onto STH-60 and go west 2.3 mi. At CTH-CC turn left and go south 2.0 mi. At CTH-E turn right and go west 1.4 mi to the Trail access just west of Glassgo Dr. Roadside parking on Glassgo Dr.

Additional Parking: (i) Carmel Rd. parking area near St. Mary of the Hill Parish. A blue-blazed spur trail leads to the Ice Age Trail. From Donegal Rd. Trail access, go west 0.1 mi on Donegal Rd. At Carmel Dr. turn right and go north 0.5 mi to parking area. (ii) Station Way Rd. picnic area. From the Menomonee Falls area take USH-41/45 north. Exit onto STH-167 and go west 7.3 mi. At Station Way Rd. turn left and go south 0.1 mi to the picnic and parking area. The Ice Age Trail follows the north edge of the picnic area. (iii) STH-167 roadside parking with spur trail to Ice Age Trail. (iv) Shannon Rd. parking area, 0.5 mi east of CTH-K. A blue-blazed spur trail leads to the Ice Age Trail. (v) Pleasant Hill Rd. eastern Trail access (**WA13**); roadside parking.

THE HIKE

From Donegal Road to the STH-167 Trail access, the segment passes through a mostly forested landscape across the glacial terrain that surrounds Holy Hill. The segment route offers just a few openings with views of glacial kame Holy Hill and the shrine and monastery that sits atop it, 1350 feet above sea level. Glacial geologists estimate at the time of the Wisconsin Glaciation, the thickness of the glacial ice extended another 1000 feet above Holy Hill. Glacial erratics are a common trailside sight in this area and several spur trails offer vistas of the surrounding landscape. A blue-blazed spur trail (**WA16**) north of Holy Hill leads to both a parking area near St. Mary of the Hill Parish and a large glacial erratic perched at the top of a kame.

At STH-167 (**WA15**) the segment continues north, crossing an intermittent stream on a board bridge built as an Eagle Scout project and then winding through grasslands of a previous agricultural era with multiple stone fence remnants along the way. Just south of the Shannon Road Trail access (**WA14**), a blue-blazed spur trail leads west to a DNR parking area on Shannon Road.

North of Shannon Road, the segment passes through a pine plantation and then continues north along the edges of two fields. At Pleasant Hill Road, hikers should turn right and follow the blazed telephone poles east for 0.5 miles. The segment departs north from Pleasant Hill Road (**WA13**), crosses a field along the edge of a small wetland, climbs two hills with a kettle pond in between, passes through a large wetland on a long, elevated boardwalk and then emerges onto Waterford Road after passing by a farm field and house.

North of Waterford Road, the segment passes several deep kettles in a mature mixed forest, then follows along the edge of farm fields, and then through a field before reaching an intersection (**WA12**) with Glassgo Drive. The segment follows the road northeast for 0.3 miles before departing off-road to the northwest on a short section that leads to the segment's terminus on CTH-E.
Mobile Skills Crew project site, 2006

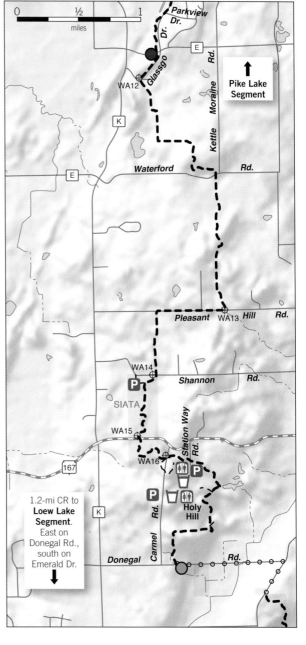

AREA SERVICES

Holy Hill Shrine and Monastery: Restaurant (seasonal), lodging (call ahead). On Trail (262-628-1838, holyhill.com).

Local Area: Restaurant. From the STH-167 Trail access go east 3.8 mi to Bilda's Friess Lake Pub at the intersection of STH-167 and STH-164 (262-628-3454).

Hartford: See Pike Lake Segment, Slinger Segment and Cedar Lakes Segment, p. 296. From the STH-167 Trail access go west and north ~7 mi.

Kettle Moraine State Forest Pike Lake Unit: See Pike Lake Segment, Slinger Segment and Cedar Lakes Segment, p. 296. From the STH-167 Trail access go west and north ~6 mi.

Pike Lake Segment, Slinger Segment and Cedar Lakes Segment (Atlas Maps 84f, 85f)

Pike Lake Segment—3.3 miles: CTH-E to STH-60

Slinger Segment—1.5 miles: STH-60 to Kettle Moraine Dr.

Cedar Lakes Segment—2.8 miles: Kettle Moraine Dr. to CTH-NN

 The **Pike Lake Segment** passes through the family-friendly Pike Lake Unit of the Kettle Moraine State Forest and offers outstanding views from the top of the nearby Powder Hill observation tower.

 At Pike Lake Unit facilities.

 From Pike Lake.

Pike Lake Unit walk-to campsites (reservations required) between Powder Hill Rd. and CTH-CC.

Pike Lake Unit campground.

Dogs are not permitted at park facilities.

Pike Lake Unit trail network loops and spurs.

 The short **Slinger Segment** mostly follows roads and sidewalks through this "Trail Town."

 At Community Park.

Portions of this segment may be suitable for those using wheelchairs or similar devices.

 The **Cedar Lakes Segment** features the Polk Kames, the second largest cluster of kames in the state.

No reliable sources of water.

A white-blazed loop trail.

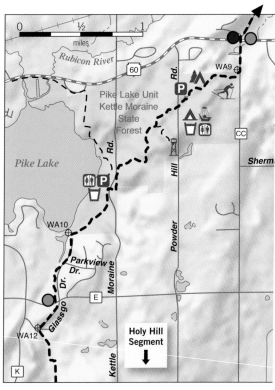

CTH-E: From USH-41 exit onto STH-60 and go west 2.3 mi. At CTH-CC turn left and go south 2.0 mi. At CTH-E turn right and go west 1.4 mi to the Trail access just west of Glassgo Dr. Roadside parking on Glassgo Dr.

CTH-NN: From USH-41 take Exit 66 onto STH-144 and go north 0.4 mi. At CTH-NN turn right and go east 0.4 mi to the parking area on the south side of the road.

Additional Parking: (i) Pike Lake Unit Swim Area on Kettle Moraine Rd. (ii) Pike Lake Unit Black Forest Nature Trail parking area on Powder Hill Rd. The Ice Age Trail passes through the east end of the parking area. (iii) Roadside parking in Slinger. Please do not park along Cedar Creek Rd.

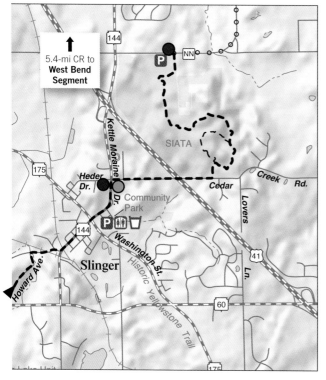

THE HIKE

The **Pike Lake Segment** heads north from its starting point on CTH-E, paralleling and then following quiet Glassgo Drive 0.3 miles to the southern property boundary (**WA10**) of the Kettle Moraine State Forest's 446-acre Pike Lake Unit. Most of the segment here follows the edge of a glacial ridge through heavily forested maple and beech woods. Pike Lake is a spring-fed kettle with a very popular sandy beach; the segment reaches the swimming area parking lot 0.5 miles after first entering the unit.

The segment crosses Kettle Moraine Road and makes its way uphill for 0.9 miles to an intersection with a spur trail. The spur climbs 0.2 miles to the top of 1,350-foot Powder Hill, one of the larger kames in the area. A lookout tower on top offers spectacular 360-degree views. From the intersection with the spur trail the segment continues another 0.25 miles to Powder Hill Road, joining the Black Forest Nature Trail along the way.

East of Powder Hill Road the segment passes a spur trail to the Pike Lake Unit campground and turns north to pass through the east end of the Black Forest Nature Trail parking area. From here, the segment travels north and east through a heavily wooded area. Walk-to campsites are located in this area. The segment continues east to CTH-CC at a spot marked with an Ice Age Trail signpost on the west side of the road (**WA9**). At this point, hikers should turn left and head north on CC for 0.3 miles to the segment's endpoint at the CTH-CC/STH-60 intersection.

The **Slinger Segment** starts from the CTH-CC/STH-60 intersection by heading northeast on an abandoned road that leads to Howard Avenue. Hikers should head east and then north on Howard Avenue to Hartford Road, where the segment heads east to Kettle Moraine Drive (STH-144).

At Kettle Moraine Drive (STH-144) the segment heads northeast and takes hikers through the village of Slinger. Slinger was an important trading center for Native Americans. Over the years, it has been at the crossroads for many trails and roads such as the Winnebago Trail, which was the easiest route through the Kettle Moraine, and the Yellowstone Trail, America's first coast-to-coast automobile highway. It was originally named Schleisingerville after the first general store owner, but changed to Slinger after World War II. Along Kettle Moraine Drive (STH-144) the segment passes Community Park before reaching its endpoint at the Cedar Creek Road intersection.

The **Cedar Lakes Segment** highlights several of the Polk Kames while traversing agricultural fields, wetlands and mixed forest of old oaks, sugar maple, white birch and beech. During the winter, the north and east sides of the kames retain snow later in season. The spring months present a scattered display of woodland and prairie wildflowers, including trillium, wood anemone, mayapple, violets, jack-in-the-pulpit and many ferns. During the warmer days of the year, frog-laden ponds create an early morning and late evening chorus echoing between the kames. The fall colors here are not to be missed. A few Ice Age Trail informational signs are placed along the segment.

From the intersection of Kettle Moraine Drive (STH-144) and Cedar Creek Road the segment follows Cedar Creek Road east for 0.7 mi. The segment departs the road and heads north along the edge of a farm field and enters the woods, soon arriving at a junction with the 0.8-mile white-blazed Kame Loop trail, which curves around a prominent kame and allows hikers to see the west side of the kame; look for a large area of shooting stars on a hilltop north of the kame. From this junction the segment heads east and then north, passing by a bench and informational sign on the east side of the kame. The segment then reaches the north junction with the white-blazed loop trail and skirts the eastern sides of a second kame. Volunteer-built puncheons and rock-lined water drainage structures highlight this portion of the segment.

The segment bends west and passes by the north side of the northern kame. The segment continues west and then north, passing through a mix of forest and farm fields before reaching its endpoint at the Trail access on CTH-NN.

Mobile Skills Crew project site, 2004, 2009

AREA SERVICES

Kettle Moraine State Forest Pike Lake Unit: Camping. On Trail (262-670-3400, dnr.wi.gov/topic/parks/name/pikelake; reservations: 888-947-2757, reserveamerica.com).

Hartford: Restaurant, grocery store, convenience store, lodging, camping, library, medical care. From the STH-60 Trail access go 2.5 mi west on STH-60. INN Style program lodging at the Jordan House B&B (262-673-5643, jordanhousebandb.com) and at Westphal Mansion Inn B&B (262-673-7938, westphalmansioninn.com). Area info available from the Hartford Chamber of Commerce (262-673-7002, hartfordchamber.org).

Slinger: Restaurant, grocery store, convenience store, library. On Trail along Kettle Moraine Dr. or from the STH-60 Trail access go 1.5 mi east on STH-60.

West Bend Segment and Southern Kewaskum Segment (Atlas Maps 85f, 86f)

West Bend Segment—6.5 miles: Paradise Dr. to CTH-D

Southern Kewaskum Segment—1.1 miles: CTH-D to Wildwood Rd.

 The rolling **West Bend Segment** *highlights scenic suburban parks with many additional hiking options.*

At Ridge Run County Park.

From Lucas Lake and Silver Creek.

 No dogs on the portion between Washington St. (STH-33/144) and CTH-D.

 Portions overlap with a gravel driveway and sidewalks. A small portion in Glacial Blue Hills Recreation Area is open to mountain biking.

 Several spur trails and three white-blazed loop trails.

 Largely passing under a power transmission line, the **Southern Kewaskum Segment** *highlights a beech-maple forest.*

No reliable sources of water.

 At nearby Timber Trail Campground (see Area Services).

Portion overlaps with Friendly Dr.

A short white-blazed loop trail.

Paradise Dr.: From West Bend take USH-45 south. Take Exit 68 onto Paradise Dr. and go west 1.0 mi to the parking area on the north side of the road.

Wildwood Rd.: From West Bend take USH-45 north. Take Exit 73 onto CTH-D (Lighthouse Ln.) and go west 0.9 mi. At Wildwood Rd. (CTH-B) turn right and go north 0.2 mi to the parking area on the east side of the road.

Additional Parking: (i) Ridge Run County Park, both north and south entrances. (ii) Washington St. (STH-33/144) commercial parking area near Culver's. (iii) Glacial Blue Hills Recreation Area off Beaver Dam Rd. (iv) CTH-D Trail access; roadside parking on the south side of the road. (v) Friendly Dr. Trail access (**WA4**); roadside parking.

From its starting point on Paradise Drive the **West Bend Segment** meanders north and soon intersects with a short white-blazed loop trail that bubbles off to the east of the main segment. The segment bends west and enters the heavily wooded property of the Girls Scouts' Camp Silverbrook at the south end of Lucas Lake. It continues past an esker and then drops to a marshy area with a bridge over Silver Creek, which flows northward from Paradise Valley Lake into Lucas Lake.

From here, the segment makes its way up a steep ridge and bends north, passing over lands protected by the Cedar Lakes Conservation Foundation. Farther on, the segment reached Wheat Ridge Lane and the southern boundary of Ridge

Run County Park.

The segment enters the park and curves around past an artesian well and small pond near a picnic area, crosses over a water-filled kettle/wetland on a boardwalk (**WA6**) and soon heads north along picturesque Silver Creek and its chain of lily filled ponds and lakes. Continuing on, the Trail partially circles a ridge, then climbs the ridge, turns east and exits Ridge Run County Park, briefly following a driveway to connect with University Drive near its intersection with Chestnut Street. The segment heads north and follows sidewalks along University Drive for a half-mile. The segment then crosses busy Washington Street (STH-33/144) to a Trail access area on the north side of the road next to a large commercial area with most services. From here, the segment heads north ascending a forested ridge.

The segment passes through the scenic Glacial Blue Hills Recreation Area traversing rugged terrain as it goes along a moraine and dips between ridges on its way toward the segment terminus at CTH-D. Shortly after crossing Park Avenue, the segment skirts a kettle and climbs to the top of an esker (**WA5**), following the crest of the esker to Beaver Dam Road. The Recreation Area features a network of hiking and biking trails, including two white-blazed loop trails.

The **Southern Kewaskum Segment** begins by crossing CTH-D and following Friendly Drive north for 0.3 miles. The segment departs (**WA4**) Friendly Drive and heads west, following a power line right-of-way over rolling hills while highlighting agricultural fields and mature beech–maple woods where hikers will find many spring and summer wildflowers. A portion roughly halfway from either segment

2.2-mi CR to **Kewaskum Segment**. North on Wildwood Rd., north on Town Hall Rd., west on Ridge Rd.

5.4-mi CR to **Cedar Lakes Segment**

Glacial Blue Hills Rec. Area

Albecker Natural Area

Ridge Run County Park

West Bend

Lucas Lake

Paradise Valley Lake

½   1
miles

terminus is usually wet in spring and difficult to hike through. Climbing out of this low area, the segment briefly leaves the right-of-way and enters the beech-maple woods to connect with a short white-blazed loop trail. Continuing west there is a small footbridge over a small ephemeral stream before reaching the segment terminus at Wildwood Road.

AREA SERVICES

West Bend: Camping, restaurant, grocery store, convenience store, general shopping, lodging, library, medical care. On Trail. Most services along Washington St. (STH-33/144) and 0.7 mi east of the segment on Paradise Dr. INN Style program lodging at Isadora's Bed & Breakfast (262-306-8468, isadorasbedandbreakfast.com). Camping at Timber Trail Campground (262-338-8561, timbertrailcampground.com). From the CTH-D Trail access take CTH-D west 1.2 mi and go north 0.6 mi on Good Luck Ln. Call ahead for availability; ask to speak with the manager if full. For West Bend area info, contact the West Bend Park and Recreation Department (262-335-5080, ci.westbend.wi.us) and the West Bend Area Chamber of Commerce (888-338-8666, wbchamber.org).

Kewaskum Segment and Milwaukee River Segment
(Washington County) (Atlas Map 86f, 87f)

SNAPSHOT

Kewaskum Segment—2.1 miles: Ridge Rd. to Eisenbahn State Trail

Milwaukee River Segment (Washington County)—6.8 miles (6.7 IAT, 0.1 CR): Eisenbahn State Trail to Kettle Moraine Dr.

The **Kewaskum Segment** features the Otten Preserve and its scenic overlooks.

 No reliable sources of water.

 At the Dispersed Camping Area on the Otten Preserve (**WA21**).

 Portion of segment crossing private land between Ridge Road and STH-45 is closed during gun deer season.

 Portion overlaps with Prospect Dr. and briefly overlaps with the multi-use Eisenbahn State Trail (EST).

 Loop trails at the Otten Preserve. The EST extends north and south from the segment.

The hilly **Milwaukee River Segment (Washington County)** highlights forested woodlands and sunny meadows.

 From a hand-pump water well (**WA24**) near Backpack Shelter 1 and at the nearby New Fane Trails parking area.

 From the Milwaukee River.

At a walk-to trailside shelter (**WA1**, reservations required).

 At nearby New Fane Trails parking area.

 At Backpack Shelter 1 (please respect those who have reserved the shelter) and nearby New Fane Trails parking area.

 Segment includes a brief connecting route roadwalk.

 Spur trail to Backpack Shelter 1.

TRAIL ACCESS AND PARKING

Ridge Rd.: From Kewaskum at the intersection of USH-45 and STH-28, take USH-45 south 1.8 mi. At the stoplight for Badger Rd. turn right and go west 0.3 mi. At Prospect Dr. turn left and go south 1.0 mi. The road curves west and changes to Ridge Rd. Continue on Ridge Rd. west 0.6 mi to the parking area.

Kettle Moraine Dr.: From Kewaskum at the intersection of STH-28 and USH-45, take STH-28 east 2.5 mi. At Kettle Moraine Dr. turn left and go north 2.0 mi. No parking at the Trail access on Kettle Moraine Dr. Instead, park at New Fane Trail Area 0.2 mi south on Kettle Moraine Dr. and 0.3 mi east on County Line Dr. A spur trail leads from the northwest corner of the parking area to the Ice Age Trail.

Additional Parking: (i) Sunburst Ski Area parking area (**WA2**). (ii) CTH-H parking area on the south side of the road. (iii) STH-28 parking area. (iv) East Moraine Dr. parking area.

THE HIKE

The area traversed by the **Kewaskum Segment** has a rich Native American history. The word Kewaskum means "crooked river" in Algonquin, the language of the Potawatomi who once inhabited the area. The Potawatomi claim to the land ended with a treaty in 1833 and the Nation was resettled to Oklahoma. Years later, only a few returned.

The Kewaskum Segment heads north from its starting point on Ridge Road through the 125-acre Roman and Mercedes Otten Preserve, home to not only the main segment route but also an additional 2.5 miles of loop trails. The main segment route features light forests and upland fields with spectacular views of the Otten Preserve and the surrounding areas. From the hilltops, hikers can look for Kewaskum and Campbellsport to the north and the Dundee Kame and Kettle Moraine State Forest to the northeast. This portion of the segment is a magnet for birds and hikers should keep an eye out for meadowlarks, bobolinks, turkeys and several birds of prey. In spring, the woods are filled with a gorgeous display of trillium and jack-in-the-pulpit, and in late summer, there are many areas of gooseberry and raspberry patches. A Dispersed Camping Area (**WA21**) for long distance hikers is located 0.5 miles from the parking area on Ridge Road.

After passing through the Otten Preserve, the segment continues east across the Sunburst Ski Area property (covering a prominent kame) on an easement granted by the Summit Ski Corporation. The segment intersects (**WA2**) with Prospect Drive, where hikers should turn left and follow the road 0.3 miles north. The segment departs Prospect Drive heading east along a field edge, crosses a boardwalk, then skirts the southern edge of the "tank farm" before arriving at USH-45. The segment crosses under USH-45 via an underpass built specifically for the Ice Age Trail. After periods of heavy rains, the underpass is often swamped with water. Therefore, as conditions warrant, hikers should carefully cross at the level of the highway.

East of USH-45, the segment intersects with the Eisenbahn State Trail, a state-owned multi-use recreation trail on the former C & NW Railroad right-of-way. Twelve of the 24.0 miles of the abandoned former rail corridor are maintained, extending from the city of West Bend to Eden in Fond du Lac County. "Eisenbahn" is German for "iron road," harkening back to this rail line's heritage and original construction in 1871. The segment very briefly follows the Eisenbahn

302   **Ice Age Trail Guidebook 2014**

State Trail north to the segment's terminus where the Ice Age Trail heads off the Eisenbahn State Trail to the east.

From the Eisenbahn State Trail, the **Milwaukee River Segment (Washington County)** heads east then south, skirting a wetland mitigation site. The Trail crosses a boardwalk, cuts through woods and along the edge of a field and then

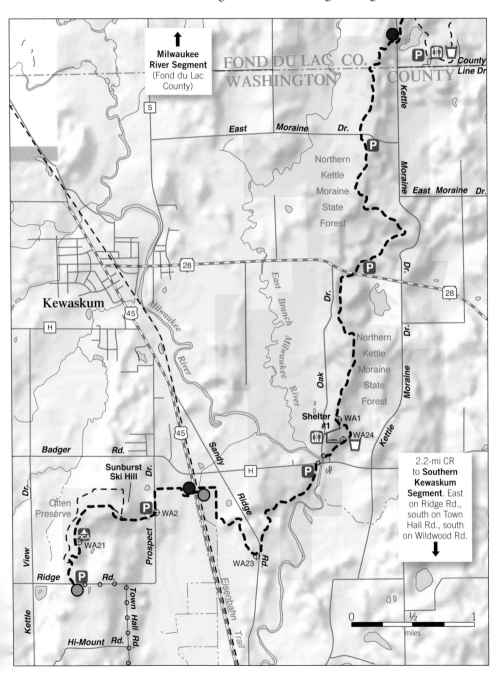

enters a forested area. As the segment meanders through the forest it crosses a wet area on a curving boardwalk and travels below and alongside a ridge, gradually climbing the ridge until the segment reaches an open field (**WA23**) just before crossing Sandy Ridge Road. The open field offers nice, long views of the surrounding fields and forested hills in the distance.

After crossing the road, the Trail passes through some more open area then drops down into the woods and courses through a more hummocky area passing by grassy depressions and wetland openings. Along the way, the segment enters the Kettle Moraine State Forest's Northern Unit. Continuing on, the segment primarily cuts across agricultural areas until it reaches the CTH-H parking area.

Hikers should turn east on CTH-H and cross over the Milwaukee River using extreme caution on the bridge, then head north on Oak Drive until the segment heads off-road to the east.

The segment continues into the dense forest and hummocky area of the south end of the Kettle Moraine State Forest's Northern Unit. The Kettle Moraine landscape dates back to the last Ice Age when the Green Bay Lobe and the Lake Michigan Lobe flowed into the area. As these lobes side-swiped each other and retreated, they created the rugged but beautiful high relief hummocky topography that makes up the landscape today, including numerous ridges, valleys, outwash plains, kettles, eskers and kames.

After leaving Oak Drive, the Trail soon comes to a trailside hand-pump water well (**WA24**), shortly followed by an intersection (**WA1**) with a short spur trail that leads to Backpack Shelter 1. Dedicated to Raymond T. Zillmer, founder of the Ice Age Trail Alliance, the shelter has a pleasant, lofty perch.

The segment continues northward through the high relief hummocky topography landscape highlighting many trailside kettles and kames in a beautiful blend of deep forest and sunny meadows. The forest offers quite solitude with a wide diversity of plants and fungal life along the Trail; the meadows offer great bird watching opportunities. The segment ends when it reaches Kettle Moraine Drive, just north of the Washington/Fond du Lac county line.

Mobile Skills Crew project site, 2013

AREA SERVICES

Kewaskum: Restaurant, grocery store, convenience store, general shopping, lodging, camping, library, medical care. From the STH-28 Trail access go west 2.0 mi on STH-28. Most services on USH-45. Lodging at Bonne Belle Motel (900 Prospect Dr., http://bonnebellemotel.com, 262-626-8414). Area info available from the Kewaskum Area Chamber of Commerce (262-626-3336, kewaskum.org).

Eisenbahn State Trail: On Trail (262-335-4445, dnr.wi.gov/topic/parks/name/eisenbahn).

KMSF Northern Unit Backpack Shelter 1: Camping. On Trail. Reservations (available only by calling 888-947-2757) are required to use the shelter and only one group per shelter per night is allowed.

West Bend: See West Bend Segment and Southern Kewaskum Segment, p. 299. From the USH-45 Trail access go south ~6 mi.

DAVE CALIEBE

Milwaukee River Segment.

Washington County

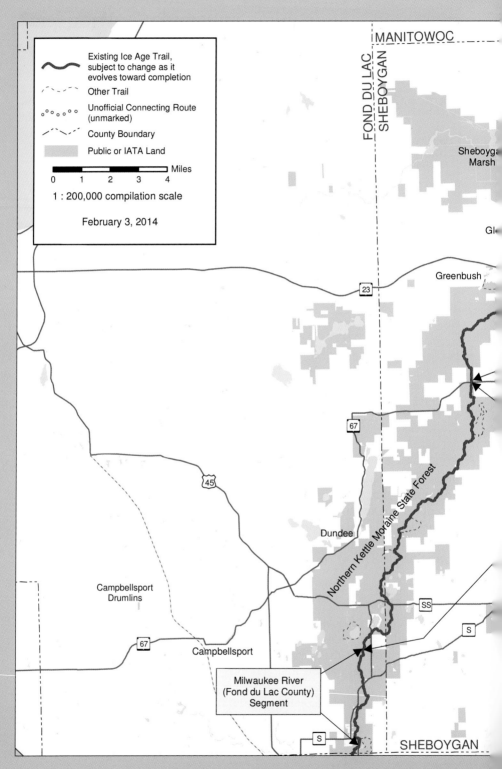

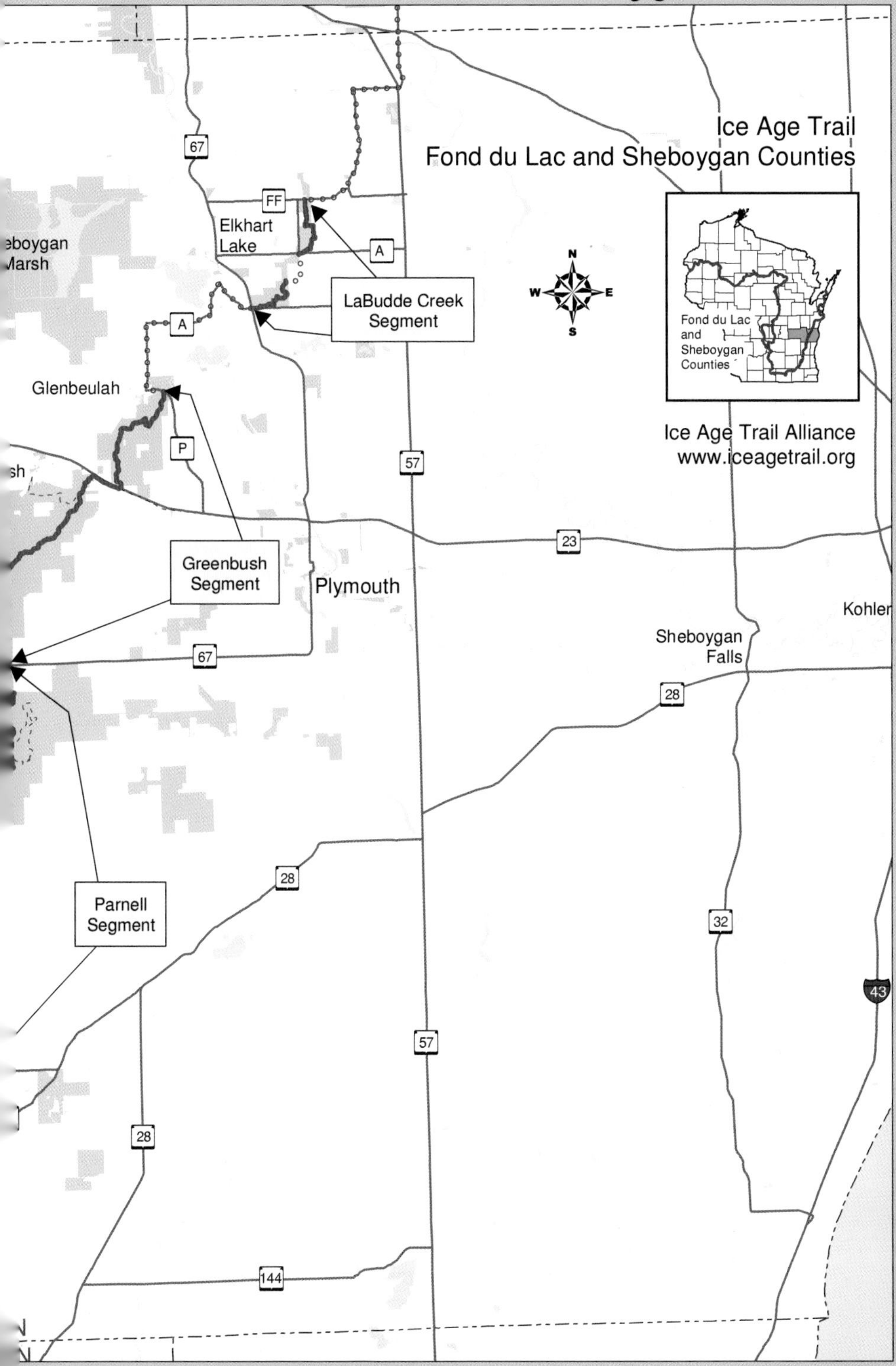

Ice Age Trail
Fond du Lac and Sheboygan Counties

67

FF

Elkhart
Lake

A

**LaBudde Creek
Segment**

eboygan
Marsh

A

Glenbeulah

P

**Greenbush
Segment**

Plymouth

67

57

23

Sheboygan
Falls

Kohler

28

28

32

**Parnell
Segment**

57

28

144

43

Fond du Lac
and
Sheboygan
Counties

Ice Age Trail Alliance
www.iceagetrail.org

Fond du Lac & Sheboygan Counties

Trail miles: 29.7
Connecting route miles: 10.0

The Interlobate Moraine (more commonly known as the Kettle Moraine) was formed when the Green Bay and Lake Michigan tongue-shaped glacial lobes met and formed a valley of ice. South-flowing meltwater cascaded into crevasses and carried sand, gravel and erratics, leaving a 120-mile-long series of kettles and ridges. The last remaining ice blocks eventually melted, creating kettles, many of which filled with water resulting in kettle lakes. The Ice Age Trail meanders within the Kettle Moraine topography through Fond du Lac and Sheboygan counties. Large and small wetlands intersperse the many forested uplands.

The Ice Age Trail in the Northern Unit of the Kettle Moraine State Forest (KMSF) highlights the formation of glacial features such as kettles, kames and eskers. This State Forest unit is 29,000 acres of rolling, wooded hills dotted with serene lakes. It offers year-round nature programs and hiking, biking, equestrian and cross-country ski trails. Developed campgrounds and backpack shelters are available for camping along the Ice Age Trail. It is this area that inspired Ray Zillmer to conceive of the Ice Age Trail. During the mid-1950s, he pursued government officials at all levels to recognize, preserve and establish a 1,000-mile national park. He envisioned this national park to be a conservation and recreation area featuring the glacial landscape that tells the story of the Ice Age.

CHAPTER INFORMATION

The Lakeshore Chapter was formed when volunteers from the old Door/ Kewaunee County, Manitowoc County and North Kettle Moraine chapters of the IATA merged the three chapters into one. Chapter members actively work together on Ice Age Trail promotion, planning and maintenance in addition to sponsored hikes held at various locations throughout the year. Hikers can become members of the "Hall of Kamers" by hiking the Northern Unit of the Kettle Moraine State Forest Ice Age Trail segments. See the IATA website or contact the chapter for more information.

COUNTY INFORMATION

Fond du Lac Area Convention and Visitor Bureau: 920-923-3010, fdl.com

Sheboygan County Chamber: 920-457-9491, sheboygan.org

Kettle Moraine State Forest Northern Unit: 262-626-2116, dnr.wi.gov/ topic/parks/name/kmn

Towering oaks on the Mauthe Lake Segment.

Fond du Lac & Sheboygan Counties

Milwaukee River Segment
(Fond du Lac County) (Atlas Map 87f)

4.3 miles: Kettle Moraine Dr. to Mauthe Lake Recreation Area

 This segment parallels the Milwaukee River through densely wooded hillsides and highlights the topography of the Kettle Moraine State Forest's Northern Unit.

 At the New Fane Trails and Mauthe Lake Recreation Area.

 At a walk-to trailside shelter (**SF7**, reservations required).

 At Mauthe Lake Recreation Area.

 At the New Fane Trails, Mauthe Lake Recreation Area and Backpack Shelter 2 (please respect those who have reserved the shelter).

 Portion briefly overlaps with a snowmobile trail.

 Spur trails to the New Fane Trails parking area and to Backpack Shelter 2.

Kettle Moraine Dr.: From Kewaskum at the intersection of STH-28 and STH-45, take STH-28 east 2.5 mi. At Kettle Moraine Dr. turn left and go north 2.0 mi. No parking at the Trail access on Kettle Moraine Dr. Instead, park at New Fane Trails parking area, 0.2 mi south on Kettle Moraine Dr. and 0.3 mi east on County Line Dr. A spur trail leads from the northwest corner of the parking area to the Ice Age Trail.

Mauthe Lake Recreation Area: From Kewaskum at the intersection of STH-28 and STH-45, take STH-28 east 0.4 mi. At CTH-S turn left and go north 6.1 mi. At CTH-GGG turn left (north) and go 1.0 mi to Mauthe Lake Rd. Turn left and go a short distance to a parking area at the entrance station. The Trail access is just west of the entrance station.

This segment follows an irregular hummocky sand and gravel ridge for most of its length, crossing through densely forested, terrain with some open prairie-like areas. The segment offers quiet passage through the forests, distant views from a ridge and opportunities to observe a variety of wildlife, including birds, plants and woodland flowers.

The segment starts where the Ice Age Trail crosses Kettle Moraine Drive at a point about a quarter-mile north of the Fond du Lac/Washington county line. A short distance (~0.3 miles) from the start, after passing over rolling hills and prairie grasses, the segment intersects (**SF8**) with a spur trail that leads to the New Fane Trails parking area. The segment continues through hardwood forests with some clearings. Just before reaching CTH-DD, the segment parallels a well-worn bike path.

After crossing CTH-DD, the segment climbs uphill and soon reaches a bench (**SF10**) in a clearing with views of kames to the west. The Trail continues on a mostly forested, hummocky ridge and crosses a snowmobile trail twice; at the second crossing, the segment and the snowmobile trail briefly overlap for about 50 feet. A short distance farther, a path to the snowmobile trail running parallel to the segment is visible. Hikers should pay close attention to blazes to avoid wandering off the Ice Age Trail.

The segment crosses CTH-S and soon reaches the southern end (SF7) of a loop trail that leads to Backpack Shelter 2. Continuing on, the Trail comes to the northern end of the loop trail as it courses through hummocky, forested topography, eventually dropping down to cross over some wetland areas. After crossing a boardwalk, the segment follows a wide, grassy tread before reaching its terminus at the Mauthe Lake Recreation Area entrance road, just west of the Recreation Area entrance station.

AREA SERVICES

KMSF Northern Unit Backpack Shelter 2: Camping. On Trail. Reservations (available only by calling 888-947-2757) are required to use the shelter and only one group per shelter per night is allowed.

KMSF Northern Unit Mauthe Lake Recreation Area: Convenience store, camping. On Trail (262-626-4305; reservations: 888-947-2757, www.reserveamerica.com). A convenience store with pizza is on CTH-GGG either 0.2 mi north of the Mauthe Lake entrance station or 0.3 mi south of the CTH-GGG Trail access.

KMSF Northern Unit Long Lake Recreation Area: See Parnell Segment, p. 312. From the Mauthe Lake Recreation Area go north and west ~8 mi.

Kewaskum: See Kewaskum Segment and Milwaukee River Segment (Washington County), p. 301. From the Mauthe Lake Recreation Area go south and west ~8 mi. Also see Trail Access and Parking directions, above.

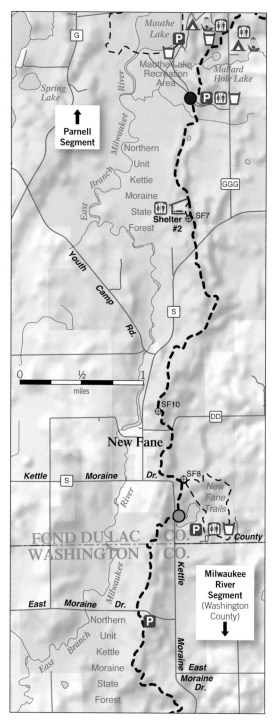

Parnell Segment (Atlas Maps 87f, 88f, 89f)

SNAPSHOT

13.9 miles: Mauthe Lake Recreation Area to STH-67

 This long segment highlights remarkable glacial formations including the world-famous Parnell Esker.

 At the Mauthe Lake Recreation Area, Butler Lake and the Parnell Observation Tower.

 From numerous lakes and streams.

 At two walk-to trailside shelters (**SF6**, **SF4**, reservations required).

 At Mauthe Lake Recreation Area and nearby Long Lake Recreational Area and private campground on Crooked Lake (see Area Services).

 At Mauthe Lake Recreation Area and nearby Long Lake Recreation Area.

 At Mauthe Lake Recreation Area, Parnell Observation Tower parking area and Backpack Shelters 3 and 4 (please respect those who have reserved the shelter).

 Backpack shelter spur trails, Butler Lake Loop Trail and Parnell Tower Loop Trail.

TRAIL ACCESS AND PARKING

Mauthe Lake Recreation Area: From Kewaskum at the intersection of STH-28 and STH-45, take STH-28 east 0.4 mi. At CTH-S turn left and go north 6.1 mi. At CTH-GGG turn left (north) and go 1.0 mi to Mauthe Lake Rd. Turn left and go a short distance to a parking area at the entrance station. The Trail access is just west of the entrance station.

STH-67: From Plymouth at intersection of STH-23 and STH-67, take STH-67 south then west 8.3 mi. Park in the grassy parking area on the south side of STH-67 next to the Trail.

Additional Parking: (i) CTH-SS parking area north of Little Mud Lake. (ii) Butler Lake Trail parking area on Butler Lake Rd. (iii) Parnell Observation Tower parking area on CTH-U.

THE HIKE

The segment starts at the Mauthe Lake Recreation Area entrance road Trail access, just west of the Recreation Area entrance station. In 1926, the Milwaukee Chapter of the Izaak Walton League protected Mauthe Lake, known as Moon Lake at the time. This initiative was a precursor to the development of the Kettle Moraine State Forest and the Ice Age Trail. Ray Zillmer, founder of the Ice Age Trail Alliance, was a long-time member and president of the League.

The segment heads north from the entrance road and skirts along the eastern edge of the Mauthe Lake campground. Be careful not to get confused by the frequent side trails that connect the campground to the Ice Age Trail. The segment cuts by Forest Lake with scenic views from the southern shore. As the Trail makes its way to CTH-SS it drops down for a couple of stream crossings, climbs up a hummock then again drops down to follow the crest of a small esker.

North of CTH-SS, the segment skirts the western side of Crooked Lake Wetlands State Natural Area, which provides habitat for various forest and plant communities and diverse nesting bird and waterfowl populations. The segment passes west of the three small Kellings Lakes. Parts of the Trail in this area can be steep and a rocky tread can lead to unsure footing. The segment soon intersects with a spur trail (**SF6**) that leads 0.6 miles west to Backpack Shelter 3. The segment continues through forests that include maple, birch, hickory, pine and oak trees.

The segment crosses CTH-F and soon meets up with the Butler Lake Loop Trail and then crosses a bridle trail as the segment makes its way to Butler Lake, which lies between two prominent eskers and is part of the Butler Lake Flynn's Spring State Natural Area. Fed from nearby Flynn's spring, Butler Lake is surrounded on three sides by a bog. A wide variety of flora and fauna are present here including rare species such as the unicorn clubtail dragonfly and the swamp spreadwing. The Butler Lake Loop Trail traverses the SNA and shares portions of the Ice Age Trail route.

Before reaching Butler Lake, the Ice Age Trail climbs to the crest of the Parnell Esker and follows it through the Butler Lake area. The Parnell Esker is a four-mile esker which ranges

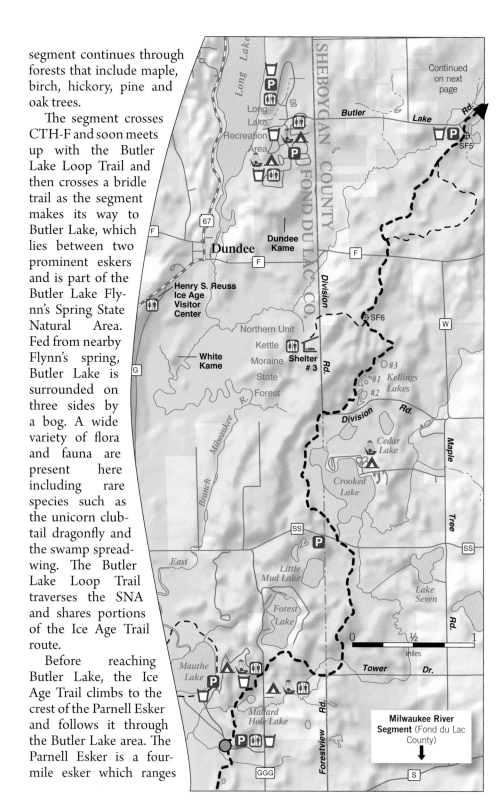

Continued on next page

from 5 to 30 feet in height and runs southwest–northeast. The esker is described on a geologic marker near the Butler Lake Trail parking area. At a high point on the esker (**SF5**) hikers will find a bench overlooking scenic Butler Lake.

From the Butler Lake area, the Trail travels across an open prairie-like area and then continues to the northeast through beautiful forested terrain going up, down and around kettles, ridges and hummocks. The area between the Trail westward to STH-67 contains one of the most striking and world-famous collections of kames in the world. Hills on the western horizon are drumlins. Hikers may catch an occasional glimpse of some of these kames and hills through the forest.

From the intersection with the Parnell Tower Loop, the segment and the loop trail head north together. Just before the northern split of the Ice Age Trail and the Parnell Tower Loop Trail, the segment intersects (**SF4**) with a short spur trail that leads to Backpack Shelter 4, which is visible from the Trail.

Continuing on, the segment passes through progressively less hummocky forested terrain, parts of which is strewn with rocks and boulders. Along the way to its terminus on STH-67, the Trail crosses a snowmobile/bridle trail twice and a power line right-of-way. Hikers should pay attention to Trail signage in these areas. Toward the end of the segment the Trail follows a wide grassy path in a more open area and reaches its terminus in a clearing at STH-67.

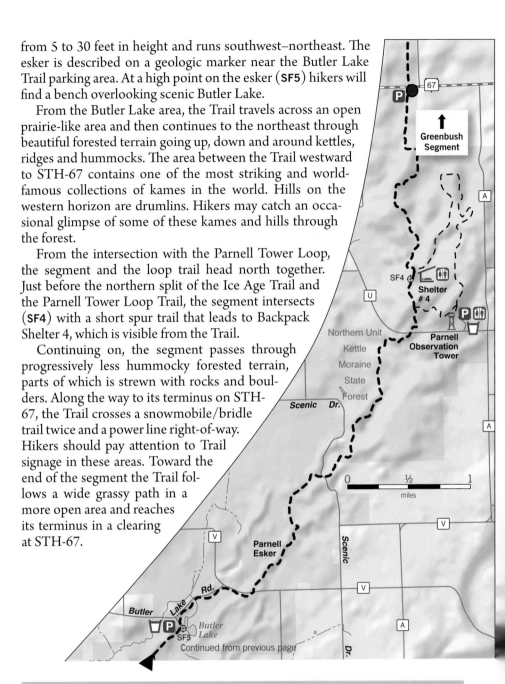

POINTS OF INTEREST

Henry S. Reuss Ice Age Visitor Center: From the Ice Age Trail at CTH-F go 2.5 mi west on CTH-F then south on STH-67 (920-533-8322, http://dnr.wi.gov/topic/parks/name/kmn/naturecenter.html).

At the Center hikers can view exhibits to learn about the frozen history of Wisconsin and the gifts of the glacier. There is a great view of the landscape from the Center and a naturalist is available to answer questions. The Center is open April through October, weekdays (8:30 am–4 pm) and weekends (9:30 am–5 pm). Hours vary November through March.

KMSF Northern Unit Mauthe Lake Recreation Area: Convenience store, camping. On Trail (262-626-4305; reservations: 888-947-2757, www.reserveamerica.com). A convenience store with pizza is on CTH-GGG either 0.2 mi north of the Mauthe Lake entrance station or 0.3 mi south of the CTH-GGG Trail access.

KMSF Northern Unit Backpack Shelters 3 and 4: Camping. On Trail. Reservations (available only by calling 888-947-2757) are required to use the shelter and only one group per shelter per night is allowed.

Plymouth: See Greenbush Segment, p. 316. From the STH-67 Trail access go east and south 8.3 mi. Also see Trail Access and Parking directions, above.

KMSF Northern Unit Long Lake Recreation Area: Camping. From the Butler Lake Trail parking area go 1.2 mi west on Butler Lake Rd. (920-533-8612; reservations: 888-947-2757, reserveamerica.com).

Dundee: Restaurant, convenience store. From the CTH-F Trail crossing go 2.0 mi west on CTH-F.

JO ELLARSON

Participants at Ice Age Trail Alliance volunteer events work hard, work safely and, above all, have a good time. Contact the Ice Age Trail Alliance (800-227-0046, iceagetrail.org) to see how you can join the fun.

TIM MALZHAN

Greenbush Segment (Atlas Map 89f)

SNAPSHOT

8.8 miles: STH-67 to CTH-P

🏔️ *This segment dips into deep valleys and traverses ridges through forests of basswood, oak, maple and pine.*

 From hand-pumped well near Backpack Shelter 5, at Greenbush Trails and Old Plank Road Trail (OPRT) parking area.

 At a walk-to trailside shelter (**SF2**, reservations required).

 At Backpack Shelter 5 (please respect those who have reserved the shelter), Greenbush Trails and OPRT parking area.

 The OPRT is open to biking, horseback riding and snowmobiling.

 Greenbush Trails network, blue-blazed spur trail to Greenbush and other short spur trails. The OPRT extends east and west from the segment.

TRAIL ACCESS AND PARKING

STH-67: From Plymouth at intersection of STH-23 and STH-67, take STH-67 south then west 8.3 mi. Park in the grassy parking area on the south side of STH-67 next to the Trail.

CTH-P: From Plymouth at the intersection of STH-23 and STH-67, take STH-23 west 2.0 mi. At CTH-P turn right and go north 2.3 mi to the parking area.

Additional Parking:: (i) KMSF Greenbush picnic area on Kettle Moraine Dr. 1.3 mi north of STH-67. (ii) KMSF Greenbush Trails on Kettle Moraine Dr. 2.5 mi north of STH-67. (iii) Old Plank Road Trail parking area on Plank Rd. 0.25 mi west of the Ice Age Trail.

THE HIKE

Heading north from STH-67 initially on relatively flat outwash, the segment reaches the Greenbush Kettle area (**SF1**) after about a mile. The kettle, just a short hike from the Trail, is one of the most symmetrical deep depressions in the area. A short distance from the kettle is a hand-pumped well and Backpack Shelter 5 (**SF2**). The Trail passes through a picnic area and continues north through hummocky topography toward Kettle Moraine Drive.

Just south of its crossing of Kettle Moraine Drive, the segment passes Greenbush Outdoor Group Camp. Right before the campground, a short unmarked spur trail leads off to the campground's parking area. This area is also a jumping-off point for the Greenbush Trails, a system of loops for mountain biking, hiking and cross-country skiing. Deep forests near the Greenbush Trails are a good place to see the hooded warbler, a rare migratory bird.

After crossing Kettle Moraine Drive, the segment travels through forested high-relief hummocky topography going up, down and around kettles and ridges as it makes its way to STH-23. The region is marked by its rich domination of red oak and shagbark hickory, which as preserved will evolve to an old growth forest.

In addition to the red oak and shagbark hickory, the dry-mesic forest canopy also consists of basswood, sugar maple, white ash, white oak and black cherry trees. The understory attracts rare birds such as Acadian flycatcher, red-shoul-

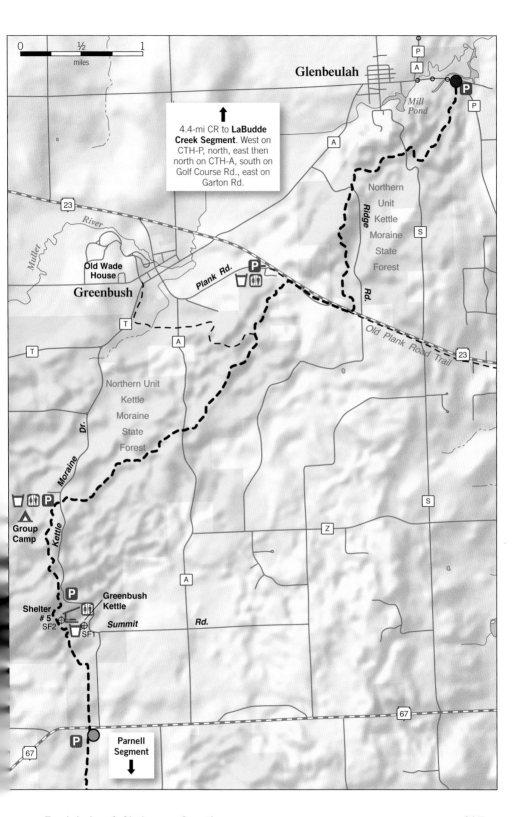

Glenbeulah

0   ½   1
miles

4.4-mi CR to **LaBudde Creek Segment**. West on CTH-P, north, east then north on CTH-A, south on Golf Course Rd., east on Garton Rd.

Mill Pond

P
A
P

23

River

Muller

Old Wade House

Greenbush

Plank Rd.

A

P

Ridge Rd.

Northern Unit Kettle Moraine State Forest

S

Old Plank Road Trail

23

T

A

T

Northern Unit Kettle Moraine State Forest

Moraine Dr.

Kettle

Group Camp

P

S

Z

A

P

Greenbush Kettle

Shelter #5

SF2

SF1

Summit

Rd.

67

Parnell Segment

P

67

dered hawk and cerulean warbler. A variety of plant species thrive in the shady area such as ferns, orchids, trillium and mayapples. The segment enters the Kettle Moraine Red Oaks State Natural Area at CTH-A.

As the segment nears STH-23, it intersects with a blue-blazed spur trail that leads 1.6 miles to the village of Greenbush and the Wade House Historic Site (see Points of Interest, below). Just south of STH-23, the segment intersects a snow-mobile/equestrian trail before connecting with the Old Plank Road Trail. This 19th century historic stagecoach route linked Sheboygan and Fond du Lac. The segment follows the Old Plank Road Trail 0.6 miles east along a paved route par-alleling STH-23, then separates at the point where the Trail crosses busy STH-23; use caution when crossing the highway.

From STH-23, the segment heads north through a mature red pine woods then again into forested high relief hummocky topography with oak, maple and hickory trees being dominant. The Trail follows a roller coaster serpentine course as it ascends and descends and curves around kettles and ridges, crosses two qui-eter roads and makes it ways to the segment's terminus at the Trail access kiosk and parking area at CTH-P.

POINTS OF INTEREST

Wade House: In Greenbush south of STH-23 and accessible from the Ice Age Trail via a 1.6-mi spur trail (920-526-3271, wadehouse.wisconsinhistory.org).

The Wade House, an 1860s New England–style stagecoach inn, served travelers of the Civil War era. From the Wade House, a short walk will take you to the Wesley Jung Carriage Museum which houses the state's largest collection of fine carriages and pioneer wagons. Also on site is the recon-structed historic Herrling Sawmill. The working water-powered mill portrays a vital component of the 19th century frontier settlement. The new Wade House Visitor Center and Carriage Museum opened in June 2013. There is a fee and hours vary by season.

AREA SERVICES

KMSF Northern Unit Backpack Shelter 5: Camping. On Trail. Reservations (available only by calling 888-947-2757) are required to use the shelter and only one group per shelter per night is allowed.

KMSF Greenbush Outdoor Group Camp: Camping. Within the Greenbush Trails area on Kettle Moraine Dr. (group camping only; reservations by calling 888-947-2757).

KMSF Northern Unit Long Lake Recreation Area: See Parnell Segment, p. 312. From the STH-67 Trail access go west and south 7.0 mi.

Plymouth: Restaurant, grocery store, convenience store, lodging, camping, medical care. From the STH-23 Trail access go east ~4 mi on STH-23 and CTH-C. Or from the STH-67 Trail access go 8.3 mi east then north on STH-67. INN Style program lodging at Spring Tulip Cottage (920-892-2101, springtulip.com). Area info available from the Plymouth Chamber of Commerce (888-693-8263, plymouthwisconsin.com).

Glenbeulah: Restaurant, convenience store, camping. From CTH-P Trail access go 0.5 mi west on CTH-P (Glen Rd.).

Elkhart Lake: See LaBudde Creek Segment, p. 320. From the CTH-P Trail access go west and north 4.0 mi.

Parnell Segment.

Fond du Lac & Sheboygan Counties

LaBudde Creek Segment (Atlas Map 90f)

THE HIKE

This segment passes through the 426-acre LaBudde Creek Fishery Area. The LaBudde Creek area is home to several species of game birds including ruffed grouse, ring-necked pheasants and woodcock, as well as a variety of songbirds such as the yellow throated and yellow warblers, catbirds, woodpeckers and brown thrashers.

The segment starts at the intersection of STH-67 and Garton Road with a 1000-foot road walk east on the shoulder of Garton Road. Leaving the road, the segment heads east and north through upland brush and grasslands/wetlands with colorful sumacs and nice views, crossing a short boardwalk along the way.

Just north of the Garton Road parking area the segment intersects with a side trail that leads to the LaBudde Channel (**SF9**), a glacial meltwater channel that was formed along the eastern edge of the Kettle Moraine and the western edge of the Lake Michigan Lobe. Continuing on its way to Badger Road, after crossing a second boardwalk (80-feet long) the segment enters a forest containing aspen, pine and cedar trees followed by mature hardwoods.

Once on Badger Road hikers will take a short connecting route 0.3 miles east on Badger Road then 0.5 miles north on Little Elkhart Lake Road before the Ice Age Trail resumes again northeast of the intersection of Little Elkhart Lake Road and CTH-A.

From here the segment crosses an open grassland, skirts along the edge of a mature hardwood forest and cuts through another upland brush area. At Keystone Road, hikers should follow the road west 0.2 miles then turn north, heading through a wetland and along a row of pine trees with views of LaBudde Creek to the east before reaching the segment terminus at CTH-FF.

Mobile Skills Crew project site 2008, 2009

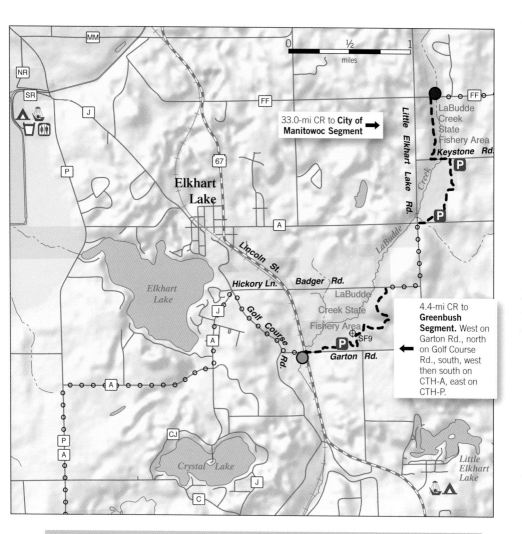

33.0-mi CR to **City of Manitowoc Segment** →

4.4-mi CR to **Greenbush Segment.** West on Garton Rd., north on Golf Course Rd., south, west then south on CTH-A, east on CTH-P.

AREA SERVICES

Plymouth Rock Campground: Camping. From Garton Rd./STH-67 intersection go 1.6 mi south on STH-67, then left on Lando St. for 0.1 mi (920-892-4252, plymouthrock-resort.com).

Elkhart Lake: Restaurant, grocery store, convenience store, lodging, camping, library. From Garton Rd./STH-67 intersection go 1.5 mi north on STH-67. INN Style program lodging at Tauschek's B&B (920-876-5087, tauscheksbedandbreakfastloghome.com). Area info available from the Elkhart Lake Chamber Area Chamber of Commerce (920-876-2922).

Broughton Sheboygan Marsh County Park: Restaurant, camping. From Garton Rd./STH-67 intersection go 1.3 mi north on STH-67. At CTH-J turn left and go 1.8 mi northwest to CTH-SR. Park entrance is on the left (920-876-2535, park vendor website: threeguysandagrill.com/grill/camping.html).

Plymouth: See Greenbush Segment, p. 316. From the STH-67 Trail access go south ~6 mi.

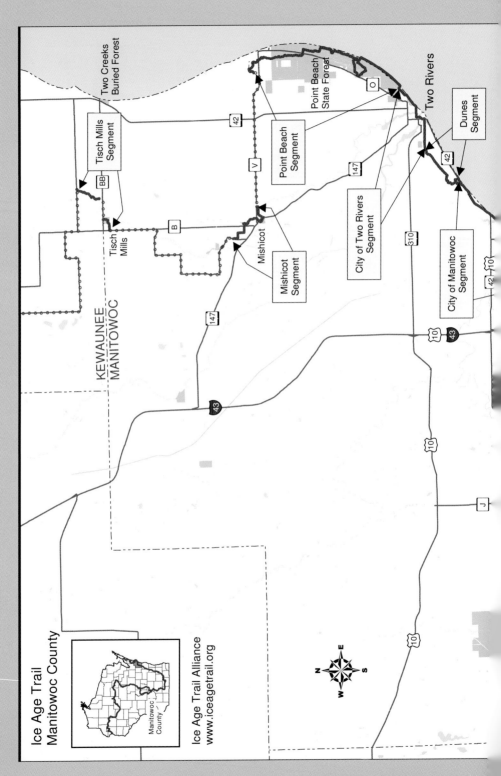

Ice Age Trail
Manitowoc County

Ice Age Trail Alliance
www.iceagetrail.org

Manitowoc County

Two Creeks Buried Forest

Tisch Mills Segment

Point Beach State Forest

Two Rivers

Dunes Segment

Point Beach Segment

City of Two Rivers Segment

Mishicot Segment

City of Manitowoc Segment

Tisch Mills

Mishicot

KEWAUNEE
MANITOWOC

Manitowoc County

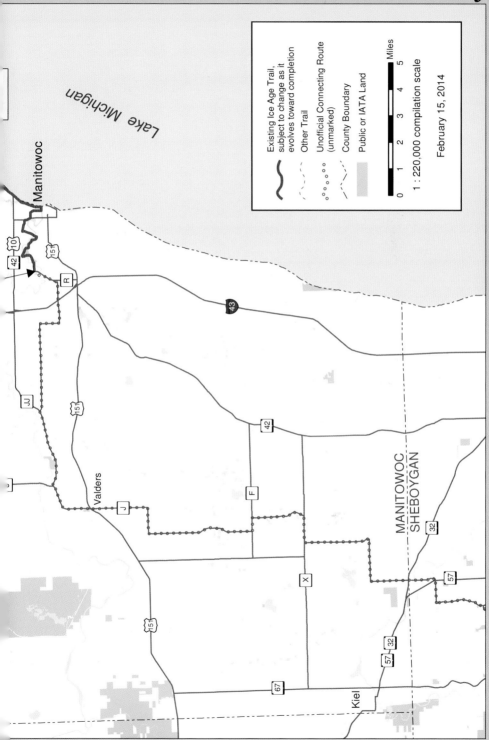

Lake Michigan

Manitowoc

Existing Ice Age Trail,
subject to change as it
evolves toward completion

Other Trail

Unofficial Connecting Route
(unmarked)

County Boundary

Public or IATA Land

Miles

0 1 2 3 4 5

1 : 220,000 compilation scale

February 15, 2014

Valders

MANITOWOC
SHEBOYGAN

Kiel

Manitowoc County

Trail miles: 27.3
Connecting route miles: 42.3

D uring the Wisconsin Glaciation, Manitowoc County was covered by both the Green Bay Lobe and the Lake Michigan Lobe. The Niagara Escarpment divided the two lobes. In the southwestern corner of the county lies the Kettle Moraine, with its hummocky terrain. Drumlins near Valders have a north–south trend giving evidence of the direction the ice sheets flowed. The soils here are reddish brown and rich in silt and clay from the Lake Michigan Lobe advancements. In the northern part of the county, the East Twin River valley occupies a channel that formed along the ice margin. The West Twin River is part of an early drainage outlet of Glacial Lake Oshkosh. Shoreline remnants of ancient Lake Nipissing, a higher-level postglacial ancestor of Lake Michigan that existed 5,000 years ago, can be seen in Manitowoc County. Glacial debris was deposited in the form of eskers, erratics, kettles and drumlins now scattered throughout the county. Exposed dolomite, scraped of soil by glaciers, dots the countryside.

Hikes through the cities of Manitowoc and Two Rivers highlight rich maritime histories and provide an opportunity to walk along the shore of Lake Michigan. The county is considered a premier birding area because of its position on the lakeshore migratory bird route.

CHAPTER INFORMATION

Lakeshore Chapter volunteers actively work on Ice Age Trail promotion, planning and maintenance in addition to sponsoring hikes held at various locations throughout the year.

COUNTY INFORMATION

Manitowoc Area Visitor and Convention Bureau: 800-627-4896,
  manitowoc.info

Tisch Mills Creek on the Tisch Mills Segment.

Manitowoc County

City of Manitowoc Segment (Atlas Map 95f)

SNAPSHOT

7.3 miles: Rapids Rd. (CTH-R) at Broadway St. to STH-42 at Taylor St.

 This urban segment highlights the city of Manitowoc and its rich maritime history and includes a lengthy stretch along the shores of Lake Michigan.

 At Henry Schuette Park, the Manitowoc Chamber of Commerce and the wayside south of Memorial Drive (STH-42) between Woodland Drive and Taylor Street.

 At Henry Schuette Park.

Hikers will not have any interaction with hunting on this segment.

Much of the segment is on sidewalks and multi-use recreation trails.

The Mariners Trail extends north from the segment.

 Portions of this segment may be suitable for those using wheelchairs or similar devices.

TRAIL ACCESS AND PARKING

Rapids Rd. (CTH-R) at Broadway St.: From I-43 take Exit 149 onto USH-151 and head east toward Manitowoc. At S. Rapids Rd. (CTH-R) turn left and go north 1.8 mi to Broadway St. Roadside parking.

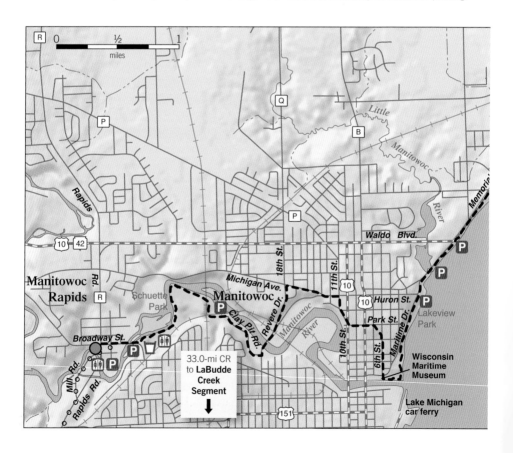

STH-42 at Taylor St.: From I-43 take Exit 152 onto STH-42/USH-10 and head east then north 6.2 mi. No parking at the Taylor St. intersection. Instead, park at the Aurora Medical Center complex access from Taylor St. and Lake View Ave. in the hospital or clinic parking area. An Ice Age Trail sign is on the northeast corner of the clinic parking area.

Additional Parking: (i) Henry Schuette Park. (ii) West of the Lake Gardens, 915 Memorial Dr. (STH-42). (iii) Mariners Trail parking areas along Maritime Dr. and Memorial Dr. (STH-42).

THE HIKE

From the segment's starting point at the intersection of Rapids Road (CTH-R) and Broadway Street, the route heads east on Broadway Street for 0.3 miles. At Clay Pit Road (the access road for Henry Schuette Park), hikers should turn left and head north along the road for 0.2 miles to the park's lower parking area. Here the segment departs Clay Pit Road and meanders through the park for 1.3 miles, mostly along the Manitowoc River, on the park's gravel roads and footpaths. *Note: Most of the facilities for Schuette Park are in the upper parking area, which is slightly off the segment route. The upper parking area is on Broadway Street just southeast of the intersection of Broadway Street and Clay Pit Road.*

The segment connects up again with Clay Pit Road and heads southeast to its intersection with South 21st Street (Revere Drive). From here, hikers should take the following route through the city of Manitowoc: Head north on Revere Drive (which changes to North 18th Street as it crosses the river) past the Eternal Light Veterans Memorial to Michigan Avenue. Turn right and head east on Michigan Avenue (which turns into Huron Street). Turn right and head south on 11th Street (which turns into North Water Street). Turn left and head east on Park Street. At the Park Street/North 7th Street intersection, turn right and walk southeast through Union Park to the North 6th Street/State Street intersection. Head south on North 6th Street for 4 blocks.

The segment departs North 6th Street and heads south across Maritime Drive in the area of the Wisconsin Maritime Museum, which is near the outlet of the Manitowoc River into Lake Michigan. The museum offers interactive educational exhibits that explore the maritime history of Wisconsin and the Great Lakes, and includes a tour of the World War II submarine the USS *Cobia*. Manitowoc residents are proud of the fact that the Manitowoc Shipbuilding Company holds the unique distinction of being the only inland shipyard to build submarines for the U.S. Navy in World War II.

Near the museum south of Maritime Drive, the segment picks up a paved path and heads east along the river a short distance, offering views of the Manitowoc Breakwater Light situated on the north breakwater. The light has a 165-year history of guiding ships in and out of Manitowoc Harbor. During the summer months, hikers may catch a view of the SS *Badger* as it sets out across the lake, ferrying cars and people to Ludington, Michigan.

The segment then turns north along the shore of Lake Michigan to the Manitowoc Marina. This is the official southern terminus of the Mariners Trail (**marinerstrail.net**). The Mariners Trail connects the cities of Manitowoc and Two Rivers on sidewalks and paved blacktop with a guardrail to protect pedestrians from the traffic on Memorial Drive (STH-42). With the waves and shoreline of Lake Michigan to the east, the Mariners Trail boasts the longest continuous scenic view of Lake Michigan in Wisconsin. Along the way, several waysides offer parking areas and trailside benches, and some even have free telescopes to gaze at ships passing by. Restaurants and "mom and pop" motels dot the west side of the highway.

Along the route of the Mariners Trail the segment passes by West of the Lake Gardens, which are open seasonally to the public with free admission. Situated on 6 acres next to Lake Michigan, the area offers a peaceful respite featuring ornate gardens and lovely fountains.

The segment continues northeast on the Mariners Trail past the Manitowoc Chamber of Commerce building. Between the chamber building and the next wayside hikers are welcome to leave the Mariners Trail and explore the Lake Michigan beach. The segment ends a short distance northeast of the wayside at the stoplight at the Taylor Street/Memorial Drive (STH-42) intersection.

AREA SERVICES

Manitowoc: Restaurant, grocery store, convenience store, general shopping, lodging, library, medical care. On Trail. Most services on STH-42, USH-151 and USH-10. INN Style program lodging at the Westport B&B (888-686-0465, thewestpoint.com). For area info, contact the Manitowoc Chamber of Commerce (920-684-5575, chambermanitowoccounty.org).

Rahr Memorial School Forest boardwalk on the Point Beach Segment.

Manitowoc County

Dunes Segment and
City of Two Rivers Segment (Atlas Maps 95f, 96f)

Dunes Segment—2.6 miles: STH-42 at Taylor St. to Columbus St.

City of Two Rivers Segment—2.8 miles: Columbus St. to Park Rd.

 *The **Dunes Segment** highlights Woodland Dunes Nature Center and Preserve, an oasis of marshland, swamps, sandy meadows and wooded ridges.*

 At the Aurora Hospital cafe and Woodland Dunes Nature Center, 1.0 mi north of the Trail.

 All trails in Woodland Dunes Preserve are closed during gun deer hunting season.

By law, dogs are required to be on leash. Dogs are permitted on the Ice Age Trail through Woodland Dunes but are not permitted on other trails through the preserve.

 A short portion follows paved surfaces near the Aurora Medical Center.

 Woodland Dunes Preserve trail network.

 *On the **City of Two Rivers Segment**, hikers can experience the city's claims to fame—home of the original ice cream sundae and maritime history at the Historic Rogers Street Fishing Village.*

 At nearby Zander Park and at Neshotah Park (seasonal).

 At nearby Seagull Marina campground.

 Hikers will not have any interaction with hunting on this segment.

Much of the segment is on sidewalks.

 Portions of this segment may be suitable for those using wheelchairs or similar devices.

TRAIL ACCESS AND PARKING

STH-42 at Taylor St.: From I-43 take Exit 152 onto STH-42/USH-10 and head east then north 6.2 mi. No parking at the Taylor St. intersection. Instead, park at the Aurora Medical Center complex access from Taylor St. and Lake View Ave. in the hospital or clinic parking area. An Ice Age Trail sign is on the northeast corner of the clinic parking area.

Park Rd.: From Two Rivers at the intersection of Washington St. and 22nd St., take 22nd St. east until it ends. (Note that 22nd St. turns right at Neshotah

Park across from the water tower.) At Neshotah Rd. turn left and go north 0.1 mi. At Park Rd. turn right and go north 0.3 mi to the end of the road. Roadside parking.

Additional Parking: (i) Woodland Dunes Preserve parking area at the east end of Goodwin Rd. (ii) Columbus St. roadside parking. (iii) Neshotah Park parking area on Zlatnik Dr.

THE HIKE

From the starting point of the **Dunes Segment** at the intersection of Taylor Street and Memorial Drive (STH-42), hikers should cross cautiously at the stoplight and head north on Taylor Street. The segment heads west at Lake View Avenue to the Aurora Medical Center. Hikers should watch carefully for signage leading the way through the complex. There is an Ice Age Trail sign at the northwest corner of the medical building (not the hospital) parking lot.

North of the medical center the segment crosses inactive railroad tracks and enters 1,200-acre Woodland Dunes Nature Center and Preserve. The preserve represents a "tension zone" between two distinct areas of natural growth; found here are a tremendous amount of both northern and southern species of plants and birds. The resulting habitat makes it one of the premier birding areas in the country. Within the preserve is the Woodland Dunes State Natural Area. It has shoreline remnants of post-glacial Lake Nipissing, seen as ridges and swales. Many of these ridges have white birch, aspen, beech and hemlock trees.

The nature center at Woodland Dunes offers educational nature programs and the preserve has miles of hiking and nature trails. The Ice Age Trail route is concurrent with the preserve's Trillium Trail for much of its length within the property.

The segment exits the preserve and reaches its endpoint at the intersection of 12th Street and Columbus Street.

Continuing on the **City of Two Rives Segment**, hikers should take the following route through the city of Two Rivers: From the Columbus Street/12th Street intersection, head east for 1.0 mile on 12th Street. Along the way at Monroe Street pass by the free Historic Farm Museum that is part of the Two Rivers Historical Society. At Washington Street (STH-42), turn left and head north for 0.1 miles, crossing the West Twin River. At East River Street turn right and go northeast for 0.2 miles. At Jefferson Street turn left and go north 0.2 miles to 17th Street. At this intersection hikers will find the historic Washington House (free admission, donations welcomed), home of the original ice cream sundae. This old hotel has beautiful murals and a ballroom on the second floor; antiques, restored period rooms and interesting collections are also on display.

At 17th Street hikers should turn right and go east across the East Twin River. At the intersection of 17th Street and Zlatnik Drive, hikers should turn left and continue northeast into Neshotah Park.

At the intersection of Zlatnik Drive and 22nd Street hikers should turn right and go east 100 feet, then turn left onto Neshotah Road and go north 0.1 miles, then turn right on Park Road and walk 0.3 miles to the segment's endpoint.

POINTS OF INTEREST

Historic Rogers Street Fishing Village: From the Trail's route on 17th St. on the east side of the East Twin River, go north a few blocks on Jackson St. (920-793-5905, rogersstreet.com).

The Historic Rogers Street Fishing Village is listed on the National Register of Historic Places. The museum village and historic park showcase over 170 years of commercial fishing with the Great Lakes Coast Guard Shipwreck Exhibit and many other historic artifacts, including climbable and symbolic 1886 North Pier Lighthouse.

AREA SERVICES

Two Rivers: Restaurant, grocery store, convenience store, lodging, camping, library, medical care. On Trail. Most services on Washington St. (STH-42). Meals at M&M Lunch (1210 Washington St., 920-794-7616). Camping at Seagull Marina (1400 Lake Street; 920-794-7533). INN Style program lodging at Red Forest B&B (888-250-2272, redforestbb.com). Area info available from the City of Two Rivers (920-793-5592, two-rivers.org).

Manitowoc: See City of Manitowoc Segment, p. 326. From the STH-42 Trail access go south ~4 mi.

I was overwhelmed with the utter kindness of people along my trip.
I had no idea how I would be received walking into towns carrying
my life on my back. After the initial glares and odd glances people
seemed to naturally want to do something to make my life easier.

ADAM HINZ, ICE AGE TRAIL THOUAND-MILER

Point Beach Segment (Atlas Map 96f)

SNAPSHOT

10.0 miles: Park Rd. to Lake Shore Rd.

This segment highlights both the ancient and current shorelines of Lake Michigan.

At Point Beach State Forest (PBSF) entrance station, campground/nature center and outdoor group campground.

From Lake Michigan and Molash Creek.

At PBSF campground and nearby private campground (see Area Services).

At PBSF campground/nature center area.

By law, dogs are required to be on leash and not permitted within PBSF facilities.

Portions overlap with park road, bike and XC trails. Hike off to the side of ski trails when groomed.

PBSF and School Forest trail networks.

TRAIL ACCESS AND PARKING

Park Rd.: From Two Rivers at the intersection of Washington St. and 22nd St., take 22nd St. east until it ends. (Note that 22nd St. turns right at Neshotah Park across from the water tower.) At Neshotah Rd. turn left and go north 0.1 mi. At Park Rd. turn right and go north 0.3 mi to the end of the road. Roadside parking.

Lake Shore Rd.: From Two Rivers take STH-42 and follow it north out of town for ~ 6 mi. At CTH-V turn right and go east 1.8 mi. At Lake Shore Rd. turn left and go north 0.2 mi. Roadside parking on the east side of the road.

Additional Parking: (i) Viceroy Rd. (CTH-VV) parking area on the north side of the road, near its junction with Sandy Bay Road (CTH-O). (ii) Within Point Beach State Forest (PBSF), east and north of the entrance station. (iii) PBSF Red Pine Trail parking area on the west side of Sandy Bay Road (CTH-O) across from the main entrance road.

THE HIKE

From its starting point at the end of Park Road, the segment travels through a wooded area and across sand dunes atop a cord walk installed to help protect the fragile environment to the beach along Lake Michigan. At an Ice Age Trail marker at the top of the beach, the segment turns north and follows the shoreline for 2.0 miles to another Trail marker (**MN14**) at the top of the beach. (Note there are no other Trail markers or signage along the beach walk.) This Trail marker can be difficult to spot; a sure sign hikers have gone too far along the beach is if they reach the mouth of Molash Creek, which always requires a ford.

From the Trail marker (**MN14**), the segment heads west (inland) and crosses sand dunes atop another cord walk, then heads briefly north. The segment connects with PBSF's scenic Molash Creek Trail and continues southwest along Molash Creek, crosses over a marshy area on a short boardwalk, then heads northwest. Along the way, the segment offers nice views of the creek and surrounding wetlands in a generally forested landscape.

As the segment nears Sandy Bay Road (CTH-O), it intersects (**MN13**) with

PBSF's Rawley Point Bike Trail. The segment follows the bike path north across a bridge over Molash Creek, then in about 0.4 miles departs the bike path and heads east in a mixed conifer/hardwoods forest to an intersection (**MN12**) with the Yellow Loop of PBSF's Ridges Trail.

From this point, the segment follows a series of PBSF's trails as it traverses over ancient beach ridges and swales left behind from Lake Nipissing, the predecessor of Lake Michigan. The Trail travels generally north in this unique area through mixed forests, with occasional glimpses of and openings to the dunes at the top of the beach, and cuts across ridges and marshy swales. Hikers should pay attention to Ice Age Trail signage.

From the intersection with the Yellow Loop, the segment continues briefly south then north on the Yellow Loop

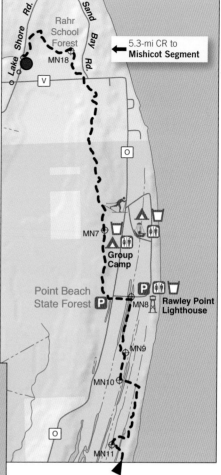

which, then transitions (**MN11**) onto the Blue Loop. Farther on, at a junction (**MN10**) the segment switches onto the Red Loop and follows it north. The segment eventually leaves (**MN9**) the Red Loop to follow a narrow, winding tread on a ridge between marshy swales under a red-pine canopy to PBSF's main entrance road (**MN8**).

For a short side trip, hikers can head east on the entrance road past the park's headquarters parking area to a trail leading to the working Rawley Point Lighthouse. At 113 feet, it is the tallest octagonal skeletal light tower and the only one of its kind on the Great Lakes. At the northern end of PBSF off Rawley Point lies Lake Michigan's most famous shipwreck, the *Rouse Simmons* "Christmas Tree Ship." In 1912, the ship, bound for Chicago with a cargo of evergreens, sank in a storm.

The segment continues west on the entrance road, crosses Sandy Bay Road (CTH-O) and makes its way through the Trail access parking area for PBSF's Red Pine Trail. From here the segment heads back into the woods from the northwest corner of the parking area. The segment intersects with trails of the Red Pine Trail system at several unmarked junctions. At one of these trail junctions (**MN7**), about 0.5 miles from the Red Pine Trail parking area, an unmarked wide, grassy trail leads 0.25 miles east to the PBSF group campsite.

Continuing north, at a signed boundary the segment leaves PBSF and enters the Manitowoc Public School District's Rahr Memorial School Forest, a 300-acre parcel with a network of hiking trails. Hikers should watch carefully for Ice Age Trail signage to navigate through the network of trails as the segment makes its way across CTH-V and meanders to its endpoint on Lake Shore Road. Of particular interest north and west of the CTH-V Trail access is the School Forest's boardwalk, a 0.3 mile curving walkway that crosses a swamp/wetland full of trees, wildflowers, frogs, turtles, salamanders, ducks and other wildlife. A boardwalk donor board (**MN18**) marks the beginning of the boardwalk, which was designed to preserve the delicate swamp/wetland ecosystem.

Mobile Skills Crew project site, 2006

AREA SERVICES

Point Beach State Forest: Camping, seasonal concession stand. On Trail (920-794-7480, dnr.wi.gov/topic/parks/name/pointbeach; reservations: 888-947-2757, reserveamerica.com). Note: For large groups, there is an outdoor group camp and group cabins available for rent.

Scheffel's Hideaway Campground: Camping. On CTH-O just south of its intersection with Viceroy Rd. (920-657-1270, scheffelshideawaycampground.net).

Two Rivers: See Dunes Segment and City of Two Rivers Segment, p. 330. From the Point Beach State Forest entrance road go south ~5 mi. Also see Trail Access and Parking directions, above.

Mishicot: See Mishicot Segment, p. 336. From Point Beach State Forest Trail entrance road go north and west 8.5 mi.

People ask me what made me decide to hike the [entire] Trail. I always like to say that in the later part of August, my wife mentioned something about getting the garage painted... and there I was... GONE!

TOM TEEPLES (AKA "LRRP"),
ICE AGE TRAIL THOUSAND-MILER (STARTED HIS HIKE ON SEPTEMBER 1ST)

Mishicot Segment (Atlas Map 97f)

2.9 miles: CTH-V at Woodlawn Dr. to Princl Rd.

Note: It is anticipated that at a 2014 Mobile Skills Crew project, volunteers will build a new section of Trail between Rock Ledge Road and Hillview Road. The new route will highlight the East Twin River and its floodplain, farmland and towering white cedars. A 400-foot-long boardwalk is in the construction plans. Parking for this new section will be at Hillview Road. The new route is shown as "Future Trail" on the accompanying map; there is a potential for an extension north to Tapawingo Road in years to follow. Check with the Ice Age Trail Alliance (800-227-0046, iceagetrail.org) for more details.

 *This segment travels through the village of Mishicot, highlighting the village Riverwalk and a covered bridge over the East Twin River, and traverses an esker.*

 From the East Twin River.

At Mishicot Village Park.

 Portion of segment crossing private land between CTH-B and Princl Rd. is closed during gun deer season.

 About one-third of the segment is on sidewalks, roads or urban paths.

TRAIL ACCESS AND PARKING

CTH-V at Woodlawn Dr.: From I-43 take Exit 164 and follow STH-147 south 8.0 mi to the village of Mishicot. At CTH-V (Randolph St.) turn left and go east 0.6 mi to Woodlawn Dr. Roadside parking.

Princl Rd.: From I-43 take Exit 164 and follow STH-147 south 6.8 mi toward the village of Mishicot. Just west of the village, take Princl Rd. north 0.4 mi. Look for IAT signage on the east side of the road. Roadside parking.

THE HIKE

The segment begins in Mishicot at the intersection of Woodlawn Drive and CTH-V (Randolph Street). Mishicot is a "Trail Town" rich in amenities for its size and has a number of interesting historical buidings. The village is named after Chief Abraham Meshigaud, born in 1831, who was the leader of the Potawatomi community and friend of village founder Daniel Smith. The segment heads south on Woodlawn Drive for 0.1 miles, then turns and heads west on Washington Street for 0.5 miles. Hikers should cross Main Street (STH-147) and head south across a bridge to the Mishicot Village Park. A path to the right curves down to the Mishicot Riverwalk along the south side of the East Twin River.

At Rockway Street the segment turns right and heads north 0.2 miles, crossing the East Twin River on a picturesque covered bridge. At CTH-V (Randolph Street) the segment heads east briefly before turning north onto Oak Street. The segment splits off Oak Street and heads northwest on Pit Road. Look for Trail signage after about 0.5 miles on the right where the segment leaves the road and climbs and traces along the top of a thirty-foot esker. A Leopold bench offers nice views from the top. The segment then crosses CTH-B and zigzags along the edges of farm fields. Hiking this portion of the segment may be rough in summer due to high weeds. The segment passes by a wooded area and reaches its endpoint on Princl Road.

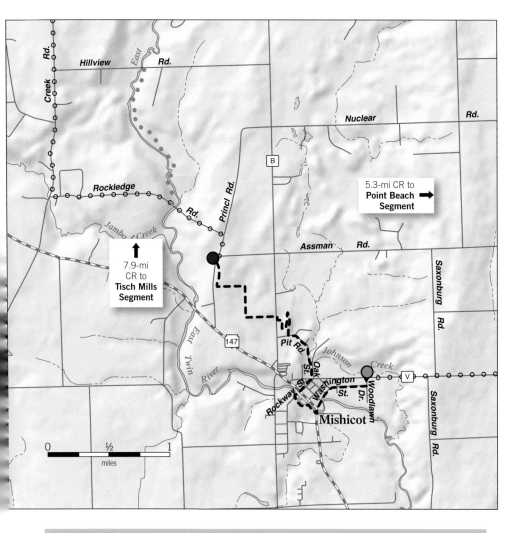

AREA SERVICES

Mishicot: Restaurant, convenience store, lodging, medical care. On Trail. Most services located on STH-147 (Main St.) and CTH-V (Randolph St.). Lodging at Fox Hills Resort (250 Church St., 800-950-7615, foxhillsresort.com). For additional information visit the Village of Mishicot website (mishicot.org).

Two Rivers: See Dunes Segment and City of Two Rivers Segment, p. 330. From the CTH-V at Woodlawn Dr. Trail access go south and east ~8 mi.

Tisch Mills Segment (Atlas Map 98f)

2.6 miles (1.7 IAT, 0.9 CR): CTH-B to Nuclear Rd.

 This charming segment ducks into a white cedar forest and highlights both Tisch Mills Creek and the East Twin River.

From Tisch Mills Creek and the East Twin River.

At a Dispersed Camping Area (**MN17**) east of the Tisch Mills Creek crossing.

 Portion of segment crossing private land between Mill Ln. and Nuclear Rd. is closed during gun deer season.

 A blue-blazed spur trail west of Tisch Mills Creek and a spur trail to the Dispersed Camping Area.

TRAIL ACCESS AND PARKING

CTH-B: From Two Rivers at the intersection of Washington St. (STH-42) and 22nd St. (STH-147), take STH-42 north 12.5 mi. At CTH-BB turn left and go west 5.0 mi through the village of Tisch Mills. At CTH-B turn left and go south 0.25 mi. No parking.

Nuclear Rd.: From Kewaunee at the intersection of STH-42 and STH-29, take STH-42 south 9.3 mi. At Nuclear Rd. turn right and go west 3.5 mi. Trail access is 100 ft west of the East Twin River. No parking.

Additional Parking: (i) CTH-BB western trail access (**MN1**); roadside parking. (ii) CTH-BB eastern trail access; roadside parking at the north end of Mill Ln. in Tisch Mills.

THE HIKE

The portion of the Tisch Mills Segment in Manitowoc County starts on CTH-B at an access point marked with a brown Carsonite post (on an elevation above the road) with the Ice Age Trail logo and blaze. The segment heads east along an agricultural field property line into a densely wooded area where the route makes good use of boardwalks that span wet areas. Wildflowers grow under the wooded canopy in this small oasis from the surrounding farmland.

Just west of its crossing of Tisch Mills Creek the segment reaches a junction with a blue-blazed spur trail that veers left and leads north following an old fence line to CTH-BB. The blue blazes may be sparse but the spur trail is fairly well defined and easy to follow. Farther along on the main segment the route crosses the creek at a spot where there's no bridge but a wooden sign reading "Wading would be safer than walking on rocks." Hikers may want to use the blue-blazed spur during times of high water as it avoids the creek altogether. East of the segment's creek crossing hikers will encounter a spur trail (**MN17**) leading to a Dispersed Camping Area (DCA) for use only by multi-day long distance hikers. The segment continues on past a memorial to the Weber family before emerging onto CTH-BB (**MN1**).

At CTH-BB, hikers should turn right and head east 0.7 miles through the village of Tisch Mills on a connecting route, then head north 0.2 miles on Mill Lane, which parallels the East Twin River.

Prior to hiking the Kewaunee County portion of the segment, hikers are advised to check with the IATA for current conditions. At times of heavy rainfall

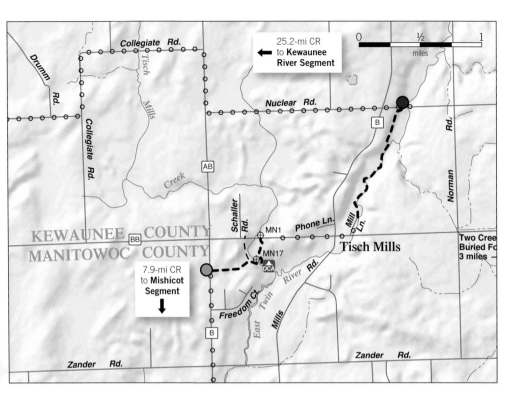

and in spring this portion of the segment tends to be very wet and occasionally flooded.

From Mill Lane the segment heads north along the west bank of the East Twin River, which in this area represents the front of the Two Rivers Moraine. The riverside walk offers hikers an opportunity to observe many types of waterfowl in this vast wetland. The segment departs from the riverbank about a quarter-mile south of the segment's endpoint and follows a fence line across a field until it reaches Nuclear Road.

POINTS OF INTEREST

Two Creeks Buried Forest: From Kewaunee, take STH-42 south 10.5 mi to the junction with CTH-BB at the Kewaunee County line. Park in the lot immediately east of the intersection and south of the restaurant. Walk southeast into the natural area (dnr.wi.gov/topic/Lands/naturalareas/index.asp?SNA=50).

Two Creeks Buried Forest is a unit of the Ice Age National Scientific Reserve. It is world-famous among geologists because it provides a unique, precise record of glacial advances and retreats during the Wisconsin Glaciation. The layers of glacial till and buried forest can be seen on the side of the steep bluff along the lakeshore due to wave erosion. Some features may be harder to see during the summer months because of ground cover. Wood from the forest has been radiocarbon-dated at 11,850 years before present. Removal of any material is strictly prohibited.

AREA SERVICES

Tisch Mills: Restaurant, grocery store, convenience store. On Trail. A convenience store is located at the intersection of CTH-B/CTH-AB/CTH-BB.

Mishicot: See Mishicot Segment, p. 336. From the Tisch Mills Trail access on CTH-B go west and south ~6 mi.

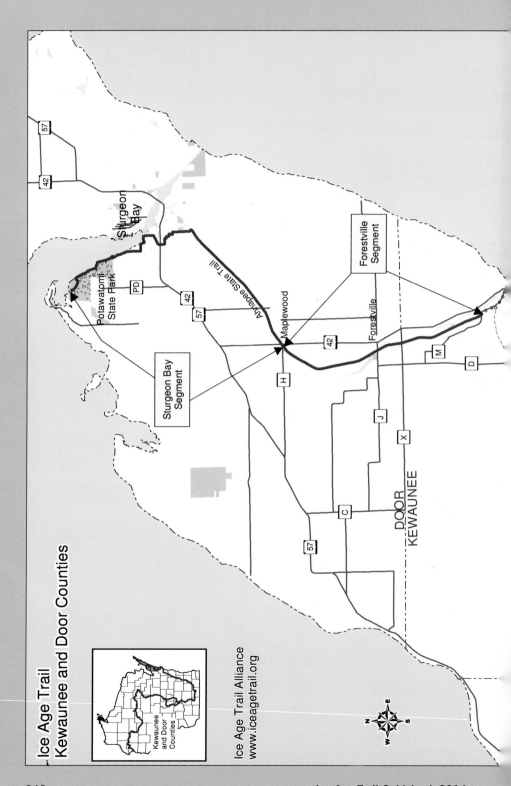

Ice Age Trail
Kewaunee and Door Counties

Ice Age Trail Alliance
www.iceagetrail.org

Kewaunee
and Door
Counties

Sturgeon Bay

Potawatomi
State Park

Sturgeon Bay
Segment

Forestville
Segment

Ahnapee State Trail

Maplewood

Forestville

DOOR
KEWAUNEE

Kewaunee & Door Counties

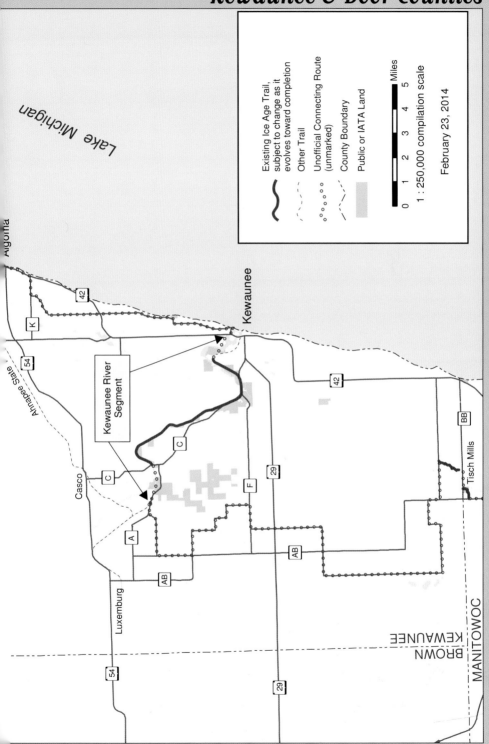

Kewaunee & Door Counties

Trail miles: 31.0
Connecting route miles: 42.5

Door County's shape is due to the 400-million-year-old dolomite rock at its base, known as the Niagara Escarpment. The erosion-resistant rock extends in a broad arc from the east side of Horicon Marsh and Lake Winnebago through Door County, Michigan and Ontario, and forms the crest of Niagara Falls. Blocks of Niagara dolomite, carried by glacial ice, are scattered through the counties to the south.

Door County is the location of the most recent Ice Age event along the Ice Age Trail. As the front of the Green Bay Lobe slowly melted northward, Glacial Lake Oshkosh formed in a large area of today's Fox River Valley. The Niagara Escarpment bound its waters on the east. Once the Green Bay Lobe melted to what is today Potawatomi State Park, Glacial Lake Oshkosh catastrophically drained into Lake Michigan through what is now Sturgeon Bay. Remnants of larger phases of Lake Michigan can be seen in the county and particularly in Potawatomi State Park. These ancient shorelines of Lake Algonquin, from 11,000 years ago, and Lake Nipissing, from 5,000 years ago, rise as much as 20 to 60 feet above modern-day Lake Michigan.

The Ice Age Trail shares the route of the multi-use Ahnapee State Trail in Kewaunee and Door counties. The route passes through drumlins, farmlands, wetlands and forests and follows parts of the Kewaunee River Valley and Ahnapee River Valley. After making its way through Sturgeon Bay the Ice Age Trail reaches its eastern terminus at the observation tower in Potawatomi State Park.

These counties have significant maritime history as told in the towns the Trail visits along the shores of Lake Michigan.

CHAPTER INFORMATION

Lakeshore Chapter volunteers actively work on Ice Age Trail promotion, planning and maintenance in addition to sponsoring hikes held at various locations throughout the year.

COUNTY INFORMATION

Door County Chamber of Commerce: 920-743-4456 or 800-527-3529, doorcounty.com

Kewaunee County Promotions & Recreation Department: 920-338-0444, kewauneeco.org

D. BLONDHEIM

Along the Forestville Segment.

Kewaunee & Door Counties 343

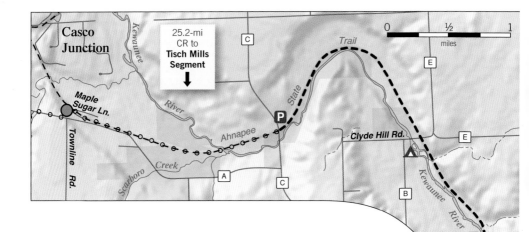

Tisch Mills Segment

This segment is located in both Kewaunee and Manitowoc counties and is described in the Manitowoc County section of this book (see p. 338).

Kewaunee River Segment (Atlas Maps 100f, 101f)

SNAPSHOT

11.2 miles (8.2 IAT, 3.0 CR): Ahnapee State Trail at Maple Sugar Lane to Hathaway Dr. Access Road

1 **1** *This segment follows the Kewaunee River section of the Ahnapee State Trail, a crushed limestone rail-trail.*

 At Bruemmer County Park.

 From the Kewaunee River.

 At nearby private campgrounds (see Area Services).

At Bruemmer County Park and the nearby C.D. Besadny Anadromous Fish Facility.

 By law, dogs must be on leash on the Ahnapee State Trail.

 The Ahnapee State Trail (AST) is open to horseback riding, snowmobiling and biking.

 The AST extends west from the segment.

 Portions of this segment may be suitable for those using wheelchairs or similar devices.

TRAIL ACCESS AND PARKING

Ahnapee State Trail at Maple Sugar Lane: From Kewaunee at the intersection of STH-42 and STH-29 (Ellis St.), take STH-29 (Ellis St.) west 1.0 mi. At the CTH-C/STH-29 fork, veer right onto CTH-C (Ellis St.) and continue northwest 1.4 mi. At CTH-C/CTH-F intersection turn right and go northwest 4.8 mi. At CTH-A turn left and go west 1.8 mi. At Maple Sugar Ln. turn right. Roadside parking. Do not block road.

Hathaway Dr. Access Road: From Kewaunee at the intersection of STH-42 and STH-29, take STH-42 north 0.6 mi. At Hathaway Dr. turn left and go west then north 0.2 mi to the shared Ice Age Trail/Ahnapee State Trail access. Roadside parking.

Additional Parking: (i) Harold Rickelberg Park in Casco Junction at Sunset Rd. and CTH-A. By foot, it is located 1.0 mi northwest of Maple Sugar Ln./CTH-A junction on the rail-trail. (ii) CTH-C western

Trail access parking area on the northeast side of CTH-C. (iii) Bruemmer County Park parking area. (iv) CTH-C eastern Trail access parking area on the north side of CTH-C. (v) Dodge St. Park: From central Kewaunee at the intersection of STH-42 and STH-29, take STH-29 (Ellis St.) west one block. At Dodge St. turn right and go north 3 blocks to the Ahnapee State Trail parking area and skateboard park. Walk the trail west 1.2 mi. (vi) Parking area for the Kewaunee Nature Walk on the corner of Hathaway Dr. and STH-42.

THE HIKE

The Ahnapee State Trail is a multi-use rail-trail that was converted for recreational use in 1975. The trail was named for the Ahnapee & Western Railroad, which served major industries in Algoma, Sturgeon Bay and Casco Junction dating back to its origin in 1892. It connected to Green Bay and Kewaunee at Casco Junction via the Green Bay and Western railway. Steam and diesel powered locomotives hauled lumber, shipbuilding materials, dairy products, petroleum products and other commodities. During World War II, the A&W transported German prisoners of war to Door County to work the fruit harvest season. In the early 1970s, costs and alternative routes of shipping forced the A&W Railroad to abandon the line. The portion of the Ahnapee State Trail along the Kewaunee River is fairly new to the state's rail-trail network and has been described as one of the most scenic sections of rail-trail in Wisconsin.

The segment starts near the point where the rail-trail passes by (unmarked) Maple Sugar Lane near its intersection with CTH-A. Hikers should look for a trail mileage sign with the text "Casco—2 miles, Kewaunee—10 miles, Luxemburg—4 miles."

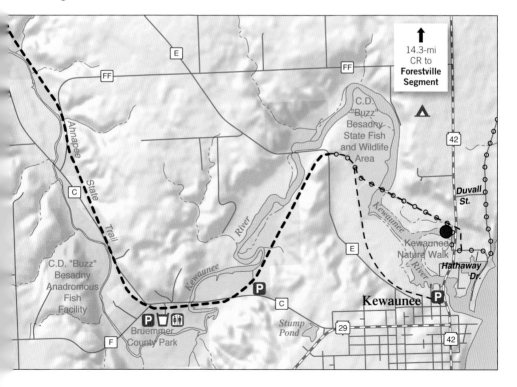

From Maple Sugar Lane, the segment passes through mostly wooded, rolling terrain. Heading east the segment, for its entire length, follows the Kewaunee River, although the river is not always visible from the Trail. The Trail crosses the Kewaunee River and Scarboro Creek on three refurbished wooden trestle bridges and passes by and through the various tracts of the C.D. "Buzz" Besadny State Fish and Wildlife Area.

On the outskirts of Kewaunee the segment passes by Bruemmer County Park. Hikers looking for an off-trail adventure can explore the C.D. "Buzz" Besadny Anadromous Fish Facility (details below in the Points of Interest section). Back on the segment route, the Trail follows a low area along the river through wetland and wooded areas. Just north of Kewaunee at Mile 0.9 of the rail-trail the segment reaches a junction where a spur angles south and leads 1.2 miles into Kewaunee, where parking is available at the Dodge Street trailhead. The Ice Age Trail heads east from this junction and crosses the Kewaunee River a final time before reaching the segment endpoint at the Hathaway Drive access road.

POINTS OF INTEREST

C.D. "Buzz" Besadny Anadromous Fish Facility: From the Ice Age Trail at the intersection with CTH-F head west on CTH-F for 0.5 mi then north a short distance on Ransom Moore Ln. (920-388-1025, dnr. wi.gov/topic/fishing/hatcheries/cdbesadny.html).

The Fish Facility is a spawning trout and salmon egg collection and harvesting facility. Following informational and educational displays, visitors can take a self-guided tour and obtain basic information on trout and salmon life history, facility operations and other related subjects. During spawning, visitors can watch trout and salmon swim up the Kewaunee River. Underwater windows offer views of the fish jumping and splashing their way up a fish ladder to large holding ponds. The Fish Facility grounds are open spring, summer and fall during daylight hours. The Facility building is open March 15 to December 15, M–F; hours vary. Call ahead to determine what fish are at the facility; fish are not always present.

AREA SERVICES

Ahnapee State Trail: On Trail (920-388-0444 or 920-746-9959, dnr.wi.gov/topic/parks/name/ahnapee/).

Kewaunee: Camping, restaurant, grocery store, convenience store, lodging, library, medical care. From the Hathaway Dr. Trail access take Hathaway Dr. and STH-42 south 0.8 mi. Camping at Cedar Valley Campground just south of Clyde Hill Rd. (N5098 Cedar Valley Road; 920-388-4983, cedarvalleycampground.com) and Kewaunee Village RV Park and Campground just west of STH-42 (333 Terraqua Dr.; 920-388-4851, kewauneevillage.com).

How sad it is that people live in this beautiful state their entire life and they never take the opportunity to experience Wisconsin. I can think of no better way to see the beauty and the diversity of this state than to hike the Trail.

DAWN MATOTT, ICE AGE TRAIL THOUSAND-MILER

Tunnel under Clyde Hill Road, Kewaunee River Segment.

Kewaunee & Door Counties

Forestville Segment (Atlas Maps 103f, 104f)

SNAPSHOT

9.1 miles: CTH-M to CTH-H

 This segment follows the multi-use Ahnapee State Trail through an area that is part of the Great Wisconsin Birding and Nature Trail.

From the Ahnapee River and Forestville Flowage/Mill Pond.

 At nearby Timber Trails and Ahnapee River Trails campgrounds (see Area Services).

 At Blahnik Heritage Park, Forestville Dam County Park and town hall in Maplewood.

 At Forestville Dam County Park.

 On Ahnapee State Trail just north of CTH-M Trail access, at Blahnik County Park and Forestville Dam County Park.

 By law, dogs must be on leash on the Ahnapee State Trail.

 The Ahnapee State Trail is open to horseback riding, snowmobiling and biking.

 Trail network at Blahnik Heritage Park.

 Portions of this segment may be suitable for those using wheelchairs or similar devices.

TRAIL ACCESS AND PARKING

CTH-M: From Algoma take STH-42 north. At CTH-S turn left and go west 0.7 mi. At CTH-M turn right and go north 0.7 mi to the parking area on the north side of the road.

CTH-H: From Sturgeon Bay, take STH-42 south 9.0 mi to CTH-H in Maplewood. Roadside parking.

Additional Parking: (i) Blahnik Heritage Park parking area on Washington Rd. (ii) Forestville Dam County Park parking area on Main St. (CTH-J).

THE HIKE

The Ahnapee State Trail, a wide, hardpacked limestone multi-use trail, got its start in the 1890s as the Ahnapee and Western Railroad, transporting lumber and dairy products. Due to financial problems, most of the rail line was abandoned in the early 1970s. A number of years later it was con-

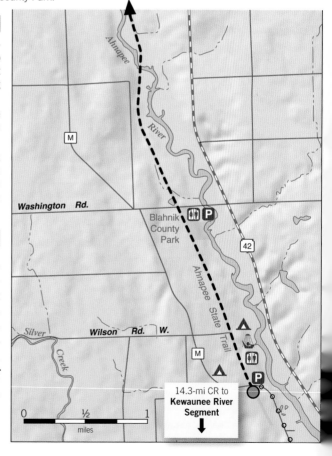

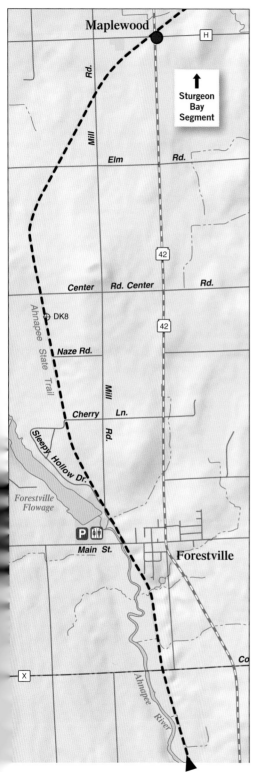

verted to a recreational trail. It is a well used trail with good signage and a number of benches placed along the way.

From its starting point at CTH-M the segment heads north on the west side of the Ahnapee River. After 0.5 miles the segment skirts the end of Wilson Road, site of the Ahnapee River Trails Campground. Farther north, at the intersection with Washington Road, the segment passes by Blahnik Heritage Park.

West of Forestville the segment passes by Forestville Dam County Park. Continuing north, the segment passes through an area (**DK8**) burned by the Great Peshtigo Fire, the most devastating forest fire in American history. On October 8, 1871, the fire destroyed more than 1.25 million acres and killed more than a thousand people. Today, mature hardwood stands erase all signs of the conflagration in the Ahnapee River Valley.

The segment reaches its endpoint in the village of Maplewood at STH-42 and CTH-H.

AREA SERVICES

Algoma: Restaurant, grocery store, convenience store, lodging, camping, library, medical care. From the CTH-M Trail access, take CTH-M south 0.7 mi. Continue south and east on CTH-S for 0.7 mi. Camping at Timber Trail Campground at the Ahnapee State Trail/CTH-M crossing north of Algoma (920-487-3707, timbertrailcamping.com) and Ahnapee River Trails Campground at the Ahnapee State Trail at Wilson Rd. (920-487-5777, ahnapee.com). Area info available from the Algoma Area Chamber of Commerce (920-487-2041, algomachamber.org).

Forestville: Restaurant, convenience store, library. From the CTH-J (Main St.) Trail access take CTH-J east 0.3 mi. The library has limited hours.

Sturgeon Bay: See Sturgeon Bay Segment, p. 350. From CTH-H/STH-42 go north ~9 mi. Also see Trail Access and Parking directions, above.

Ahnapee State Trail: See Kewaunee River Segment, p. 344.

Sturgeon Bay Segment (Atlas Maps 104f, 105f)

13.7 miles: CTH-H to Ice Age Trail Eastern Terminus in Potawatomi State Park

This segment offers hikers three widely varying experiences representative of the overall Ice Age Trail experience and is therefore a good place to wrap up or start a thousand-mile journey on the Trail. The segment starts with a rail-trail hike, transitions into an urban hike through a city with a rich cultural history, then finishes with a quiet, forested trek through a state park.

At Cherry Blossom Park and various locations in Potawatomi State Park (PSP).

From Sturgeon Bay.

At PSP and nearby private campground (see Area Services).

At the S. Neenah Ave. Trail access (**DK6**), Cherry Blossom Park, Otumba Park and PSP.

By law, dogs are required to be on leash on the Ahnapee State Trail and in PSP. Dogs are not permitted in PSP facilities or on groomed ski trails.

Portions overlap with the multi-use Ahnapee State Trail. Other portions overlap with sidewalks and roads and with PSP trails open to biking and skiing. Hike off to the side of ski trails when groomed.

PSP trail network.

Portions of this segment may be suitable for those using wheelchairs or similar devices.

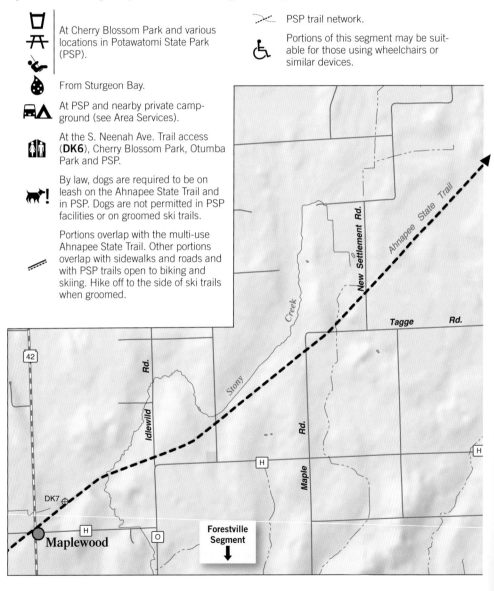

CTH-H: From Sturgeon Bay, take STH-42 south 9.0 mi to CTH-H in Maplewood. Roadside parking.

Eastern Terminus in Potawatomi State Park: From Sturgeon Bay take STH-57/42 southwest to CTH-PD (Park Dr.). Turn right and go north 2.4 mi to Potawatomi State Park. Follow the park's entrance drive 3.5 mi to the Ice Age Trail eastern terminus at the observation tower. Park at the Ice Age Trail long-term parking area at the old ski hill (**DK2**), located 3.3 mi from the main entrance. An un-blazed spur trail leads from the parking area to the Ice Age Trail at the observation tower.

Additional Parking: (i) S. Neenah Ave. Ahnapee/Ice Age Trail access parking area (**DK6**). (ii) Cherry Blossom Park. (iii) Bayview Park. (iv) Otumba Park. (v) Potawatomi State Park parking areas along Shoreline Road.

THE HIKE

From its starting point on CTH-H in Maplewood, the segment heads northeast on its way to Sturgeon Bay, sharing the route with the Ahnapee State Trail, a wide, hardpacked limestone multi-use recreational trail that was formerly the rail bed of the Ahnapee and Western Railroad. The route quickly traverses the southern extent of the Maplewood Swamp (**DK7**), a unique peat swamp where waterlogged soil prevents dead vegetation from fully decomposing, creating a spongy layer of peat. As it continues northeast, the segment passes by Stoney Creek Swamp and crosses the creek itself. Dark swamp water creeps within a foot of the raised trail bed as it cuts through these swamps. From here, the segment bends gently through forests, orchards and farmland, sometimes under the cover of overhanging trees and sometimes in openings.

Shortly after crossing Neenah Avenue, the segment arrives at a trailhead for the Ahnapee State Trail (**DK6**). From the trailhead area the segment heads north along Neenah Avenue for 0.7 miles. The segment departs Neenah Avenue and heads west and north on a path that skirts and weaves through an industrialized area between Neenah Avenue and Lansing Road, eventually arriving at Yew Street. The route follows Yew Street west briefly, then Lansing Road north briefly, before heading west off-road and following the southern perimeter of Cherry Blossom Park, a grassy neighborhood park. The Trail continues beyond the park and through the adjoining neighborhood to Hudson Road.

At Hudson Road the segment turns north and follows the road under STH-42/57 to Green Bay Road, where it then heads east through a commercial area. On the southwest corner of the Green Bay Road/Lansing Road intersection the segment arrives at an Ahnapee State Trail/Ice Age Trail access area (**DK5**) marked with an Ice Age Trail sign and a brown-and-white Ahnapee Trail sign. This is where the City Trail Extension of the Ahnapee State Trail ends. From here, hikers may wish to take an interesting side trip to the Cardy Paleo-Indian Camp archaeology site (see Points of Interest, below).

From the Green Bay Road/Lansing Road intersection hikers should cross to the north side of Green Bay Road and continue east. The road curves north and becomes Madison Avenue. Downhill, over the roofs of stores and restaurants, hikers can see shipyards, dry docks, towering cranes and the city's old steel bridge. At the intersection of Madison Avenue and Larch Street the segment angles northwest through Bayview Park, which highlights the Sturgeon Bay Canal. Since 1882, Great Lakes freighters from Green Bay have bypassed going around the tip of the Door County peninsula, known as "Death's Door," and have instead traveled through the canal to Lake Michigan. Not only is it a safer passage, it reduces the travel distance from Green Bay to Milwaukee and Chicago by 150 miles.

The segment exits the park and follows Juniper Street west, Joliet Avenue north and Hickory Street west to Duluth Avenue. It follows Duluth Avenue north to the end of the road (**DK4**), where there is a large Ice Age Trail sign as the Trail continues north into Potawatomi State Park. A nearby informational sign shows a map of the park with marked trails.

Potawatomi State Park is named after the Native Americans who inhabited Green Bay's shores and islands. Potawatomi means "Keepers of the Fire," a reference to the Council of Three Fires, a Potawatomi alliance with the Ojibwe and Ottawa. Bedrock outcrops of the Niagara Escarpment can be found throughout the area among cedar, birch, maple and pine forests. In the southern portion of the park, the segment route overlaps with the park's Hemlock Loop; in the northern portion, the segment shares the park's Tower Loop. A highlight of the segment's route through the park is a set of rock steps in Niagara dolomite (**DK3**) constructed by Ice Age Trail Alliance volunteers in 2002.

From the end of Duluth Avenue, the segment heads east briefly toward Sturgeon Bay before resuming a northward course along the shoreline. Near Picnic Area 4, the segment joins up with the Hemlock Loop and continues north between Shoreline Road and Sturgeon Bay. The segment crosses Shoreline Road and angles west toward the park campground. The Trail then departs from the Hemlock Loop and turns north, crossing Shoreline Road again and continuing along between the road and the bay, passing near the campground's South Camp Area and then the North Camp Area. Hikers can enjoy several bay vistas along the way. The segment joins up with the Tower Loop near the North Camp Area. A little farther on, hikers should skip a Tower Loop cutoff trail and continue north.

The segment crosses Shoreline Road a final time and heads inland climbing steeply into a forested area, eventually emerging onto Norway Road and the park's observation tower. From the tower, an unblazed spur trail leads to the Ice Age Trail long-term parking area (**DK2**) at the old ski hill. Situated atop a 150-foot dolomite bluff, the park's 75-foot tower, built in 1932, offers views of Sawyer Harbor, Sturgeon Bay, Green Bay and the surrounding area. At the base of the tower the Ice Age Trail eastern terminus is marked with an official terminus marker (similar to that found at the western terminus) affixed to a large rock.

Mobile Skills Crew project site, 2002

POINTS OF INTEREST

Cardy Paleo-Indian Camp Archaeological Site: From the Ice Age Trail at the intersection of Green Bay Rd. and Lansing Rd., head north on Lansing Rd. then turn left at Spruce St. and walk west 0.2 mi to 322 W. Spruce St.

The Cardy Paleo-Indian Camp archaeological site, listed on the National Register of Historic Places, is considered one of the most important archaeological finds in Wisconsin. The Cardy Site, marked by a kiosk and plaque, preserves the remains of a campsite used by Native Americans at the end of the Ice Age. An extensive dig in 2003 unearthed spear points, tools, a fire pit and other artifacts. Archeologists believe that Native Americans lived and worked in this area 11,000 years ago near the shore of Glacial Lake Algonquin and within walking distance of the receding continental ice sheet. This camp is unusual for its far north location. Glacial Lake Algonquin occupied the Lake Michigan and Lake Huron basins at the end of the Ice Age and would have been about 25 feet higher than Green Bay is today.

AREA SERVICES

Maplewood: Restaurant. From the CTH-H Trail access go west 0.2 mi on CTH-H.

Sturgeon Bay: Restaurant, grocery store, convenience store, general shopping, lodging, camping, library, medical care. On Trail. Most services located on Green Bay Rd. (STH-42/57) and downtown at Michigan St. and 3rd Ave. INN Style program lodging at the White Lace Inn (877-948-5223, WhiteLace-Inn.com) and the Black Walnut Guest House (877-255-9568, blackwalnut-gh.com). Camping at Tranquil Timbers Camping Resort located just south of Potawatomi State Park (920-743-7115, tranquiltimbers.com). Area info available from the Sturgeon Bay Visitor Center (920-743-6246, sturgeonbay.net).

Potawatomi State Park: Camping. On Trail (920-746-2890, dnr.wi.gov/topic/parks/name/Potawatomi; reservations: 888-947-2757, reserveamerica. com). There are several other state parks in Door County.

Ahnapee State Trail: See Kewaunee River Segment, p. 344.

DAVE CALIEBE

View of Sturgeon Bay from the observation tower at the Ice Age Trail's eastern terminus.

Appendix

Mecan River Segment.

Dells of the Eau Claire Segment, Marathon County.

Glossary

Barrens Areas where pine and stunted oaks grow. Barrens made up 12% of the state's original landscape. Found in prairie-like areas with sandy, infertile soil. Animals that inhabit barrens include whitetail deer, grouse, prairie chicken, redheaded woodpecker and timber wolf.

Bog A wetland of spongy ground or peat, often with tamaracks and sphagnum moss.

Continental Glaciation The formation, movement, recession and related effects of colossal, nearly continent-sized ice sheets. Though common during the Pleistocene (or most recent) Ice Age, the only ice sheets that today approach the enormity of those existing during the Ice Age are in Antarctica and Greenland. Continental glaciation sculpted a quarter of the Earth's landmass and dramatically changed the Earth's climate, oceans, plants and animals.

Dells/Dalles A gorge cut by torrents of meltwater released by a melting glacier or draining of glacial lakes. Some dramatic examples: the Dells of the Eau Claire, the Wisconsin Dells and the Dalles of St. Croix.

Dispersed Camping Area (DCA) A minimally developed camping area for long-distance hikers. To help increase camping opportunities for Ice Age Trail long-distance hikers, the Ice Age Trail Alliance and its partners are working to establish DCAs, especially in areas (i.e., the southern two-thirds of the Trail) where convenient camping options are otherwise limited for long-distance hikers. DCAs are not "campgrounds" or even "campsites" in the traditional sense; instead, they are typically nothing more than a cleared area where hikers may legally camp for a night. Use of DCAs is restricted to those on multi-night long-distance hikes.

Dolomite A rock similar to limestone consisting largely of calcium magnesium carbonate.

Driftless Area The southwestern quarter of Wisconsin is unglaciated or shows no signs of past glacial activity. It is a landscape deeply cut by ancient streams into narrow, angular valleys and several-hundred-million-years-old ridges. The best place along the Trail to see the Driftless Area is Dane County between Mineral Point Rd. and Table Bluff Rd., west of the end moraine.

Drumlin An elongated, teardrop-shaped hill. These streamlined hills were sculpted in the direction of the glacial ice movement. They often occur in groups known as *swarms*. Because drumlins generally form miles behind, or up-ice, from an end moraine, they are rare along the Trail. The Farmington Drumlins, in Waupaca County, is the largest swarm of drumlins along the existing segments of the Trail. A small group of drumlins is in Door County between Maplewood and Sturgeon Bay. STH-60, between Columbus and Hartford, and I-94, between Madison and Sussex, cross one of the largest drumlin swarms in the world.

End Moraine A type of moraine formed at the outer edge of a glacier or glacial lobe where it paused or stopped. Prominent end moraines along the Trail can be witnessed at Prairie Moraine County Park in Dane County, Devil's Lake State Park in

Sauk County and the range of hills north and east of Antigo in Langlade County. End moraines define the general route of the Trail.

Ephemeral Ponds (*also* **Vernal Ponds**) Small isolated wetland depressions or pools of water that dry occasionally or are temporary. They can be deep or shallow with vegetation around them and occur in habitats such as sandhill, natural pinelands, dry prairies and other related communities. Lacking in fish, they are often home to insect species such as mosquitoes and mayflies and natal amphibians such as frogs and toads.

Erratics Boulders carried long distances by the glaciers and deposited when the glacier melted. They tend to be smooth and rounded. Erratics can be found along the entire Trail, except where it traverses parts of the Driftless Area. Large, famous erratics along the Trail are in Walworth, Waupaca and Langlade counties.

Esker A sinuous rounded ridge of sand and gravel deposited by the streams that flowed through tunnels at the base of the glacier. The Parnell Esker in the Kettle Moraine State Forest's Northern Unit is the most notable example along the Trail. Other excellent eskers are in Polk and Taylor counties.

Extinct Glacial Lake A glacial lake that drained, often catastrophically, when a glacier or glacial lobe melted back. Extinct Glacial Lake Wisconsin's lakebed remains visible in Adams and Juneau counties. Much of the Fox Valley was for a time under Glacial Lake Oshkosh.

Fen An area of low, flat marshy land where decomposing plants accumulate, forming peat.

Ford A shallow place in a river or stream where one can cross by wading.

Hummocky Describing hilly, knob-and-kettle topography.

Ice Age National Scientific Reserve Unit Areas administered by the Wisconsin Department of Natural Resources to protect, preserve, and interpret the outstanding examples of glaciation in Wisconsin. There are nine units (Interstate State Park, Chippewa Moraine, Mill Bluff, Devil's Lake, Cross Plains, Horicon Marsh, Campbellsport Drumlins, Kettle Moraine, and Two Creeks Buried Forest) and all but three (Mill Bluff, Horicon Marsh, Campbellsport Drumlins) are on or near established Ice Age Trail segments.

Ice Sheet A large, continental glacier that is not confined by underlying topography. The northeastern quarter of North America was covered over a dozen times by the Laurentide Ice Sheet during the Ice Age, between 10,000 and 2.5 million years ago. Today, ice sheets are found only in polar regions such as Greenland and Antarctica.

Ice-Walled Lake Plains Mesa-like hills that were once lakes on a melting glacier. Streams flowing on the glacier deposited loads of sediment into these lakes. When the surrounding glacier had completely melted, the lake bottoms became the hilltops. Ice-walled lake plains are showcased at the Chippewa Moraine National Scientific Reserve in Chippewa County.

Kame A conical hill composed primarily of water-rounded sand and cobbles that were deposited by streams that flowed downward through shafts in the glacial ice. The Kettle Moraine contains the largest and most important kame fields in the world, particularly between Dundee and the Parnell Tower, near Slinger and at Holy Hill. Kames are intriguing because of their shape and the way they were formed, not because of their size.

Karner Blue Butterfly (*Lycaeides melissa samuelis*) On the federal endangered species list. Wisconsin has the largest remaining population. It is slightly larger than a postage stamp with a wingspan of approximately 1 inch. It is seen in the beginning of June and again in August. This butterfly feeds exclusively on wild lupine, a bright blue flower, found in dry, sandy soil, partly shaded meadows and oak savannas in central and northwestern Wisconsin.

Kettle A surface depression formed by large, detached blocks of melting ice that were buried with sand and gravel. As the ice melted, the other material collapsed, leaving a crater-like depression. Some kettles are more than 100 feet deep. Kettles can be found in many places along the Trail.

Kettle Moraine Also called the Interlobate Moraine, the Kettle Moraine is a series of ridges, 120 miles long and only a few miles wide, in eastern Wisconsin. The combined action and deposits of the Green Bay and Lake Michigan lobes of the continental ice sheet formed the Kettle Moraine. The Kettle Moraine is the birthplace of the Ice Age Trail and the subject of the first published study of interlobate glaciation in 1878.

Leopold Bench A 33- or 48-inch-long bench seen along the Trail originally designed by conservationist Aldo Leopold. He built and used the bench when he lived in central Wisconsin while writing *A Sand County Almanac*. Design plans can be found by entering "Leopold Bench" into an internet search engine.

Lobe A tongue-like extension of an ice sheet. Six major lobes during the late Wisconsin Glaciation covered portions of Wisconsin. These lobes were the Superior, Chippewa, Wisconsin Valley, Langlade, Green Bay and Lake Michigan lobes. The Des Moines Lobe extended slightly into western Polk County.

Mammoth An extinct species of elephant with hairy skin and long tusks curving upward that roamed North America, Europe and Asia. It is the Ice Age Trail mascot.

Moraine A ridge formed by unsorted gravel, sand and boulders carried by the glacier and deposited at the outer edge, or front, of the glacier. Some are only 10 feet high, while others rise 250 to 300 feet. Moraines can be found in many places along the Trail.

Outwash Plain A sandy plain formed when glacial meltwater streams in front of glaciers spread over a very wide, flat area. The water swept the sand into both glaciated and unglaciated areas. Between Hancock and Plover, I-39 crosses part of a vast outwash plain. Another example is the Antigo Flats of Langlade County, visible along the Trail from the Harrison Hills of Lincoln County.

Pitted Outwash An area of outwash that is dimpled with kettles. These areas were formed by meltwater-carried blocks of ice that were deposited with sand and gravel and later melted in place, leaving kettles.

Portage A route to carry a boat overland to get from one body of water to another or to avoid a water obstacle. Two well-known historic portage routes along the Trail are in the city of Portage on the land between the Fox and Wisconsin Rivers and at Grandfather Falls in Lincoln County.

Potholes A smooth bowl carved into bedrock by the grinding action of stones whirling around in a river eddy. Many potholes were formed by torrents of glacial meltwater during the Ice Age. The best place to see these along the Trail is near the western terminus in Interstate State Park. These potholes were formed when the St. Croix River was much deeper than today. Small potholes at Devil's Lake State Park formed before the Ice Age.

Riparian Zone The area of thick vegetation that runs along the bank of a river. It is characterized by shrubs, vines, trees and grasses. Important to a watershed, they help maintain streams and rivers in their natural state. During heavy rains they help prevent flooding by slowing the flow of water both into the river and along the river banks. In addition, by acting as a buffer between the land and the water, chemicals such as fertilizers and pesticides which are applied to the land, are absorb through many of the river area's plant roots.

Sedge Meadow A wetland that is dry in late summer and composed mostly of sedges. Sedges are plants that look like grasses but feel rough when stroked.

State Ice Age Trail Area (SIATA) A property owned by the Wisconsin Department of Natural Resources (DNR) and managed for the Ice Age Trail.

Swale A hollow or depression at the beginning of a valley that often has wet soils.

Terminal Moraine A type of end moraine where a glacier or glacial lobe reached its maximum extent and melted back.

Thru-Hike To hike an entire long-distance trail, such as the Ice Age Trail, end to end in one season or continuous journey.

Tunnel Channel Created by a fast moving river under a glacier that carves a valley. After the glacier has melted, the valley often contains a series of lakes. Prominent tunnel channels can be seen along the Trail in the New Hope Segment in Portage County and the Straight River Segment in Polk County.

Wisconsin Glaciation A period of the Earth's history at the end of the Pleistocene Ice Age, between 10,000 and 75,000 years ago. All glacial lobes and landforms described in the Guide occurred or were created during the last part of the Wisconsin Glaciation, unless otherwise noted.

Bibliography

Bolles, Edmund Blair. *The Ice Finders: How a Poet, a Professor and a Politician Discovered the Ice Age*. Washington D.C.: Counterpoint. 1999.

DeLorme. *Wisconsin Atlas and Gazetteer*. Yarmouth, ME: DeLorme. 2011.

Dott, Robert H., Jr. and John W. Attig. *Roadside Geology of Wisconsin*. Missoula, MT: Mountain Press Publishing Company. 2004.

Hansen, Eric. *Hiking Wisconsin*. Guilford, CT: Globe Pequot Press. 2002.

Ice Age Trail Alliance. *Ice Age Trail Atlas*. Cross Plains, WI: Ice Age Trail Alliance. 2014.

Lapham, Increase A. *Wisconsin: Its Geography and Topography*. North Stratford, NH: Ayer Company Publishers. 1846 (reprint 1999).

Mickelson, David M., et al. *Geology of the Ice Age National Scenic Trail*. Madison, WI: University of Wisconsin Press. 2011.

Morgan, John and Ellen. *50 Hikes in Wisconsin*. Woodstock, VT: Backcountry Guides. 2004

Reuss, Henry S. *On the Trail of the Ice Age*. Sheboygan, WI: Ice Age Park & Trail Foundation, Inc. 1990.

Smith, Bart. *Along Wisconsin's Ice Age Trail*. Madison, WI: The University of Wisconsin Press. 2008.

Wisconsin Department of Natural Resources. *Wisconsin, Naturally, A Guide to 150 Great State Natural Areas*. Wisconsin Department of Natural Resources. 2003.

*A more complete bibliography can be found on the IATA website (**iceagetrail.org**).*

Useful Addresses & Phone Numbers

Ice Age Trail Alliance
2110 Main St.
Cross Plains, WI 53528
800-227-0046
info@iceagetrail.org
iceagetrail.org

Wisconsin Department of Natural Resources—Bureau of Parks and Recreation
PO Box 7921
Madison, WI 53707-7921
608-266-2181
DNRWisconsinParks@wisconsin.gov
dnr.wi.gov/topic/parks
For camping reservations at state parks:
888-WIPARKS [947-2757],
reserveamerica.com

National Park Service—Ice Age National Scenic Trail
700 Rayovac Dr., Suite 100
Madison, WI 53711
608-441-5610
nps.gov/iatr

Wisconsin Department of Tourism
800-432-TRIP [8747]
travelwisconsin.com

Wisconsin road conditions:
511 (in Wisconsin) or 866-511-9472

Greyhound Bus Line
800-231-2222
greyhound.com

Badger Coaches
Milwaukee to Madison
608-255-1511
badgerbus.com

Van Galder Bus Co./Coach USA
Bus service to Madison, Janesville, Chicago, Milwaukee and Minneapolis.
800-747-0994
coachusa.com/vangalder

Jefferson Lines
Bus service to Midwest cities including Minneapolis, Rice Lake, Baraboo, Madison, Milwaukee, Manitowoc and Green Bay
800-451-5333
jeffersonlines.com

Megabus
Low-cost bus service to Midwest cities including Minneapolis, Madison, Milwaukee and Chicago
megabus.com

Amtrak
Empire Builder route includes Chicago, Milwaukee, Portage and the Twin Cities
800-USA-RAIL [872-7245]
amtrak.com

Index

Segment Names

ICE AGE TRAIL SEGMENT	ATLAS MAPS	COUNTY	PAGE
Gibraltar Segment	62f	Southern Columbia	202
Grandfather Falls Segment	28f	Lincoln	101
Grassy Lake Segment	7f	Barron & Washburn	34
Greenbush Segment	89f, 90f	Fond du Lac & Sheboygan	316
Greenwood Segment	51f	Waushara	167
Groves-Pertzborn Segment	62f, 63f	Southern Columbia	205
Harrison Hills Segment	30f, 31f	Lincoln	108
Hartland Segment	82f	Waukesha	282
Hartman Creek Segment	48f	Portage & Waupaca	158
Harwood Lakes Segment	15f, 16f	Chippewa	57
Hemlock Creek Segment	10f, 11f	Barron & Washburn	42
Highland Lakes Eastern Segment	33f	Langlade	120
Highland Lakes Western Segment	32f, 33f	Langlade	122
Holy Hill Segment	84f	Washington	294
Indian Creek Segment	5f	Polk & Burnett	22
Indian Lake Segment	64f	Dane	214
Janesville Segment	74f	Rock	246
Janesville to Milton Segment	75f	Rock	249
Jerry Lake Segment	22f, 23f	Taylor	71
John Muir Park Segment	56f	Marquette	178
Kettlebowl Segment	35f, 36f	Langlade	130
Kewaskum Segment	86f	Washington	301
Kewaunee River Segment	100f, 101f	Kewaunee & Door	344
LaBudde Creek Segment	90f	Fond du Lac & Sheboygan	320
Lake Eleven Segment	20f–22f	Taylor	68
Lapham Peak Segment	81f, 82f	Waukesha	278
Lodi Marsh Segment	63f	Southern Columbia and Dane	207
Loew Lake Segment	83f, 84f	Washington	292
Lumbercamp Segment	34f, 35f	Langlade	128
Madison Segment	66f	Dane	220
McKenzie Creek Segment	4f, 5f	Polk & Burnett	20
Mecan River Segment	51f, 52f	Waushara	171
Merrimac Segment	61f, 62f	Sauk	198
Merton Segment	83f	Waukesha	285
Milton Segment	75f	Rock	251
Milwaukee River Segment (Fond du Lac County)	87f	Fond du Lac & Sheboygan	310

ICE AGE TRAIL SEGMENT	ATLAS MAPS	COUNTY	PAGE
Milwaukee River Segment (Washington County)	86f, 87f	Washington	301
Mishicot Segment	97f	Manitowoc	336
Monches Segment	83f	Waukesha	285
Mondeaux Esker Segment	23f	Taylor	76
Monticello Segment	68f, 69f	Green	234
Montrose Segment	67f, 68f	Dane	227
New Hope–Iola Ski Hill Segment	45f	Portage & Waupaca	150
Newwood Segment	26f, 27f	Lincoln	96
Northern Blue Hills Segment	11f	Rusk	46
Old Railroad Segment	33f, 34f	Langlade	124
Parnell Segment	87f–89f	Fond du Lac & Sheboygan	312
Parrish Hills Segment	31f, 32f	Langlade	116
Pike Lake Segment	84f, 85f	Washington	296
Pine Lake Segment	4f	Polk & Burnett	17
Pine Line Segment	24f	Taylor	80
Plover River Segment	39f, 40f	Marathon	138
Point Beach Segment	96f	Manitowoc	333
Portage Canal Segment	57f	Northern Columbia	184
Rib Lake Segment	25f	Taylor	84
Ringle Segment	41f, 42f	Marathon	143
Sand Creek Segment	5f, 6f	Polk & Burnett	24
Sauk Point Segment	61f	Sauk	192
Scuppernong Segment	80f, 81f	Waukesha	274
Skunk and Foster Lakes Segment	47f	Portage & Waupaca	154
Slinger Segment	85f	Washington	296
Southern Blue Hills Segment	11f, 12f	Rusk	48
Southern Kewaskum Segment	86f	Washington	299
St. Croix Falls Segment	1f	Polk & Burnett	6
Stony Ridge Segment	80f	Waukesha	270
Storrs Lake Segment	75f, 76f	Rock	251
Straight Lake Segment	3f	Polk & Burnett	14
Straight River Segment	3f, 4f	Polk & Burnett	17
Sturgeon Bay Segment	104f, 105f	Kewaunee & Door	350
Table Bluff Segment	64f, 65f	Dane	216
Thornapple Creek Sgment	40f, 41f	Marathon	140
Timberland Hills Segment	6f	Barron & Washburn	30
Timberland Wilderness Segment	26f	Lincoln	94

ICE AGE TRAIL SEGMENT	ATLAS MAPS	COUNTY	PAGE
Tisch Mills Segment	98f	Manitowoc and Kewaunee & Door	338
Trade River Segment	3f	Polk & Burnett	14
Turtle Rock Segment	28f	Lincoln	101
Tuscobia Segment	8f–10f	Barron & Washburn	38
Underdown Segment	29f, 30f	Lincoln	105
Valley View Segment	65f, 66f	Dane	220
Verona Segment	66f	Dane	224
Waterville Segment	81f	Waukesha	276
Waupaca River Segment	47f, 48f	Portage & Waupaca	154
Wedde Creek Segment	52f	Waushara	174
West Bend Segment	85f, 86f	Washington	299
Whitewater Lake Segment	78f	Walworth & Jefferson	257
Wood Lake Segment	25f, 26f	Taylor	86

Points of Interest along the Trail

PLACES	ATLAS MAPS	COUNTY	PAGE
Ahnapee State Trail	102f–105f	Kewaunee & Door	346
Also Leopold Legacy Center	58f	Sauk	196
Badger Prairie County Park	66f	Dane	224
Badger State Trail	67f–70f	Dane and Green	229
Broughton Sheboygan Marsh County Park	90f	Fond du Lac & Sheboygan	321
Brunet Island State Park	16f, 17f	Chippewa	62
CD "Buzz" Besadny Anadromous Fish Facility	101f	Kewaunee & Door	346
Camp New Wood County Park	28f	Lincoln	101
Cardy Paleo-Indian Camp Archaeological Site	105f	Kewaunee & Door	353
Chequamegon National Forest	20f–24f	Taylor	70
Chippewa Lobe Interpretive Loop	22f	Taylor	74
Chippewa Moraine National Scientific Reserve and David R. Obey Ice Age Interpretive Center	15f	Chippewa	56
Circus World Museum	60f	Sauk	190
Cross Plains National Scientific Reserve	65f	Dane	219
Cushing Memorial Park and Wisconsin Veterans Memorial Riverwalk	82f	Waukesha	281

PLACES	ATLAS MAPS	COUNTY	PAGE
Dells of Eau Claire County Park	40f	Marathon	142
Devil's Lake State Park	61f	Sauk	197
Eisenbahn State Trail	86f, 87f	Washington	304
Emma Carlin Trails—Southern Unit Kettle Moraine State Forest	79f, 80f	Walworth & Jefferson and Waukesha	262
Fort Winnebago Surgeon's Quarters	57f	Northern Columbia	185
Gandy Dancer State Trail	1f–3f	Polk & Burnett	12
Gibraltar Rock	62f	Southern Columbia	202
Glacial Blue Hills Recreation Area	86f	Washington	299
Glacial Drumlin State Trail	81f	Waukesha	281
Grandfather Falls Dam and Hydroelectric Plant	28f	Lincoln	101
Greenbush Trails—Northern Unit Kettle Moraine State Forest	89f	Fond du Lac & Sheboygan	316
Hartland Marsh	82f	Waukesha	282
Hartman Creek State Park	48f	Portage & Waupaca	157
Henry S. Reuss Ice Age Visitor Center	88f	Fond du Lac & Sheboygan	314
Historic Rogers Street Fishing Village	96f	Manitowoc	332
Holy Hill Shrine and Monastery	84f	Washington	295
Ice Age Trail Alliance Headquarters	65f	Dane	216
Indian Agency House	57f	Northern Columbia	184
Indian Lake County Park	64f	Dane	214
Interstate State Park	1f	Polk & Burnett	9
Iola Winter Sports Club	45f	Portage & Waupaca	150
John Muir Memorial County Park	56f	Marquette	178
John Muir Trails—Southern Unit Kettle Moraine State Forest	79f	Walworth & Jefferson	259
Kewaunee River section of the Ahnapee State Trail	100f, 101f	Kewaunee & Door	344
Lake Country Recreation Trail	82f	Waukesha	278
Lapham Peak Unit—Kettle Moraine State Forest	81f, 82f	Waukesha	281
Loew Lake Unit—Kettle Moraine State Forest	83f, 84f	Washington	293
Long Lake Recreation Area	88f	Fond du Lac & Sheboygan	312
Mariners Trail	95f	Manitowoc	326
Mauthe Lake Recreation Area	87f	Fond du Lac & Sheboygan	311
Merrimac Ferry (*Colsac III*)	62f	Sauk	199
Merrimac Preserve	62f	Sauk	198
Military Ridge State Trail	66f	Dane	227

PLACES	ATLAS MAPS	COUNTY	PAGE
Milton House Museum	75f	Rock	253
Mondeaux Dam Recreation Area	23f	Taylor	78
Mountain-Bay State Trail	41f, 42f	Marathon	144
Murphy Flowage Recreation Area	10f, 11f	Barron & Washburn and Rusk	43
Murry Creek Loop Trail	48f	Portage & Waupaca	160
Naga-Waukee County Park	82f	Waukesha	
New Fane Trails—Northern Unit Kettle Moraine State Forest	87f	Washington and Fond du Lac & Sheboygan	278
New Glarus Woods State Park	69f	Green	235
New Hope Pines State Natural Area	45f	Portage & Waupaca	150
Northern Unit—Kettle Moraine State Forest	86f–90f	Washington and Fond du Lac & Sheboygan	301
Observatory Hill State Natural Area	56f	Marquette	179
Old World Wisconsin	80f	Waukesha	271
Ottawa Lake Recreation Area	80f, 81f	Waukesha	275
Parfrey's Glen State Natural Area	61f	Sauk	193
Pike Lake Unit—Kettle Moraine State Forest	84f, 85f	Washington	295
Point Beach State Forest	96f	Manitowoc	335
Potawatomi State Park	105f	Kewaunee & Door	354
Prairie Moraine County Park	66f, 67f	Dane	224
Ridge Run County Park	85f, 86f	Washington	299
Robert Cook Memorial Arboretum	73f, 74f	Rock	242
Rotary Botanical Gardens and Lions Beach	74f	Rock	248
Scuppernong Hiking and Skiing Trails—Southern Unit Kettle Moraine State Forest	80f, 81f	Waukesha	274
Southern Unit—Kettle Moraine State Forest	78f–81f	Walworth & Jefferson and Waukesha	257
Straight Lake State Park	3f	Polk & Burnett	14
Sugar River State Trail	69f–71f	Green	235
St. Croix National Scenic Riverway	1f	Polk & Burnett	9
Timm's Hill National Trail	25f	Taylor	84
Tuscobia State Trail	8f–10f	Barron & Washburn	40
Two Creeks Buried Forest	98f	Manitowoc	339
Underdown Recreation Area	29f, 30f	Lincoln	107
University Ridge Golf Course	66f	Dane	220
UW-Waukesha Field Station	81f	Waukesha	276

PLACES	ATLAS MAPS	COUNTY	PAGE
Veterans Memorial Park	34f	Langlade	125
Wade House Historic Site	89f	Fond du Lac & Sheboygan	318
West of the Lake Gardens	95f	Manitowoc	328
Whitewater Lake Recreation Area	78f	Walworth & Jefferson	259
Wisconsin Conservationists' Hall of Fame	81f–83f	Waukesha	268
Wisconsin Maritime Museum	95f	Manitowoc	327
Wood Lake County Park	26f	Taylor	88
Woodland Dunes Nature Center and Preserve	95f, 96f	Manitowoc	330

KEY TO MAP SYMBOLS (see also Segment Snapshot symbol key, opposite)

Water

🥛	**Drinking Water** May be available only seasonally.

Camping

⚑	**Backpacking Campsite** A hike-to campsite (varying levels of development) established for backpackers.
⬚	**Primitive Camping** Areas where hikers may practice Leave No Trace primitive camping. See p. xxvi for Leave No Trace guidelines.
DCA	**Dispersed Camping Area (DCA)** A minimally developed area where long-distance hikers may legally camp. DCAs are established by the Ice Age Trail Alliance and its partners in areas where convenient camping options are limited.
⌂	**Kettle Moraine Backpacking Shelter** Trailside shelters in the Northern (5) and Southern (3) Units; reservations required.
⛺	**Car-Camping Campsite** A traditional campground reachable by either car or foot.

Amenities

🅿	**Parking Area**
🚻	**Toilet** May be available only seasonally.
⛷	**Cross-Country Ski Trails**
🚿	**Shower** May be available only seasonally and/or for a fee.

Trail

⸺	**Ice Age Trail** Marked with yellow blazes.
∘ ° ∘ ∘	**Unofficial Connecting Route** Unmarked.
• • • •	**Future Ice Age Trail** Approximate route.
⸺	**Select Other Trails**

Other Map Features

▪	**Publicly Owned or IATA-Owned Areas** Open to public access. Those labeled SIATA are State Ice Age Trail Areas, properties owned by the Wisconsin Department of Natural Resources and managed for the Ice Age Trail.
⟙	**Tower** Includes fire towers with no public access.
●—●	**Gate** A locked gate or berm that does not permit public motor vehicle access.
⚶	**Unreliable Water Source**

KEY TO SEGMENT SNAPSHOT SYMBOLS (see also map symbol key, opposite)

Elevation & Ruggedness	
◣3	This segment is: 1 (mostly flat) through 5 (very hilly).
2👢	Factoring in signage, maintenance and/or layout challenges; water hazards or crossings; remoteness and logging, this segment is: 1 (not rugged) through 5 (very rugged).
Water	
▯	Drinking water is available on this segment from a pump or spigot with potable water. May be available only seasonally.
💧	Drinking water is available on this segment from a natural source; filtration required.
✕	Drinking water is NOT available on this segment.
Camping	
🚶▲	Backpack Camping—Segment has hike-to camping options further defined by map symbols. See map symbol key (opposite) for detailed descriptions.
🚗▲	Car Camping—A traditional campground is located on or within a few miles of the segment.
Amenities	
🧺	Picnic areas are available on or near the segment.
🛝	Child-friendly amenities like playgrounds and/or swim areas are available on or near the segment.
🚻	Restrooms are available on or near the segment. May be available only seasonally.
Hunting & Dogs	
⊘	Hikers will not have any interaction with hunting on this segment.
🚫	Segment crosses private land and portions or the full segment may be closed to hikers during hunting season(s).
🐕!	Segment has special regulations for hiking with dogs. (In general, dogs are permitted but must be leashed and under control.)
Shared, Spur & Accessible Trails	
▰▰▰	Portions of the segment overlap with biking, snowmobiling or groomed cross-country skiing trails or roads and/or sidewalks.
⋯⤸⋯	Other hiking trails (spurs, loops or lollipops) are present off the main segment route.
♿	Portions of this segment may be suitable for those using wheelchairs or similar devices.

Symbol Keys

Hike Locator

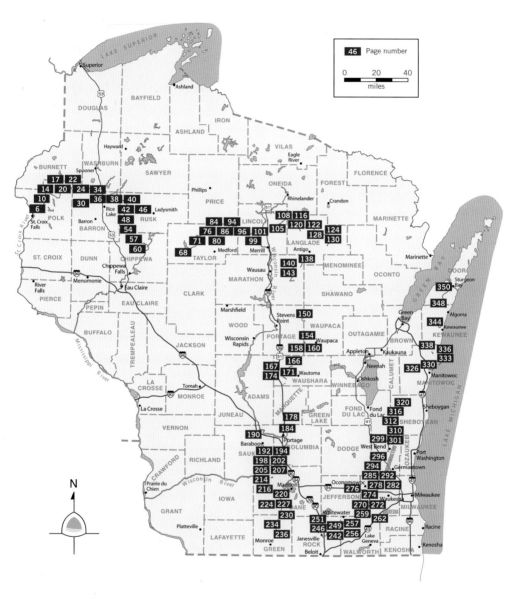

Note: All hike maps are oriented with north up and printed at the same scale.

Ice Age Trail Guidebook 2014